Financial Cold War

A View of Sino-US Relations from the Financial Markets

James A. Fok

WILEY

This edition first published 2022

Copyright © 2022 by James A. Fok.

Registered office

John Wiley & Sons Ltd, The Atrium, Southern Gate, Chichester, West Sussex, PO19 8SQ, United Kingdom

For details of our global editorial offices, for customer services and for information about how to apply for permission to reuse the copyright material in this book please see our website at www.wiley.com.

Wiley publishes in a variety of print and electronic formats and by print-on-demand. Some material included with standard print versions of this book may not be included in e-books or in print-on-demand. If this book refers to media such as a CD or DVD that is not included in the version you purchased, you may download this material at http://booksupport.wiley.com. For more information about Wiley products, visit www.wiley.com.

Library of Congress Cataloging-in-Publication Data is Available:

ISBN 978-1-119-86276-5 (hardback)
ISBN 978-1-119-86278-9 (ePub)
ISBN 978-1-119-86277-2 (ePDF)

Cover Design: Wiley
Cover Image: © suns07butterfly/Shutterstock
SKY8AC4B287-94B9-429D-BE2E-8FF6B39D1581_111921

For Peter & Harry

Contents

Preface

Among my earliest memories was a visit to a stockbroker's office with my father. Growing up in Hong Kong, every Chinese New Year children would receive 'red packets' containing small sums of money from relatives and family friends. Each year, my father would gather up the haul that my siblings and I had collected to invest in stocks. In the *go-go* years of Hong Kong in the 1980s, people from all walks of life seemed to hang on every fluctuation of the stock market. Although I had very little knowledge of financial markets back then, I suppose I was instilled early in life with a sense of their power.

Later, as a teenager, I struggled with my studies in classical Chinese texts. Taking pity on me, my godmother offered to tutor me, and I started going up to her office twice a week for tutorials. Auntie Sue – as she is known to me – was a successful lawyer who had co-founded a law firm with my father. However, by that stage she had become a little bored of the law and had taken up a side-line in trading stock options. I found Confucian and Mencian philosophy rather tedious and often diverted these tutorial sessions to discussions on stocks and options trading. Over time, Auntie Sue taught me the basic principles of securities valuation and options pricing that, as an adolescent with dreams of riches, I absorbed with enthusiasm.

In my first year at university, with savings from part-time work and various entrepreneurial ventures, I opened an online trading account and began investing in the markets myself. It was in the middle of the Dot-com boom and I had some initial success but, ultimately, this was to lead to one of my first great lessons in the pitfalls of overexuberance. Nonetheless, my interest in financial markets wasn't extinguished.

As an undergraduate in Beijing in the 1990s, I got to experience first-hand how market reforms were transforming China. I witnessed the launch of Starbucks, Walmart and the trappings of American consumer culture in the country. A huge number of Chinese students aspired to post-graduate studies in the United States (US) and I was regularly asked by fellow students to help them study for the GRE English test, success in which was a prerequisite for acceptance to American colleges (although, frankly, most of them scored far higher than I would have done). At that time, it seemed to me that the 'Chinese Dream' was pretty similar to the 'American Dream' and, like many observers, I expected economic growth would ultimately lead to political reforms and a more liberal democratic society.

I also glimpsed some of the hangovers from China's traumatic past. When five US guided bombs hit the Chinese embassy in Belgrade during the Balkans conflict in 1999, people were quickly whipped up into a nationalistic frenzy. US authorities claimed that this incident, in which three Chinese citizens were killed, was due to a CIA mistake. China has never accepted this explanation. In the days that followed, angry crowds demonstrated outside the US embassy. One evening shortly afterwards, I was out with a friend from Korea. Conversing in English, we were mistaken for Americans and chased after by a mob. That certainly left an impression on me that populist nationalism is a pretty scary thing.

On completing university, I joined the graduate programme of an American investment bank in London. I rapidly specialised in advising financial services clients and learned top-down and bottom-up about the international financial system.

For almost a decade until mid-2021, I worked at the centre of Hong Kong's financial markets at Hong Kong Exchanges and Clearing Limited (HKEX). HKEX is the sole exchange and clearing house operator in the most successful initial public offerings (IPOs) market in the world. I landed there because, back in early 2012, I found myself between jobs with time on my hands. A social acquaintance who was running Business Development for HKEX at the time asked if I might come and help out on a corporate takeover the Exchange was contemplating. I had been due to join another investment bank several months later and my wife told me I should just relax and enjoy my time off. However, although I had previously worked on transactions involving banks, insurers and asset managers, I had never seriously looked at how exchanges work, and curiosity got the better of me. The transaction turned out to be the competitive auction for the London Metal Exchange (LME), the world's leading venue for trading industrial metals, with a history tracing back over four centuries.

From the outside in, HKEX in those days looked like a sleepy and bureaucratic organisation. On my first day in the office, I discovered that the company did not have international direct dialling from the desktop phones. To make an overseas call, you had to find a secretary to come and input a long series of codes before being able to dial out. The first-round bids for the LME were due in a couple of weeks. When I got home that night, I told my wife that I would be able to resume my time off after that. *Famous last words. . .*

HKEX was then in the early stages of a transformation to broaden its focus from stock trading. Notwithstanding the company's inexperience in international takeovers, the then Chairman and CEO were determined to win the race to acquire the LME. In the latter stages of the transaction, I was asked whether I might stay on in a full-time position. My wife was sceptical about the idea. We were thinking about starting a family and working for the Exchange would involve a meaningful pay cut. However, somehow it just felt like the right move.

Hong Kong is a small town and I already knew a number of people at HKEX. Most importantly, the Exchange was one of the few sizeable financial institutions that is Hong Kong-based. HKEX sits at the heart of Hong Kong's financial ecosystem, which is integral to the city's success and prosperity. It was attractive to me to be putting my energies towards building a company that can make a big difference to Hong Kong, and where the key decisions were made locally, rather than far away in Frankfurt, London or New York.

Hong Kong's *raison d'être* since it was ceded to the British in 1842 following the Opium War has been as a centre of trade, connecting

China and Western markets. Over time, the trade in goods was supplemented by trading in securities and derivatives. Following the return of sovereignty to China in 1997, Hong Kong's role as the leading financial centre connecting China and international markets has continued to grow.

HKEX has grown alongside Hong Kong, expanding its role in the past decade from serving as the leading platform for Chinese companies to raise investment from international investors to trading in fixed income, currencies and commodities. The company has also cooperated with Mainland Chinese market infrastructure operators to expand and deepen the connections between China and international markets.

Initially, I worked as Chief of Staff to the CEO. Later I took over running Group Strategy for the organisation. Through my work on the formulation and execution of HKEX's strategy, I found myself at a fascinating intersection of global geopolitics and financial markets at what is arguably one of the most pivotal points in international relations in my generation. From this perch, I had the opportunity not only to interact with the top managements of the major global banks, corporate issuers and investors who are HKEX's customers, but also to work closely with regulators and policymakers in Hong Kong, Mainland China, and around the world. This opened my eyes to the broader geopolitical considerations surrounding financial markets policy and regulation.

In most parts of the financial services industry, the main challenges are to work out how to get something done and how to make money doing it. Due to their central position in the marketplace, exchanges and other market infrastructures that constitute the 'plumbing' of the global capital markets overlap with regulation and policy to a much greater extent than other financial organisations. For regulators and policymakers, making money is only a secondary or even tertiary concern. What they care about are the *rules of the game*. Very subtle changes in these can have a huge bearing on a wide range of national interests.

Following China's economic rise over recent decades and emergence as a global power, there has been much speculation about a 'gathering storm' in Sino-US relations. Academic and policy debate has raged over whether China and America can avoid the 'Thucydides Trap'. This is the theory first posited by the ancient Athenian historian

Thucydides in his *History of the Peloponnesian War* between Athens and Sparta (431–404 BC) that the fear of a rising power challenging the leadership of an incumbent power would inevitably lead to war. Indeed, in the majority of instances where a rising power has challenged the supremacy of the dominant power over the past five hundred years, war has followed – as in the case of Germany versus Great Britain in 1914.[1]

In the euphoria of the years following the end of the Cold War, such a conflict between two major powers was almost unimaginable. And yet, in the wake of the 2008 Global Financial Crisis (GFC), we have seen a return to populist and nationalist politics, including the open expression of appalling prejudices, that had previously been unknown and regarded as unthinkable to my generation in the liberal democracies of the West. Brexit and the Sino-US trade war are conspicuous examples of this phenomenon, where public opinion and government policies have been heavily influenced by economic factors. At the time of writing, the full long-term effects of the Covid-19 pandemic are yet to be known, but tensions have been escalating.

This book is an attempt to synthesise the financial and economic factors that have brought us to our current predicament, analyse the geopolitical realities underlying financial markets today, and to suggest some solutions that balance the many varying interests, so as to avert the calamities that befell earlier generations. In this attempt, I am conscious of Maslow's caution that 'It is tempting, if the only tool you have is a hammer, to treat everything as if it were a nail'. Financial markets cannot provide solutions to all the complex problems that arise in Great Power relations – indeed, policies that excessively favoured markets at the expense of communities may have contributed to many of the problems in the first place.

That said, I haven't yet come across an analysis that considers fully, from both a top-down and bottom-up perspective, how the global financial system as we know it today is contributing to geopolitical tensions. Even less attention is paid to the diverse range of policies, regulations, infrastructures and conventions that support it. Without an appreciation of these and the history of how the system has come about, it is difficult to understand the full scope of the systemic financial challenges facing the world's two leading powers, much less devise effective strategies for navigating the treacherous waters we're in.

A number of leading authorities from different fields have recommended a variety of paths that could lead to a peaceful rebalancing of the Sino-US relationship. This book does not try to usurp those, but to supplement their specific perspectives with a practical perspective from the field of financial markets. What I can say with confidence though is that, without addressing the sources of financial and economic tensions, it is unlikely that other sources of conflict can be eliminated. I hope this book might help increase mutual understanding and offer some insights to assist policymakers in both the East and the West in the extremely difficult task of smoothing the course of China's integration into the international financial system during a tricky period of geopolitical adjustment.

However, the book is not only targeted at policymakers. Be it in a liberal democracy or any other political system, leaders govern on behalf of their people. Every citizen has an interest in understanding the issues his or her country faces, so as to help ensure that leaders act in the best interests of society as a whole. The book has therefore been written in a way to make it accessible, without shying away from complexity. I hope it will be helpful in particular to those with an interest in international relations, finance, economic history, sociology and political science.

Being of mixed Chinese and British heritage, I owe my very existence to globalisation and to the particularly tempestuous period of history that created China and Hong Kong as they are today. This has undeniably influenced my viewpoints. Another stroke of serendipity that has enriched my outlook – and my life more generally – was to have met my wife Yeone, an American with a love of her country. Through her, I have had the opportunity to better understand the US and re-examine some of my preconceptions. Having had the privilege of experiencing the best – and, on occasions, the worst – of contemporary China and America, I have a deep affection for both countries. Moreover, our two young sons will grow up both Chinese and American and, if for no other reason, this alone gives me an enormous vested interest in seeing the two nations thrive in harmony with each other. Yet, putting sentimentality aside, I believe that setting the right policies depends on making objective assessments of the facts.

At this point, readers should note that I held positions of influence in Hong Kong's financial markets strategy and policymaking between

2012 and mid-2021. Through this, I was directly involved in certain Chinese policy steps towards financial markets internationalisation that are discussed in this book. While I have made every effort to maintain objectivity, where there are failings in this regard, I hope that readers will be compensated through the insights afforded by a first-hand perspective.

Over the course of human history, extreme inequality in the distribution of resources has tended to lead to conflict. The evolution of international trade and investment has, when conducted on the basis of sound rules and with the object of mutual benefit, raised humanity's collective standard of living and contributed to more peaceful coexistence between societies. Listening to the political rhetoric of late, it seems that some of our leaders may need a reminder of the lessons of history. This is my small contribution to that cause and I hope that readers will find this book entertaining, informative and thought-provoking.

That all said, I am an optimist and believe firmly that, if we can successfully navigate the next steps of global financial integration, we can all look forward to a bright era of greater prosperity and security. We have no choice. The alternative is simply not something we want to contemplate.

–James A. Fok
Hong Kong
10 September 2021

Acknowledgements

My first thanks must go to my wife Yeone, who initially encouraged me to write this book as a way of passing some spare time while stuck at home during the Covid-19 pandemic. She probably hadn't imagined that it would become such an engrossing diversion as to cause me to neglect most of my familial duties for many subsequent months. As I disappeared (at least mentally) into the research and writing, she only very occasionally complained about having to shoulder most of the burden of looking after our five-year-old twins. On top of that, Yeone reviewed the first draft of each section, asked a ton of questions, and pushed me to add colour to illustrate my arguments. I hope that the final work at least partially justifies her sacrifices.

My next thanks go to Mark Bentley. Mark gave me my first job in financial services and has been a consistent friend and mentor ever since. While working on this book, I spent countless hours in conversation with him discussing many of the ideas contained in it. Mark and I have very different perspectives (he is an ardent free marketeer who talks of Milton Friedman in the same reverent tones reserved for saints of the church), but his impressive ability to dissect arguments and challenge the flaws in them undoubtedly improved the final work considerably.

This book also owes a huge debt to the work of the many authors and writers whose books, research papers and articles are listed in the bibliography. I now realise what an enormous amount of effort goes into all of this, and I am extremely grateful to each of them.

Along the way, I have had a lot of help. Much of what I have learned about financial markets has come from former colleagues, business partners, professional advisors, regulators and clients. There are far too many to name each of them here, but I am deeply grateful to all those who have shared the highs and supported me through the lows of my career thus far, and to each and every one who has made my work so much fun over the years.

Specifically in relation to this book, thanks go to Bryan Cheuk and Kenneth Lock, who helped with research on the economic and financial data that appear in it. I am also grateful to Alokik Advani, Andrew Bernard, Cheah Cheng Hye, Rebecca Chua, Fu Hao, Jeremy Grant, Patrick Jacquelin, Sue Johnson, Kai Keller, Paul Kennedy, Michael Lam, Li Yingying, Max Lummis, George Magnus, Michael Moser, James Muir, Edmund Ng, Lisa O'Connor, Matt O'Neill, Ketan Patel, Patrick Young and Zhou Bo, who reviewed various chapters and provided helpful feedback and encouragement.

There are a number of people to whom I am particularly indebted for their extensive comments and advice.

Mustansir Barma provided very detailed feedback on the draft manuscript and corrected several factual errors.

Roland Chai urged me to consider more deeply how digital currencies might affect the future development of the global financial system. Adam Wielowieyski then introduced me to a wide range of research in this area and was exceedingly patient in answering my many questions. This effort was not only interesting and rewarding, but it also led me to change some of my final conclusions.

Jonathan Chow provided insightful feedback on the structure of the book and editing advice, which put better focus on the key arguments. He also gave me some helpful suggestions on the title of the book and various sections.

Nick Gardiner sent me pages of meticulously typed notes on the manuscript, with a huge number of valuable questions and suggestions.

Katie Kolchin was a wealth of information on US financial statistics and much more. Her eye for detail helped significantly improve the chapters covering the development of the US market.

After I thought I had a near-final draft of the manuscript, a mutual friend suggested that I ask Henny Sender to take a look at it for me. I had met Henny a number of years before and knew her to be very thoughtful and knowledgeable about China's financial markets. I was incredibly fortunate that Henny not only *looked* at the draft for me, but drilled into the manuscript, pushing me to clarify each passage with a sort of nurturing iron discipline I had not encountered since visits to the school matron's surgery at boarding school. Without a doubt, this resulted in a far more polished work than I could ever have accomplished on my own.

Several others provided very helpful comments and advice on the manuscript, but would prefer to remain anonymous. I am deeply grateful to each of them.

Ronald Chan, Uther Charlton-Stevens, Mark Makepeace, Sophie Chen Keller and Shan Weijian gave me extensive advice on the publishing process and were extraordinarily generous with their contacts. I ultimately chose to work with Wiley because of the incredible enthusiasm that Gladys (Syd) Ganaden showed in the project right from the start. Syd, together with Purvi Patel, Sylvie Docherty, Philo Antonie Mahendran and the entire Wiley team were friendly, professional and a delight to work with throughout the process. I am also very grateful to Amita Haylock and Cheng Hau Yeo of Mayer Brown for their professional support and practical advice.

Finally, I must thank Stephanie Tsui for her daily support over many years. Without her efficiency in organising my life, this book would never have been completed.

That all said, any errors, omissions or other failings in this final work (of which I am sure there are many) are my responsibility. I must also stress that the views expressed herein are mine alone, and do not claim to represent those of any of the individuals who have provided advice or support. Nor do they represent the views of any of my former employers or other organisations with which I am associated.

–James A. Fok
Hong Kong
4 October 2021

Abbreviations

9/11	11 September 2001
AIDS	Acquired Immunodeficiency Syndrome
AIIB	Asian Infrastructure Investment Bank
ANZUS	Australia, New Zealand, United States Security Treaty
ASEAN	Association of Southeast Asian Nations
B2B	Business-to-Business
B2C	Business-to-Consumer
BCCL	Bond Connect Company Limited
BIS	Bank for International Settlements
BRI	Belt and Road Initiative
CBDC	Central Bank Digital Currency
CBOE	Chicago Board Options Exchange
CBOT	Chicago Board of Trade
CCDC	China Central Depository and Clearing
CCP	Chinese Communist Party
CDS	Credit Default Swap
CEO	Chief Executive Officer

CFA	Court of Final Appeal (of the Hong Kong Special Administrative Region)
CFETS	China Foreign Exchange Trading System
CFFEX	China Financial Futures Exchange
CFIUS	Committee on Foreign Investment in the United States
CGB	Chinese Government Bond
CIA	Central Intelligence Agency
CIPS	Cross-Border Interbank Payment System
CME	Chicago Mercantile Exchange
CMU	Central Moneymarkets Unit (of the Hong Kong Monetary Authority)
CNH	Offshore Chinese Yuan
CNY	Onshore Chinese Yuan
CSRC	China Securities Regulatory Commission
DTC	The Depository Trust Company
e-CNY	Digital Yuan
ECB	European Central Bank
EEC	European Economic Community
ETF	Exchange-traded Fund
EU	European Union
FATCA	Foreign Account Tax Compliance Act (of the United States)
FCC	Federal Communications Commission (of the United States)
FDI	Foreign Direct Investment
FDIC	Federal Deposit Insurance Corporation (of the United States)
FDR	Franklin Delano Roosevelt
Fed	Federal Reserve (of the United States)
FINSIDER	Società Finanziaria Siderugica
FSTB	Financial Services and Treasury Bureau (of the Hong Kong Special Administrative Region)

G-10	Group of 10
G-7	Group of 7
GATT	General Agreement on Trade and Tariffs
GDP	Gross Domestic Product
GFC	Global Financial Crisis
GNP	Gross National Product
GPS	Global Positioning System
GRE	Graduate Record Examination
GSE	Government-sponsored Enterprise
HFT	High Frequency Trader
HIV	Human Immunodeficiency Virus
HKEX	Hong Kong Exchanges and Clearing Limited
HKMA	Hong Kong Monetary Authority
HKSCC	Hong Kong Securities Clearing Corporation
ICB	International Clearing Bank
ICE	Intercontinental Exchange
ICSD	International Central Securities Depository
IET	Interest Equalisation Tax (of the United States)
IMF	International Monetary Fund
IMM	International Monetary Market
INSTEX	Instrument in Support of Trade Exchanges
IPE	International Petroleum Exchange
IPO	Initial Public Offering
IRI	Istituto per la Ricostruzione Industriale
IRS	Internal Revenue Service (of the United States)
JCPOA	Joint Comprehensive Plan of Action
JFK	John Fitzgerald Kennedy
LBJ	Lyndon Baines Johnson
LCH	London Clearing House
LDC	Less Developed Country
Legco	Legislative Council (of the Hong Kong Special Administrative Region)

LME	London Metal Exchange
LTCM	Long-Term Capital Management
M&A	Mergers and Acquisitions
MAD	Mutually Assured Destruction
MBS	Mortgage Backed Security
MFN	Most Favoured Nation
MMF	Money Market Fund
MMT	Modern Monetary Theory
MOU	Memorandum of Understanding
MPT	Ministry of Posts and Telecommunications (of the People's Republic of China)
MTN	Medium-term Note
NAFMII	National Association of Financial Markets Institutional Investors (of the People's Republic of China)
NASD	National Association of Securities Dealers
NATO	North Atlantic Treaty Organisation
NAV	Net Asset Value
NEO	Net Errors and Omissions
NGO	Non-governmental Organisation
NPC	National People's Congress (of the People's Republic of China)
NPL	Non-performing Loan
NSL	National Security Law (of the Hong Kong Special Administrative Region)
NYMEX	New York Mercantile Exchange
NYSE	New York Stock Exchange
OECD	Organisation for Economic Co-operation and Development
OPEC	Organisation of Petroleum Exporting Countries
PAC	Political Action Committee
PBOC	People's Bank of China
PhD	Doctor(ate) of Philosophy

PIIGS	Portugal, Italy, Ireland, Greece and Spain
PLA	People's Liberation Army
PNP	Pacific Newport Partners
PRC	People's Republic of China
QDII	Qualified Domestic Institutional Investor
QDII2	Qualified Domestic Individual Investor
QFII	Qualified Foreign Institutional Investor
R&D	Research and Development
RQFII	Renminbi Qualified Foreign Institutional Investor
S&P	Standard and Poor's
SARS	Severe Acute Respiratory Syndrome
SASAC	State-owned Asset Supervision and Administration Commission (of the People's Republic of China)
SAT	State Administration of Taxation (of the People's Republic of China)
SCH	Shanghai Clearing House
SDR	Special Drawing Right
SEATO	Southeast Asian Treaty Organisation
SEC	Securities and Exchange Commission (of the United States)
SEHK	Stock Exchange of Hong Kong
SEZ	Special Economic Zone
SFC	Securities and Futures Commission (of the Hong Kong Special Administrative Region)
SNB	Swiss National Bank
SOE	State-owned Enterprise
SWF	Sovereign Wealth Fund
SWIFT	Society for Worldwide Interbank Financial Telecommunication
TAF	Term Auction Facility
TARP	Troubled Asset Relief Programme
TPS	Transactions Per Second
TVE	Township and Village Enterprise

TWh	TeraWatt Hour(s)
UCITS	Undertakings for Collective Investment in Transferable Securities
UK	United Kingdom
UN	United Nations
US	United States (of America)
USSR	Union of Soviet Socialist Republics
WMD	Weapons of Mass Destruction
WTI	West Texas Intermediate
WTO	World Trade Organisation
WW1	World War I
WW2	World War II

Chapter 1

Introduction

今天，我主要讲一个问题，就是解放思想，开动脑筋，实事求是，团结一致向前看。

－ 邓小平，1978 年中共中央工作会议

Today, I mainly want to discuss one question, namely, how to emancipate our minds, use our heads, seek truth from the facts and unite as one in looking to the future.

– Deng Xiaoping, Central Party Work Conference 1978

On Christmas Day 1991, the hammer and sickle flag was lowered over the Kremlin for the last time. It was a dry, still Wednesday morning and the temperature hovered around one degree above freezing, mild by Moscow standards for that time of year. With that, the Cold War had ended.

History would go on to record it as a triumph of capitalism over communism, and of liberal democracy over dictatorship. The euphoria of the period was famously captured in Francis Fukuyama's 1989 essay and subsequent book, declaring 'The End of History', with America's brand of capitalist democracy standing as 'The Last Man'.[1] Indeed, the US had become the sole superpower and the world basked in the glow of the *Pax Americana*. Even as the US was at the apex of its power, however, the seeds of future crises had been sown.

'Free market' ideology had been a major factor in America's victory in the Cold War and, by the fall of the Soviet Union (USSR), US financial markets, with the dollar at their core, had long since attained global leadership. The whole world had become dependent on an American-dominated financial system.

The victory of free market capitalism over communism was so convincing that political parties of the left had to become more centrist – if not outright *right-wing* – in order to win power. The epochal phrase 'It's the economy, stupid' was coined by campaign strategist James Carville during Bill Clinton's successful 1992 presidential campaign and summed up the prevailing mood in the US. Across the Atlantic, in 1995 Tony Blair's Labour Party in Great Britain abandoned Clause IV of the party's constitution, which had previously committed Labour to 'common ownership of the means of production'. This was seen as a decisive step on the path towards Blair's election victory in 1997.

A significant outgrowth of this free market ideology were the monetarist economic policies advocated by Milton Friedman and economists of the Chicago school. Their popularisation was, in many ways, a reaction against the dominance of redistributive Keynesian economics that had prevailed since the end of World War II (WW2) but which had failed to meet economic challenges faced in the 1970s. The influence of monetarist economics was to have a profound impact on government and central bank policies around the world. The increased role for central banks in managing the money supply within economies de-emphasised fiscal policy and governments' role in economic management.

Of course, the impact of the collapse of the Soviet Union was not just felt in economic and financial policy. As the sole superpower, the US was much freer to pursue and implement its strategic objectives across many spheres. When Saddam Hussein invaded Kuwait in August 1990, President George H.W. Bush took painstaking care to build broad international support through the United Nations (UN) Security Council and assembled a coalition of 35 nations before launching Operation Desert Storm to repel Iraqi forces from Kuwait. When his son, President George W. Bush, invaded Iraq in 2003, he did so notwithstanding explicit objections from UN Security Council members Russia and France, and amidst widespread international condemnation.

American military supremacy owes much to the role of the dollar in international trade and finance. US Treasuries make up roughly 60 percent of global central bank reserves,[2] enabling the US government to finance its fiscal deficits cheaply and without any currency mis-match risk between its revenues and liabilities. Gradually, US policymakers came to realise that, through effective control of the global financial system, the dollar itself could be wielded as a weapon against strategic rivals.

The use of financial pressure and 'geo-economic' power in international diplomacy is nothing new. When Britain and France supported Israel's 1956 invasion of Egypt in a bid to topple Egyptian president Gamal Abdul Nasser and regain Western control of the Suez Canal, President Eisenhower used the threat of dumping British Gilts[3] to force the withdrawal of the British and French troops. However, in the post-Cold War period, the exploitation of the dollar to achieve US diplomatic and strategic objectives was extended significantly.

Meanwhile, unlike the leaderships of the former Warsaw Pact countries, the Chinese Communist Party (CCP) continued in power beyond the end of the Cold War. Nevertheless, the CCP had also seen a wave of protests that had threatened its rule in the form of the 1989 student movement. Deng Xiaoping's decision to crack down on that movement in Tiananmen Square on 4 June 1989 has been described as 'one of the most consequential decisions in recent world history'.[4] Whatever the morality of that decision, it was influenced both by China's own history of internal chaos when the central government had been weak, and by the experience of Gorbachev's *Perestroika* movement, which had led to significant political upheavals while failing to generate meaningful economic growth.

China had been pursuing gradual market and political reforms since Deng had come to power in 1978 and announced his 'reform and opening up' (改革开放) policies. In the wake of Tiananmen, however, the Chinese government significantly accelerated market reforms, or what China's leadership has called 'socialism with Chinese characteristics' (中国特色社会主义), while political reforms were for the most part shelved.

As China embarked upon on its own unique path of reform and growth, Chinese policymakers were able to draw on lessons learned from the West. They also paid close attention to developments in Russia in the years following the fall of communism, as well as to Japan's slump into economic stagnation following the end of the Japanese economic miracle. The resulting improvement in living standards for the Chinese population was unprecedented in history, with hundreds of millions of people being lifted from extreme poverty into the middle class within a generation.

The economic policies China has pursued since the 1990s have led to growth that has far exceeded the expectations of their original architects. Following its accession to the World Trade Organisation (WTO) in 2001, China's export growth accelerated rapidly, and the country became the factory of the world. For some in the developed West, this provided great benefits, including low inflation, access to reasonably priced consumer goods and, increasingly, a huge new market for goods and services. For others, competition from China has led to displacement, wage stagnation and unemployment. Some, including many in the US, argue that China has engaged in unfair trade practices, such as suppressing the value of its currency to make its exports more competitive.[5] Others argue that it is America's high cost structure that has made its exports uncompetitive, so it has only itself to blame.[6] The truth, as is often the case, lies somewhere in the middle.

It is not unreasonable for China's leadership to pursue policies that improve the Chinese people's standard of living. The path that China followed was not substantially different to that followed by Japan and West Germany during their post-WW2 recoveries. In this regard, the CCP has done a pretty good job. As China's prosperity has increased, the government has tightened environmental codes and raised minimum wages. These are hardly the actions of a government that is pursuing a narrowly mercantilist trade agenda. At the same time, as trade and other imbalances grew, China's leadership was not proactive enough in addressing other countries' concerns. Escalating tensions were exacerbated by the 2008 Global Financial Crisis (GFC) and its aftermath.

Legacy of the GFC

The 2008 GFC was a watershed event in post-WW2 history. Its significance lies not in the crisis itself, which shared a pattern with countless other financial crises, but in its causes and consequences, as well as a major turning point that it marked.

The ostensible causes of the GFC were the excesses that had been allowed to build up in the US subprime mortgage market. It was a story of greed, hubris, regulatory failures and policy missteps. However, casting a broader eye over the history of the build-up of these excesses, it becomes apparent that the origins of the GFC lay in structural imbalances that had built up in the global financial system over many decades. These are explored in more detail in Chapter 3.

The consequences of the GFC have been far-reaching and, whether we are conscious of them or not, they will continue to impact societies around the world economically, politically and diplomatically for a long time to come.

First, the direct financial impact of the crisis was devastating to a huge number of people. Livelihoods, security and community all suffered. Faith in a financial and social system that had promised stability and prosperity for decades was shattered. And we have yet to identify a system to replace it.

Second, although America had already done much to undermine the legitimacy of its global leadership through unilateralist and aggressive post-Cold War international policies, the GFC brought issues into much sharper focus. Other countries began to question the *status quo* of the global order and it became a spur to action. Reduced willingness to follow America's lead has complicated and slowed down the process of decision making on matters of global importance. The pursuit by other countries of alternatives to US-dominated international organisations has also generated diplomatic tensions.

Third, policy actions during and subsequent to the crisis have, for the most part, treated the symptoms rather than the root causes of the disease. Regulatory reforms have made the banking system less vulnerable to financial shocks. However, more fundamental underlying problems have not been tackled. Continued reliance on monetary policy and market self-correction mechanisms has failed to revitalise key parts of the economy. In addition, the prolonged application of some treatments, such as extraordinarily low interest rates, have contributed to a widening wealth gap. This, in turn, has stoked greater societal tensions.

Fourth, as these domestic and international tensions have simmered, we have witnessed a descent into more populist and nationalistic politics in many countries. This is spreading tensions and conflicts across many spheres.

Looking back at the crisis and events since, it is also clear that the GFC marked a major turning point in Sino-US relations. The illusion of American omnipotence was shattered, and China's own self confidence increased. This increased China's willingness to challenge the US where it felt its own interests were at stake and ushered in a more assertive attitude in the conduct of its international affairs.

The focus of this book is the escalation in tensions between the US and China. There is a severe risk that a misdiagnosis of key sources of tensions will lead to the wrong treatments being applied, allowing conflicts to spread and become more aggravated. It is therefore critical to carefully examine the history of the Sino-US relationship, including its financial dimensions, to correctly identify the key issues that must be addressed.

Modern History of Sino-US Relations

After the CCP came to power in 1949, a rift opened between the US and China along the ideological lines of capitalism versus communism. As the Cold War got under way, the US applied the same strategy of 'containment' towards China that it employed with the Soviet Union. For three decades, the US did not officially recognise the People's Republic of China (PRC) and sought to limit its influence in and recognition by the outside world. For its part, China treated the US as a strategic enemy and sought to spread communist revolution in Southeast Asia, threatening US interests. The countries stood on opposing sides in two wars: in Korea (1950–1953) and in Vietnam (1955–1975).

The impetus for the thaw in relations that started with Henry Kissinger's secret visit to China in 1971 was their common desire to counterbalance the threat from the Soviet Union. It was a relationship based not on common ideals, but on a common enemy. The eventual normalisation in relations that came in 1978 left open the important question of the future of Taiwan. However, vast US military superiority meant that there was little immediate prospect that differences over the territory would boil over. Moreover, Deng Xiaoping was preoccupied with economic reforms after the ravages of decades of civil strife.

As the threat from the Soviet Union declined during the 1980s, both because of Mikhail Gorbachev's rise to power in 1985 and due to the implosion of communism itself, the basis of the Sino-US relationship evolved into one of commerce and trade. Trade was mutually beneficial in many ways, and China's economic reforms transformed the lives of most of the Chinese people for the better. However, the two countries' social and political models remained poles apart. In 1989, a wave of protests erupted in China, calling for faster political reforms. The violent suppression of these became a flashpoint in Sino-US relations, since the CCP's actions offended American sensibilities over human rights and democracy.

In retrospect, comparing China's trajectory to that of Russia in the years since, it is hard to argue that a different course of action at that time would have resulted in a better outcome for the Chinese population as a whole. Reforms of the size and scope that China was pursuing had created significant internal conflicts both within the CCP leadership and across wider society. Deng's historic Southern Tour (南巡) in 1992 signalled his continued commitment to economic reforms. This was critical in overcoming internal opposition within the CCP and broader society to continuing reforms. George H. W. Bush took the decision not to leave China ostracised and out in the cold and, with the skilled stewardship of Zhu Rongji (朱镕基) – first as vice premier, then as premier – huge leaps forward were made in China's economic transformation. These included the introduction of market-based pricing mechanisms, monetary reforms to rein in runaway inflation, and privatisation of some of the sprawling state-owned enterprises (SOEs). He also successfully negotiated China's entry into the WTO, spurring a surge in foreign investment and exports.

Throughout this period, China's record on human rights was a recurring theme in the dialogue between the two countries. In part, this reflected public opinion in the US and its commitment to liberal democratic values. In part, it also served as a useful pretext when the US needed leverage in negotiations on other matters. Taiwan's continuous transformation into an ever more vibrant liberal democracy presented problems for both sides.

US actions in other parts of the world in the post-Cold War period significantly coloured China's views about US foreign policy. A number of events heightened insecurity among China's leadership. During the 1991 Gulf War, the ease with which US-led forces overran Saddam Hussein's army – then the fourth largest in the world – shocked China's military leaders.[7] It highlighted the backwardness and vulnerability of the People's Liberation Army (PLA). Their insecurity was reinforced by Bill Clinton's decision to send two aircraft carriers to Taiwan during the Taiwan Strait crisis in 1996.[8] China had become a net importer of crude oil that year. With 80 percent of China's oil imports passing through the narrow waterway connecting the Indian Ocean and the South China Sea, known as the Malacca Strait,[9] American dominance of the sea lanes in close proximity to China posed a threat that key supplies would be cut off in the event of conflict. This focused the Chinese leadership's minds on maritime security.

The US-instigated North Atlantic Treaty Organisation (NATO) bombings of Yugoslav troops during the Kosovo War in 1999 also set a worrying precedent for China's leadership, who had strenuously opposed the action alongside Russia as interference in the internal affairs of another sovereign country. The pretext of humanitarian intervention, given continuous US attacks on China's human rights record, was a cause for serious concern to the CCP. The Bush Administration's pursuit of an invasion of Iraq in 2003 further compounded insecurities. The Chinese leadership saw little option other than to pursue comprehensive military modernisation as economic growth provided the financial means.

During the 1997 Asian Financial Crisis, in contrast to other countries in the region, China resisted devaluing the renminbi. It was hoped that currency stability would demonstrate China's financial discipline and help maintain confidence in its economy, but it also served to bolster regional economic stability. As its balance of payments surplus, particularly versus the US, surged after the turn of the millennium, China then drew heavy criticism from US policymakers for holding *down* the value of its currency. China's manufacturing growth contrasted with a decline in America's manufacturing capacity and it became easy to blame China for the loss of American jobs. However, on closer inspection of China's manufacturing exports, the picture becomes rather less clear cut.

A high proportion of China's exports is in the processing trade and contains high import content. One estimate shows that, of the 7.4 percent GDP growth that China saw in 2014, consumption and investment accounted for 3.8 percent and 3.0 percent, respectively, meaning that net exports only contributed 0.6 percent to China's GDP growth that year.[10] What is more, by 2018, although China's trade surplus with the US had reached $419 billion, its trade with the rest of the world was roughly balanced. That is to say that, while China has a huge balance of payments surplus versus the US, this is offset by a deficit that it is running with other nations and territories, including raw material exporters such as Australia and Brazil; and suppliers of intermediate goods and components, such as Korea and Taiwan.[11] The US balance of payments deficit versus China is therefore more accurately depicted as a deficit that the US is running against the rest the world.

This deficit can be explained partly by America's comparative advantage in high technology, where core research and design are carried out in the US, while lower value manufacturing and assembly have been offshored to lower cost locations. Apple is a classic example of this. A China-assembled iPad that is sold in the US for $499 generates only around $8 for Chinese labour.[12] In contrast, the Chinese market has generated huge profits for American companies such as Boeing, Nike, Starbucks and Disney.[13]

That is not to say that the US does not have valid grievances against China in areas of trade and financial policy. Foreign businesses operating in China have long complained that Chinese government policies discriminate against them, citing lack of regulatory transparency; inadequate protection of intellectual property; difficulty obtaining local licenses; and limited protections for their commercial secrets. There is a strong case that there is indeed a highly uneven playing field for foreign businesses in China.[14] Given China's high level of domestic savings, there is also a legitimate complaint about the asymmetry between the relative ease of foreign investment into China's capital markets and the still-limited channels for foreign companies to raise capital from Chinese investors.

Many of these issues arise from the fact that China continues to feature a relatively overbearing state. This and continuing shortcomings in the transparency and consistency of the legal and regulatory system are problems that China's growing population of private businessmen and entrepreneurs also increasingly chafe against. The strength of Hong Kong's IPO market provides a good illustration of this. HKEX has been the top IPO venue globally in five of the 10 years up to the end of 2020, with Mainland Chinese companies accounting for 85 percent of the funds raised over that period.[15] Although Chinese businesses seeking to raise money from public markets would reap far higher valuations by listing in Shanghai (上海) or Shenzhen (深圳),[16] many private businessmen still prefer to IPO their companies in Hong Kong. The reasons for this include Hong Kong's relatively reliable legal and regulatory system; the ability for them to raise funds in a currency that is easily convertible; and the desire to protect their wealth from the Chinese authorities by moving part of it offshore.

The Chinese government is not unaware of the many problems and has been pursuing gradual reforms. Many of these reforms have been market-oriented and have better aligned China's practices with international norms, including the lowering of barriers to capital flows between China and international markets. However, given the flaws in the US financial and economic model highlighted by the GFC, many in China's leadership have become even more sceptical than before about US free market ideology. To successfully bring about further financial and economic reforms now, the case needs to be stronger than in the past. US coercion has had some impact but is likely to be met with continual resistance. Ultimately, it is likely that domestic forces will be the most effective in pushing the Chinese government towards change.

In the aftermath of the GFC, Chinese officials have no doubt displayed some level of conceit and a greater degree of assertiveness in their interactions with other countries.[17] Following President's Xi Jinping's (习近平) coming to power in 2012, China has also stepped up the scale of its international ambitions, notably through the Belt and Road Initiative (BRI, 一带一路), a grand infrastructure development strategy encompassing a large number of developing countries and trading partners. China's Made in China 2025 (中国制造 2025) strategy also seeks to upgrade China's industrial base from low value export manufactures to high technology value products and services. To a great extent, these initiatives are a far-sighted recognition, triggered by the GFC, that China cannot indefinitely depend on growth in exports to Western markets in light of the structural economic headwinds that those countries face. However, China's increasing international ambitions have been seen as a threat to the US, particularly as Xi's administration appears to be centralising more power within the CCP.

Since the Trump Administration launched its trade war with China in January 2018, the scope of the conflict has been widened from a pure focus on trade and tariffs. Sanctions have been applied against Chinese technology companies. US allies have been pressured to remove Chinese manufactured components from their telecommunications networks on national security grounds. Further, Chinese companies from sensitive sectors have been denied access to US capital markets. Officials from both countries have recently hurled incendiary accusations at each other and engaged in an unseemly war of words over the origins of the Covid-19 pandemic and interference in Hong Kong affairs.[18] Some commentators believe that the US and China have entered – or are entering – into a 'New Cold War' or 'Cold War II'.[19] Some have even gone so far as to suggest that there are reasons to welcome this, believing that multidimensional Great Power competition will provide an impetus for human progress and help the US confront its recent political dysfunction.[20]

The Financial Roots of Sino-US Conflict

This book rejects the notion that the current Sino-US conflict is a New Cold War for three reasons.

First, there is a critical difference in the factors underlying tensions between China and the US today and those that precipitated the 20th century Cold War. In the late 1940s, there was no meaningful trade or investment between the US and the Soviet Union that could give rise to frictions. The primary driver of the Cold War was ideological, whereas financial factors have played a major role in stoking current Sino-US tensions. While it is undeniable that there are significant ideological differences between China and the US, far from seeking the overthrow of global capitalism, China has adopted significant aspects of the capitalist economic model and, although it has not fully embraced America's brand of free market ideology, it is today no more socialist than a great many European social democracies. These hardly present a threat to America's capitalist way of life.

Second, the Cold War was characterised to a great extent by strategic disengagement between the two principal protagonists, as both worked in parallel to demonstrate the superiority of their respective economic models. Since there was virtually no economic relationship to begin with, there was little to lose. In contrast, given the high level of economic interdependence between China and America today, disengagement – or 'decoupling', as some would have it – would be highly damaging to both nations' prosperity. That is even if complete disengagement were actually possible. Globalisation has interwoven and integrated economies and supply chains around the world to an extent that would make a decoupling between China and the US not only economically damaging but also quite likely to lead to a cascading set of conflicts with other countries. Australia, against which America runs balance of payments surpluses, can afford to pay for US imports due, in large part, to the surpluses it runs versus China.[21] Ironically, therefore, Sino-US disengagement could compound existing economic stresses and elevate the risk of hostilities ratcheting up.

Third, to the extent that a state of 'Cold War' exists today, it is hardly 'new'. A central theme of this book is that widening wealth and income inequality in both countries has been a major factor underlying current Sino-US tensions. At the root of rising inequality are the cumulative imbalances created by the structure of the global financial system and national economic policies, which have built up over many decades. That is not to say that there are not other sources of tensions between the two countries. Great Power relations are inextricably tied to historical contexts and are influenced by numerous internal and external factors, as well as the characters of political leaders. Some focus on a schism between America's liberal democracy and China's one-party state. However, while this difference in political models is a determinant of how the two societies individually operate and can be mobilised, it is not in itself an inherent source of conflict. Instead, throughout the history of human civilisation, the division of material wealth and resources *between* and *within* societies has repeatedly been found at the heart of major clashes, and this is the dimension of Sino-US relations on which this book is focused.

Tracing back to the end of WW2, as the Cold War was getting under way, the world was unwittingly entering into a *Financial Cold War*, in which it has been engaged ever since. The opening shot of this war was the Bretton Woods Agreement of 1944, which lodged the US dollar at the centre of the global monetary system. Financial systems, like all ecosystems, thrive on equilibrium. The dollar's centrality in the financial order created by Bretton Woods spawned an imbalance that has since grown and multiplied. The Financial Cold War has played out over two key battlefronts.

The first has been the division of resources *between* countries. The dollar-centric global financial system has created international demand for dollars that has provided the US with low-cost capital without any currency mis-match risk. Other countries, notably emerging markets that have needed to insure against periodic dollar exchange rate volatility, have borne a high cost for this. However, to keep the world supplied with sufficient dollar liquidity, the US was required to run continual balance of payments deficits. The lack of any structural mechanism for revaluing the currencies of countries with persistent large balance of payments surpluses has forced America to become the world's 'consumer of last resort'. This has transferred productive capacity to other countries and, unless the US is able to constantly expand its economy faster than its cumulative balance of payments deficits, the rising debt burden will drag on future growth. It was fortuitous that America's lead in the information technology revolution allowed it to maintain strong growth with low inflation for a quarter of a century. However, in recent years, rapidly rising public debt has given rise to concerns over America's long-term financial stability, exacerbated global financial imbalances, and created tensions with large foreign holders of US public debt, including China, due to the risk of monetary inflation.

The second battlefront has been over the distribution of wealth *within* countries. The billionaire Warren Buffett candidly told a *CNN* interviewer in 2011 that 'there's been class warfare going on for the last 20 years, and my class has won'.[22] He was right. Structural overvaluation of the dollar due to the level of foreign demand for the currency has weakened the competitiveness of American exports in international markets. The wealthy have benefited disproportionately from the migration of manufacturing to lower-cost centres of production, while US workers have paid the price. This is not just a matter of monetary policy, however. Extreme ideological leanings towards free market policies since the 1980s have benefited wealthy and corporate interests through a range of policies, including lower taxation and less rigorous antitrust enforcement. The negative social impacts have been far-reaching. Rising wealth concentration has dragged on American economic vibrancy and undermined the legitimacy of the political system.

China's rapid growth over the past four decades, and the consequent improvement in living standards, has insulated it from this second battlefront so far. In unleashing this growth, a number of highly talented statesmen have had to balance a great many conflicting interests. However, as it has pursued market-oriented reforms, growing wealth inequality in China is also generating greater social tensions. As economic growth slows from the heady rates of earlier years and demographic pressures from the country's aging population continue to rise, these tensions will only grow more acute. China's governance structure and economic model, credited with fostering the country's development during the early years of its economic transformation, may now be holding it back from adapting to new realities.

At its most fundamental level, therefore, the Financial Cold War is the invisible conflict, embedded in national financial policies and the structure of international financial markets, over the distribution of wealth. Worryingly, however, this has been spilling over into wider conflicts.

In the face of growing domestic social tensions arising from wealth and income inequality, the political elites in both countries have resorted to populist nationalism. This is discussed further in Chapter 6. The result has been escalating Sino-US tensions, with the Financial Cold War recently heating up in the form of a widening geopolitical clash being played out in the financial and economic spheres.

Conventionally, there are considered to be seven economic tools suited to geopolitical application: trade policy; investment policy; economic and financial sanctions; financial and monetary policy; economic aid; cyber; and energy and commodities.[23] The latter two have certainly been applied in Sino-US geopolitical context but, since these verge on the domain of conventional warfare, they fall outside the scope of this volume, which is focused on the financial and economic dimensions of the relationship that are stoking tensions. Nevertheless, as highlighted in this book, each of the other tools in the economic arsenal has been mobilised in an escalating Sino-US conflict.

The trade war launched by Donald Trump in early 2018 has been the focus of much attention. However, this was neither the opening salvo in the geo-economic clash between the US and China, nor is trade even the most pertinent battlefront. While trade flows were at the fore-front of policymakers' thinking at Bretton Woods,[24] the huge growth in global financial markets since then means that today the trade in goods and services has been vastly superseded by financial flows, which now account for roughly 90 percent of cross-border capital movements.[25] It is therefore to the capital markets that we must look to fully understand the scope of the geo-economic conflict between the two countries.

As the geo-economic campaign between China and the US unfolds, we face a substantial risk that this will spill over into broader conflicts that could result in disaster for both nations and the rest of the world.

The Financial Path Out of Conflict

The evolution of markets has been a major civilising force for human-ity. Financial markets provide a vital means for capital to be allocated to where it can be most productively used and have enabled the sharing of risks, such that mankind has been able to undertake giant ventures beyond the capacity of any individual or small group. This has contrib-uted to a reduction in conflict and to huge advances for humankind.

Nevertheless, markets operate within institutional frameworks and are subject to the incentives that they create. When policies are calibrated to encourage competition and foster enterprise, markets can be powerful drivers of innovation and progress. Financial markets are complex eco-systems, however. Poorly designed incentive structures and lax regulatory enforcement can give rise to serious imbalances. When imbalances occur, their impact can stretch far beyond the financial sphere, with significant social, political and diplomatic repercussions.

Since finding resolutions must begin with understanding, this book reviews in detail the history of how the global financial system today has come about, as well as the ideological and practical underpinnings of different financial and economic policies.

Part One of the book focuses on the US. It first gives an account of how the dollar came to dominate the global financial system, and explains the policies, regulations, infrastructure and market conventions that perpetuate the dollar's global role. It then questions whether the costs of that role to both the US and the rest of the world may now outweigh the benefits.

Part Two focuses on China. Given the very long historical perspective through which Chinese policymakers frame policy, it is necessary to have a broad perspective of Chinese history to appreciate the context of today's financial and economic policies. This part therefore first takes readers on a whistle-stop journey through six centuries of Chinese history, from the height of China's relative global economic power during the Ming Dynasty (明朝, 1368–1644) through to the ravages of the Cultural Revolution (文化大革命, 1966–1976) and the country's economic climb back in the decades since. It then goes on to give an account of the development of China's modern financial markets and examines the financial and economic challenges facing the country today.

Part Three examines the true nature of the current Sino-US conflict and possible ways to reduce tensions between the two countries. It first critically assesses the New Cold War narrative and looks at the financial and economic sources and dimensions of conflict. It then looks at the role of financial markets today and how, in many instances, contemporary policies, regulations and incentives have subverted the proper functioning of markets. The final chapter concludes with a discussion of potential reforms to US and Chinese policies and to the global monetary system that could help rebalance the world economy and de-escalate Sino-US tensions.

The sheer scale of the imbalances that have built up means that they cannot be quickly unwound and many of the challenges are not well understood. Reforms will require key decision makers in China, the US and other major nations to put their heads together, seek truth from the facts, and cooperate with each other in designing appropriate policies. It will be a daunting task. However, for the sake of our future peace, stability and prosperity, it is a task that we can no longer put off.

PART ONE

THE COLOUR OF MONEY TURNS GREEN

Chapter 2

How the US Dollar Took Over the World

Dollar bills have absolutely no value except in our collective
imagination, but everyone believes in the dollar bill.

– Yuval Noah Harari

If we were to imagine the global economy as a human body, then
you could say that America controls its circulatory system. Flowing
through the arteries and veins of the global financial system are US
dollars, which serve as the primary means of exchange in international
trade and investment, and as a universally recognised store of economic
value. The dollar was used for around 39 percent of all global payments
and dollar-denominated securities (largely in the form of US Treasuries) made up roughly 60 percent of global foreign exchange reserves in
2020,[1] far exceeding America's share of either world trade (11 percent[2])
or nominal global GDP (24 percent[3]). In other words, the US currency

plays a role in the world that stretches way beyond US borders and has, in effect, become a global utility.

At least one former US Treasury Secretary has acknowledged that the dollar's role is a source of great power for the US, since it has allowed the US government to 'pay lower rates . . . than it otherwise would' on its borrowings and 'enables the country to run larger trade deficits, reduces exchange-rate risk, and makes American financial markets more liquid'.[4] Another commentator put it more bluntly: 'By generating a steady flow of customers who want to hold the currency . . . it allows the privileged country to . . . *fund a lifestyle well beyond its means*'.[5]

At one time, the dollar was backed by a fixed quantity of gold; however, since President Nixon's abandonment of the gold standard in 1973, the currency has had no intrinsic value beyond ink, paper and faith in the US government and its financial system. That the rest of the world continues to confer what former French president Valéry Giscard d'Estaing called this 'exorbitant privilege' on the US undoubtedly reflects the fact that the dollar-based global financial system has had benefits for other countries as well. However, as we shall see in Chapter 3, many stakeholders within that system are increasingly questioning whether the costs may now outweigh the benefits.

Although it seems firmly entrenched, the primacy that the dollar enjoys today is, in historical terms, a relatively recent phenomenon. For most of the 1800s, America's economy was predominantly agrarian and inward looking. It was not until 1916, with Europe heavily weighed down by World War I (WW1), that the US economy overtook the British Empire to become the largest in the world.[6] Even then, the role the dollar played in global trade and investment was only roughly equivalent to that of sterling up until WW2 and the throbbing heart of international finance continued to be the City of London, whose banking fraternity looked down on their US counterparts as 'unsophisticated kinsmen, too rich for their own good'.[7]

While it may be tempting to draw a correlation between the growth of the US economy during and after WW2 and the rise in the dollar's global status, much as it is now speculated that China's economic growth will inevitably lead to the renminbi becoming the dominant global currency, this interpretation would be overly simplistic and inaccurate. If GDP size were the sole factor determining the relative global importance of a nation's currency, then both the euro and the renminbi would already be close to usurping the dollar – a prospect that remains distant today. Instead, the dollar's present dominance is rooted in historical circumstance and perpetuated through four pillars of the US system: the rule of law; international trade and macroeconomic policies; the deepest and most open financial markets in the world; and established capital markets infrastructure supporting the global financial system. All too often, this fourth pillar is overlooked by economists and policymakers. This is a serious oversight for, without a solid understanding and appreciation of the 'plumbing' of the global financial system, it is impossible to foresee the impact of market evolutions or to design effective financial policies. Before attempting to diagnose the problems of our current global financial order, let alone determining the feasibility – or even desirability – of any major changes to it, we must first understand how it came about and its structural underpinnings.

The story of the US dollar's rise over the last century is inextricably intertwined with the geopolitics of the era, but it is also one of financial and technological innovation. At certain times, domestic and international policies drove this innovation; at other times, geopolitics were driven by structural shifts in the markets. Some significant factors that contributed to the dollar's dominance actually arose out of American policy mistakes, policy choices by other governments, or financial entrepreneurialism that policymakers initially weren't even aware of. There are, of course, many aspects to American power besides the dollar, and the currency has always had a relationship of symbiosis and mutual reinforcement with these. However, as the other sources of US power have waned, the dollar has become ever more important in relative and, paradoxically, absolute terms. There has been a price for this though – one that the original architect of the dollar's leadership perhaps didn't sufficiently take into account.

An Ad Hoc Position

It is said that success has many fathers and so it is with the astonishing success of the US dollar over the past hundred years, but if any one man can be credited with having laid the foundation stone upon which the dollar's empire was built, that man would be Harry Dexter White. As a senior US Treasury Department official in the 1940s, White was the key architect of the Bretton Woods system that governed the international economic order for almost three decades after WW2.

Born in 1892, White was the son of Lithuanian Jews who had fled the tsarist pogroms in 1885 and settled in Boston. Harry was the youngest of seven children and was educated in local public schools, where he was not an exceptional student. His mother had died when he was aged just nine. His father Jacob was a peddler who made a living dealing in hardware and crockery. Through hard work and thrift, the family had eventually come to own four hardware stores by the time Jacob died, just two months after Harry graduated from high school. After school, he initially worked as a clerk in the family business, but upon President Woodrow Wilson's declaration of war on Imperial Germany in April 1917, the 25-year-old Harry White enlisted in the US Army and was commissioned as an infantry first lieutenant.

Stationed in France in training and supply camps, White had an uneventful war and returned home in November 1918. However, no longer satisfied by the life of a small businessman, he set his sights on an academic career and enrolled at Columbia University in 1922 to study government. He transferred the following year to Stanford, from which he graduated 'with great distinction' in economics.[8] From Stanford, he moved on to pursue a PhD at Harvard and it was there that he appeared to develop a fascination for the relationship between the workings of the international monetary system and the performance of the real economy. He taught for six years at Harvard but, aged 40 and unable to secure a tenured position, he took up an assistant professorship at Lawrence College in Appleton, Wisconsin in 1933.

Harry White's path from Wisconsin to the US Treasury came via an invitation in the summer of 1934 from Jacob Viner, a respected University of Chicago economics professor. Viner was at the time advising Treasury Secretary Henry Morgenthau and asked White to assist him on a three-month study of monetary and banking legislation and institutions. Once in Washington, White never looked back. Following completion of the Viner study, he took another temporary position with the US Tariff Commission but returned to the Treasury just three weeks later when a position as principle economic analyst in the Division of

Research and Statistics opened up. This was again a temporary position paid for, fatefully, out of profits from an emergency fund set up to stabilise the dollar's exchange rate. Remarkably, White's employment at the Treasury would continue on this tenuous *ad hoc* basis for another 12 years until he was finally made a fully-fledged civil servant in 1945.[9]

In the early 1930s, the world was mired in the Great Depression and the prevailing monetary orthodoxy for countries to tie the value of their currencies to a fixed quantity of gold had broken down. With great reluctance, Britain had abandoned the gold standard in September 1931 and devalued sterling. Twenty-five other nations followed suit shortly thereafter. The US held out for a time but was ultimately forced to give up the dollar's fix to gold in April 1933, shortly after President Franklin D. Roosevelt took office. There followed a period during which the dollar's exchange rate seemed to fluctuate arbitrarily, as the President took to setting a target exchange rate from his bed each morning, mostly based on whim rather than scientific method. While the thought of befuddled bankers rather tickled Roosevelt's sense of humour, concerns were raised from within the Federal Reserve and the Treasury, where some considered FDR to be acting beyond his presidential authority in buying gold at a price above the level fixed by statute. Roosevelt ultimately relented and, under the Gold Reserve Act, re-fixed the dollar's exchange rate to gold in January 1934 at $35 per ounce, 59.06 percent below its previous level.[10]

As countries battled with the Depression era's high unemployment, they turned to competitive devaluations and tariff barriers in an effort to make their exports more competitive and to limit imports. These 'beggar-thy-neighbour' policies led to a collapse in global trade, significantly worsening the economic hardship. In the subsequent years and decades, the international trade and monetary policies of the interwar years became widely viewed as a major factor contributing to the outbreak of WW2.

At the Treasury, Harry White gained a reputation as an able economist and carved out a critical role for himself in international policy. He was also known to be quick-tempered and impatient, though he 'was meticulously civil to anyone in a position to afford him access to the powerful'.[11] The focus of his work reflected the major trade and monetary issues of the time, into which he threw himself energetically.

Competitive currency devaluations and their impact on global trade was an issue with which he concerned himself especially. He argued that a stabilisation in international monetary policy was required to increase foreign trade, which was an important factor in achieving the economic recovery that the Roosevelt Administration sought to bring about. This would require a new form of international monetary diplomacy. Competition between the Treasury and the State Department over control of this function was to open to White a huge opportunity.

Henry Morgenthau Jr. was a long-time friend and neighbour of FDR at his Hyde Park estate in upstate New York. He had no background in economics and, upon his appointment as Treasury Secretary in 1934, the prominent New York donor Gladys Straus quipped that Roosevelt had managed to find 'the only Jew in the world who doesn't know a thing about money'.[12] White rapidly made himself indispensable as the intellectual force behind Morgenthau's expanding power base, while Morgenthau served as a powerful patron for the ambitious White.

In 1935, Morgenthau despatched White on a trip to Europe to engage in fact-finding and exploratory talks on the matter of exchange rate stabilisation. This trip was to have great significance in Harry White's career, as his meetings with politicians, businessmen, bankers, civil servants and economists would help to position him later as the obvious candidate to coordinate and lead America's international negotiations on the post-war monetary system. It was also on this trip that he first met John Maynard Keynes, the famed British economist with whom he would later joust in the run-up to and during the 1944 Bretton Woods conference.

The Barbarous Relic

In contrast to Harry White, Maynard Keynes had a privileged upbringing. Born into an affluent academic family in Cambridge, his father Neville was a lecturer in moral sciences and a fellow of Pembroke College, while his mother, who had been educated at Newnham College, became the city's first female mayor. Educated at Eton, he had gone on to study mathematics at King's College Cambridge, where he was elected to a lifetime fellowship in 1908, at the age of 26. A liberal with a mischievous anti-establishment streak, he was a leading member of the Bloomsbury Set that included intellectuals and artists such as Leonard and Virginia Woolf, as well as Duncan Grant, Keynes' one-time lover.

During WW1, Keynes served in the British Treasury and had a front row seat in the 1919 Paris Peace Conference, where the terms of the peace were hammered out. He quit in disgust three weeks before the Versailles Treaty was signed and went on to publish a highly critical account of those negotiations under the widely acclaimed title *The Economic Consequences of the Peace*. In this book, he painted withering portraits of the three leading figures of the conference – American President Woodrow Wilson, British Prime Minister David Lloyd George, and French Prime Minister Georges Clémenceau. Among Keynes' key criticisms of Versailles was the high level of war reparations imposed. He had argued that, if the defeated Germany was 'to be "milked"', then she 'must first of all not be ruined'.[13] Indeed, popular resentment of the economic hardship that reparations imposed on the German population was later exploited by the Nazis in their rise to power in the 1930s.

Keynes had seen the question of reparations as being inextricably tied to the debts that the European Allies had taken on to finance the war. He had therefore proposed that the peace treaty include a financial package that would have linked the reparations paid by Germany to the level of repayments by the Allies to each other and to the US. The US had lent $12 billion to the Europeans during WW1, of which around $5 billion was owed by Great Britain and $4 billion by France. In turn, Britain was owed $11 billion by 17 countries, including some $3 billion due from France and $2.5 billion due from Russia, which had become uncollectible following the Bolshevik revolution in 1917.[14] Understandably, the Americans were reluctant to take a write-down on their loans to the Allies and Woodrow Wilson dismissed Keynes' proposal, insisting that reparations and war debts be treated as two separate matters.

Reparations and war debt, however, were not the greatest villains in the cast that Keynes held responsible for the global economic ills of the interwar period. The leading role, as his thinking developed through the 1920s, was reserved for gold.

The expansion of global trade during the 19th century had been underpinned by the fixing of the value of currencies against gold.

Issuers of currency on the so-called gold standard committed themselves to holding reserves of physical gold against the paper money that they issued. This provided an assurance that the issuer would not erode the value of its currency by simply printing more notes. Expansion of the money supply, therefore, was restricted by the pace of new gold discoveries, which were relatively infrequent.[15]

Of course, in periods of distress such as times of war, governments can be tempted to expand the money supply by way of the printing presses in order to meet their obligations. Britain had last done this during the French Revolutionary War in 1797, when the threat of invasion had led to mass withdrawals of gold from the Bank of England. However, in the years 1815–1821, following Napoleon's defeat at Waterloo, the Bank had withdrawn around half the paper money in circulation, driving prices down by 50 percent, and restored the gold standard. Though those six years had witnessed riots and economic distress, Britain's monetary discipline was seen as having set sterling apart from all other currencies in Europe. This in turn was credited for the country's emergence as the world's leading economic power over the half-century that followed.[16] As trade surpluses from Britain's lead in manufacturing exports generated excess capital searching for investments, London emerged from the 19th century as the banker to the world and sterling the pre-eminent global currency.

During the four years of WW1, European governments had incurred total war spending of around $200 billion, or roughly half of their aggregate GDP. In addition to borrowing from their own citizens and from overseas, they had raised taxes and printed more money. By the end of the war, the money supply in Britain had doubled, in France it had tripled, and in Germany it had quadrupled.[17] In the early 1920s, in the face of social and fiscal pressures, Germany resorted to uncontrolled money printing, leading to massive hyperinflation that decimated the value of middle-class savings. Britain, still vested with the pride of a great imperial power, chose the opposite route and sought to restore the value of sterling to the pre-war level.

Before WW1, the British pound's exchange rate to the US dollar, fixed by the gold standard, had been $4.86. Having untethered itself from gold during the war, sterling's exchange rate had fallen to as low as $3.20. In 1920–1921, the Bank of England, led by its conservative governor Montagu Norman, chose to deflate the economy via high interest rates in order to reverse wartime inflation. Prices fell by 50 percent from their wartime highs and the pound recovered to $4.35 by the autumn of 1924. However, while the country rebounded from a recession in 1921, growth remained muted and the exchange rate struggled to recover to the 1914 level.[18]

Keynes, back in Cambridge after the war and having acquired celebrity status on account of the success of *The Economic Consequences*, became a prolific columnist writing on economic issues. He also dabbled in speculation on currencies and commodity prices. While the rest of the country was struggling with unemployment rates of around 10 percent in 1923, these pursuits provided him with a handsome living. The main target of his writings was the Bank of England and its stubborn quest to restore the old dollar parity. He argued eloquently and with acerbic wit that the Bank was mistaken in its belief that wages were sufficiently flexible to adjust as rapidly as prices, and that the short-term pain caused by its policies was bringing Britain to the 'verge of revolution'.[19]

Notwithstanding Maynard Keynes' impassioned assault on gold, the Conservative Party's victory in the 1924 general election heightened expectations of a return to the gold standard. Winston Churchill, who had roamed the political wilderness since spearheading the Gallipoli debacle in 1915, was surprised to find himself appointed Chancellor of the Exchequer in Stanley Baldwin's government. This meant that the decision about sterling's link to gold fell to him. While no intellectual laggard, Churchill never mastered the details of monetary policy and relied on advice from experts in the field. Although Keynes was among those whom he consulted, the establishment orthodoxy prevailed. In his budget of April 1925, Churchill announced Britain's return to the gold standard at the pre-war rate. This soon proved to be a mistake that he came to regret.

At the level at which it was fixed to gold, sterling was significantly overvalued, making Britain's exports uncompetitive. France, on the other hand, returned to the gold standard in 1928 at one-fifth of the 1914 parity, significantly *undervaluing* the franc and thereby making French exports far more attractive.[20] As a consequence, capital flooded into France with its undervalued currency and into the US, which was experiencing a stock market boom, while uncompetitive British industry was starved of investment.

In a series of articles, pamphlets and books written and published between 1923 and 1936, Keynes launched an intellectual attack on the classical economic orthodoxy and its reliance on gold, which he called a 'barbarous relic'. These works addressed not just monetary policy, but its relationship with employment, prices and trade. His theories were to form an intellectual basis for economic policies that predominated in the West in the post-war years up until the 1970s.

He argued that gold as a foundation for the monetary system had only worked during the 19th century because new mining discoveries had fortuitously kept pace with economic growth. The operation of monetary policy to avoid the loss of gold reserves, as was the prevailing practice, entailed raising interest rates at times of economic weakness, which served to raise savings and exacerbate falling consumer demand, further compounding falling profits. Given the fluctuating pace of economic growth and variances between different trading partners, he believed that central banks were much better positioned to manage a country's monetary affairs without gold as a reference. This is, in fact, the system commonly followed today with floating fiat currencies, but was a revolutionary concept at the time.

Keynes also explained that inflation and deflation, more than just a rise and fall in prices, were a means of wealth transfer between different groups and social classes within society. Classical economic theory held that, in a free market, wages would naturally adjust to a level at which there would be full employment. Keynes debunked this theory and showed that there was no natural tendency for full employment. For structural and even psychological reasons, wages do not necessarily adjust in line with falls in prices and profits. Further, since falling wages themselves removed economic demand, deflation could actually worsen unemployment. This meant that high unemployment could persist indefinitely unless governments intervened to boost consumption demand. Crucially, he argued that such government spending would have a 'multiplier' effect, since it would stimulate other economic activity. This therefore justified governments' use of deficit spending at times of rising unemployment as a means of 'pump priming' the economy to induce a return to growth.

Citing his famous remark that 'In the long run, we are all dead',[21] critics of Keynesian economic theory have often accused him of advocating policy short-termism and irresponsible government spending that would lead to ever rising deficits. This is inaccurate, as Keynes actually believed strongly in balanced budgets over an economic cycle. However, governments have tended to lack the political will or discipline to rein in their budgets in the good times.

There is no doubt that Keynes' theories were founded on Britain's particular economic circumstances at the time. Nevertheless, it became clear that the rigidity of the gold standard was a major underlying contributor to the *worldwide* breakdown in trade and economic hardship of the 1930s. The need to maintain fixed exchange rates forced central banks to raise interest rates to prevent outflows of gold just as economic demand was already shrinking. Due to the nature of fractional reserve banking systems,[22] the impact of withdrawals of gold was magnified through the reduction in banks' capacity to lend. In turn, this caused asset prices to tumble, which led to loan defaults that further compounded economic weakness. As panic set in, scenes of depositors queued up outside banks to withdraw their savings became commonplace. Some 9,000 banks in the US failed during the 1930s.[23]

Via the transmission mechanisms of international trade and investment, economic problems in one country spread to others and prosperity declined globally. Even countries that had run large trade surpluses suffered. France had maintained strong exports by keeping the franc undervalued, but the Banque de France incurred huge losses on its sterling balances when Britain was forced to devalue the pound in 1931.

Keynes was convinced that the global monetary order needed to be radically reformed. Instead of society adjusting to the requirements of the gold standard, he believed that it was monetary policy that needed to adapt to the natural tendencies of society. In his vision, there needed to be a more flexible mechanism of international exchange rates to allow for periodic adjustments in response to imbalances in trade or capital flows, and the role of the barbarous relic in monetary policy needed to be gradually phased out. And this is precisely the plan that he drew up.

Two Competing Plans

Hitler's invasion of Poland in September 1939 precipitated the commencement of WW2 in Europe. Even before America was drawn into the war by the Japanese attack on Pearl Harbour in December 1941, it was already entangled via the Lend-Lease programme, through which it was providing material and financial support to a cash-strapped Britain. Churchill described America's Lend-Lease programme as a 'most unsordid act',[24] but it was also one of calculated self-interest since, if Britain were to be defeated by Germany, the US would be left standing alone against a fascist-controlled Europe. For Britain, however, it meant it would face a costly debt to the US after the war.

Keynes returned to the Treasury as an unpaid advisor to the Chancellor of the Exchequer after WW2 started. By this time, he was becoming a part of the establishment that he had previously derided. He was elected to the Court of the Bank of England in 1941 and then ennobled as Baron Keynes of Tilton the following year. Understanding the implications of his country's financial position and the need to plan ahead for its changed circumstances after the war, he began work in August 1941 on a plan for a new post-war global monetary order.

Anxious to avoid a repeat of the policy mistakes of the 1920s and 1930s, his plan sought to replicate the stability of the gold standard within a more flexible framework. There were two key elements to his proposal.

First, there was to be a new global reserve currency created, which he called *Bancor* (French for 'bank gold'). Bancor was to have a fixed exchange rate against all members' currencies and gold, but it was provided that countries with persistent balance of payments deficits would be subject to automatic devaluations, while countries running persistent surpluses would be subject to upwards adjustments of their exchange rates. This created a 'pegged but adjustable' currency system that enabled changes in countries' relative balance of payments to be reflected in their exchange rates over time.[25]

Second, it involved setting up a new global central bank that he called the International Clearing Bank (ICB), which would take on the role of issuing Bancor. Central banks were to buy and sell their own currencies among themselves through a system of debits and credits in their ICB 'clearing accounts', with the ICB providing overdraft facilities to cover any temporary balance of payments shortfalls.[26] This would avoid the chronic shortage of gold reserves that wrought global financial instability in the interwar years. Although Keynes had accommodated gold within the system in recognition of its historic monetary role, it was provided that the ICB could issue new Bancors in exchange for gold, but that there would only be one-way convertibility, thereby gradually withdrawing gold from its monetary role over time.

Almost in parallel, Harry White had begun work on a competing plan, the first draft of which was completed in March 1942. Though they had worked independently and, initially, without either of them knowing that the other was even working on such a plan, the contours of White's proposal were remarkably similar to Keynes'. However, the White plan also reflected key American interests. Among these were the opening up of international markets for US exports and the elevation of the dollar to become the global unit of exchange.[27]

The White plan continued to place gold at the centre of the monetary system, alongside dollars. Each currency was to be fixed to the dollar, which was in turn fixed to gold. Currency devaluations under this system were to be rare and would entail significant penalties on the devaluing country. He also provided for two new agencies: a United and Associated Nations Stabilisation Fund (later to become the International Monetary Fund (IMF)) and a Bank for Reconstruction and Development of the United and Associated Nations (later to become the World Bank). The Fund, like Keynes' ICB, would allow members to buy currency to cover balance of payments shortfalls, but only against adequate collateral in the form of gold or other currencies. Compared with the Keynes plan, therefore, the White plan provided for a far more rigid system of global exchange rates. The mechanism for temporary liquidity support was also far less flexible than the one Keynes had proposed.

White's continued adherence to gold at the centre of the system was, in part, because he simply did not believe that the world was ready to accept that the dollar could play the global role he envisioned without the backing of gold.[28] However, the fact that the US held two-thirds of the global reserves of monetary gold also gave it an incentive to ensure that its monetary value was protected. America's large gold holdings at that time nevertheless legitimised the dollar to be 'as good as gold' and, by setting all other currencies' exchange rates by reference to the dollar, the dollar's role at the centre of the global monetary system would be cemented.

White's plan also reflected America's position as a large balance of payments surplus country at that time. Keynes' proposal would have made surplus nations unsecured creditors to deficit countries that made use of the ICB's liquidity support facility. This was unacceptable to the Americans, as was Keynes' proposal that countries running persistent large surpluses be subject to automatic upwards revaluations of their currencies, since this would have served to penalise the US. This may seem ironic in light of fierce American criticism of China's large trade surpluses in recent years.

The change in US circumstances was something that Jacob Viner actually foresaw in a July 1943 letter to Keynes, in which he wrote: 'The expectation that the US will be alone or almost alone as a creditor is plausible for the first period' but 'Over the long pull . . . I think that the US is as likely to be short as to be long of foreign short-term funds.[29]

Keynes' plan equally reflected British interests. In light of Britain's strained economic circumstances, it was not realistic for sterling to play the central role as a global reserve currency that it had before. However, Keynes was opposed to the idea that another national currency should do so. Beyond the question of national interests, there was simply a fundamental conflict between the role of a national central bank and that of an issuer of a global reserve currency. The global reserve issuer, as an international liquidity provider, would need to take into account financial conditions in *all countries* around the world, whereas a national central bank's mandate and allegiance are purely domestic.

It took two years of sometimes heated negotiations between the British and the Americans before the representatives of 44 nations finally, in July 1944, congregated on the Mount Washington Hotel in Bretton Woods, New Hampshire to ratify the historic international agreement. The Bretton Woods conference itself was largely a formality, since most of the terms had been hammered out beforehand. The three-week event had a jovial atmosphere about it, fuelled by the flow of alcohol.

The countries taking part included an eclectic mix of Allied Powers, governments in exile, British colonies, and emerging markets. Some were just happy to be there, without really understanding much of what was going on.

America's far stronger negotiating position meant that, on almost all key elements, White's proposal prevailed over the Keynes plan. Even so, Harry White took painstaking care to choreograph every detail of the conference to ensure that the dollar-based monetary order that he had advocated was ratified. History would later vindicate Keynes' reservations about the White plan, however.

The Bretton Woods system would ultimately break down amidst the Vietnam War, when US deficits made the dollar fix to gold no longer tenable. By that time though, the dollar had already been firmly embedded at the heart of the global monetary system and, after the gold standard was abandoned in 1973, the dollar itself simply supplanted the role of gold in the global monetary hierarchy. Harry White was to die in 1948 under the shadow of a Congressional investigation into his espionage activities on behalf of the Soviet Union. Despite his vehement denials, later revelations from both US and Soviet archives confirmed that he had been passing sensitive information to the Russians since the 1930s.[30] Nevertheless, he had undeniably achieved for the dollar a feat of financial alchemy that sterling had never accomplished in its century as the leading global reserve currency.

Bretton Woods ushered in a long period of growth and prosperity in the 1950s and 1960s. The dollar's special status under that system enhanced its role as a currency of lending and borrowing in international markets. Under the previous gold standard, a dollar that flowed out of the US represented a unit of gold outflow that would reduce the lending capacity of the US banking system. However, under the Bretton Woods system, a dollar that left the country had a high probability of finding its way back into a deposit at a US bank, amplifying the amount of credit that US banks could lend out. This should have placed New York at the centre of this international dollar market. However, through a remarkable confluence of circumstances and opportunism, the financial centre that won out was not New York, but that familiar financial capital of the old world: London.

A British Innovation

If governments had laid the foundation at Bretton Woods, it was markets that then took over the next phase of the construction of the dollar's towering role in global finance. It was in capital raising and investment that the dollar would come into its most widespread international use. The spread of the dollar as the dominant currency of international borrowing and investment provided the channels for worldwide transmission of US financial and monetary policies. Further, the dollar-based globalisation of financial markets spurred the development of networks and infrastructure that would give the US unprecedented geopolitical power in the financial sphere. It is therefore all the more surprising that this market for the offshore dollar – otherwise known as the 'Eurodollar'[31] – developed almost entirely outside the purview of American regulators.

The origins of the Eurodollar market are somewhat murky, as there were no published statistics on it until 1963. Although customers had long been allowed to deposit US dollars and other currencies at banks in London and such deposits had been growing during the interwar years, the birth of the Eurodollar market is generally acknowledged to have been in the 1950s. A number of factors contributed to its evolution.

In the immediate aftermath of WW2, the industrial base of Europe was either destroyed or had been given over to the manufacture of war supplies. Due to its geographic position, the US had been spared much of this destruction and had seen its economy grow to account for roughly half of global GDP. US exports were in strong demand and the need to pay for these in dollars meant that the rest of the world faced a dollar shortage. Through Marshall Plan aid, the US injected $17 billion into Europe in the form of reconstruction grants. Around $4.4 billion in similar aid was given towards the reconstruction of Japan.[32] Between 1947 and 1958, the US encouraged the outflow of dollars in order to provide liquidity to the international economy and, from 1950, began running a balance of payments deficit. As the post-war recovery took hold, offshore dollar balances began to accumulate. Initially, these were deposited with European banks, which in turn placed them back into the US banking system via their US branches, subsidiaries or correspondent banks.

With the rise in Cold War tensions, the Soviet Union and countries within the Eastern bloc became concerned that the US government might confiscate or freeze their dollar deposits, so they began to transfer these holdings from New York to London and Paris. The first such transfer by the Soviet Union was to the Paris-based Banque Commerciale pour l'Europe du Nord, which had the telegraphic address 'Eurobank'. It is said that the term 'Euro-dollar' traces its origins to this.[33]

There were other attractions to holding dollar deposits offshore, however. Offshore dollar deposits were not subject to US reserve requirements that forced banks to hold a certain proportion of their deposits in non-interest-bearing accounts with the Federal Reserve. Furthermore, Eurodollar deposits fell outside the jurisdiction of the Federal Reserve Board's Regulation Q, which was promulgated in 1933 to avoid the excessive competition that had been deemed partially responsible for bank failures during the Great Depression. Between 1935 and 1956, Regulation Q capped the interest rates that US banks could pay on deposits to one percent for 30-day deposits and to 2.5 percent for 90-day deposits.[34] Therefore, so long as offshore banks could lend the dollars out at market rates, they could afford to pay higher interest rates to depositors than domestic US banks.

An innovative product offering by a British bank also played a key role. Britain had devalued the pound by 30 percent in September 1949 under the weight of its balance of payments deficit but began loosening exchange controls that had been imposed at the outset of the war in the early 1950s, in line with the Bretton Woods objective of freer global trade. In 1954, restrictions on British banks operating in the forward exchange markets were lifted. When, in 1955, sterling interest rates were raised above US rates, a profitable opportunity opened up for arbitrage between sterling and dollar interest rates. Midland Bank, one of the major British clearing banks, began offering 1⅞ percent on 30-day dollar deposits, or ⅞ percent above the Regulation Q capped rate of one percent. It then sold the dollars in the spot market[35] and bought them back in the forward market for a premium of 2⅛ percent, giving Midland sterling funding at 4 percent (1⅞ percent plus 2⅛ percent) versus the prevailing Bank Rate of 4.5 percent.

The Bank of England initially raised some concerns at the rapid growth in Midland's foreign currency deposits, which appeared unrelated to its commercial transactions, but decided not to restrict the activity. Maurice Parsons, who later went on to become deputy governor from 1966 to 1970, rationalised that 'it is impossible to say to a London bank that it may accept dollar deposits but may not seek for them.' Threadneedle Street's[36] sanguine attitude towards Midland's innovation was likely influenced at least in part by the beneficial impact of these dollar inflows on Britain's balance of payments position – in June 1955 alone, the dollar deposits Midland attracted reduced the fall in the country's foreign exchange reserves from $56 million to $6 million.[37] As with most financial innovations, other banks quickly copied what Midland was doing.

In the wake of the Suez crisis, sterling was hit with renewed distress, prompting the Chancellor of the Exchequer to impose new foreign exchange controls in the third quarter of 1957. The use of sterling to finance foreign trade between third parties was banned and refinance credits in sterling were outlawed. Prevented from using their sterling deposit bases for international lending, resourceful British banks began to use their dollar deposits.

Meanwhile, US multinational companies were making large investments to expand their overseas operations. Though US balance of payments deficits had been modest from 1950 to 1957, from 1958 to 1962 US deficits reached levels of between $2.5 billion and $3.8 billion.[38] In 1961, the Federal Reserve began expressing concerns that the growing Eurodollar market may 'constitute a danger to stability',[39] but by that time the Bank of England had grasped the importance of this market in developing international trade and to restoring the City of London's role as a leading international financial centre. By 1963, the Bank for International Settlements (BIS) estimated the size of the Eurocurrency market to be $12.4 billion, of which three-quarters was in US dollars. This large base of offshore dollar deposits soon became the target of bankers helping corporations to raise funds via bond issues.

The Coupon Express

In the post-war years, New York had been the principal financial centre where borrowers went in search of investment. The first international bond issue after WW2 was by the World Bank in the

New York-based foreign dollar bond market (or, as it came to be known, the 'Yankee' market). This was largely a public sector market, with issuers including governments, government agencies and municipalities. Issues were required to comply with the 1933 Securities Act and be registered with the Securities and Exchange Commission (SEC). Regulations also required that a US investment bank acted as lead manager on the issue and that there be a US domestic underwriting syndicate. Many US public pension funds were not permitted to buy these foreign securities and US insurance companies were restricted on the amount they could hold, so these issues were increasingly bought by European investors through discretionary private banking accounts with Swiss or Benelux banks, or via London brokers. Towards the end of the 1950s, *three-quarters* of these issues were being bought by European investors.

It was galling to the European intermediaries that, although they were handling much of the distribution, US underwriters were earning most of the new issue fees. European distributors therefore began to look for a way to handle the entire new issue process by themselves.

At the time, Switzerland would have seemed the natural home for what would become the massive Eurobond market, since most of the early issues of US foreign dollar bonds were placed there. Switzerland itself had a sizeable market for foreign bonds issued in Swiss francs, which had started in 1947 and, by 1963, had the equivalent of around $790 million outstanding – slightly larger than the amount owed by European borrowers in the New York market.[40] White, Weld & Co., a New York-based firm that was one of the most prominent players in the foreign dollar bond market, formed a close relationship with Crédit Suisse and based its European activities in Zurich. So, *what led the market to come to be centred on London?*

As with most such decisions in international finance, it ultimately came down to questions of regulation and tax. Switzerland imposed a 35 percent withholding tax on interest paid on domestic issues to non-residents, but foreign issues were exempt from this. What weighed far more against Switzerland though was the tax authorities' refusal to exempt bond trading from Swiss stamp taxes, and a Swiss Federal issue tax of 1.2 percent that made it unattractive for Swiss banks to underwrite and manage issues in Switzerland themselves.

For tax reasons, US banks initially flocked to set up operations in Paris. Morgan Guaranty and Morgan Stanley together had set up Morgan et Cie there to underwrite new issues. Merrill Lynch based their first European headquarters in the French capital, as did Dillon Read. However, a number of European countries grew concerned at the rapidly expanding pool of stateless Eurodollars and took steps to limit its growth. In the early 1960s, France, along with Switzerland, Germany and Italy, prohibited interest payments on foreign deposits.

London had been a far-from-obvious candidate for becoming host to this foreign securities market. An executive with SG Warburg at the time recalled that 'London was a pretty miserable place to be, beset with post-war gloom, exchange controls and the narrow parochial attitude of the City'.[41] However, because of the concentration of banks in London holding Eurodollar deposits, the British authorities began to see an opportunity for the City to 'fill a vacant role in Europe in mobilising foreign capital for world economic development'.[42] That Britain still operated exchange controls that had created a highly regulated onshore domestic economy may in fact have helped create common ground between City firms and the British regulators in pursuing business in this offshore currency market. Stanislas Yassukovitch, then an executive at White Weld and who would go on to be appointed CEO of the European Banking Company and Deputy Chairman of the London Stock Exchange, among other prominent positions, pointed out:

> Paradoxically it was because there was exchange control. As a result of the Exchange Control Act, the Bank [of England] could allow traffic in foreign currency securities on its capital market, and activity in foreign currencies, because it was completely isolated from the management of the domestic currency mass.[43]

For the first Eurobond issue out of London to take place, however, there was a myriad of legal, regulatory and tax issues to overcome. The firm that led the way on this was SG Warburg.

SG Warburg had been founded in London in 1936 by Siegmund Warburg, a scion of the German-Jewish banking dynasty who had fled from Hamburg to Britain after Hitler had come to power. The company was originally named New Trading Company, or 'Nutraco', and began by financing the growth of small businesses and offering corporate finance advice. In its early years, it comprised a small group of German-Jewish *émigrés*, whose leading members were known as the 'Uncles'. The company's internal language was German and, in the German tradition, the Uncles were extremely formal, addressing each other by their last names even after decades of close acquaintance. SG Warburg was not among the leading City firms, but in 1956 acquired a small merchant bank, Seligman Brothers, through which it became an Accepting House recognised by the Bank of England and gradually made a name for itself over the following decade.

SG Warburg was not a major distributor of Yankee bonds, but Siegmund Warburg was familiar with the market through his family's relationship with the US investment bank Kuhn, Loeb & Co. His cousins Paul and Felix Warburg were both senior partners at the New York firm and Siegmund himself served as a partner and Executive Director of Kuhn Loeb from 1953 until 1964. As far back as 1958, Warburg had bemoaned the fact that American underwriters were receiving the lion's share of fees on Yankee issues, notwithstanding the fact that most of the distribution was carried out by European banks. In the early 1960s, he and his partners set out to overcome the barriers to launching a Eurobond out of London. The borrower that served as the test case with the British authorities was the builder and owner of Italy's motorway network, Autostrade.[44]

The reason why Autostrade was chosen traces back to its relationship with the Italian public holding company Istituto per la Ricostruzione Industriale (IRI). IRI had been set up in the 1930s to rescue and restructure companies that had become insolvent during the Great Depression. When a Warburg banker approached IRI with the idea of a Eurodollar financing, it was keen to test out the idea to raise urgently required funds for the Italian steel company Società Finanziaria Siderugica (FINSIDER). However, FINSIDER's statute did not permit it to pay bond coupons without first deducting Italian tax. Such withholding taxes, which were common at the time, would have made the bond unattractive to foreign investors, as they meant investors could be taxed twice on the same coupon: once via the withholding tax; and then again when they declared the income in their country of residence. Double tax treaties were not widespread at the time and, even where taxes could be reclaimed, the process could take months. Autostrade was exempt from all Italian taxes and could pay coupons gross, so FINSIDER's finance director made an arrangement with Autostrade to issue the bond as a front for FINSIDER, presumably for a fee.[45]

Exemption from withholding taxes was just one of many issues that had to be resolved though. Over a period of six months, Warburg executives and their lawyers, Allen & Overy, engaged in extensive negotiations with the Inland Revenue, the Stamp Office, the Bank of England, and the London Stock Exchange.

For a dollar bond issued outside the US, there was no requirement for it to be registered with the SEC. However, an arbitrary choice of the location of registration might have impacted investors from outside that jurisdiction. It was therefore determined that the bonds would be issued in bearer form, which meant that there would be no registered owner, and no records of the identity of the owner or changes in ownership. The bearer nature of Eurobond securities would give rise to the popular stereotype of the 'Belgian dentist'. In Belgium, interest on domestic bond issues were taxed at source, so the Belgian dentist came to symbolise the affluent European investor who would invest in these issues via an account in a neighbouring country and, given the anonymity of the bearer structure, then evade taxes by failing to report the income to his home tax authority. Investments were often made via banks based in Luxembourg, which would clip the coupons[46] on behalf of the investor and deposit the income into his account. The briefcase-bearing Belgian dentist, often accompanied by his wife or mistress, could be seen most weekdays riding the morning train between Brussels and Luxembourg City, nicknamed the 'Coupon Express'. After a substantial lunch and a visit to his bank, he could then be seen returning to Brussels on the evening train.

In recalling the hoops that the bankers had to jump through on the Autostrade issue, former SG Warburg executive Ian Fraser wrote:

> For instance there was a British stamp duty of 4% on the capital value of all bearer bonds in Britain: so we decided to issue them on Schiphol Airport in Holland, in which country there was no such impost. The British Inland revenue would insist on deducting 42½% income tax from all coupons cashed whether by UK residents or foreigners; so we arranged for the coupons to be cashed in Luxembourg and several other places abroad. Most of the banks in the syndicate that [SG Warburg director Gert] Whitman was

putting together would not underwrite unless we put in place a listing on a major stock exchange such as London. After a lot of hard work we persuaded Throgmorton Street to admit our bonds to the official list even though they could not be 'delivered' (in settlement of a transaction) in Britain but only in Brussels or Luxembourg. Then we had major difficulties with the central banks of France, Holland, Sweden, Denmark and of course Britain, about the exchange control consequences of allowing the bonds to be underwritten, purchased, sold and coupons cashed and ultimately the bonds redeemed all in a foreign currency – US dollars. Finally we could not find any printing firm to do the security printing of the bonds to a standard required by the rules (written in the 1920s) of the London Stock Exchange, until at the last moment De La Rue, the playing card printers, came forward and said they had two aged Czech engravers whom they could bring out of retirement who could do it for us.[47]

As a result of their painstaking efforts, the Autostrade bond was finally launched on 1 July 1963. The issue was for $15 million and had a term of 15 years, paying a coupon of 5.5 percent per annum. So pleased with the issue was the Autostrade executive who signed the deal that he promised Fraser a gold badge that would entitle him to lifetime free travel on all Italian motorways. However, such was the excitement of the issue that the Italian executive had a heart attack and died, so Fraser never received his badge.

Intrepid British bankers had gotten the ball rolling, but the growth of Eurobond issuance in London thereafter was accelerated by a development on the other side of the Atlantic that same month. The capital outflow from the US that had created the Eurodollar pool was raising concerns. American authorities began to exhort European borrowers to desist from raising capital in the US and to do so in their home markets instead. Nevertheless, Yankee bond issuance grew from $1.2 billion in the whole of 1962 to over $1.5 billion in the first half of 1963.[48] On 18 July 1963, President Kennedy announced a range of measures to Congress to address the balance of payments situation, key among which included the imposition of an Interest Equalisation Tax (IET) for a period of two years. The IET was levied on the purchase price of a foreign security bought by a US citizen, and was set at levels that ranged from 2.75 percent on bonds with a maturity of less than three and a half years up to 15 percent for long-dated securities.[49] The IET was eventually signed into law by Lyndon Johnson after Kennedy's assassination, but it was applied retroactively from the date of its announcement to Congress and had an immediate chilling effect on Yankee issuance. Morgan Guaranty Chairman Henry Alexander commented to colleagues at the time that 'This is a day you will remember for ever. It will change the face of American banking and force all the business off to London'.[50] US investors' purchases of foreign securities fell from $1 billion in the first half of 1963 to $250 million in the second half of the year. Meanwhile, new dollar-denominated Eurobond issuance grew from $35 million in the second half of 1963 to $545 million in 1964.[51]

In 1965, with the US balance of payments position coming under further pressure due to the Vietnam War, Lyndon Johnson extended the IET for a further two years. He also introduced voluntary restrictions on the transfer of funds overseas by US corporations and on foreign loans and investments by US financial institutions. The purpose of these restrictions was to encourage US companies to borrow overseas to finance their international investments. US corporations therefore started to look to the Eurobond market for financing.

As issuance passed the $1 billion mark in 1967, the US announced further measures to stem its negative balance of payments position. Voluntary restrictions were replaced by mandatory ones, which limited US companies' overseas investments to set quotas. This meant that US multinationals now had no choice but to borrow overseas. US issuance in the Eurobond market jumped from $527 million in 1967 to almost $2 billion in 1968 and more US investment banks set up operations in London.[52] During the six years that these mandatory restrictions remained in force, US issuers accounted for 271 issues and raised almost $7 billion, or around one-third of the total new Eurobond issuance over that period.[53] Soon, the accompanying explosion in international securities trading would place strains on the cross-border settlement infrastructure.

Plumbing the World's Financial Markets

In the late 1960s, Stanley Ross, resident managing director of Kidder Peabody Securities in London, had a problem.

Ross was one of the most experienced traders in the Eurobond market. The son of a London bus conductor, he had left school at 15 to join the Royal Air Force. After a brief period in the service, he left in 1951 and headed to the City, where he had joined the stockbroking firm Strauss, Turnbull & Co. In 1963, on a routine inspection of the office, Julius Strauss found the young Stanley Ross reading a translation of Marcel Proust's *À la Recherche du Temps Perdu*. Impressed with this display of intellect, Strauss promoted him to the equity trading department. From there, he was appointed to trade the Autostrade issue and was, therefore, one of the first people to trade the Eurobond market. He joined Kidder Peabody in 1967 and there oversaw the rapidly expanding trading in Eurobonds.

Although London was establishing itself as the home of secondary trading in Eurobonds, in 1967 New York remained the centre where they were settled. The settlement process was still highly manual, and the rapid expansion in the volume of trades had created a logjam. Each night, the clerks would send a telex to the firm's bank in New York listing the bonds it should receive and deliver on its traders' behalf. Kidder Peabody's New York bank Schroder would report payments that it had made on its behalf against bonds received. The problem was that there never seemed to be any corresponding reports for cash received when the traders had sold bonds. At a time of rising interest rates, Kidder Peabody's overdraft costs were skyrocketing, eating up all the trading profits.

Ross flew to New York to find out what was happening. His bank sent him down to the vaults where the bond certificates were held. There, he was handed a tatty folder containing all his firm's settlement instructions. When he opened the file, hundreds of delivery instructions flew up in the air and fluttered to the floor. Schroder had simply cut up all the telexes and acted on the instructions to receive bonds but left the delivery strips in the folder. *There were all the profits!*

Ross put his head in his hands and moaned: 'Oh my God. Oh my God'. Just then, he heard a voice behind him say: 'Never mind, Stanley. I am here since [*sic*] six weeks and I've turned a $7 million debit into a $16 million credit'.[54] It was Wolfgang Kron of Deutsche Bank, a fellow trader who was there dealing with the same problem. The logjam in the settlement system was affecting most of the broker dealers across the market. US broker Weeden & Co. had to temporarily withdraw from the Eurobond market in 1969 after finding $50 million — around three times its entire capital — tied up in failed settlements.

After returning from his visit to the vault, Ross told his colleagues that they should sue Schroder for negligence and refuse to pay the interest charges. The firm's leadership laughed it off and instructed him to pay the charges and to absorb them into his profit and loss account.

Traders weren't the only ones afflicted by the paperwork crisis, however. The market was unregulated and unscrupulous banks would frequently exploit the inefficiencies in the settlement infrastructure. The Belgian dentist and his ilk, who represented around 90 percent of market demand, sometimes wouldn't see their bonds for up to two years after paying for them. When they were finally delivered, it would often be without the intervening coupon payments. If this situation were allowed to continue, it would eventually kill the market.

The logjam in New York only affected US dollar-denominated Eurobonds. Luxembourg, which had long historic, linguistic and commercial ties to its neighbours, had emerged as an offshore banking centre within Europe. By the late 1960s, Luxembourg banks had developed a thriving business in bond settlements and might have seemed poised to capture more business from New York. However, operations there too were paper-based and involved the transportation of bond certificates between various banks in armoured vehicles, which was a costly process prone to settlement errors. A greater problem in Luxembourg though was its paucity of fine dining venues.

The closing lunch was something of a ritual in the Eurobond market in those days. The closing of a Eurobond issue required the physical handover of the bond certificates by the borrower, once it had confirmation that the lead manager had paid over the issue proceeds. This would usually involve a small ceremony, followed by a gourmet lunch. French tax law precluded Paris as a venue for closings, while stamp taxes ruled out London. In the search for an alternative, one banker approached the head of Morgan Guaranty's securities department in Belgium to see if Morgan might be able to host closings in Brussels. The city possessed the requisite standard of cuisine and had good transport links with major European cities. Thus, in 1965, Morgan Guaranty began to host closings in Brussels.

By 1966, in the face of the paperwork crisis in New York, executives at Morgan Brussels began to consider offering a service whereby it would hold the bonds until maturity and facilitate settlement in-house between buyers' and sellers' accounts at Morgan Guaranty. This would eliminate the costs of transporting bond certificates between different locations and reduce the risk of failed settlements. With the enthusiastic support of then president of the Morgan Guaranty Trust Co. in New York, John M. Meyer Jr., the service was launched in July 1967. By December 1969, this had evolved into Euroclear.

Euroclear was the first international central securities depository (ICSD). ICSDs play a critical role in global securities markets through a number of functions. First, they serve as a depository for the safekeeping of securities. Second, they facilitate secure settlement between buyers and sellers by way of book entries in their respective accounts, obviating the need to physically transfer the certificates. Third, because the ICSD holds a range of securities in a client's security account as well as cash deposits in the client's cash account, where there is a shortfall in cash to settle a purchase, the ICSD is able to provide a loan collateralised against the client's other securities in order to settle the trade, thereby avoiding settlement failure. Finally, ICSDs facilitate the placing and acceptance of securities as collateral between third parties which, among other things, has enabled the growth of the now $1 trillion per day US 'repo'[55] market that is a fundamental source of liquidity in global capital markets.[56]

Stanley Ross was an enthusiastic early adopter of this service and Kidder Peabody became the first major trading firm to insist that anyone wanting to deal with it would have to become a member of Euroclear. The ICSD quickly became a significant profit centre for Morgan, since it paid little interest on the large and stable amounts of cash held in its clients' cash accounts and was able to invest this cash to reap substantial income.

Concerned that Euroclear would give Morgan Guaranty key insights into its competitors' activities, a group of Luxembourg and foreign banks established Cedel in Luxembourg in September 1970. Bitter competition and rivalry between Euroclear and Cedel would serve to drive down settlement fees further, much to the benefit of customers.

To allay the competitive concerns, Morgan Guaranty sold Euroclear to its users in 1972, though it continued to profit from providing credit to Euroclear's customers until Euroclear set up its own bank in 2000. Cedel was fully acquired by Deutsche Börse in 2002 and is now known as Clearstream.

Meanwhile, to deal with the continuing paper jam in the US market, the New York Stock Exchange (NYSE), the American Stock Exchange and the National Association of Securities Dealers (NASD) cooperated to set up The Depository Trust Company (DTC) in 1973. John M. Meyer Jr., who served as chairman of Morgan Guaranty from 1969 to 1971, was again an instrumental influence behind this development.

In a contemporaneous and not-entirely-unrelated development, 239 banks from 15 countries began cooperating to establish the Society for Worldwide Interbank Financial Telecommunication (SWIFT) in 1973. SWIFT is a not-for-profit cooperative that was founded to standardise payment instructions between financial institutions. Up until SWIFT's launch in 1977, payment instructions between banks had been communicated via telex. Often, it would require up to 10 messages back and forward in order to effect a single transaction. The problem was that message formats differed between institutions, making the system costly and prone to error. The Brussels-headquartered Society is not a bank or a settlement institution and does not hold or operate accounts on behalf of customers; it is simply involved in the organisation and distribution of data, providing a secure and trusted telecommunications network for the transmission of sensitive financial information. Within a year of SWIFT's launch, 10 million messages had been sent. By 2020, the system was facilitating cash and securities transfers for over 11,000 users located in more than 200 countries around the world.[57]

The arrival of these international payments and settlement infrastructures solved the paperwork crisis for traders like Stanley Ross in the late 1960s and came just in time to foster the continued growth of the nascent Eurobond market. That market in December 2019 was estimated to be around $25 trillion in size, around 24 percent of the total bonds outstanding globally.[58] This harnessing of savers' capital for use by governments and corporations has created jobs, supported public services and provided for the development of public infrastructure around the world. For savers and investors, it also opened up new international investment opportunities that could improve their returns and help diversify their exposures.

These organisations, colloquially known as the 'plumbing' of the world's financial markets, enabled unprecedented growth and globalisation of the international capital markets by driving down the costs and increasing the reliability of cross-border transactions. With the dollar already the predominant currency of international borrowing and investment, they provided a network that would allow it to further extend its reach. In turn, this would further amplify the transmission of US economic and monetary policy to other countries via global investment and liquidity, in addition to trade. This is a trend that would be accelerated further still by a series of shocks in the 1970s.

Niksonu Shokku

Richard Milhous Nixon's most celebrated foreign policy achievement was the initiation of Sino-US rapprochement, the highlight of which was his February 1972 visit to China to meet with Chairman Mao Zedong (毛泽东). This diplomatic masterstroke fundamentally reshaped the Cold War balance of power in America's favour. It forced the Soviet leadership to the negotiating table on *détente* and paved the way for America's exit from a demoralising Vietnam War. For US allies in East Asia though, this sudden and unexpected development following Nixon's enunciation of the Guam Doctrine in 1969 was unsettling.[59] For none was it more so than Japan, whose government received only two hours' notice before Nixon's 15 July 1971 announcement that Henry Kissinger had made a clandestine visit to China to meet with Zhou Enlai (周恩来). This was one of a series of US diplomatic blows to Satō Eisaku's government that the Japanese media dubbed the *Niksonu Shokku*, or 'Nixon Shocks'. However, it was not just in the realm of foreign policy that the 37th president was to create long-lasting tremors. The financial shocks he delivered also left a profound legacy in global capital markets.

The better known of these financial shocks was the suspension of the dollar's convertibility to gold in 1971. This effectively brought an end to the Bretton Woods system.

Though the US had been running a current account surplus of around one percent of GDP throughout the 1950s, it was running an overall balance of payments deficit due to the flow of American capital into investments overseas. By the latter part of the decade, foreigners saw that the dollar was overvalued and began to exercise their rights to convert their dollar holdings into gold. Between the end of 1957 and the end of 1959, US gold reserves fell by around 15 percent. Fears of inflationary government spending under a Kennedy presidency led to a further nine percent decline in US gold reserves in 1960.[60] In short, more and more dollars were being backed up by falling reserves of gold.

When the London gold price jumped to almost $40 per ounce in October 1960, the Federal Reserve and the Bank of England were forced to intervene to bring the dollar back in line with the official exchange rate of $35. Thereafter, the US undertook a number of measures to stem the balance of payments deficit and discourage the outflow of dollars. These included the IET to discourage American purchases of foreign securities; the issue of Treasury bonds in foreign currencies[61] to discourage Europeans from calling in gold; and coercion of European allies to help stabilise the value of the dollar.

This drew consternation from other countries, particularly after the escalation of US involvement in Vietnam. Among the most vocal critics was Charles de Gaulle, who complained that the dollar's supremacy allowed the Americans to indulge in costly foreign wars without having to curtail spending at home. In September 1963, he ordered the Banque de France 'to demand from the Americans that eighty percent of what they owed us by virtue of the balance of payments should henceforth be repaid in gold'.[62] France subsequently went so far as to send a battleship to collect its gold from the vaults of the New York Fed.

Germany, while more circumspect in its public statements, had revalued the Deutschmark in 1961 and 1969, but continued to see speculative inflows. In May 1971, the German government decided to allow its currency to float. Although this curbed speculative flows into Germany, it did little to stem capital outflows from the US. By that year, US dollar liabilities of $70 billion were backed by just $13 billion in gold.[63]

In reality, de Gaulle was not entirely accurate when he suggested that the US did not bear a cost for its exorbitant privilege. Post-war recovery meant that European and Japanese exports had begun competing with US manufactures and this was already eroding America's share of global manufacturing, but there is little doubt that the overvalued dollar was accelerating this process. By the 1970s, this would be manifested in rising US unemployment.

As early as 1962, British Prime Minister Harold MacMillan suggested to JFK halving the rate at which the dollar could be converted into gold to $70 per ounce. However, even if Kennedy had acted on that suggestion, it would have merely deferred the problem of inadequate gold reserves and would have done nothing to address the issue of falling US export competitiveness. This is because, under Harry White's system, the values of *all other currencies* had been fixed against the dollar.

At the heart of the matter was a fundamental conflict that persists to this day: the US desire for balance of payments equilibrium is incompatible with the dollar's role as a global currency and the consequent need to supply dollar liquidity to the whole world. This conflict created by the Bretton Woods system was first identified in the 1950s by Belgian-American economist Robert Triffin and has come to be known as the 'Triffin Dilemma'. It was not possible for the US to simultaneously issue enough dollars to satisfy the trading needs of the entire world and maintain a fixed exchange rate against gold. For one thing, as Keynes had pointed out in the 1930s, new supplies of gold were not keeping pace with the growth in the economy and in trade. And to keep the world supplied with sufficient dollar liquidity, the US must continue to run a balance of payments deficit. Failure to do so would starve the rest of the world of dollars and precipitate a liquidity crunch similar to the one in gold that had contributed to the Great Depression (see Chapter 3 for further discussion).

In the face of economic pressures and speculative attacks on the dollar, Nixon went on national television on 15 August 1971. In the grainy analogue broadcast, he announced in a calm tone that the US was suspending the dollar's convertibility to gold. In the height of irony, he told viewers that 'The effect of this action . . . will be to *stabilise* the dollar'.[64] At the same time, he announced a 90-day wage price freeze to combat inflation and demonstrate to other countries that the US was taking its share of pain, as well as a temporary 10 percent import surcharge to protect US manufacturers from near-term currency fluctuations.

Nixon's announcement stunned the world. The President hadn't even forewarned the IMF. The US subsequently met with the other Group of 10 (G-10) countries at the Smithsonian Institute in Washington DC in December that year and, following two days of tough negotiations, announced that the dollar would, on average, be devalued by 10 percent, while the Deutschmark was revalued upwards by 13.6 percent and the yen by 16.9 percent. The dollar was pegged at $38 per ounce of gold and the permitted fluctuation from the new parities was widened to 2.25 percent. However, the Smithsonian Agreement did not hold. Nixon was not interested in being tethered to the new parities and, following his resounding election victory over George McGovern, attempts by the G–10 to re-establish a system of fixed parities were abandoned in 1973. The dollar would, henceforth, be a freely floating fiat currency without any fixed reference to gold or any other asset.

By ditching the shackles of gold, Nixon had established America's absolute monetary sovereignty. No longer would the US government be constrained in the amount of currency it could issue by its holdings of gold. And contrary to Harry White's concerns, the dollar maintained its role as the global reserve currency. By that time, the dollar was already too entrenched in the global monetary system and there was no obvious alternative to it. The freely floating dollar introduced volatility into the foreign exchange market that had not existed under the Bretton Woods system. It also allowed the dollar to depreciate based on America's relative economic performance versus its trading partners. However, as discussed in Chapter 3, steps taken by foreign central banks to maintain the stability of their currencies has limited the extent to which the dollar has actually been allowed to fall.

The second financial policy shock initiated under Nixon's administration was a domestic one. This was the move to abolish fixed brokerage commissions for trading shares on the NYSE.

For 183 years, pursuant to the Buttonwood Agreement of 17 May 1792 (so-called after the legendary buttonwood tree outside 68 Wall Street, under which the NYSE was established), brokers of the NYSE set a minimum level for the trading commissions they charged to their clients. By the 1960s, this clubby arrangement was the subject of increasing investor criticism. Moreover, an alternative over-the-counter (OTC) market was emerging as an avenue for investors to avoid paying fixed commissions. A heated debate between the Justice Department, the SEC, the NYSE and Wall Street brokers developed over the issue. However, in 1973, the SEC finally faced down diehard opposition from the brokerage community and initiated the process to put an end to fixed commissions. On 1 May 1975, which came to be known as 'May Day' within the industry, commissions for trading shares on the NYSE were finally deregulated.

At first, brokers clung to their previous commission levels. However, over time, competition dramatically reduced the cost of trading on the NYSE as discount brokers like Charles Schwab emerged, charging clients a fixed dollar amount per trade irrespective of the number or value of shares traded. The fall in trading costs contributed to huge growth in trading volumes in the following decades.

As the profitability of the old fixed commission structure disappeared, US brokers sought to scale up in order to extract cost efficiencies. Throughout the 1950s and 1960s, there had been four mergers between major US securities firms. Between 1975 and 1980, there were 29 such mergers and the pace accelerated throughout the 1980s and 1990s. Names like White, Weld & Co. were swallowed up by Merrill Lynch, while Kidder Peabody was merged into Paine Webber, which itself was acquired by the Swiss bank UBS in 2000.

These enlarged US firms were also incentivised to seek out new markets overseas and to develop new business lines. The international expansion of US financial institutions contributed to the further globalisation of the dollar. However, it was the expansion of a particular new type of financial product that was to turbocharge the growth of dollar-based finance.

In a money-based economy, the price of all assets is referenced to the money unit of account. In allowing the dollar to fluctuate freely, Richard Nixon had unleashed far greater volatility in *all* financial assets. This created a need for producers, consumers and investors to hedge the risk of large price swings. It also created huge opportunities for financial speculators. With the end of their fixed commission structure in share trading, Wall Street firms were to discover a huge new profit centre in derivatives.

Volatility

Up until the 1970s, derivatives had been a specialised and arcane area of financial markets. They had largely been employed by producers and consumers of commodities to fix the price at which they would transact in the future, so as to manage the risk of intervening price movements. For example, a farmer could use a futures or forward contract to lock in a price at which he could sell his grain to a store owner. If there was a bumper crop and the price of grain falls due to oversupply, then the farmer will have benefited by having been able to sell his crop at a higher price than he would have gotten otherwise. On the other hand, if there was a drought resulting in widespread crop failures, then the price of grain would be expected to rise, and the store owner will have benefited.

In the US, Chicago has been the traditional hub for derivatives trading, owing to its location close to the farmlands and cattle country of the Midwest and its role as a transportation and distribution hub for agricultural produce. The Chicago Board of Trade (CBOT) was formed in 1848 as a forwards market for corn. The Chicago Produce Board, later renamed the Chicago Butter and Egg Board, was founded in 1874. This was later reorganised as the Chicago Mercantile Exchange (CME) in 1919.

Over in New York, a group of Manhattan dairy merchants launched the Butter and Cheese Exchange of New York in 1872. As the products traded widened to include poultry, dried fruit and canned goods, its name was changed in 1882 to the more grand-sounding New York Mercantile Exchange (NYMEX). Other regional exchanges trading different commodities sprang up around North America. Eventually, most would demutualise and consolidate into larger exchange groups. By 2008, CME, CBOT and NYMEX had been amalgamated to form the CME Group, which is today the largest derivatives exchange in the world.

Derivatives have an even longer history outside the US. In Japan, the Dōjima Rice Exchange was established in Ōsaka in 1697 and began trading a form of futures contract in 1710. In Great Britain, the LME traces its origins back to 1571. Derivatives exchanges have played a critical role in the development of banking systems, trade and commerce around the world. However, President Nixon's 1971 decision to suspend the dollar's convertibility to gold converged with significant breakthroughs in academia and technology that would catalyse massive growth in the use of derivatives and transform financial markets.

★★★

In 1962, a Californian mathematics professor by the name of Edward Thorp published a book entitled *Beat the Dealer*, in which he applied advances in probability theory to the game of blackjack. His method assigned a value to each card in the deck and required remembering the value of cards that had been played. In simple terms, when the value of the remaining cards in the deck implies favourable odds, the gambler should increase his or her bet sizes to profit from this statistical advantage. The book was a sensation and inspired legions of card counters seeking their fortunes in Las Vegas. Thorp's work on probability to validate his method involved a large number of mathematical calculations that were carried out on an IBM 704, the first mass produced computer. This machine required calculations to be inputted on punch cards and, by today's standards, was painfully slow. Nevertheless, the dawn of the computer age was a critical development that allowed derivatives to take off, for it enabled complex mathematical calculations to be solved quickly and accurately.

Having found himself barred from casinos after his success at the blackjack tables, Thorp went on to apply his energies to financial markets. In 1969, he teamed up with a young New York stockbroker to form Princeton Newport Partners (PNP), an early quantitative hedge fund that went on to produce compound annual returns of almost 20 percent net of fees until it was wound up in 1989.[65] PNP's extraordinary success was owed to its ability to exploit statistical mispricing of derivatives through arbitrage strategies. Academic honours for the model that accurately priced derivatives would go to others, while Thorp quietly made a fortune for himself and his investors.

The maths for calculating a derivative's price are based on four factors: the price of the underlying asset; the length of time until its expiry date; market interest rates; and volatility. If all of these quantities are known, then the price of a derivative instrument can be calculated with scientific accuracy. However, while the price of the underlying asset, duration and interest rates can be known, future volatility is a prediction based on historic experience. Traders who forget that the past is not always a good guide to what will happen in the future often suffer catastrophic losses. Ironically, Robert Merton and Myron Scholes, the academics who shared the 1997 Nobel Prize in economics for inventing the famous Black-Scholes model for pricing options, learned this lesson the hard way. Just a year after their Nobel award, the hedge fund Long-Term Capital Management (LTCM), in which they were partners, had to be bailed out by Wall Street banks under Fed supervision after suffering spectacular losses.[66]

Notwithstanding its inventors' later misadventures, the advent of the Black-Scholes model in 1973, coupled with developments in computer technology, brought about a revolution in the financial services industry. Before that, trading required few academic qualifications and there were many examples of mailroom clerks who had risen to untold riches in the rough and tumble of the markets. Nowadays, trading rooms have been taken over by mathematicians and scientists holding advanced degrees.

***

President Nixon's abandonment of the dollar's fix to gold sparked demand for hedging currency volatility that had previously been subdued by the Bretton Woods system. This was a void that CME's energetic chairman Leo Melamed moved rapidly to fill.

Melamed was born into a Jewish family in Bialystok, Poland in 1932. His father was a mathematics teacher. At the outbreak of WW2, the family fled to Lithuania and were one of the fortunate Jewish families to receive a life-saving transit visa issued by Japanese vice-consul Sugihara Chiune in 1940. After a long passage via Siberia to Japan, the family eventually crossed the Pacific to the US and settled in Chicago. Melamed trained as a lawyer but, while attending John Marshall Law School, he answered a job advertisement for a position at Merrill Lynch, Pierce, Fenner & Beane. Thinking that a firm with such a lengthy name could only be an established law partnership, he inadvertently found himself working as a trading floor order-runner on the CME. He became hooked on the markets and it was not long before he bought his own membership seat on the exchange. By 1969, he had risen to become chairman.

Melamed had long subscribed to the free market theories espoused by University of Chicago economics professor Milton Friedman. He saw that the end of Bretton Woods created the conditions for a market in foreign exchange rates, and immediately began to think about launching currency futures on the CME. However, many of the exchange's members at that time did not believe that financial futures could succeed and thought that the CME should stick to its traditional agricultural futures products. Indeed, the New York Produce Exchange had renamed itself the International Commerce Exchange in April 1970 and launched currency contracts targeted at small-time speculators, but these had not found success. Nevertheless, that had been before Nixon's August 1971 bombshell and Melamed was convinced that *that* crucial development would enable global currency futures to take off.

To build credibility for his cause, he enlisted Friedman's help. Over breakfast at the Waldorf Astoria in November 1971, Melamed explained his idea to the famed economist. Friedman agreed that, with the suspension of the Bretton Woods Agreement, conditions were ripe for developing a market in currency futures. Melamed asked Friedman if he would be willing to put his opinion in writing, to which the economist answered: 'Yes, but I am a capitalist'. For a fee of $7,500, Friedman agreed to write a feasibility study on 'The Need for a Futures Market in Currency' and submitted it to the CME in December 1971. With this endorsement, Melamed launched the International Monetary Market (IMM) in May 1972 and began offering futures contracts on seven currencies against the US dollar.[67] The currency futures achieved rapid success and, with the backing of Friedman's academic prestige, the IMM received regulatory support for the launch of interest rate futures on US Treasury bills in 1975.

Volatility ushered in by the end of Bretton Woods was not just restricted to currency markets. As global oil demand increased in the years after WW2, the US had found itself becoming increasingly dependent on oil imports, particularly from the Middle East. Prior to the 1970s, the international oil companies had been vertically integrated operations, carrying out all the functions from oil exploration to distribution to end customers. However, the end of colonialism and rising nationalism had seen a wave of nationalisations of these natural resources by oil-exporting countries. Consequently, the oil companies no longer owned the oil in the ground and the commodity became increasingly traded through world markets. The devaluation of the dollar angered the exporters, who effectively received less in return for their oil. Meanwhile, price controls in the US discouraged new exploration and boosted consumption, leading to tighter supply. When the Arabs initiated an oil embargo in October 1973 in response to US military assistance to Israel during the

Yom Kippur War, prices rocketed. Panic buying saw the posted price for Iranian oil shoot up from $2.90 a barrel in mid-1973 to as high as $22.60.[68]

Such a steep increase in energy prices set off global inflation and led to deep economic hardship in much of the developed world. Although the embargo was ended in March 1974, oil prices remained elevated versus their previous level and volatility persisted. The overthrow of the Shah of Iran by Ayatollah Khomeini in 1979 set off a second oil price shock, with oil prices doubling over 12 months to $39.50 a barrel.[69] Faced with this price volatility, businesses from airlines to utilities scrambled to hedge the cost of their oil. NYMEX started offering trading in futures contracts on home heating oil and gasoline to meet this demand.

In March 1983, NYMEX launched a futures contract on light sweet crude oil delivered to tanks located in Cushing, Oklahoma. This grade of oil, known as West Texas Intermediate (WTI), became a global standard for oil prices. The benefit of a standardised benchmark is that it serves as a reference against which other grades of oil can be priced and concentrates trading liquidity, so as to enable traders to transact large quantities of oil without causing major price swings. In 1988, the International Petroleum Exchange (IPE) in London launched futures contracts on Brent Crude, a heavier grade of oil extracted from the North Sea. The IPE was acquired by the Atlanta-based Intercontinental Exchange (ICE) in 2001 and Brent has now overtaken WTI to become the benchmark used to price over three-quarters of the world's traded oil.

Growth in derivatives trading from the 1980s has been explosive. This was fuelled by a set of factors that each reinforced the others: growth in financial markets; consequent greater demand for hedging tools; product innovations by the financial industry; a larger supply of graduates with the necessary quantitative skills; and technology-enabled electronification of financial trading. The pros and cons of this growth are explored in Chapter 7; however, the development of these derivatives has been critical in consolidating the dollar's global position.

As of the end of 2020, the total notional value outstanding of all derivatives contracts was estimated to be $667 trillion.[70] This compares to the $110 trillion combined market capitalisation of all stock markets in the world[71] and $139 trillion in total debt outstanding in global bond markets.[72] It is also roughly 7.9 times the size of global GDP.

These contracts are vital to the smooth functioning of international trade and financial markets, as they allow businesses and individuals to manage their risks across foreign exchange, interest rates, credit, stocks and commodity prices. To be effective risk management tools, derivatives must be liquid and, preferably, supported by infrastructure such as clearing houses to help minimise counterparty risks.[73] Given the sheer size of this ecosystem of products and infrastructure, it would be extremely difficult for this system to be replaced. And since the vast majority of these derivatives are priced in US dollars, the growth and standardisation of derivatives contracts in the past half-century has powerfully entrenched the role of the US currency.

Unlike stocks, bonds or other assets, derivatives have a peculiar characteristic. Since the value of a futures or options contract is inherently derived by reference to the price of the underlying asset or to a particular event, for every winner on a derivatives contract, there must be a loser. In contrast, investors holding a stock that goes up can all benefit from the increase in the stock's value. However, in order to go long on a derivative (in other words, to bet that its value will go up), there must be someone on the other side of the trade willing to go short (or bet that its value will go down). During the term of the contract, the price of the reference asset may fluctuate significantly. In order to protect against the default of one or other party, when the price moves against one side of the contract, the losing party is usually required to post collateral in order to provide security that they can meet their obligation. The growth of derivatives markets has, therefore, multiplied the demand for high quality assets that can be posted to meet collateral requirements.

Further, not all investors seeking to avoid market volatility risks are able to do so using derivatives. This has spawned demand for secure and highly liquid assets that can be held as insurance against sudden and large funding needs. The largest issuer of such assets in the world is the US Treasury.

'Risk Free' Assets

As of the end of 2020, the total amount of US Treasury securities outstanding stood at $27.8 trillion.[74] These securities represent the cumulative amount of money raised by the US federal government to fund its spending requirements over and above what it collects in taxes. They are the largest and most liquid asset class in the world, with around one-third of the public debt owned by overseas investors.[75] Although the number seems staggeringly large, there is theoretically no risk that the US government will default on this debt. This is because all of its outstanding debt is denominated in US dollars and, since Nixon took the US off the gold standard, the US Treasury can simply print more dollars to meet its repayment obligations as they fall due. For this reason, US Treasuries are considered to be 'risk free' assets.

The history of the US Treasury securities market as we know it today is surprisingly short. Up until the US entered WW1, there was only around $1 billion of Treasury debt outstanding. New offers were infrequent. The last time before 1917 that Treasury securities were issued was in 1911 to help finance the construction of the Panama Canal.[76] Prior to that, the last offering had been in 1900 for the refinancing of bonds that had been issued during the Spanish-American War of 1898.[77] Treasury bonds were issued on a project finance basis and required Congressional approval for each issue. Congress would therefore supervise all the terms of each bond, including the interest rate and the maturity. It was not until 1935 when the Roosevelt Administration was engaging in consistent deficit spending to combat the Great Depression that Congress switched to regulating the total value of bonds that could be issued, rather than the specific terms of each issue. In 1939, Congress agreed to turn over decisions regarding the issuance of Treasury securities to the Secretary of the Treasury, limiting itself to specifying only the maximum debt that could be outstanding – the so-called 'debt ceiling'.

To finance its participation in WW1, Woodrow Wilson's administration issued five 'Liberty Loans' totalling $21.4 billion, with maturities between four and 30 years. The government debt was gradually reduced during the 1920s and, by the time Franklin Roosevelt took office in 1933, the outstanding public debt stood at around $20 billion, or 20 percent of GDP.[78] From there, the size of the US deficit continued to grow through WW2 and peaked at 119 percent of GDP at the end of the war.[79] Each US administration since then has added to the balance of US Treasury debt outstanding. However, as America enjoyed strong economic growth, the debt as a percentage of GDP steadily declined to 24.6 percent of GDP in 1974.[80] From that point on, however, slower economic growth and rising government expenditure saw the US national debt grow at a much faster pace than the economy.

It's not just the government that has continually spent more than it earns; American consumers have done so too. This might never have been possible without an audacious deal negotiated by former Treasury Secretary William Simon to ensure a stable source of funding from overseas.

Born in Paterson, New Jersey in 1927, William Edward Simon was the son of an insurance executive. Handsome and athletic, he served in the US Army before attending Lafayette College in Easton, Pennsylvania, where he was a member of the Delta Kappa Epsilon fraternity. Upon graduation in 1952, he headed to Wall Street, where he eventually became the partner in charge of the Government and Municipal Bond Departments at Salomon Brothers. The chain-smoking Simon became Deputy Secretary of the Treasury in January 1973 and launched the Federal Energy Administration to address the energy crisis at the height of the Arab oil embargo. He was appointed Treasury Secretary in May 1974, after George Shultz resigned from the Nixon Administration.

In mid-1974, the economic outlook for the US was dire. The oil embargo had quadrupled oil prices and inflation soared, even as unemployment was rising. For the oil exporters, however, the sharp rise in oil prices had been a bonanza. In 1974, members of the Organisation of the Petroleum Exporting Countries (OPEC) had a balance of payments surplus of $67 billion.[81] None benefited more than Saudi Arabia which, with the largest reserves of oil in the world, enjoyed a surge in its wealth. Bedouin shepherds, whose fathers and grandfathers had ridden across the desert on camel back with Ibn Saud, were suddenly driving Datsun pick-up trucks, propelling Nissan to the number one spot in vehicle sales in the country.

On an overcast morning in July 1974, the newly appointed Treasury Secretary boarded an 8am flight from Andrews Air Force Base to embark on a secret mission. The official purpose of his two-week trip was to conduct a tour of economic diplomacy across Europe and the Middle East. However, the real mission that he and President Nixon had agreed was to take place during a four-day layover in Jeddah, Saudi Arabia.

His objectives were to neutralise oil as an economic weapon and to persuade King Faisal to help finance America's rising government deficits with his country's newfound oil wealth.

On the surface, the outspoken former bond salesman seemed uniquely ill-suited for such a delicate diplomatic assignment. Just a week before his trip to Saudi Arabia, Simon had publicly called the Shah of Iran, a close US ally, a 'nut'. Nevertheless, his earlier career had given him an appreciation of the appeal of US Treasury debt and why this would be attractive to the Saudis.

Up until that point, Saudi Arabia had been parking its petrodollar surpluses in the Eurobond market. However, the emerging market government and corporate debt that featured prominently in that market exposed the Saudi Treasury to credit risks, and those securities were far less liquid than those issued by the US government.

It took several months of negotiations after Simon's initial trip, but the US and Saudi Arabia finally reached a deal. The US agreed to buy oil and to provide the kingdom with military aid and equipment, while Saudi Arabia promised to invest billions of its petrodollar surpluses into US Treasuries to finance US government spending.

At the last minute, King Faisal demanded one key final term: that the country's purchases of US Treasuries should remain strictly secret. The US had offended Arab sensibilities just a year before with its military support to Israel, so publicity around this deal might have been embarrassing to the kingdom. The bearer nature of Eurobonds allowed the country to keep its holdings secret, and it sought the same anonymity for its investments in US Treasuries. Under the arrangement agreed between the US Treasury and Saudi Arabia, the Saudis were allowed to bypass the normal competitive bidding process for buying Treasuries and the sales were excluded from the official auction totals. By 1977, Saudi Arabia had accumulated around 20 percent of all Treasuries held overseas. Remarkably, this arrangement remained secret for over four decades until a dogged journalist from *Bloomberg News* uncovered it through a Freedom of Information Act request in 2016.

Arguably, Saudi Arabia would have received a better return if it had invested in equities or in higher-yielding bonds. However, William Simon's instincts about the attractiveness of the safety and liquidity of US Treasuries had been spot on. What is more, what the Saudi regime received in return was far more valuable than the financial yield on its holdings. Under what would become known as the Carter Doctrine, the 39th president proclaimed in January 1980:

Let our position be absolutely clear: An attempt by any outside force to gain control of the Persian Gulf region will be regarded as an assault on the vital interests of the United States of America, and such an assault will be repelled by any means necessary, including military force.

The Carter Doctrine was, in fact, a public renewal of a commitment that Harry Truman had made in a letter to King Ibn Saud in October 1950 that the US 'is interested in the preservation and territorial integrity of Saudi Arabia'.[82] America's increased thirst for Middle East oil by the 1970s committed it even more to maintaining security and stability in Saudi Arabia. William Simon's deal provided the financial means for the US to uphold that commitment.

This oil-for-dollars-for-Treasuries agreement was an early example of a type of vendor-financing arrangement that the US has effectively entered into with almost all major surplus countries with which it runs balance of payments deficits. As China emerged as an export juggernaut in the early 2000s, it too would accumulate large balances of US government securities, with holdings of US Treasuries peaking at $1.3 trillion in 2011, or just over nine percent of the US national debt at the time.[83]

These vendor-financing relationships have become politically controversial, as they are also seen as a means for large exporters to artificially hold down the value of their own currencies (by selling them to buy large amounts of dollars) in order to maintain their export competitiveness. Meanwhile, blue collar wages in the US have stagnated and manufacturing operations have been relocated to lower-cost countries. Equally, for large holders of dollar-denominated securities, continually growing US deficits have raised fears that the US would devalue their holdings through currency depreciation or higher inflation – or both.

Ironically, however, the huge amount of US Treasuries outstanding has enhanced the perception about their safety. In times of market turbulence, investors flock to US Treasuries because they are the most liquid asset class and are, in fact, safer than holding cash in the bank. In the US, the Federal Deposit Insurance Corporation (FDIC), created in 1933 to protect depositors against bank failures, insures deposit amounts up to $250,000 per depositor per insured bank.[84] For individuals or institutions with larger holdings, US Treasuries provide greater security because the US government is less likely to default than a bank. International regulations, such as the BIS's Basel III rules that govern the capital and liquidity requirements of the global banking sector, have further enhanced the demand from major financial institutions by designating US Treasuries as 'risk free' for the purpose of calculating banks' capital needs.

The massive structural demand for US Treasury securities has given the US government almost unconstrained ability to borrow from international capital markets. As discussed further in Chapter 3, however, this capacity is a double-edged sword. The lack of constraints on public spending has contributed to poor prioritisation and overspending. On the international stage, overextension of US policy has led to conflict, while the scale of US borrowings from other countries has led to an accumulation of implicit and explicit international obligations. The demand for US Treasuries has also helped magnify demand for other private US securities and prop up the value of the dollar. This mispricing of capital has, over time, fundamentally impacted the allocation of resources both *between* the US and other countries, and *within* the US itself. As imbalances persisted, financial bubbles would inflate and periodically burst with dramatic social and political consequences.

Boom and Bust

In 1980, Ronald Reagan successfully campaigned for the White House on a promise of smaller government. That promise proved to be empty, as US government deficits ballooned during his presidency. His enormous defence spending eventually exhausted the Soviet Union's ability to keep up, and it imploded amidst the popular dissatisfaction of its own people over the privations to which they had been subjected in the pursuit of dominance over the US. However, amidst the euphoria of the Wall Street boom of the 1980s and America's victorious emergence from the Cold War in the early 1990s, the US and the dollar appeared increasingly unassailable.

Reagan's free market ideology did not mean that his administration took an entirely hands-off approach to the dollar. His presidency witnessed growing domestic paranoia that Japan was poised to surpass the US economically. Following substantial dollar appreciation against other major currencies between 1980 and 1985, US manufacturers campaigned aggressively for government action to protect their export competitiveness. This led to the Plaza Accord in September 1985, under which the US entered into a joint agreement with France, West Germany, Japan and the United Kingdom (UK) to intervene in currency markets to force a depreciation of the dollar against the yen and the Deutschmark. Between 1985 and 1987, the dollar depreciated by around 50 percent against the yen.[85]

The appreciation in the yen set off a buying spree by Japanese companies overseas. In September 1989, the Sony Corporation bought Columbia Pictures for $3.4 billion in cash, then the largest acquisition in the US by a Japanese company.[86] Two months later, Mitsubishi paid $846 million for a 51 percent stake in Manhattan's Rockefeller Centre.[87] In what has been seen as a symbol of the excesses of the time, the Imperial Palace grounds in Tokyo were famously estimated to be worth more than all of California. Popular consternation about Japan 'buying up America' reached a crescendo. Then the Japanese bubble burst. Since the end of 1989, Japan has fallen into seemingly perpetual economic stagnation.

By the early 1990s, with its major economic challenger in decline and its major military and geopolitical rival collapsing, the US was at the zenith of its power. Even as new challenges began to mount up in subsequent decades, however, the dollar has gone from strength to strength.

The framework put in place by Harry White at Bretton Woods put the dollar at the heart of the global monetary system. Policies pursued by successive US administrations after WW2 enabled the widespread adoption of the dollar as the dominant currency for international capital raising and investment. Financial institutions, notably in the City of London, grasped the commercial opportunity that this offered, supported by local governments and regulators. As capital market flows came to far outstrip commercial trade flows and global payments and market infrastructure developed around the dollar-based system, the dollar's position in the global monetary order became more entrenched. By the time that President Nixon severed the dollar's tie to gold, there was no credible alternative to take its place.

Paradoxically, the very undermining of the dollar's value caused by that decision enabled the US currency's international reach to widen further. This is because it freed the US from residual constraints on its balance of payments deficits, and the volatility it unleashed in financial markets precipitated the development and proliferation of derivatives. The US dollar is now not only the reference currency in which individuals and corporations all over the world conduct commerce and account for their asset holdings, but it has also become the reference currency in which they manage their financial risks. The global payments and settlement infrastructures created in the 1960s and 1970s enabled and accelerated this process, as they facilitated secure and cost-efficient cross-border financial trading and, more importantly over time, the mobilisation of vast pools of securities as collateral around the globe.

Given how entrenched it has become, it is difficult to see how the dollar could be displaced. However, the dollar's success has generated significant challenges for other countries and has created enormous burdens for the US itself. International holdings of US financial assets, particularly Treasury securities held by foreign governments, have saddled the US with weighty international obligations. The reduced currency flexibility that the US is locked into by Triffin's dilemma has also contributed to wage stagnation and unemployment domestically. Notwithstanding the exorbitant privilege that the dollar has conferred upon the US, therefore, it might be asked whether it is the rest of the world or America that has borne the higher cost.

Chapter 3

Whose Problem?

I would as soon leave my son a curse as the almighty dollar.

– Andrew Carnegie

At a meeting of G-10 finance ministers in Rome in November 1971, US Treasury Secretary John Connally famously told his astonished counterparts that 'The dollar may be our currency, but it is your problem'.[1]

A native of Texas, John Bowden Connally Jr. was admitted to the bar after graduating from the University of Texas School of Law. During WW2, he joined the Navy and initially served on the staff of James Forrestal and Dwight Eisenhower. Later, he saw action aboard aircraft carriers in the South Pacific and was awarded the Bronze Star for bravery and the Legion of Merit for outstanding service. After his discharge in 1946, he returned to Texas to practice law. When Lyndon B. Johnson, whom he had known since before the war, was elected to the Senate, Connally headed back to Washington DC as a key aide to LBJ. He was named Secretary of the Navy under President Kennedy in 1961, then was elected Governor of Texas on the Democratic ticket in 1962. When JFK was assassinated in Dallas the following year, Connally had been riding in the President's limousine and was severely wounded. He recovered and was later appointed Treasury Secretary by Nixon in 1971, notwithstanding the fact that he hailed from the opposing political party.

Before agreeing to accept the appointment, however, Connally insisted that Nixon find a position in his administration for George H.W. Bush. He had been concerned that his appointment would embarrass the Republican Bush, who had campaigned hard on Nixon's behalf in Texas and had recently lost a hard-fought election for a seat in the Senate. To secure Connolly's acceptance, Nixon appointed Bush as Ambassador to the UN, which may have rescued the future president's political career.

At Treasury, Connally focused his energies on the country's balance of payments position in the face of high domestic unemployment and was eager to end America's 'benign neglect' of the situation. His Treasury Department completed a study in May 1971 that concluded that the dollar was overvalued by 10 to 15 percent, and recommended that the US should seek '(i) a lasting improvement in the balance-of-payments position . . . , (ii) a more equitable sharing of responsibilities for world security and economic progress, and (iii) a basic reform of the international monetary system'.

These recommendations may seem eerily similar to demands made by more recent US administrations with respect to China and the EU. At that time, the Treasury's key targets were Japan and West Germany. Both were running significant balance of payments surpluses and, while the West Germans had allowed some revaluation of the Deutschmark, the Japanese were pursuing an export-led growth model and adamantly opposed any change to the dollar exchange rate of ¥360 that had been established in 1949.[2]

Treasury staff advocated a number of measures to pressure other countries into allowing the dollar to depreciate. These included a suspension of the dollar's gold convertibility; imposing trade restrictions; diplomatic and financial pressure; and reduction of the US military presence in Europe and Japan. Connally recognised that suspension of the dollar's gold convertibility alone was unlikely to be sufficient to achieve his desired devaluation, as countries with undervalued currencies would likely pursue measures to maintain their dollar exchange rates.

He therefore pushed to introduce a 10 percent surcharge on all imports as an additional measure. Since this raised the cost of imports for US consumers, it had a similar effect to depreciating the dollar, but would most impact those countries with the highest dependence on exports to the US. Nixon announced the import surcharge on 15 August, alongside the suspension in gold convertibility.

Paul Volcker, who would later serve as Chairman of the Federal Reserve from 1979 to 1987, was at that time the Under Secretary of the Treasury for International Affairs and had been heavily involved in the decision to suspend gold convertibility. A rationalist, he had anticipated that other countries would appreciate the economic realities and accommodate US demands. He later wrote:

> In my naïveté, I thought we could wrap up exchange rate realignment and start talking about reform in a month or two. . . Instead, I got a fast lesson in big-league negotiations. . . What we found, even after we shut the gold window, was fierce resistance by key countries to their currencies floating upward against the dollar.[3]

What followed amply demonstrated the international political tensions that are inherent risks of seeking exchange rate rebalancing within the dollar-centric global monetary system, as well as the difficulties and diplomatic costs faced by the US in effecting adjustments.

As Connally foresaw, the Bank of Japan immediately began buying dollars in the currency markets to maintain the yen at the old exchange rate. Over the course of the first week after Nixon's announcement, Japan's foreign exchange reserves grew by $2.7 billion, or 30 percent. Another week later, they had grown by a further $4 billion. The Japanese government was eventually unwilling to maintain intervention on such a large scale. If the import surcharge remained, Japan also stood to suffer economically, given its large exports to the US. By the end of August, Minister of Finance Mizuta Mikio announced that Japan would allow the yen to float. However, Japan maintained a 'dirty float' with continued government intervention to slow the yen's appreciation.[4]

The import surcharge may have provided leverage against Japan, but it strained American diplomatic relationships built up over decades and risked sparking retaliatory measures that had contributed to the Great Depression in the 1930s. Although primarily targeted at Japan, the surcharge applied to all countries, including Latin American nations running balance of payments deficits against the US, and Canada, which already had a free-floating currency. The European Economic Community (EEC) filed a complaint against the US under the General Agreement on Tariffs and Trade (GATT).

Apart from the threat of trade and diplomatic retaliation, American efforts to solve its balance of payments problem also stoked tensions between other countries. West Germany would not agree to a revaluation of the Deutschmark unless the French franc was also revalued, so as not to alter the competitive position between the European neighbours. France would only agree to a revaluation of the franc if the level of appreciation of the Deutschmark was greater. German officials insisted that the yen be revalued at least four percentage points more than the Deutschmark.

Given the diplomatic considerations, Nixon indicated to Connally that he should seek a quick settlement. This was achieved via the Smithsonian Agreement in December. Two days later, Nixon lifted the import surcharge. In light of the haste to reach a resolution though, the depreciation of the dollar under the Smithsonian Agreement was insufficient to restore equilibrium to the US balance of payments position. This was subsequently attributed as a major reason why a further dollar devaluation was needed in 1973, when Nixon severed the tie to gold completely.[5]

In one area of the May 1971 Treasury recommendations, the US did appear to have some success. The agreement to return sovereignty over Okinawa, which the US had occupied since the end of WW2, in November 1971 included a contribution from Japan towards the cost of continued US defence presence in the country. Between 1970 and 1975, America's share of total defence spending by NATO countries fell from around 77 percent to 60 percent.[6] Nevertheless, in the context of the Cold War, the US was constrained in the extent to which it could cut back on its worldwide military commitments. Even today, US spending on defence continues to exceed that of all other NATO members combined, and critics have long complained that the US provides a 'free ride' to Japan on regional security.[7]

The dollar-based international monetary system has put the US at the centre of the financial system in which all other nations have to operate. This has given the rest of the world a profound interest in

US financial and economic policy. Every move by US financial policymakers has the potential to seriously affect their economies and the prosperity of their people. Meanwhile, to allow the dollar to play the international role that it does, the US has had to surrender significant powers of influence over its domestic economy. The rest of the world's need for dollar liquidity has also created a temptation for both the US government and American consumers to spend far beyond their means. For consumers, the imbalances that this generated blew up spectacularly in the GFC, causing grave economic and social hardship. As yet, there has been no overt reckoning over the extent of US government borrowing, but the lack of constraints has contributed to serious policy errors.

Half a century after John Connally made his famous remark to the G-10, the dollar remains a big problem for the rest of the world. However, has it now become a bigger problem for America?

The Unipolar Moment

In the autumn of 1990, the influential columnist and political commentator Charles Krauthammer penned an article entitled 'The Unipolar Moment'. At the time, it was apparent that the Soviet Union as a Great Power rival to the US was in structural decline. Krauthammer predicted that the 'bipolar' US and Soviet dominated world of the Cold War era would give way to a 'unipolar' world in which, for a historical 'moment', possibly lasting several decades, America would be the sole superpower. To illustrate his point, Krauthammer drew on the events that were unfolding in the Persian Gulf at the time.

In the early hours of 2 August 1990, Saddam Hussein launched a surprise invasion of Kuwait. One hundred thousand Iraqi troops met little resistance as their tanks rolled down the six-lane highway towards Kuwait City. The tiny Kuwait held huge oil reserves. If he held Kuwait, the ruthless Iraqi dictator would directly control 20 percent of both OPEC production and global oil reserves.[8] He would also be in a position to threaten neighbouring Saudi Arabia, the world's largest oil producer. Oil prices, which had fallen in the 1980s as new supplies came online and geopolitical risks subsided, shot up towards $40 a barrel, more than double the price just before the invasion.[9]

Iraq was a large oil producer, but had been financially strained by the protracted Iran-Iraq War that had ended with a UN-brokered ceasefire in 1988. The war had cost the country half a million lives and, with 30 percent of its GDP still going towards military spending, Iraq was struggling to pay its international bills. Hussein railed against low oil prices, which he blamed on other OPEC members such as Kuwait, accusing them of not observing production quotas.

Iraq had been the largest arms purchaser in the world since 1985 and had pursued development of nuclear and chemical weapons. The timing of Hussein's invasion of Kuwait was calculated. The collapse of communism in Eastern Europe had left the Soviet Union grappling with internal problems. Europe was similarly distracted with the reintegration of East and West Germany. Saddam Hussein sought to exploit these developments to gain hegemony over the Persian Gulf and become the predominant oil power. He did not believe that the US had the stomach to send troops into battle. That was a critical miscalculation.

George Herbert Walker Bush was one of the best-prepared presidents ever to occupy the White House. He had been the youngest navy fighter pilot in the Pacific in WW2. He was later elected to the House of Representatives, where he served from 1967 to 1971. After serving as Nixon's Ambassador to the UN, he had chaired the Republican National Committee before being stationed in Beijing from 1974 to 1975 as America's top diplomat in China. He then served as Director of the CIA prior to being chosen as Ronald Reagan's vice president. He was himself elected to the top office in 1989.

Bush understood the wide range of issues at stake. Oil security was no doubt a major factor, but the risk that inaction posed to the post-Cold War order was also a key consideration. He thought back to the catastrophic consequences of European appeasement of Hitler in the Rhineland in 1936 and in Czechoslovakia in 1938 and resolved to act.

He also wanted to avoid 'another Vietnam' and, although the US was militarily capable of taking on Saddam Hussein's forces alone, he sought to build international support for action through the UN. Bush rapidly deployed forces to provide security to Saudi Arabia on 7 August, then drew on his deep network of personal relationships and took the time to assemble a coalition of 35 nations to force Iraq to withdraw. After deploying sanctions and securing a UN Security Council resolution on an ultimatum on 29 November, the US-led UN coalition forces launched Operation Desert Storm on 16 January 1991.

It took just 43 days for Kuwait to be liberated. A highly effective US-led air campaign meant that the ground war lasted just 100 hours.[10] Notwithstanding the overwhelming victory, Bush decided not to risk loss of life or a splintering of the coalition by advancing onto Baghdad to overthrow Saddam Hussein.

It was likely that domestic political considerations were also a factor in this decision. In his article, Krauthammer attributed Bush's strenuous efforts to build an international coalition more to domestic concerns. Broad international support was needed to establish legitimacy among Americans for military action against the backdrop of resurgent isolationist sentiment. Nevertheless, the decision to go to war had been met with large demonstrations in both the US and Western Europe.[11]

The Gulf War highlighted starkly that, in the immediate post-Cold War world, there was no international power that came close to challenging the US militarily. This was a fact not lost on other countries – not least China, for whose leadership the Gulf War became a catalyst for military modernisation. The low level of casualties raised US confidence in its military prowess, emboldening subsequent US administrations, which did not exercise the same deft diplomacy and restraint that George H. W. Bush had demonstrated. Freed from concerns about external threats, the US political elite gradually became complacent and more prone to polarisation in domestic politics. Krauthammer's fears of a return to isolationism were borne out when Bush was not elected for a second term in 1992. One of the key reasons for Bill Clinton's victory in that election was a greater focus on domestic economic issues amidst slowing growth and rising unemployment.

Any illusion that America could safely retreat into isolationism, however, was shattered on 11 September 2001. The terrorist attacks by Al Qaeda operatives on the twin towers of the World Trade Centre and on the Pentagon were the first strikes the US had suffered on home soil since the Japanese attack on Pearl Harbour in December 1941.

In contrast to the powers of the Eurasian land mass, the US is geographically blessed by being large, resource-rich and protected by wide oceans to its east and west. It also has the most formidable military capability the world has ever seen. However, none of those advantages could insulate the country against the shadowy threat of terrorism. The events of that single day transformed the national psyche and, suddenly, Americans felt physically vulnerable at home.

By then, George H. W. Bush's son George Walker Bush was in the White House. Bush Jr. quickly responded by declaring a 'War on Terror'. On 7 October, the US launched an invasion of Afghanistan, where the Sunni Islamic fundamentalist Taliban regime was sheltering Al Qaeda's leader Osama bin Laden. At this point, world sympathy was largely with the US.[12]

By 2002, with Afghanistan seemingly under control, Washington turned its sights on a new target. In his State of the Union address that January, Bush branded Iran, Iraq and North Korea as an 'axis of evil' and his administration began planning for a war on Iraq. Although there was no direct link between Iraq and the 9/11 attacks, there were a number of reasons why Bush's administration wanted to oust the Iraqi regime.

There was still a sense of unfinished business from the 1991 Gulf War. Vice President Dick Cheney had served as Secretary of Defence under Bush's father and had played a key role in decision-making during that campaign. A factor behind the decision not to invade the Iraqi capital in 1991 had been the assumption that Saddam Hussein would be toppled by forces within his own country. However, Hussein had survived and launched a bloody crackdown against a Kurdish uprising in northern Iraq.

The Iraqi dictator also had a history of seeking to develop chemical, biological and nuclear weapons. UN weapons inspectors had frequently met with lack of cooperation from Hussein's regime, leaving suspicions that he may have been continuing to develop weapons of mass destruction (WMD). Hussein himself did nothing to alleviate these suspicions by conveying ambiguity over his possession of such weapons on the apparent belief that, if the truth were known, it would have weakened his regime versus both Iran and domestic opponents.[13]

Notwithstanding the humanitarian case and suspicions about Iraq's WMD programme, France, Germany and Russia vehemently opposed a war with Iraq on the UN Security Council. There was significant scepticism about intelligence information alleging that Saddam Hussein possessed WMD and the American threat of action met with condemnation from around the world. Close ally Canada refused to engage in a war on Iraq without UN sanction. The Arab League condemned the war, and the European Parliament passed a non-binding resolution on 29 January 2003 opposing unilateral US military action against Iraq.

British Prime Minister Tony Blair was Bush's strongest supporter and committed UK forces to the US invasion. However, Blair faced fierce domestic resistance. Two million people took to the streets of London in the largest peace rally in the country's history.[14] British Foreign Secretary Robin Cook took a principled stand and resigned, telling a silenced House of Commons that 'what has come to trouble me most in recent weeks is the suspicion that if the hanging chads in Florida had gone the other way, and Al Gore had been elected, we would not now be about to commit British troops to the Middle East'.[15]

A month before the US-led invasion of Iraq commenced on 20 March 2003, as many as 50 million people marched for peace in cities all over the world.[16]

By 9 April, US forces had captured Baghdad and images of American soldiers helping Iraqis pull down a statue of Saddam Hussein were broadcast around the world. Aboard the USS *Abraham Lincoln*, Bush stood in front of a banner that read 'Mission Accomplished' and declared that 'the United States and our allies have prevailed'.[17] Notwithstanding the triumphalism, things soon began to unravel.

Failure to discover WMD further discredited the Bush Administration's rationale for going to war in the first place. Inadequate planning by the US for post-war reconstruction in Iraq then left a power vacuum that soon resulted in chaos and civil war. Reports also began to emerge about widespread abuses of prisoners by the US military at detention centres and prisons in the country. The most notorious of these took place at the Abu Ghraib prison, where prisoners were subjected to torture, humiliation and sexual abuse. This added to widespread condemnation of the US over human rights abuses committed during the War on Terror. These included extrajudicial transfers of prisoners to a US detention camp located at the Guantánamo Bay Naval Base at the south-eastern end of Cuba, where captives were held indefinitely and denied their rights under the Geneva Conventions.

For strategic and other rivals of the US, America's willingness to act outside established multinational frameworks such as the UN set a post-Cold War precedent that heightened insecurity. Even for allies, America's disregard for the rules-based order, which the US itself had established in the post-WW2 era, reduced America's moral standing. It was again Robin Cook who captured international public sentiment most eloquently:

> *If we believe in an international community based on binding rules and institutions, we cannot simply set them aside when they produce results that are inconvenient to us.*[18]

The direct financial costs of the War on Terror between its launch and 2020 are estimated to have been $5.4 trillion. The obligations to care for the veterans of the war are expected to add at least another $1 trillion to that figure in the coming decades.[19] The entire cost of the War on Terror was funded through US government borrowing, and the costs of servicing the additional debt burden will weigh on the federal budget for decades to come.[20] At the same time, the Bush Administration continued with a series of tax cuts that reduced America's fiscal revenues. If the US government had not had such unconstrained ability to borrow, would it have pursued such a costly war?

History may look back on America's unipolar moment as the beginning of its slide towards imperial overstretch. More immediately, however, the huge financial burden of the war and how that burden has been shared between the different segments of US society have exacerbated simmering domestic social tensions.

The Almighty Mr. Market

Economics is classed as a science. However, unlike most other areas of science, in which theories can be proven or disproved conclusively through experimentation, economics is imprecise. Outcomes of economic experiments are almost always impacted by the ambiguous intricacies of human social interaction and a multitude of other externalities. Economic policy, therefore, reflects society's beliefs and values. Economic theories can and do influence policymakers. However, often economic ideas are simply co-opted as a means of justifying policies driven by particular political ideologies.

Keynesianism was popularised in America through its association with Franklin Roosevelt's New Deal policies, which were implemented to combat the Great Depression. Whether Keynesian theories inspired the New Deal or were merely used to provide intellectual justification for FDR's policies is contested,[21] as is their effectiveness. Nobel prize-winning economist Paul Krugman argued in a *Playboy* magazine article that it was not the New Deal, but the outbreak of WW2 that ended the Great Depression.[22] Nevertheless, Keynesian economics replaced the previous economic orthodoxy of *laissez faire* and, in the several decades following WW2, dominated policymaking in North America and Western Europe.

Implicit within Keynesian economic theory is a trade-off between inflation and unemployment. When unemployment is high, government stimulus spending can help stoke a recovery. Excessive stimulus, however, leads to inflation. Monetary tightening policies, such as higher taxes and interest rates, can serve to rein in inflation, but the consequent reduction in consumption leads to an increase in unemployment. This relationship, described in the 1950s by New Zealand-born economist Bill Phillips, is known as the 'Phillips curve'. However, in the 1970s this relationship broke down. Suddenly, across America and Western Europe, rising unemployment was accompanied by *higher* inflation.

The reasons for this phenomenon, which became known as 'stagflation' (stagnation combined with inflation), were many.

Productivity growth is the apotheosis of economic development. The increase in productive output per hour of labour creates a virtuous circle in which higher productivity leads to higher profits, allowing wages to be improved, stimulating higher consumption, and increasing government tax receipts. In the post-WW2 years, rising urbanisation, improved manufacturing techniques and increases in scale all contributed to steady growth in productivity. However, by the 1970s, productivity increases had fallen off and it would not be until the introduction of mass computing in later decades that there would again be a sustained period of high productivity growth in the developed world.[23]

At the end of WW2, US industry had little competition due to the devastation in many other countries. As Western Europe and Japan recovered though, their manufacturers began to compete against US goods in international markets. This put pressure on US workers' wages, as lower labour costs in other countries meant that foreign goods were more price competitive.

Specific factors relating to the early 1970s converged with these broader trends. Succumbing to political pressure, Federal Reserve Chairman Arthur Burns had kept monetary conditions loose, so as to help President Nixon's re-election prospects in 1972.[24] This served to elevate inflation.

The oil price shock that followed in 1973 then further added to inflationary pressures. The growth in the West's energy dependence on oil since the end of WW2 meant that increases in the price of oil fed through into almost all segments of economic activity. The world had become accustomed to stable supplies of cheap oil. The sharp increase in oil prices, therefore, had a material and widespread impact on inflation.

The post-WW2 years had also seen a relatively balanced distribution of the benefits of economic growth between labour and the owners of capital. Supported by rising productivity, American workers had become accustomed to regular increases in their wages that were above the rate of growth in the economy. Trade unions had strong powers of collective bargaining and, as inflation drove the cost of living up, they pushed for higher wage increases for their members. The virtuous circle of the post-WW2 decades gave way to a vicious circle, where the *expectation* of higher inflation drove rising wage demands, which in turn fed through into higher inflation.

At the time, economists struggled to explain what was untethering the anchors of prevailing economic theory. Arthur Burns told Congress that 'the rules of economics are not working the way they used to'.[25] Into this void stepped the monetarists.

★★★

Monetarism is closely associated with the Economics department of the University of Chicago, among whose alumni and academic staff have numbered no fewer than 31 Nobel laureates. The most well-known among these was Milton Friedman, who has been described as the 'father of monetarism'.

Milton Friedman was born to Hungarian Jewish immigrants in Brooklyn in 1912. Shortly after he was born, the family relocated to

Rahway, New Jersey. A gifted student, he graduated high school aged 16 and was awarded a competitive scholarship to study mathematics and economics at Rutgers University, where Arthur Burns was one of his professors. Upon graduating in 1932, the young Friedman went on to pursue graduate work at the University of Chicago.

During the 1930s, Friedman worked for the National Resources Planning Board in Washington DC, just as the Roosevelt Administration was pursuing its New Deal policies. Given the circumstances of the Great Depression, Friedman supported the New Deal's job-creation programmes, but was critical of price controls, which he believed interfered with an important signalling mechanism for resource allocation. He later said of the New Deal that it was 'the wrong cure for the wrong disease'.[26] He would go on to take up positions at the University of Wisconsin and at Columbia University before returning in 1946 to the University of Chicago, where he would remain for the next 30 years.

The diminutive Friedman became an intellectual leader of the Chicago school, winning the John Bates Clark Medal for the most outstanding American economist under 40 in 1951. A staunch libertarian, he rejected Keynesian government intervention. Among a large body of academic work, he is best known for his quantity theory of money. In the book *A Monetary History of the United States 1867–1960*, he and co-author Anna Schwartz concluded that the Great Depression had been caused by excessively tight monetary policy, which had choked off the supply of credit to businesses. This supported a rejection of the use of fiscal policy to manage economic demand, and the use of monetary policy instead – most notably through the management of the money supply.

Although he rejected a role in the Eisenhower Administration, believing that it would require too much 'compromise' with his anti-government views,[27] he was active in and highly influential upon public policy, and was a key advisor to the Reagan Administration.

Like Keynes, Friedman's theories reflected the circumstances of his era. Keynesian theories had rejected *laissez faire* policies that had resulted in high concentrations of wealth. In advocating government spending and intervention, Keynesianism was inherently redistributive. Between 1950 and 1975, the share of federal government spending on welfare rose from 26 percent of the budget to 55 percent.[28] Through the 1950s,

1960s and 1970s, the top rate of federal income tax remained high, never dipping below 70 percent.

Ronald Reagan believed that high taxation and government spending were restricting free enterprise. Friedman's theories supported reducing the role played by government and slashing taxes – which Reagan duly did. During his presidency, he cut the top rate of income tax from 70 percent down to 28 percent, while the lowest tax rates came down from 14 to 11 percent.[29] Although taxes were cut across the board, the wealthy clearly directly benefited the most. As John Kenneth Galbraith observed, 'the age of John Maynard Keynes gave way to the era of Milton Friedman'.[30]

The 'free market' philosophy Friedman advocated and the enthusiasm with which it was adopted were in part a reaction against the problems brought on by the extreme application of Keynesian policies. It was the pendulum swinging back. However, when taken over by ideological fervour, sound ideas about reforms were pushed to the opposite extreme.

One idea advanced by Friedman that has been particularly controversial is in the area of business ethics. In an essay entitled 'A Friedman Doctrine: The Social Responsibility of Business Is to Increase Its Profits', which was published in the New York Times in 1970, the economist argued that a corporate executive is an 'agent' for the shareholders 'who own the corporation' and that 'his primary responsibility is to them', rather than to pursue what he might deem to be the 'social responsibilities' of the business.[31]

Prominent opponents of this view include Klaus Schwab, who founded the World Economic Forum, which hosts the annual Davos gathering of global elites, partly as a counterbalance to the rise of Friedman's 'shareholder capitalism'. Schwab has promoted 'stakeholder capitalism', which demands that businesses should take into account all interests, including those of customers, employees and the communities in which they operate.[32]

Critics blame the rise of shareholder capitalism for a decline in corporate ethics that has given rise to high profile scandals such as the accounting fraud that brought down the corporate giant Enron.[33] One study that presented an ethics case to business students found that 20 to 30 percent of them could not even identify the ethical issue. The author of the study colourfully opined that 'far too much of the world's corporate leadership is driven by moral midgets who have been educated far beyond their capacities for good judgment'.[34] While containing a large kernel of truth, such views ignore a number of considerations.

Social responsibilities are hard to define, and different individuals have different views. Corporate managers are appointed by shareholders and can be removed by them, so are inherently incentivised to act in accordance with shareholders' wishes. Friedman's doctrine provides a clarity of objective and implicitly rejects the notion that an individual manager or small group of executives should be the arbiters of a company's social purpose. Where the owners of a business wish the company to pursue objectives other than profit maximisation, they can direct the management accordingly. However, in the case of large publicly listed corporations, widely distributed ownership among a large number of disparate public shareholders may make this infeasible. Friedman's 1970 essay addresses this problem by stating that the 'one and only social responsibility of business' is 'to increase its profits *so long as it stays within the rules of the game*',[35] thereby putting the onus on governments, which represent society more broadly, to define the social responsibilities of businesses by enacting them into laws and regulations. It is here that something of a conflict arises in Friedman's philosophy.

Milton Friedman opposed excessive government interference in markets. This supported a political drive towards deregulation. In many areas, this drove significant improvements in efficiency. For example, the deregulatory Staggers Rail Act of 1980 led to a doubling of the ton-miles moved by railways since it was enacted, and the industry now uses far fewer resources of all types.[36] Airline deregulation initially led to increased competition, which helped drive down the price of air travel for consumers.[37] However, as governments increasingly deferred to markets, free market ideology became a pretext for abdication of government responsibility even where it was apparent that intervention was necessary.

In 1904, Teddy Roosevelt initiated an investigation into anticompetitive practices in the petroleum industry. This led to a break-up of John D. Rockefeller's Standard Oil in 1911, which marked an end to the era of the 'robber barons'. However, the unprecedented boom in mergers and acquisitions (M&A) over the past several decades surpasses even the peak of the Gilded Age.[38] Over a period of 15 years between 1997 and 2012, *two-thirds* of US industries became concentrated in the hands of just a few companies.[39]

The rise in corporate consolidation has had a number of detrimental effects. Monopolies and oligopolies tend to result in higher prices for consumers. Where a small number of companies dominate an industry at the national or local level, they can also more effectively hold down wages for workers. Dominant players make it harder to enter an industry, resulting in fewer start-ups, lower investment and less innovation. This contributes to less diversity and lower productivity across the economy.[40]

In his 1970 *New York Times* essay, Friedman acknowledged the need for 'open and free competition'. However, by 1999, his antipathy towards any form of state regulation led him to argue that, far from promoting competition, antitrust laws 'tended to do exactly the opposite'.[41] While excessive regulation can act as a barrier to competition, insufficient regulation can lead to abuses. It is incumbent upon policymakers to strike a balance. It is hard to conclude anything other than that, by the late 1990s, free market ideology had overtaken common sense. However, fanning the flames of this ideological fervour in all aspects of public life was the increasing influence of moneyed interests on US politics.

★★★

In his 1861 essay 'On Representative Government', the English philosopher John Stuart Mill wrote:

> *There has never yet been, among political men, any real and serious attempt to prevent bribery, because there has been no real desire that elections should not be costly. Their costliness is an advantage to those who can afford the expense, by excluding a multitude of competitors. . .*[42]

Money has always had a strong influence on politics. Even where there is no explicit corruption, corporate leaders and the wealthy tend to move in the same circles as the political elite, so have greater opportunities to influence policy. However, there is strong evidence that the level of influence wielded by moneyed interests on the US political system has increased in recent decades.

Political action committees (PACs) in the US pool campaign contributions from members and donate these funds to campaigns for or against candidates running for office. They also ballot initiatives and legislation. In 1974, there were just 89 corporate funded PACs. By 1982, there were 1,467 of them lobbying for various corporate interests.[43]

In 2016, the top 0.01 percent of Americans in terms of wealth contributed 40 percent of total campaign donations. It has been argued, with some justification, that the ability of corporate entities to finance politicians in the US, coupled with the lack of significant limits on private contributions, gives the wealthy a disproportionate influence on American politics and leads to policies that favour the top of US society.[44]

However, it is not just direct political contributions that have increased the influence of wealthy and corporate interests. The US now has more well-funded strategic think tanks than any other country. They have become a deeply embedded part of the Washington DC ecosystem, with a 'revolving door' of personnel that moves between think tanks, government service and private industry. This situation gives rise to two serious concerns. First, notwithstanding America's liberal values and long-standing tradition of free speech, the incentive structures created by this system make the policy establishment prone to 'groupthink'. Given the prospect of lucrative careers in private industry, individuals working in the system are disincentivised from straying outside the 'respectable' consensus. Second, 'threat inflation' tends to prevail, as think tanks that offer less alarming appraisals on issues tend not to be as well-funded and are less influential. This raises particular concerns with respect to US foreign and defence policy.[45]

In Eisenhower's farewell address on leaving office in 1961, he presciently warned his countrymen about this risk:

> We have been compelled to create a permanent armaments industry of vast proportions. Added to this, three and a half million men and women are directly engaged in the defence establishment. We annually spend on military security more than the net income of all United States corporations. The conjunction of an immense military establishment and a large arms industry is new in the American experience. . . We must guard against the acquisition of unwarranted influence, whether sought or unsought, by the military-industrial complex. The potential for the disastrous rise of misplaced power exists and will persist.[46]

The sinister risks inherent in the US military-industrial complex have been well documented. Defence contractors have allocated manufacturing facilities to all key Congressional districts in the US, creating a conflict of interest for members of Congress who want to preserve jobs in their constituencies and who also decide what weapons systems will be produced for the US military.[47] In one reported instance in 2003, a chairman of the Defence Policy Board expressed support for a contract with Boeing just 16 months after Boeing had committed to invest \$20 million in his venture capital firm.[48] Although 22,785 individuals were referred for prosecution for official corruption that year, just 12 of these referrals were related to revolving door offenses, and only two of those resulted in prosecution.[49] The complex system of lobbying employed by defence contractors not only threatens the legitimacy of the US political process but, combined with the propensity for threat inflation in Washington think tanks, has also created dangerous incentives for American military adventures overseas.

As the level of influence of wealthy and corporate interests increased in US politics, even left-leaning political parties became more concerned to pander to corporations and the *diktats* of free market ideology. During his campaign for the White House, Bill Clinton had promised greater investment in jobs, education and public infrastructure, and to cut taxes for the middle classes by 10 percent. However, partly as a result of the Gulf War, budget deficits were running at \$290 billion a year at the time he came into office.[50] This was an unpleasant surprise and created a problem, as Clinton had also pledged to balance the national budget by 1997, and his economic advisors did not want his new administration to lose fiscal credibility.

Less than a fortnight before his inauguration, Clinton met with his appointee as Secretary of the Treasury, former Goldman Sachs chairman Robert Rubin, and other members of his economic advisory team at the Governor's Mansion in Little Rock, Arkansas. During the course of a six-hour meeting, his advisors made the case that he should scale back his plans. Lower deficits, they said, would convince the bond markets to bring interest rates down, and savings that the American middle class would get through lower payments on their borrowings would support the broader economy and leave them better off than if they were to receive a tax cut. This in turn would help bring down unemployment.

Clinton vented his frustration to the assembled group, saying: 'You mean to tell me that the success of my programme and my re-election hinges on the Federal Reserve and a bunch of f★★★ing bond traders?'.[51] Despite his irritation, he ultimately gave in to the demands of the market.

An underlying factor at play was the continuing march of globalisation. National boundaries were being lowered by technological advances, greater mobility of people and capital, and prevailing political trends. It became easier for corporations and individuals to relocate to locations offering more favourable policies. This meant market-unfriendly policies risked businesses taking their operations offshore, further compounding the fiscal problems.

Thus, the Clinton years became characterised by fiscal conservatism and tax policies continued to favour the wealthy. Fortuitously, thanks to strong economic performance and the Dot-com boom, the Clinton years were ones of prosperity. By the time he left office, median household income had increased by $6,000[52] and the country had enjoyed several years of budget surpluses.

The Clinton Administration also continued the deregulatory agenda, including passing the Financial Services Modernisation Act in 1999. This repealed the Glass-Steagall Act of 1932, which had forced a separation between commercial and investment banking activities following a wave of bank failures during the Great Depression. This opened the door for the merger of the insurance group Travelers (which had acquired Wall Street firm Salomon Brothers in 1997) with Citicorp, to create the banking giant Citigroup. A wave of M&A in the banking sector followed.

Riding on the surpluses that Clinton had built up, his Republican successor George W. Bush launched the biggest tax cuts in a generation, featuring $40 billion in tax rebates in 2001 and increasing to $70 billion a year thereafter.[53] These cuts overwhelmingly favoured the wealthy and were maintained notwithstanding escalating budget deficits generated by the costs of the War on Terror.

Ever one to deliver an insightful quip, James Carville said of the power that markets exerted over the Clinton Administration: 'I used to think that if there was reincarnation, I wanted to come back as the president or the pope or as a .400 baseball hitter. But now I would like to come back as the bond market. You can intimidate everybody'.[54]

If Bill Clinton felt that America was a prisoner of financial market forces, however, emerging markets had it a lot worse.

Emerging Markets Crises

By 1977, OPEC oil revenues had reached $128 billion. *What were they doing with all that cash?* The answer was that three-quarters of the surplus was being invested in industrialised countries, with a quarter of it going to the US alone.[55] William Simon's deal with King Faisal meant that a lot of it was now being invested in US Treasury bonds, but there was still a lot left over. Much of the dollar surpluses was being deposited into US and foreign banks.

The banks receiving these dollar deposits faced a conundrum. The US recession meant that many consumers and small businesses didn't want to borrow. The ones that did generally had questionable credit. Meanwhile, large corporations were now able to borrow more cheaply by issuing bonds directly to investors. *What could the banks do with all the deposits?*

The answer to the banks' problem was increased lending to less developed countries (LDCs), or what we nowadays call 'emerging markets'. This was not an entirely new phenomenon. LDCs were a popular destination for US bond investors prior to the Great Depression. Unsurprisingly, those investments did not turn out well. However, by the 1970s, a whole new generation of bankers who had not lived through that experience were ready to give it another go, attracted by the fat margins they could earn on lending to LDC governments.

To be fair to the bankers, there was also some subtle pressure from US government officials to expand lending to LDCs. The US ran a balance of payments surplus against Latin American countries, so the 'recycling' of OPEC surpluses through lending to the developing world provided the financing for those countries to continue buying US exports. A top economic advisor in the Ford Administration, Bill Seidman, candidly admitted that banks had been told that it was their 'patriotic duty' to recycle petrodollars to the LDCs.[56]

The growing exposure of US banks to LDCs did not go unnoticed. A staff report issued by the Senate Subcommittee on Foreign Relations in 1977 expressed concern about the risks this posed to the 'stability of the US banking system and by extension the international financial system'. Federal Reserve Chairman Arthur Burns was also critical of the banks for extending too much credit to over-indebted countries.[57] However, these warnings went unheeded.

By mid-1982, US bank loans to South America totalled $82.5 billion.[58] The nine largest American banks had lent a total of $83 billion to LDCs, of which $51 billion was to Latin America alone. A 1981 *Wall Street Journal* article openly expressed concern about these exposures, describing them as 'starkly ominous', with the potential to precipitate 'a chain reaction of country defaults, bank failures and a general depression matching that of the 1930s'.[59] Notwithstanding the rising concerns, bankers remained nonchalant. Even on the eve of crisis, Citicorp Chairman Walter Wriston brushed caution aside, declaring that 'countries don't go bankrupt'.[60]

In 1982, Mexico, which was a large oil exporter, announced that it could no longer service its debts on the original terms. Other highly indebted countries soon followed. The LDC crisis had begun.

The LDCs' high level of borrowing was only one factor in precipitating the crisis, however. Another major factor was the appointment to the chairmanship of the Federal Reserve in 1979 of a man with a mission to slay US inflation.

***

Paul Adolph Volcker Jr. was the son of a civil servant, who had grown up in New Jersey. In high school, on account of his 6-foot and 7-inches in height, he'd played on the varsity basketball team. On graduating from high school, he tried to enlist in the Army, but was rejected because he was an inch too tall. He therefore applied to Princeton University, where he studied economics, politics and history. In his senior year, he wrote his thesis on 'The Problems of Federal Reserve Policy Since World War II', arguing that the Fed needed to act more firmly to control inflation.

After Princeton, Volcker went on to further studies at Harvard's School of Public Administration. Two years later, he won a scholarship to write his doctoral thesis at the London School of Economics, affording him the opportunity to travel around Europe. On his return to the US, he first took up a position as a staff economist at the New York Fed but was then recruited to work at Chase Manhattan. There he served as special assistant to David Rockefeller, who was at that time the bank's vice chairman.

Volcker was first lured to Washington DC in 1962 by his old boss at the New York Fed, who had joined the Kennedy Administration.[61] He started as an advisor to the Treasury and went on to serve three presidential administrations there, rising to Under Secretary for International Affairs. In that role, he was a key figure in Nixon's decision to close the gold window in 1971. When he left the Treasury in 1974, he had intended to return to Wall Street, but Arthur Burns persuaded him to become President of the New York Fed. There, he watched with frustration as the Federal Reserve failed to rein in inflation.

William Miller replaced Burns at Fed Chairman in 1978. When Jimmy Carter decided to do a cabinet reshuffle in 1979, he tapped Miller to serve as Treasury Secretary. Paul Volcker was reported not to be Carter's first choice as Fed Chairman. When the job was offered to him in the Oval Office, the cigar smoking Volcker slumped on the couch. Pointing at Miller, who was also present, he told Carter that 'You have to understand, if you appoint me, I favour a tighter policy than that fellow'.[62]

The job as Fed Chairman involved significant sacrifices for Volcker. It paid about half as much as the role of President of the New York Fed. His wife, who suffered from debilitating rheumatoid arthritis and diabetes, remained in New York to be near her doctor, as did their son, who was born with cerebral palsy. The famously frugal Volcker moved into an apartment building populated by George Washington University students and would take his laundry to his daughter's house in the Virginia suburbs.

A dedicated public servant and fiercely independent, Volcker wasted little time in making good on his word to the President. Inflation at that time was exceeding one percent per month. On the evening of Saturday, 6 October, he called a news conference in the grand boardroom at the Federal Reserve headquarters to announce a major shift in the conduct of monetary policy.

Pope John Paul II was visiting Washington at the time. When the television network *CBS* informed the Fed that it didn't have a spare camera crew to cover the Fed Chairman's announcement, Volcker's spokesman told the *CBS* producer: 'Send your crew here. Long after the pope is gone, you'll remember this one'.[63]

Volcker's message was a declaration of war on inflation. Drawing on the strategy advocated by Milton Friedman, the Federal Reserve Chairman announced that, going forward, the Fed would aim to control the supply of money. Previously, Fed policy had aimed to control interest rates – the price of money. From that point on, the Fed would determine how much money was available, with markets setting the price. Limiting the money supply would cause interest rates to go up, but the Fed would no longer target a specific increase.

The immediate result was a huge surge in interest rates. The prime rate charged by banks to their most creditworthy customers almost doubled, peaking at 21.5 percent. The public backlash was substantial. Indebted farmers drove their tractors through the capital and blockaded the Federal Reserve headquarters. Car dealers mailed in keys for cars they could not sell. A builder who was put out of work sent in a two-by-four block of wood, on which he had written: 'Where will our children live?'.[64]

The pain was not just felt by US borrowers though. The LDCs, which had borrowed from the banks in US dollars, found that the interest rates they paid on those loans shot up. Furthermore, higher interest rates in the US attracted capital inflows, pushing up the dollar's exchange rate. This meant that the value of LDC borrowers' loans also increased significantly in local currency terms, making it even harder for them to repay.

★★★

There has continued to be a steady stream of emerging markets crises over recent decades: the Tequila crisis (Mexico, 1994); the Asian Financial Crisis (1997); the Russian financial crisis (1998); and the Argentine debt default (2001) – to name but a few of the most prominent. Contrary to popular perceptions of irresponsible emerging market governments and poor institutional controls, the stories are far more nuanced.

In certain cases, emerging market governments borrowed in foreign currency to expand government spending and go on consumption binges, rather than investing in productive capacity. This was the case in various Latin American countries. When this behaviour led to financial crises, it is fairly clear that the cause was poor government policy.

However, prior to the Asian Financial Crisis, most governments in Asia had run what appeared to be sound fiscal policies. Strong economic growth and rising exports had attracted inflows of foreign capital. Money flowed in from overseas to local stock markets, as well as in the form of lending to local corporations and banks. In South Korea in 1997, it was borrowing by domestic corporations in dollars that proved problematic because their earnings were in Korean won. When the won plunged in the crisis, their debt burden in local currency terms surged. This, in turn, threatened the stability of the Korean banking system, embroiling South Korea's government and the whole country in the crisis.

The level at which borrowing might be deemed excessive defies precise definition. For example, the year before Argentina defaulted on its sovereign debt in 2001, the country's government debt-to-GDP ratio was just above 40 percent.[65] This compares with Japan's debt-to-GDP ratio of well over 200 percent in 2019.[66] Notwithstanding the enormous size of the Japanese government's borrowing, nobody expects Japan to default anytime soon. The problem for Argentina was that 80 percent of Argentine private debt was in dollars, while only 25 percent of the country's economy was export-oriented.[67] Japan, on the other hand, can borrow a large portion of what it needs from Japanese savers in its own currency.

Contagion is another major problem. What precipitated the Asian Financial Crisis in 1997 was a decision by the Thai government to float the Thai baht, as it no longer held enough foreign currency to maintain its peg to the US dollar. Capital flight ensued immediately, setting off a chain reaction that engulfed nations across the entire region, notwithstanding large degrees of variation between their stages of development, economic structures and fiscal positions.

Some observers have blamed the phenomenon of 'crony capitalism' for the crises in Asia and elsewhere.[68] This is where large and politically well-connected firms obtain preferential access to foreign financing, irrespective of their productivity relative to other potential uses of the capital. This is true in some instances up to a point, but is hardly the whole story.

Looking at all the various emerging markets financial crises, it can be said that each had its own peculiar symptoms, but all shared a certain common pathology: high levels of dollar borrowing in the system, accompanied by currencies tied to a rising US dollar.

Emerging market governments were not blind to the dangers of debt, but access to capital is critical to fund development. Foreign investors typically shun lending in emerging markets' local currencies, as they worry that the governments could simply print more money and erode the value of the debt.[69] Even where governments are trusted, foreign investors prefer to receive payment in hard currencies (usually dollars) and the cost of hedging against local currencies can significantly reduce returns for investors (or, more likely, increase the cost for borrowers). In some cases, emerging market governments peg or fix their local currency's exchange rate to a hard currency in order to help attract foreign investment. Even then, the large demand for risk free assets such as US Treasuries (discussed in Chapter 2) can often crowd out demand for alternative investments and make it difficult – or, at least, far more expensive – for emerging markets to access capital.

The Asian Financial Crisis caused much human suffering and distress. As currency values slumped, banks and businesses collapsed, and an estimated 22 million people were plunged into poverty. In Indonesia, the rupiah fell to just 15 percent of its pre-crisis exchange rate and the country saw a 13.8 percent fall in GDP in 1998. In Thailand, where the crisis had first started, the unemployment rate jumped from 0.9 percent in 1997 to 5.3 percent in 1998. Cutbacks in Thailand's national budget meant that, in the midst of the battle against the HIV epidemic, spending on HIV and AIDS control was slashed by one-third in real terms.[70]

***

The dollar-centric global monetary system clearly presents financial and economic challenges for emerging market countries. However, the financial crises that they periodically face also present broader diplomatic, political and security challenges.

As laid down under the Bretton Woods system, the IMF is the first port of call for a country faced with a foreign currency liquidity crisis.

However, there is significant stigma attached to IMF rescues. This has not been helped by the sometimes high-handed manner of IMF officials and harsh conditions imposed on troubled countries. In light of the high degree of influence that the US wields over the IMF,[71] America is often viewed as being behind the organisation's decisions, which can lead to diplomatic tensions.

Understandably, the US is more willing to extend financial support where it has greater national interests at stake. In the wake of the 1994 crisis that afflicted its southern neighbour Mexico, the US quickly orchestrated a $50 billion IMF bailout. When IMF support is less forth-coming and has more strings attached – such as in the case of the Argen-tinian crisis – the perception of unequal treatment can generate negative public sentiment towards the US.[72]

During the Asian Financial Crisis, conditions imposed by the IMF in return for financial assistance were often perceived as 'a cynical, opportu-nistic attempt by Washington to exploit the crisis on behalf of American banks and contractors seeking easier access in Asian markets'.[73] Recipi-ents of IMF support were forced to commit to political and economic reforms, monetary tightening, and deep cuts in government expenditure. A lasting image of the humiliation to which Asian governments were subjected was of Michel Camdessus, then head of the IMF, standing with his arms folded 'in Schoolmarm fashion' looking over President Suharto as the Indonesian leader signed an IMF bailout agreement in January 1998.[74] Suharto's regime collapsed shortly thereafter, and the country saw a wave of violence directed at the Chinese merchant class.

In South Korea, where there were 36,000 US troops stationed near the North Korean border, Washington supported a record $57 billion IMF bailout. One of the conditions demanded in return was an increase in the ceiling on foreign ownership of Korean stocks to 50 percent. This was a major reform that would have been controversial in the best of circumstances. The IMF gave the Korean government only 12 days to comply. This precipitated widespread anti-American sentiment in South Korea, with one article in the *Korea Times* stating accusatorily: 'Every-body knows the IMF is run by the US'.[75]

The conditions imposed by the IMF on Asian economies were not entirely cynical in nature. The advice doled out reflected the prevailing American view that free market solutions were the best cure. However,

Mahathir Mohamad's government in Malaysia rejected the IMF's austerity medicine and, instead, imposed capital controls and fixed the ringgit's exchange rate at 3.80 per dollar.[76] It also undertook interest rate cuts and embarked upon a policy of reflation. Malaysia's subsequent strong recovery served to undermine the IMF's standing to a degree and, by extension, the economic model advocated by the US.

There is more at stake than foreign perceptions of the US, however. One of the most sobering episodes among the emerging markets crises of recent decades was what happened in Russia in 1998. Financial markets practitioners remember this as the crisis that precipitated the collapse of LTCM, but for those in the security establishment the crisis had far more sinister consequences.

Following the collapse of the rouble, the Russian government effectively went into collapse. In the heavily nuclear-armed state, government workers at weapons facilities went unpaid and failure to pay utility bills led to the power being cut off in some cases. The lack of electricity rendered alarms and surveillance devices at key facilities inoperative. An American team that visited the Kurchatov Institute in Moscow in September 1998 found 100 kilograms of highly enriched uranium (sufficient for several nuclear bombs) completely unguarded. There was simply no money to pay for a guard. In December of that year, the head of the Russian Federal Security Service in Chelyabinsk reported that workers had been found trying to steal 18.5 kilograms of weapons grade nuclear material. It has not been possible to estimate how much deadly material from that time found its way into the international black market.[77]

Suffice it to say that, far from abstract economic phenomena, financial crises have serious real-world consequences. Imbalances in the global financial system that lead to frequent structural recurrences of such crises, therefore, potentially imperil the entire planet.

★★★

Major crises tend to elicit regulatory and policy reactions. The emerging markets crises led to some significant developments in this regard. In the financial sphere, two stand out due to the reverberations they would have later on.

The first was the advancement towards international bank capital requirements.

Following the LDC crisis in the early 1980s, the market value of the loans that banks had made to LDCs fell significantly, reflecting a high probability that many of them would not be repaid. However, a number of banks continued to hold the loans on their balance sheets at the original book value. With the tacit acquiescence of their regulators, they maintained a fiction for much of the rest of the decade that they would eventually be repaid. If they had recognised the losses, it is likely that many of these banks would have been insolvent, which would have triggered a banking crisis in the US.

Bank capital comprises the equity paid in by shareholders and the accumulated retained earnings of the bank. Unlike industrial companies, the assets that banks hold are not factories and machinery, but rather the loans they lend out to borrowers. To fund these loans, they use the money provided by their depositors. These deposits constitute the banks' liabilities. Typically, banks lend for a fixed duration – say, a 30-year mortgage – but it is unlikely that depositors are willing to tie up their money for such a long time. This gives rise to a mis-match between the time when banks will receive repayment on their loans and the time when depositors might want to withdraw their funds. Banks count on a constant flow of depositors being willing to keep enough money in the bank, so that they aren't faced with more people wanting their money back than they can pay out.

Interest rates on longer-term loans tend to be higher than on short-term deposits. The difference between what a bank receives on money it lends out and what it pays on money deposited by its customers generates the bank's profits. However, if a borrower defaults on a loan, then the bank might incur a loss. This is where bank capital comes in. The capital provides a buffer to help ensure that banks can absorb some losses and still meet their obligation to pay money back to their depositors.

During the Great Depression, a wave of loan defaults caused a panic by depositors, who lined up at banks to withdraw their money. The sudden demand for funds meant that many banks could not come up with enough money in time and went insolvent. This precipitated a chain reaction that significantly worsened the crisis.

There are now two ways that governments address such risks. The first is via central banks, which have the power to issue currency. Against adequate collateral, central banks will lend short-term funds to commercial banks, so that they can meet their obligations in the event of a liquidity crunch. The second is through deposit insurance, which in the US is underwritten by the FDIC. This provides depositors with reassurance that they will get their money back, thus helping avoid panics.

Such government guarantees, however, give rise to the risk of 'moral hazard'. If a bank knows there is a government backstop in the event that their loans go bad, it might be tempted to make riskier loans in the hope of reaping higher profits. If its gambles don't pay off, then taxpayers are left on the hook. In light of banks' shaky balance sheets in the 1980s, regulators and the government began to become concerned.

Before 1980, there had been no standard rule on the ratio of bank capital to bank assets in the US. That year, the Fed, the FDIC and the Comptroller of the Currency issued a set of capital-to-asset guidelines for the banking industry. These guidelines placed greater pressure on banks to maintain adequate capital but didn't have the force of law behind them. In 1983, Congress enacted the International Lending Supervision Act, which required regulators to set enforceable capital standards.

However, in a rapidly globalising banking industry, the competitiveness of US banks versus foreign players was becoming a big issue. From 1973 to 1978, the number of foreign banks operating in the US increased from 60 to 122. Over that period, their combined assets grew from $37 billion to $90 billion. Particularly aggressive were the Japanese banks. By 1988, the 10 largest banks in the world by assets were all Japanese. US regulators' concerns were made clear when, appearing before Congress, Paul Volcker stated: 'I cannot emphasise strongly enough our interest in the competitiveness of US banks'.[78]

Seeking a level playing field for banks around the world, the Federal Reserve worked with the Bank of England to initiate a drive towards a set of common international standards. The result in 1986 was a set of risk-based standards that assigned risk weights to different types of assets held by banks and set a minimum capital requirement based on the 'risk weighted assets'. Assets considered to hold no risk, such as rich country government bonds, were assigned a risk weighting of zero, while most other loans were risk weighted at 100 percent.

With this methodology in place, the two central banks then turned to the Swiss-based BIS to mandate international adoption of the standards through its Basel Committee on Banking Supervision. The Basel Committee was made up of central banks from 13 rich nations and had been established in 1974 to coordinate the oversight of banks operating internationally. In 1988, the Basel Committee agreed to adopt the Anglo-American standards for governing international banks' capital requirements. It soon became apparent, however, that there were numerous shortcomings in the Basel standards, and that their design had triggered numerous unintended consequences.

Among the key design flaws was the arbitrary nature of the risk weights. There was no differentiation between different types of consumer and commercial loans, nor adequate distinction between varying levels of country risk for sovereign debt. This meant that banks were perversely incentivised to make riskier loans in some instances. There was also no recognition of the benefits of diversifying loan portfolios, which generally reduces the overall level of risk. The standards had further omitted to define non-performing loans (NPLs) and agree to a common accounting treatment for them. This meant that banks that did not fully reflect the losses on their loan portfolios could mask their capital shortfalls. This became a particular issue with the Japanese banks in the wake of the collapse in Japanese real estate prices after 1989.

One particular unintended consequence was to further increase demand for US Treasuries. Since these 'risk free' assets required no capital to back them, banks were incentivised to increase their holdings of these securities. In the recessionary environment of 1989 to 1992, US banks *reduced* their overall lending to consumers and businesses while *increasing* their US Treasury bond holdings by almost 50 percent.[79]

In the early 1990s, the Basel Committee began work on refining the standards to address these shortcomings. This was a fraught process but, by 1999, the Committee had managed to agree on a new set of standards, known as Basel II. Given the complexity of the new rules, which ran to over 400 pages in length, the Committee allowed for a long transition period. The new standards were not scheduled to be fully implemented until 2007.

The Basel II standards introduced greater differentiation in the risk weights applied to different assets. For different types of loans and debt securities, the Committee proposed to base the risk weights on ratings provided by the major US private credit rating agencies, Standard & Poor's (S&P), Moody's and Fitch. Setting aside the obvious conflict of interest arising from the fact that these credit rating agencies are paid directly by the issuers that they assign credit ratings to, there were a number of objections raised at the time. Some countries had little experience in dealing with these agencies, so would find the new methodology difficult to implement. Others pointed out that the credit rating agencies had a poor track record on identifying major turning points in the credit cycle. As a compromise, the Basel Committee allowed the largest banks to employ their own internal systems for evaluating loan riskiness.

Political considerations were evident in a number of aspects of the new standards. One example was the Committee's decision to assign a much lower risk weight of 50 percent to residential mortgages. This was done to appease German banks, which had large exposures to real estate loans.[80]

The effect of the Basel II standards was to allow many large banks to hold *lower* levels of capital than they had held previously. Realising the shortcomings of the Basel II rules, the US put in place a parallel system that applied to US banks, including legislation that required banks to hold minimum capital-to-total assets ratios.[81] Nevertheless, many loopholes remained. One way that banks discovered they could skirt the new capital requirements was to package their loans into so-called 'off balance sheet' vehicles. These were special purpose entities set up and sponsored by the banks to purchase loans from their own books. Assets held in such vehicles did not appear on banks' balance sheets and therefore did not attract any risk weighting. The increased leverage in the banking system was an accident waiting to happen – as was discovered during the 2008 GFC.

★★★

The second highly consequential development arising from the emerging markets crises was a shift in the monetary policies of a number of emerging markets countries, particularly in Asia. Learning from the lessons of the Asian Financial Crisis, Asian governments pursued tight fiscal policies and built up huge foreign currency reserves to insure themselves against currency market volatility and the risk of sudden large capital outflows.

The accumulation of foreign currency reserves in this instance is somewhat different from the petrodollar surpluses of the oil exporters. Instead of selling commodities in return for hard currencies, such as the dollar, what these emerging market central banks were doing was selling their own currencies to buy dollars in the foreign currency markets. Like the action taken by the Bank of Japan immediately following Nixon's devaluation of the dollar in 1971, the effect of these purchases was to hold down the value of their domestic currencies. This helped keep their exports competitive in international markets, but also had the effect of building up foreign exchange reserves as insurance against the risk of a financial crisis. In the event of a sudden depreciation of their own currencies, they could sell their foreign exchange reserves to stabilise the domestic economy.

The numbers involved are simply staggering. From the end of the Asian Financial Crisis, emerging markets had built up $7.5 trillion in foreign exchange reserves by February 2021.[82] China accounted for around 44 percent of these.[83] Left relatively unscathed by the Asian Financial Crisis due to its comparatively low level of integration into the international financial system in 1997, China's exports expanded rapidly following its admission to the WTO in 2001, and the country built up huge foreign currency surpluses.

Given the size of these reserves and the need for both safety and liquidity in these holdings, the vast majority of them are held in government bonds of major advanced economies. Given the leading role that the dollar plays in the global economy, the US is the country most affected by this. This is a mixed blessing for America. Although this enormous demand for US Treasuries lowers the interest rate the US government has to pay on its borrowings, the demand for dollars pushes up its exchange rate versus other currencies. This makes US exports less competitive in international markets, deepening America's balance of payments deficits. This is not a cost-free exercise for emerging markets countries either, however.

The relatively tight fiscal policies that they have had to run to avoid capital outflow has meant lower spending on domestic infrastructure that could advance their own development. Further, there is a significant direct financial cost. This is because, if a country were to just issue more of its own currency to buy dollars, the large expansion of its domestic currency supply would lead to runaway inflation. In order to offset this, these countries issue government bonds in their own currencies to soak up the additional money supply, a manoeuvre known as 'sterilisation'. The interest rate on the government bonds issued is often far higher than the yield on the dollar bonds purchased.

For example, in 2019 government securities issued by the Indian government from 3-month to 10-year maturities had yields of 5 to 6.5 percent. The yield on equivalent US government securities was under 2 percent. This meant that the Indian government was paying more than 3 percent a year to sterilise its US dollar reserves[84] – a pretty steep cost. What is more, these reserve holdings expose Indian taxpayers to investment risks on the securities, as well as to foreign exchange losses if the US dollar depreciates against the rupee.

Self-insurance against financial crises through foreign reserve accumulation is therefore a very expensive strategy for countries that choose to pursue it. However, the alternative of being left exposed and vulnerable to financial market shocks is hardly appealing either. Thus, the dollar-based global monetary system leaves emerging markets between a rock and a hard place. For the US, other countries' accumulation of dollar reserves leads to an overvalued currency, reducing American export competitiveness. This in turn gives rise to higher US unemployment, wage depression, and escalating social issues. The resulting imbalances that have built up in the global financial system have also created significant risks of future instability.

★★★

It is not just emerging markets that have had to contend with the problems of dollar volatility unleashed since the 1970s. The desire for greater monetary stability was a significant impetus for European countries to begin the process of monetary union that would eventually lead to the creation of the euro in 1999. In the same vein as Volcker's Fed, the European Central Bank (ECB) has pursued tight monetary discipline to ward off inflationary threats.

After Volcker's shock therapy, US inflation came under control, falling below four percent in 1983. Until greater inflationary pressures surfaced in 2021 in the wake of the Covid-19 pandemic, inflation had remained consistently low for almost four decades. This silenced Volcker's earlier critics and, for a quarter of a century, America enjoyed strong growth and prosperity. However, this did nothing to address the risks to other countries arising from US monetary policy.

Ultimately, central banks owe their responsibilities to their domestic populations. Paul Volcker was a public servant of unimpeachable integrity. Notwithstanding the LDC crisis set off by Fed policies in the early 1980s and the accompanying human costs to the afflicted countries, Volcker had faithfully served the interests of the US. Asked in 2010 whether, looking back, he had made any mistakes, the former Federal Reserve Chairman cited a personal rather than a professional one:

> *The greatest strategic error of my adult life was to take my wife to Maine on our honeymoon on a fly-fishing trip.*[85]

The problem was that, given other countries' dependence on the dollar, US financial instability would inevitably trigger instability around the world. And in light of greater global trade and financial integration, economic slowdowns elsewhere tend to feed back into lower US growth. It would take a financial crisis of global proportions to jolt the US central bank out of its domestically focused view of its responsibilities, however.

The Weakest Link

The chain of causes and events that led to the 2008 GFC was very long. In fact, any one of a number of vulnerabilities could have resulted in a financial collapse at that time. It happened that the weakest link in the chain was the US subprime mortgage market. When a wave of defaults on subprime mortgages began to trigger losses, other fragilities in the financial system became apparent and a general panic followed.

The 2008 crisis and its aftermath exposed a host of regulatory failings and highlighted the excesses of the unbridled free market system. The causes of, responses to, and consequences arising from the GFC all provide insights from which we can draw.

Housing is a basic human need, ranking just below food, water and clothing. In modern capitalist societies, it is often considered that home ownership gives individuals a stake in the system, fostering social stability. For this reason, many governments have pursued policies to facilitate purchases of residential housing. In the US, an early step in this pursuit was taken in the 1930s, when the Roosevelt Administration created Fannie Mae, a government-sponsored enterprise (GSE) that encouraged banks to provide mortgages to mass market borrowers. It did so by purchasing mortgages conforming to certain specifications in the secondary market, guaranteeing the banks liquidity. Due to their backing by the US government, GSEs could borrow more cheaply than commercial banks, which also helped lower the cost of mortgages.

Facing fiscal pressures due to the Vietnam War, the US government privatised Fannie Mae in 1968. This allowed the government to remove its obligations from the federal balance sheet. Notwithstanding the privatisation, it was still assumed that the GSEs had implicit government backing due to their important role in the US housing market. This meant Fannie Mae and Freddie Mac – another mortgage-related GSE set up in 1970 – could continue to borrow cheaply in credit markets.

The GSEs borrowed money to invest in long-term mortgages that borrowers could repay at any time, which meant that they were highly exposed to interest rate fluctuations. To lay off this risk, the GSEs pioneered mortgage securitisation in 1970. Securitisation involved packaging a pool of mortgages and selling securities tied to borrowers' payments to investors. In 1977, a bond trader at Salomon Brothers named Lewis Ranieri put together the first private mortgage securitisation for a commercial bank. Ranieri and his team quickly expanded the market in mortgage-backed securities (MBSs).[86] During the 1980s, a further innovation was to tranche these mortgage securities into different levels of seniority. The more senior tranches were lower risk, thus attracting the top AAA rating from credit rating agencies and yielding lower rates of interest. The riskier lower tranches would yield a higher rate of interest. The different tranches catered to varying levels of risk appetite among investors.

The emergence of this market in securitised loans coincided with higher market volatility resulting from Nixon's floating of the dollar and Volcker's subsequent war on inflation, as well as the ban on fixed commissions on share trading in 1975. It was a market made for the investment banks, which profited hugely from the packaging, distribution and trading of these securities. The investment banks' enthusiasm helped the market soar. In 1980, 67 percent of US mortgage loans were held on the balance sheets of depository banks.[87] By the late 1990s, most of these loans had become packaged as securities that were widely held by banks, insurers, pension funds and other investors all over the world.

As the market grew, the relationship between the borrower and the bearer of the risk on the loan grew more distant. Instead of a customer borrowing from a local bank that would hold onto the mortgage for the duration of the loan, the system now involved mortgage brokers, bank or non-bank lenders, securities underwriters, ratings agencies, servicers, and a wide range of far removed investors. The intermediaries along this growing value chain had ever decreasing incentive to ensure the soundness of the underlying loans.

In the 1990s, a team at JPMorgan led by an ambitious young Cambridge graduate named Blythe Masters invented the credit default swap (CDS). A CDS is essentially an insurance product that pays out when there is a loan default. These allowed the risk of the underlying loans to be further separated from the mortgage security and distributed to the market. Banks embraced this innovation, as it not only allowed them to reduce their capital requirements under the Basel rules, but also provided another instrument to be sold and traded in the financial system.

Investment banks did not take deposits. The way they funded themselves was via the wholesale funding markets. This could be via bond issues or short-term borrowing from other banks or institutions. A major source of funding that emerged were money market funds (MMFs). These are mutual funds that hold secure, short-term liquid securities. MMFs offer investors an enhanced return versus holding cash on deposit at a bank, so are attractive to individuals and institutions looking to make a better yield on their cash balances. By the end of the 1990s, there were around $1 trillion held in such cash pools. They formed part of a global financial ecosystem in which money flowed freely across borders to where it would get the best risk-adjusted return. Not just US investment banks, but also European banks which needed access to dollars would borrow from MMFs. The ICSDs, which had been set up to facilitate cross-border settlements in the Eurobond market, facilitated this trans-atlantic flow and enabled securities to be pledged and repo'ed in return for short-term liquidity. This 'efficiency' encouraged more investors to enter the market, adding to the supply of credit.

As interest rates moderated and stabilised after the early 1980s, asset prices boomed. Securities prices generally have an inverse relationship with interest rates, so markets trended upwards. However, lower mort-gage rates also made housing more affordable and led to a boom in house prices. People began to believe that home prices would always continue to rise over the medium to long term. Meanwhile, government policy continued to support the expansion of housing finance, particularly for lower-income earners and 'underserved' minority communities.[88]

From 1999 to 2003, 70 percent of all mortgages originated still conformed to the standards of the GSEs in terms of borrower credit-worthiness. However, by 2006, 70 percent of new US mortgages were so-called 'subprime' or other 'unconventional' loans,[89] where borrowers either had poor credit histories or could not verify their incomes. In the low interest rate environment following the bursting of the late 1990s Dot-com bubble, the higher yields on subprime loans attracted a large number of lenders and investors. Even HSBC, the staid British banking group formed following the acquisition of Midland Bank by the Hon-gkong and Shanghai Banking Corporation, got into the game through its 2003 acquisition of US subprime lender Household International for $15.3 billion. Against this competition from private mortgage lenders, Fannie Mae and Freddie Mac felt pressured to get in on the act as well, purchasing $300 billion in non-agency securitised mortgages for their portfolios in 2005 and 2006.[90]

In addition to lenders looking for higher yields, there was also a surge in demand for high-grade securities. This came from oil exporters whose income was rising due to high oil prices, and Asian countries building up foreign exchange reserves. China, which was experiencing an export boom in the wake of WTO accession, was a major buyer of high-grade securities. These reserve holdings were not, for the most part, invested in MBSs. However, because reserve investors were buy-ing such a large amount of AAA securities, other investors were forced to look for alternative high-grade bonds. Investment bank structuring departments, with the complicit support of the rating agencies, met this demand through slicing subprime loans into tranches to create AAA securities. With this surge in demand for MBSs, the conventional economics of the mortgage securitisation market were turned on their head. Instead of the demand for mortgages driving the *supply* of MBSs, lenders began pushing more mortgages to fulfil the *demand* for MBSs. During this boom, irresponsible and even fraudulent behaviour among intermediaries in the value chain was rife.

In each of 2005 and 2006, $1 trillion in unconventional mortgages were issued, up from just $100 billion in 2001. On the eve of the GFC, given the cost of the War on Terror and the subprime mortgage boom, one economist noted that the 'US was absorbing nearly 80 percent of the international savings that crossed borders'.[91] Given this concentration, any hiccup in US credit markets was bound to have a far-reaching impact on the global financial system.

The result of the credit boom was a bonanza for Wall Street. In the early 2000s, the financial services sector accounted for 35 percent of all profits in the US economy. The bonus pool for New York bankers in 2006 amounted to $60 billion, rising to $66 billion in 2007.[92] In a tradition of Citigroup chairmen making ill-judged remarks that mark the peak of financial excesses, Chuck Prince brushed off any concerns, saying: 'When the music stops . . . things will be complicated. But as long as the music is playing you've got to get up and dance. We're still dancing'.[93]

The Music Stops

HSBC announced $10.5 billion in loan impairment charges for the 2006 financial year, in large part due to its exposure to the US subprime mortgage market through Household International. That was just one early sign of the troubles to come.

In the spring of 2008, the fifth largest US investment bank Bear Stearns nearly collapsed due to its exposure to subprime mortgages. It was rescued through a sale to JPMorgan in a deal that involved the Federal Reserve underwriting a portion of its losses. One by one, other major financial firms found themselves in trouble due to their subprime exposures. By early September, to save them from bankruptcy, Fannie Mae and Freddie Mac, which owned or guaranteed $5 trillion in home loans, had been put into 'conservatorship' – meaning, effectively, that they had been nationalised. A week later, Lehman Brothers collapsed in the largest bankruptcy in history. Lehman's fall triggered almost $10 trillion in losses and set off a wave of panic that would infect markets around the world. That week, the insurance giant AIG would need $85 billion in government capital to prevent it from going bankrupt. AIG had insured vast amounts of MBSs through the sale of CDSs and other derivatives, and it simply did not have enough capital to meet the wave of pay-outs that it faced.

Ironically, given the US was the epicentre of the crisis, as panicking investors dumped investments around the world, they fled to the safety of US Treasuries and the dollar. In contrast to all the crises in emerging markets, where investors had fled amidst *their* troubles, the American financial crisis had the effect of sucking money *into* the country, pushing *up* the dollar's exchange rate versus other currencies.

There remains controversy over whether, had US financial officials acted to rescue Lehman in the same way as they had done with Bear Stearns, much of the subsequent market crisis of that period might have been avoided. The key officials – Hank Paulson, another former Goldman Sachs chairman serving as Treasury Secretary; Ben Bernanke, Chairman of the Federal Reserve; and Tim Geithner, President of the New York Fed – all argued subsequently that they did not have the legal power to do so. Even if they had had the power and chosen to exercise it, it is unclear what would have happened. We shall never know for certain. However, what followed was an unprecedented series of manoeuvres, in terms of their size and scope, to rescue the global financial system from the edge of the abyss.

Much of the credit for this goes to Ben Bernanke, an academic economist from Princeton University who had succeeded the long-serving Alan Greenspan as Fed Chairman in 2006. When he was a graduate student, friends had set Bernanke up on a blind date with his future wife because they thought the pair were both so 'nerdy' that they might hit it off.[94] Bernanke's particular field of academic expertise was the Great Depression, in which he had developed a lifelong interest as a

child after listening to his maternal grandmother's stories of 1930s depri-
vation.[95] It just so happened that this nerd understood better than almost
anyone else how policy mistakes in the wake of the 1929 Wall Street
crash had turned a market collapse into a global economic calamity.

The contours of financial panics tend to be broadly similar. Financial
losses cause investors to sell assets. Selling pushes down the price of those
assets further. As asset prices fall, concerns set in about potential credit
losses. These lead lenders to withdraw lines of credit, putting a squeeze
on liquidity and further accelerating asset sales and price declines.
The resulting general loss of confidence can rapidly turn a squeeze on
liquidity into a solvency crisis, particularly where financial leverage in
the system is high – as it was just before the GFC. As credit dries up for
businesses, workers are laid off and consumption declines, turning the
financial squeeze into an economic decline. It is a vicious circle in which
fear can create its own self-fulfilling prophecy. The way to arrest this
downward spiral is to step in as early as possible with enough liquidity
to restore confidence. This is what Bernanke sought to do.

The Fed and the Treasury introduced a large number of measures,
both conventional and extraordinary.[96] The three broad strategies pursued were: liquidity support; recapitalisation; and confidence building.
The Fed slashed interest rates and extended liquidity support to banks
by extending to the edge of its legal powers the types of collateral it
would accept. After an initial angry rejection by Congress, the Treasury
succeeded in getting approval for a $700 billion Troubled Asset Relief
Programme (TARP) to support the rescue of the financial sector. Banks
were 'encouraged' to raise new capital. On Columbus Day, Hank Paulson
summoned the heads of nine leading US banks to coerce them to accept
a total of $125 billion of new capital injections out of TARP funds.[97]
Through government guarantees and asset purchases, some of the most
toxic assets were either removed from the system or ringfenced from
bank balance sheets. No longer dancing, Citigroup received the largest
bailout of all the US banks, getting a total of more than $476 billion
in capital and guarantees.[98] Later, in a confidence rebuilding exercise,
the Fed subjected US banks to stress tests to demonstrate to the public
that they were solvent and had sufficient capital to withstand further
financial shocks.

The rescue operation didn't just extend to the US financial sector, however. Bernanke understood that the globalised nature of the financial system meant stabilising US markets alone would not be enough to insulate the economy from further economic fallout. Lehman Brothers had had customers and counterparties all around the world. All of them had been impacted by its failure. Further, the role of the dollar meant that a liquidity squeeze in dollar markets would have a severe impact on liquidity in other countries as well. The shocks to overseas markets would inevitably feed back into the US. The Federal Reserve's support measures therefore took on a global dimension.

The aggregate of European banks' balance sheets had grown vastly out of proportion to the size of the overall European economy. In 2007, the three largest banks in the world by assets were all European – RBS, Deutsche Bank and BNP Paribas. Their combined total assets amounted to the equivalent of 17 percent of global GDP. In Germany and Spain, their banking sectors' balance sheets were around 300 percent of national GDP. In France and the Netherlands, this figure stood at around 400 percent of GDP. In Ireland, a relatively small country, the liabilities of its banking sector amounted to 700 percent of its GDP.[99] European banks had invested heavily in US securities markets. They had funded these dollar investments through heavy borrowing in the wholesale funding markets. Their pre-crisis funding had included around $1 trillion from US MMFs, as well as roughly another $1 trillion in interbank funding, foreign exchange swaps and other short-term funding.

On 16 September, the Reserve Primary Fund, one of the most long-standing MMFs with $62 billion under management, informed the Fed that it was about to 'break the buck'. This meant that it would be unable to pay back investors a dollar for each dollar they had invested in what was supposed to be a highly safe and liquid fund. The wholesale funding markets, which had already been drying up, went into a seizure. This left European lenders facing a massive liquidity shortfall.

The Federal Reserve put in place liquidity lines to make up for the withdrawal of commercial funding. A Term Auction Facility (TAF) provided banks with access to short-term funds that they could no longer get from the asset-backed commercial paper market. This was available to all US banks, including the US subsidiaries of foreign banks.

The total amount of TAF loans lent out rose as high as $6.18 trillion. Foreign banks accounted for well over 50 percent of this, with European banks being the primary beneficiaries.[100]

For overseas banks that did not have access to this facility, the Federal Reserve provided support through foreign central banks. In view of the size of the European banking sector, European central banks had remarkably low levels of foreign exchange reserves with which to support their banks. The Bank of England and Swiss National Bank (SNB) had less than $50 billion each. The ECB had only around $200 billion.[101] To ensure that foreign central banks would have sufficient dollar liquidity to support their own banking sectors, the Fed stepped into the role of central bank to the world. In all, it entered into swap arrangements with 14 foreign central banks,[102] accepting their currencies as collateral in return for lending them US dollars. By September 2011, total lending under the swap facilities had risen to $10 trillion, of which around 80 percent was to the ECB. Looking back, although the Europeans did not escape their own debt crisis later, things would have been far worse without the support provided by the Federal Reserve.[103]

★★★

Notwithstanding the failures that had led to the crisis, once the US regulatory authorities had understood the magnitude of the GFC, their swift and large-scale actions were highly effective in rescuing the financial system and arresting further contagion. In contrast to European banks, US banks recapitalised quickly. This allowed the US financial sector to recover relatively rapidly. In the wake of the crisis, a wide range of measures were implemented at both the domestic and international level to improve the transparency of the financial system and to reduce future risks. These included the Dodd-Frank Act in the US and new BIS bank capital rules, known as Basel III. The most significant feature of the US response to the crisis, however, was the explicit step the Federal Reserve took to act as a liquidity provider of last resort to the global financial system. No other central bank in the world had (or has) either the institutional capability or willingness to take on that role. The crisis had therefore not only demonstrated how interlinked the global financial system had become, but also how critical the US market, the dollar and American institutions had become to the entire world.

Looking at the GFC from the perspective of its consequences for the dollar's global role, the impact was mixed. The fact that the crisis occurred and that it originated in the US did much to undermine international confidence in US regulators and the American model of capitalism. However, swift and decisive action by the Federal Reserve at the height of the crisis certainly prevented it from becoming a lot worse. Moreover, it demonstrated that, in a crisis, investors around the world still flocked to the safety of US Treasuries. There was no comparable asset class in terms of safety and liquidity available.

In contrast to the Fed's decisive actions, the ECB was paralysed by both its institutional conservatism and political disagreements between European member states. From its launch in 1999, the euro had been gradually gaining credibility as a serious alternative to the dollar in global markets. In 2007, as the dollar was depreciating against the euro, the Brazilian model Gisele Bündchen had famously demanded to be paid her fees in euros instead of dollars.[104] However, the GFC and the subsequent euro crisis eliminated the euro as a serious contender to the dollar.

That did not prevent people from looking for other alternatives though. In one particularly notable proposal calling for reforms to the dollar-centric global monetary system, the governor of the People's Bank of China (PBOC) Zhou Xiaochuan (周小川) advocated for a more neutral system that made use of special drawing rights (SDRs) issued by the IMF.[105] SDRs had been created by the IMF in 1969 in response to stresses on the Bretton Woods system at the time. They are a reserve asset, whose value is based on a basket of currencies. While SDRs are not a currency per se, but rather a unit of account, Governor Zhou's proposal was that their use could be expanded to create a more balanced global monetary system. This was effectively a call to overturn the Harry White plan adopted at Bretton Woods in 1944 and to replace it with something akin to Keynes' Bancor proposal. This did not catch on at the time, but it was a bold idea that may simply be waiting for its moment.

The GFC's hit to the global economy was severe. Consumption around the world declined and international trade collapsed. In July 2008, Chinese exports had been rising at a rate of 25 percent per annum, and imports by 30 percent. Half a year later, exports were declining by 18 percent and imports by more than 40 percent.[106] Concerned at the social consequences of such a sharp decline, Beijing unleashed a huge wave of stimulus spending. This stimulus drive was so large that it had a significant effect on buoying *global* growth. However, as discussed in Chapter 5, it also exacerbated imbalances in China's domestic economy and contributed to a rise in Sino-US tensions.

Perhaps most consequentially, the GFC intensified socioeconomic strains that had already been simmering in developed countries. As wages had stagnated since the 1970s, greater credit availability had allowed Western consumers to maintain their lifestyles through higher borrowing. The GFC brought to light the mirage of prosperity they had been living in. The wealth and other social inequalities that had built up were further compounded by the effects of the crisis responses. The contrast between how highly paid bankers were treated versus the average worker in the rescue also became a lightning rod for popular resentment. This was to have a radical impact on politics.

Anyone for Tea?

As millions of workers were laid off, the economic impact of the GFC gave way to popular anger. Much of this was directed at the bankers who had precipitated the crisis with their risky behaviour. Growing anti-bailout rage was stoked by reports of large bonuses paid to executives at institutions that had been rescued from bankruptcy with taxpayers' money. Newspaper reports on 15 March 2009 that AIG would pay $165 million in bonuses to employees in its Financial Products Division, which had been responsible for the insurer's near collapse, sparked widespread anger. Charles Krauthammer reflected popular sentiment when he called for 'an exemplary hanging or two' in response to the AIG bonus payments.[107]

The Fed and the Treasury were in an unenviable position. The complexity of these derivative positions meant that they needed to keep the specialist staff in place if they were to recoup taxpayers' funds from the AIG rescue. Ultimately, the taxpayer would reap a gain of almost $23 billion on their investment in the insurer.[108] However, that did little to quell public anger at the time. The feeling that financial mismanagement and malfeasance on a massive scale had not only gone unpunished, but was being rewarded, fundamentally undermined trust in the political establishment.

Barack Obama was inaugurated in January 2009, in the midst of the crisis. An outstanding orator and the youngest president to have been elected in decades, he had campaigned on a message of hope, which had broad appeal, particularly among the young. As the first African American to hold the office, his ascent through the Democratic field to the White House symbolised change. However, it was inevitable that the financial crisis would dominate the agenda during his term in office.

The new administration set out to provide assistance to struggling homeowners. On 18 February 2009, Obama unveiled the Making Homes Affordable programme, which included two key propositions. The first was to allow underwater homeowners who were up to date on their mortgage payments to refinance onto loans with better terms and lower monthly instalments. The second was targeted at borrowers who had fallen behind on their mortgage payments, providing a subsidy from TARP funds to help them meet their monthly payments.

This relief to over-indebted borrowers proved to be the last straw for some people already outraged by taxpayer rescues of the banks. During a live broadcast from the trading floor of the CME, *CNBC Business News* editor Rick Santelli went on a rant about homeowner bailouts. In front of the camera, he turned to the CME floor traders and asked: 'How many of you people want to pay for your neighbour's mortgage that has an extra bathroom and can't pay their bills [sic], raise their hand'. A roar of 'No!' came back from the traders, then Santelli turned to the camera and asked, 'President Obama, are you listening?'[109] This was the moment the Tea Party movement was born.

The movement's name refers to the Boston Tea Party of 16 December 1773, when American colonists, angry at Britain's imposition of 'taxation without representation', dumped 342 chests of tea imported by the British East India Company into the harbour. This event kicked off the American revolution.

The modern Tea Party was a right-wing conservative movement that opposed 'big government' and what some vocal critics saw as fiscal irresponsibility. Lacking any identified leader, its supporters organised protests via social media and backed political candidates. Polls showed

Tea Party supporters tended to be white, male and over the age of 45. Its agenda was not always clear and was sometimes considered to have racist undertones, but the movement became a significant expression of popular dissatisfaction, which hindered Obama's policy agenda throughout his time in office.

The unwillingness of the two major political parties to work together compounded the problem. Senator Ted Kennedy's death in late 2009 stripped Obama of the advantage of a Congressional majority. The Republicans' landslide victory in the House the following year left him contending with a hostile and uncooperative legislature. The Democratic Senator of Indiana Evan Bayh summed up the dysfunctional state of US politics when he retired in 2010:

> For some time, I've had a growing conviction that Congress is not operating as it should. There is much too much partisanship and not enough progress; too much narrow ideology and not enough practical problem-solving. Even at a time of enormous national challenge, the people's business is not getting done.[110]

As the country recovered from the GFC, partisanship in Congress stymied any attempt to use fiscal tools to stimulate the economy where monetary policy was not effective. This meant that the Fed was left almost entirely alone in trying to maintain the recovery with low interest rates. This was a major reason for the unbalanced recovery. By keeping short-term interest rates low, banks were able to profit by buying higher yielding long-dated securities. However, low interest rates alone could not induce them to lend to the parts of the economy where capital was needed the most. Furthermore, low interest rates led to a boom in asset prices. This contributed to a widening wealth divide.

In his memoirs published in 2015, Ben Bernanke wrote that he did not believe that low interest rates favoured the rich. He justified this view by citing the fact that the wealthy have higher savings, so low interest rates on their deposits would depress their incomes.[111] However, this argument ignores the fact that, because they have a greater cushion of savings, the wealthy, unlike the poor, can afford to invest a substantial portion of their savings in higher risk assets, such as stocks and real estate. And it was these risk assets that boomed, leaving the wealthy far better off, even as workers' wages continued to stagnate.

Notwithstanding his denial that low interest rates were exacerbating wealth inequality, Bernanke clearly articulated the need for the government to shoulder part of the responsibility for the recovery through fiscal policy. However, the Obama Administration had little chance of getting such policies through a hostile Republican-controlled Congress. Having been a mainstream Republican voter before he arrived in Washington, Bernanke's frustration with the 'know-nothing-ism' of the far-right Republicans and the dysfunctional state of the political system led him to abandon both political parties altogether and declare himself a 'moderate independent.[112]

Meanwhile, things weren't much better in Europe. A government debt crisis that started in Greece in 2009 had spread to other nations in the European periphery. The episode put the spotlight on an unresolved problem in the design of the European single currency. Although the euro had committed its members to a common interest rate, each state was still responsible for its own fiscal policy. If a euro member country was facing a debt crisis, it could not devalue its currency in order to lower its debt burden. However, there was no mechanism in place for the ECB or other euro members to provide financial support. Indeed, when the crisis occurred, the northern European countries, led by Germany, were vehemently opposed to support for what they saw as profligate southern Europeans.

Nevertheless, financial interlinkages across the eurozone had tied the fates of all member countries together. Prior to the single currency, the Italian government borrowing in lira or the Spanish government borrowing in pesetas paid far higher interest rates than Germany's government did on its borrowings. This reflected the higher risk of devaluation of the lira and peseta versus the Deutschmark. After the euro's launch, interest rates on government bonds across the eurozone converged to Germany's lower rates. This had encouraged greater borrowing in the southern European countries. Given the single currency, German and French banks had become significant holders of Greek and other eurozone government bonds. A default by a eurozone member government, therefore, threatened another banking crisis in Europe.

As acrimonious disputes between European governments ensued, borrowing rates for governments in the most financially stretched countries – namely, Portugal, Italy, Ireland, Greece and Spain (collectively branded the 'PIIGS') – spiked. This further deepened Europe's economic woes and dithering by the ECB and European politicians only made the situation worse. At one stage, it threatened the very collapse of the euro itself. It was not until 2012 when ECB head Mario Draghi pledged to do 'whatever it takes' to keep the single currency together that the European crisis began to abate.[113]

Notwithstanding the relative cohesion of the US federal model, disputes over fiscal issues also engulfed America during this time. In 2011, an unnecessary act of self-harm was committed through a political stand-off between Congressional Republicans and the Obama Administration over the debt ceiling. If the ceiling was not raised, the Treasury would no longer be able to borrow money through financial markets and would run out of funds to meet its obligations to pay federal employees and service interest on its debt. The Treasury made the gravity of the situation clear in a statement that warned that a failure to raise the ceiling would 'threaten the jobs and savings of everyday Americans' and 'call into question the full faith and credit of the United States government'.[114] As the deadline drew near in late July, neither side would budge, heightening nervousness in financial markets. Financial calamity was only avoided at the very last minute on Sunday, 31 July, when the two parties reached an agreement to raise the debt ceiling and trim government spending. However, citing the risk that this 'political brinksmanship' had introduced, the rating agency S&P took the unprecedented step of downgrading the credit rating on US government debt from AAA to AA+.[115] So far, the rating downgrade does not appear to have raised the cost of America's government borrowing, but the full longer-term consequences for the dollar as the preeminent global reserve currency remain to be seen.

Conscious of the risk to America's financial standing, mainstream Republicans introduced a bill in 2013 to ensure that, in the event of a similar stand-off in the future, payment to government bondholders would get prioritised, so as to avoid the unthinkable of a US government default. However, the Full Faith and Credit Act, as it was named, soon became dubbed the 'Pay China First Act' and was voted down by the Democrats. This was to foreshadow further tensions between the US and its largest creditor later on, but ignored the fact that millions of US investors, including pension funds and charities, would be severely harmed by a default on US Treasuries – not to mention the global financial chaos that it would inevitably unleash.

As political dysfunction continued and wealth disparities widened, another movement emerged in September 2011 when protesters occupied Zuccotti Park, in the Wall Street financial district in New York. Occupy Wall Street, as the movement called itself, adopted the slogan 'We are the 99 percent' in protest against the income and wealth inequality between the richest one percent and the rest of the population. The Occupy movement particularly appealed to younger people who had struggled to find jobs and get onto the housing ladder in the wake of the GFC. The movement soon spread to London, where protesters occupied the grounds of St. Paul's Cathedral near the offices of the London Stock Exchange. In Hong Kong, Occupy Central protestors squatted in the plaza below HSBC's local headquarters for almost 10 months.

The economic malaise and polarised civic atmosphere were a breeding ground for more radicalised politics. Facing a declining standard of living, many in the developed West became susceptible to the dog whistle of populist nationalist politicians who blamed their troubles on immigrants, unfair trading practices of foreign countries, and the corruption of the media and liberal elite. In June 2016, following a campaign by Brexiteers who promised greater controls over immigration, Britons voted to leave the EU. The same year, the real estate mogul and reality television personality Donald J. Trump ran for the US presidency on the Republican nomination. He railed against 'big business, elite media and major donors' and promised to 'Make America Great Again' by fighting for 'the laid-off factory workers, and the communities crushed by our horrible and unfair trade deals'.[116] His election to the White House marked a decisive turning point in US politics, which was to have wide-ranging financial and diplomatic repercussions.

A Tipping Point?

In a televised debate with the Democratic nominee Hillary Clinton during his presidential campaign, Trump complained that 'They're using our country as a piggy bank to rebuild China', and declared: 'We have to stop our jobs being stolen from us'.[117]

Far from America serving as China's piggy bank, however, China is a large creditor to the US government. According to data published by the US Treasury Department, Mainland China held $1.07 trillion of US Treasury securities at the end of 2020, making it the second largest foreign creditor to the US behind Japan.[118]

US Treasuries make up around one-third of China's substantial foreign exchange reserves.[119] These reserves were built up as a consequence of the PBOC's sterilisation of China's trade surpluses. It is certainly true that China's policy of maintaining the renminbi's peg to the dollar from 1995 to 2005, notwithstanding the country's far more rapid growth in productivity, contributed to the accumulation of such a large amount of reserves. However, China is far from the only country to have managed its exchange rate against the dollar. From Japan in the 1970s and 1980s to the emerging markets exporters of today, many countries have sought to maintain currency stability against the dollar. It is estimated that the greenback serves as the monetary anchor for economies that make up 70 percent of world GDP, with half of those currencies being explicitly pegged to the dollar.[120]

The reasons for this extend far beyond trade competitiveness. Even a cursory glance at the relative values of global trade versus financial flows will highlight the outsized relative importance of capital markets. World trade stands at just over 60 percent of global GDP,[121] whereas the total value of cross-border financial claims is over 400 percent of world GDP.[122] Currency stability against the dollar is also important to maintaining domestic stability in many countries, since currency volatility could generate sudden large financial flows, which can lead to sizeable swings in asset prices and consumer price inflation.

Donald Trump's four years in the White House were marked by increasingly acrimonious politics and erratic policies, often emanating from the President via 'tweets' on the social media platform Twitter. Trump appeared to revel in antagonising America's friends and foes alike, dismaying long-standing US allies by withdrawing from the 2015 Paris Agreement on climate change mitigation and the Trans-Pacific Partnership, a regional trade agreement negotiated by the Obama Administration. However, from the perspectives of America's social stability and the Sino-US relationship, two initiatives of the Trump presidency particularly stand out.

The first were Trump's tax reforms. Even with the national debt and inequality riding high, the 45th US president signed into law in 2017 a set of tax cuts, 80 percent of the benefit of which went to the top one percent.[123] These were justified on the basis that they were expected to stimulate economic growth and deliver 'trickle down' benefits to American workers. Their main effects have simply been to further increase public borrowing and widen the wealth divide.

The second was the trade war against China, initiated in early 2018 with the announcement of import tariffs on certain Chinese imports. As the rhetoric ratcheted up, Trump declared a 25 percent tariff on $50 billion worth of annual Chinese imports in June that year.[124] When China threatened to retaliate with tariffs on US goods, Trump threatened to impose tariffs on a further $267 billion worth of Chinese imports.[125]

Initially, it seemed that the core of US demands was to address America's chronic balance of payments deficit. However, as negotiations went on, the US raised issues about China's trade practices and forced technology transfers. As pointed out in Chapter 1, there was certainly merit in some of the US complaints about China. However, given China's low margins on its exports, it was unlikely that a bilateral deal on trade with China would materially address America's deficit problems. Put simply, if Trump believed that America's financial relationship with China is unsustainable, that is also true of its financial relationship with the rest of the world. And the root cause of this is the dollar's role in the global financial system, which has given rise to two big problems for the US.

First, international demand for dollars has inhibited the US currency from depreciating to reflect higher levels of productivity growth elsewhere. This means that the American economy is unable to fully avail itself of a key adjustment mechanism in response to a relative decline in its productivity. This has negatively impacted the competitiveness of US exports. The major losers from this have been US manufacturing workers.

Second, to prevent liquidity in the global financial system from seizing up, the US has had to run continual current account and fiscal deficits. This is fine when US economic growth is keeping pace with the rest of the world but, when US growth lags, it can lead to growing financial imbalances. Since opinion on whether the dollar's role requires the US to run deficits is sharply divided,[126] however, this point requires some further elaboration.

Opponents of the view that the US dollar's status as a global reserve currency requires America to run continual deficits cite the examples of Japan and Switzerland to support their case. Certainly, both the yen and the Swiss franc are significant reserve currencies, notwithstanding persistent Japanese and Swiss current account surpluses. However, relative to the dollar, the yen and the Swiss franc are minnows. They respectively make up 5.9 percent and 0.17 percent of global foreign exchange reserves, compared with around 60 percent for the US dollar.[127] Less than four percent of global payments are made in Japanese yen, versus around 40 percent in dollars.[128] Essentially, global trade and financial markets can weather liquidity shortages in the yen or Swiss franc, but not in the dollar.

Importantly, US Treasuries also make up the lion's share of high quality liquid collateral supporting the global market in repos and other credit instruments. A shortage in US Treasuries can therefore have a magnified impact on global liquidity, which has knock-on effects on asset prices and activity in the real economy. In the period running up to the GFC, when the supply of US Treasuries was insufficient to meet the demand for high-grade securities, investors ended up taking on extra risk – with catastrophic consequences.

For these reasons, it is clear that, as global trade and financial market activity expand, the supply of dollars needs to expand along with it. This requires the US to run deficits. In the long run, however, it is only possible to keep expanding the absolute amount of the public debt when GDP growth is expanding at a rate at least as fast as the nominal debt is growing. Otherwise, at some point, excessive monetary inflation will cause confidence in the currency to collapse. For a long time now, America's national debt has been expanding at a far higher rate than its economic growth. Worryingly, the cracks in the system may now be impacting the stability of the whole edifice of the dollar-based global financial order.

★★★

As the severity of the Covid-19 pandemic became apparent in late February 2020, financial markets began to wobble. The sell-off in risky assets like stocks and corporate bonds was to be expected, as the darkening economic outlook caused investors to flee to the safety of highly secure and liquid investments such as US Treasuries.

On 3 March, the Federal Reserve cut interest rates to around one percent. Four days later, New York Governor Andrew Cuomo declared a state of emergency in America's leading financial hub. Around the same time, the oil price plummeted as Saudi Arabia and Russia entered into a price war, sending shockwaves through stock, currency and commodity markets. Then, something extraordinary happened: instead of buying up Treasury bonds, investors started to sell them.

The yield on 10-year Treasury bonds, which usually falls when investors look for safety, began to rise on 10 March. Investors were pulling their money out of MMFs. As outflows accelerated, the funds pulled back sharply from corporate debt markets in order to return cash to investors. Post-GFC regulations meant that banks were less willing to step in to buy these securities. This was not helped by the fact that traders were scrambling to make arrangements to adjust to working from home. That made it harder to sell everything, including Treasury debt. The drying up of liquidity in the $18 trillion market for supposedly risk free US government securities sent the market into a panic.

President Trump declared a national state of emergency on Friday, 13 March. On the Sunday, an emergency meeting of the Fed slashed interest rates to just above zero. However, selling pressure continued when the markets reopened the following day. On 18 March, the Fed announced a programme to rescue the embattled MMFs by buying hard-to-sell securities off their hands. Still, the market was choked. After a torrent of calls with the Treasury over the weekend, the Fed issued a press release at 8 o'clock in the morning on Monday, 23 March. It would step into the market to buy MBSs and corporate debt and, crucially, it pledged to buy an *unlimited* amount of US Treasury debt.[129]

Since then, the Federal Reserve balance sheet has grown at an unprecedented rate. Quantitative easing and other post-GFC monetary measures had seen the amount of assets held by the Fed grow from around $900 billion in September 2008 to just under $4.2 trillion by the end of 2019. During 2020 alone, it grew by another $3.2 trillion to almost $7.4 trillion.[130] This was remarkable.

The market strategist Michael Howell points to three development phases of the US dollar since WW2. First, there was the Gold Exchange Standard (1945–1971), created by the Bretton Woods system. This was followed by the Oil Exchange Standard (1974–1989), ushered in by William Simon's deal with Saudi Arabia, which underpinned demand for dollars. The third phase, the Emerging Market Exchange Standard (1990–), began in the wake of the fall of the Berlin Wall, when competition for international capital among high-growth countries incentivised them to demonstrate the integrity and sustainability of their currencies by building up large reserves of dollars.[131]

Arguably, a fourth phase – the Federal Reserve Guarantee – began in September 2013, with the Fed's capitulation following the so-called 'taper tantrum'. Markets had taken the 2011 political shenanigans over the debt ceiling in their stride. However, when Ben Bernanke suggested in June 2013 that improving economic conditions might warrant the Fed scaling back its monthly bond purchases under the quantitative easing programme from $85 billion to $65 billion later that year, markets skipped a beat. Treasuries sold off rapidly, causing a spike in yields. Stocks sold off as well, and liquidity in emerging markets in particular began to dry up. This was as much a test of political will as it was a monetary issue. The Fed appeared to flinch when, following the scheduled September meeting of the Federal Open Market Committee, it announced that it would leave interest rates unchanged and continue its bond buying programme at the prevailing rate.[132] That was the point at which it became clear that, henceforth, demand in the US Treasury market would be underpinned by the Federal Reserve. That decision had vast implications and was steeped in moral hazard.

America's national debt had already been growing at an alarming rate. At the turn of the century, total outstanding borrowing stood at $5.7 trillion, or 55 percent of GDP. As a result of tax cuts, wars, the GFC and, most recently, the Covid-19 pandemic, total US government debt had reached a staggering $27.8 trillion by the end of 2020, or 129 percent of GDP.[133] Since 2013, foreign reserve purchases have no longer been supporting the growth in US Treasury supply. China's holdings peaked at just over $1.3 trillion that year and fell to less than $1.1 trillion by the end of 2020. Foreign official holdings by central banks as a whole grew only marginally from $4.1 trillion in 2013 to $4.2 trillion in 2020.[134] Over the same period, the Federal Reserve's holdings of US Treasuries jumped from $2.2 trillion to $4.7 trillion, accounting for roughly 17 percent of outstanding US government debt.[135]

In March 2021, Congress approved President Biden's $1.9 trillion American Rescue Plan to support the nation's pandemic-battered economy. This stimulus programme provided much needed relief, including cheques of $1,400 each to households earning less than $75,000 per year. It also brought total pandemic-related spending by the US government to $6 trillion and heaped further debt upon the country.

The surge in liquidity provided by the Fed during 2020 drove a boom in stock and other asset prices. From a low of 2,192 in March 2020, the S&P 500 index climbed 71.4 percent to end the year at 3,756 points, up 51.1 percent for the full year.[136] With the pandemic sending unemployment to record levels, this further exacerbated wealth and income inequality. Soaring government debt and the expanding Fed balance sheet may, however, undermine confidence in the integrity of the dollar, leading to much higher inflation. Inflationary signs have already been seen in commodities and other goods, but it is not yet clear whether this is due to the monetary stimulus or supply chain disruptions or, indeed, whether this will feed through into permanently higher prices.[137] But the market is watching nervously.

Investor expectations that the Fed will always come to the rescue have also increased the complexity of exiting the stimulus. Since the price of most assets is inversely correlated to interest rates and the key reference rate in financial markets is the yield on US Treasuries, a Fed withdrawal from bond purchases would put pressure on asset prices across the board. The price and liquidity of financial assets further determine how much can be borrowed against them as collateral. A broad decline in asset prices would lead to widespread deleveraging, putting further pressure on asset prices. This would have a severe negative impact on global economic activity.

Rises in interest rates would also increase the cost of servicing the public debt, with knock-on effects on the government budget. Unless economic growth can be boosted significantly, the burden of servicing the huge public debt will weigh heavily on the population. Monetary and fiscal decisions that determine how the costs are allocated among different sections of society also have the potential to generate significant further conflict and social upheaval.

★★★

Far from being the last man standing at the end of history, America has arrived at the end of its unipolar moment a hobbled giant. Its finances overstretched, its military exhausted, its infrastructure crumbling, its society divided, and unpopular overseas, it would not be inapt to paraphrase the term used to describe the Ottoman Empire before WW1 and call the US the 'Sick Man of North America'.

In its moment of hubris, America allowed itself to indulge in exorbitantly costly military adventures, which have strained relations with the international community and undermined both America's moral legitimacy and the international rules-based order that it led the creation of. If America commits atrocities and ignores international laws when they prove inconvenient, then it invites other countries to pursue the 'law of the jungle' as well. The cost of this will be very high.

One of the key enablers of this lapse was the lack of constraints on government borrowing that the dollar-based global monetary system abetted. Even as the costs of unnecessary wars and the GFC mounted, both George W. Bush and Donald Trump's administrations persisted with tax cuts for the wealthy.

As the political system was captured by wealthy and corporate interests, both democratic and market forces were corrupted, generating greater polarisation in the distribution of income and wealth across society. Monetary stimulus further boosted the wealth of the richest in society but left the poor and the middle classes falling further behind. Because the wealthy tend to spend less of their incomes, widening wealth disparity has also dragged on economic growth.

During successive emerging markets crises and the GFC, capital continued to flow to the US at times of market volatility and dislocation. However, the Covid-19 pandemic has stretched America's national finances to an unprecedented level and, to paraphrase Keynes, markets might be able to stay irrational for longer than you can remain solvent, but they are unlikely to stay irrational forever. In its first months, the Biden Administration indicated that it understands the need to restore America's fiscal base. In addition to plans to raise more taxes for corporations and the wealthy, Treasury Secretary Janet Yellen notably called for global cooperation on a minimum corporate tax rate in April 2021 – which was quickly followed up with an agreement between the Group of 7 (G-7) two months later.[138] Having previously served as Chairman of the Federal Reserve, Yellen appreciated the pitfalls of overreliance on monetary policy and the need to use fiscal levers to help rebalance the US economy. Nevertheless, these moves seem unlikely to be sufficient to offset the additional debt piled on through stimulus measures and, concerned about the integrity of the dollar, many investors and trading partners are already actively looking for alternatives. This is further discussed in Chapter 7. *Could we now be reaching a tipping point?*

This is a challenge for both the US and the rest of the world. To redress falling US competitiveness, American policymakers can gamble on discovering a new technological or societal breakthrough that delivers a large boost to US productivity. However, such breakthroughs are unpredictable and may not emerge for a long time. The alternative is to reform the global monetary system to allow the dollar to adjust and help bring the US balance of payments back into equilibrium. Given the size of the imbalances and the global finance and trade dependencies that have built up based on the dollar-centric system, it would take a long time and an internationally coordinated effort to transition to an alternative global monetary order. The governance over any new system would also be critical. The euro crisis demonstrated clearly the risks of delay and indecision in executing monetary policies when crises occur. Would a new global monetary system based, for example, on IMF SDRs be prone to similar risks? These questions are considered further in Chapter 8. The choices for policymakers are complex – even if they are prepared to broach the subject of a managed transition away from the dollar-based order.

Complicating this problem is the cost of maintaining the ability to project military power on a global basis. Foregoing costly wars of choice like the 2003 Iraq invasion is one matter, but many countries have come to depend on a US security guarantee. Foreign funding of US government deficits has created explicit obligations or an implicit sense of entitlement. A retrenchment of the dollar's role would necessarily require other countries to bear a greater burden for their own security. The implications of this go beyond the financial realm to the question of whether this would enhance or diminish global security.

Advances in shale oil extraction technologies have given the US the ability to enjoy energy independence. Advances in renewable and other energy technologies will likely further reduce America's oil dependence in the future. The continued US security guarantee over the Middle East therefore benefits China, which is now the largest global oil importer, far more than it does the US. However, the threat from international terrorism means that the US is no longer able to retreat into safe isolationism behind two wide oceans. The rise of cyber and other new forms of military capabilities will also require ongoing investment in defence capabilities. There will necessarily be trade-offs.

As America's unipolar moment fades into ashes of history, all eyes are now fixed on China, whose rapid rise over the past four decades has inspired both hope and trepidation. But is China ready to join the US at the apex of the global financial system, or even to grasp the baton of sole leadership? And would that be desirable for the rest of the world?

PART TWO

CAPITALISM
WITH CHINESE
CHARACTERISTICS

Chapter 4

From First World to Third and Back Again

如其善而莫之违也，不亦善乎？如不善而莫之违也，
不几乎一言而丧邦乎？

－孔子

If [a ruler's words] be good, is it not also good that no one oppose
them? But if they are not good, and no one opposes them, may there
not be expected from one sentence the ruin of his country?

– Confucius

On 2 February 1421, the first day of the new lunar year, thousands
of foreign envoys, officials and military officers gathered in the seven
acre courtyard of the Gate of Receiving Heaven (*Fengtianmen*, 奉天门)
to congratulate the Emperor Yongle (永乐) on the completion of the
Forbidden City in his new capital, Beijing. The vermillion-walled
compound topped with golden coloured tiles held more than 800

rooms, including three palace residences, three main receiving halls, and over 100 chambers containing libraries, offices, archives, factories, artisan studios and storerooms. Built on a strict north-south axis, its construction involved 232,089 skilled workers from 62 trades and, in its peak construction years between 1417 and 1420, over a million general labourers. In all, it is estimated that one in 50 of China's then total population of 60 million had worked on the Forbidden City.[1] Its splendour and opulence were designed to awe and humble all who beheld it, and to leave no doubt that China was the most powerful nation on Earth.

At the time of the Ming Dynasty (1368–1644), the Chinese were by far the world's richest and most scientifically advanced people. It is thought that the cultivation of millet and rice in China began some 10,000 years ago[2] and the system of writing that is used to this day was developed during the Shang Dynasty (商朝, c.1600–1046 BC). Recorded history from the Zhou Dynasty (周朝, 1046–256 BC) describes the gradual conquest and absorption of surrounding non-Chinese-speaking peoples and, by 221 BC, Qin Shi Huang (秦始皇) had conquered seven Warring States to unify the country. Politically unified, with a stratified society and substantial agricultural surpluses, Chinese rulers were able to mobilise large labour forces to undertake giant construction projects such as the Great Wall and the Grand Canal – the world's longest canal, stretching over 1,000 miles between Beijing and Hangzhou (杭州). China's technological innovations were also impressive. It was the first country to develop cast-iron production (in around 500 BC) and its long list of inventions included efficient animal harnesses, wheelbarrows, sternpost rudders, porcelain, kites, gunpowder and magnetic compasses.[3] Having invented paper in the second century AD, the Chinese went on to develop movable type printing technology in the 11th century, roughly 400 years before Johannes Gutenberg introduced it to Europe.

China was not so much a nation state as it was a civilisation. Indeed, the modern concept of the Westphalian nation state did not exist in the consciousness of the Chinese until it was thrust upon them by the European powers in the 19th century. The foundational story of Chinese civilisation told of the legendary king Yu the Great (大禹), who built a system of dams and dykes to control flooding from the Yellow River (黄河) and to provide irrigation to the fields. Thus, from its very beginnings, political legitimacy in China has been derived from the ruler's ability to bring order. During the Zhou Dynasty, this tradition was further developed into the concept of the 'Mandate of Heaven' (*tianming*, 天命) which, conditioned on the personal righteousness of the emperor, conferred on him and his line a divine right to rule over 'All Under Heaven' (*tianxia*, 天下). This conception of the Chinese emperor's role in the cosmos, which became ingrained in the Chinese psyche as it passed down over generations, is critical to understanding some of the tensions that later arose in interactions between China and the West from the 18th century.

The moral framework governing the obligations of the emperor and his subjects was derived from the philosophy-based religions of Confucianism and Daoism. These were later supplemented with teachings from Buddhism, which was introduced to China during the Tang Dynasty (唐朝, 618–907 AD). Confucius (551–479 BC) had a particularly profound influence on political and ethical philosophy in Chinese civilisation that persists to this day. Confucianism emphasises moral correctness, justice and filial piety, and inculcates the development of wisdom over the mere accumulation of knowledge. Confucius did not consider everyone to be created equal and his teachings instruct that due respect be paid to one's elders and superiors. That is not to say that he advocated blind obedience. Indeed, where the emperor was following an incorrect course of action, Confucius deemed it to be the obligation of a loyal subject to point this out to him.

The moral-philosophical underpinnings of Chinese political power and the emphasis on the righteous ruler help, in part, to explain why modern China still struggles to introduce the 'rule of law' in the Western conception. Western legal traditions arose out of the teachings of the Christian Church, which were derived from a singular deity that stood above any individual monarch. Thus, it was natural for a European ruler to be subject to the law. In China, there was no tradition of such a higher authority to which the ruler must be subject. Instead, China's legal traditions conform to the practice of 'rule by law', and it has always been implicitly understood that the ruler would employ the law to stay in power.[4]

In the Chinese traditional perception, a ruler who neglected his duties or acted tyrannically would arouse the displeasure of heaven, resulting in chaos. The Mandate of Heaven might then be withdrawn. In the historical experience, the waning of dynasties was often accompanied by natural disasters or famine. When the state was weakened, it was exposed to internal rebellion or outside invasion. Where the incumbent ruler was overthrown, the Mandate of Heaven was considered to have passed to the successful invader or usurper. However, underlying this mystical perception of the rises and falls of dynastic regimes are recurring social, economic, political, military and environmental challenges that have been featured throughout more than three millennia of recorded Chinese history.

First, in the north, south and west, China has been surrounded by neighbouring peoples who have most often been hostile. This inherent geographic vulnerability to invasion has required considerable resources to be devoted to military defence and diplomacy.

Second, far from being a homogeneous people, China is made up of a large number of different ethnic, linguistic and religious groups. Although 92 percent of the population today identify themselves as Han (汉), China remains home to at least 56 different ethnic groups. Indeed, the narrative of a single, continuous history of the Chinese people that was promoted by the revolutionaries who overthrew the Qing Dynasty (清朝, 1644–1911) has been challenged by more recent scholarship.[5] This diverse population was also separated by a wide variety of languages and dialects. There are estimated to be around 2,000 forms of spoken 'Chinese', of which as many as 400 are mutually unintelligible.[6] It was not until late in the 20th century that a standardised spoken language – *Putonghua* (普通话, literally meaning 'common language') – became widely adopted. And, unlike the peoples of the Mediterranean world, China had no single unifying religion, much less the monotheism of the Abrahamic religions that helped underpin the identities of the nation states that developed in Europe.

Third, the logistical burden and manpower requirements involved in governing such a vast territory are substantial. Until modern communications and transport were introduced in the 20th century, the large distances that separated the capital and the outer reaches of the empire meant the central government often had little idea of what was going on in many areas it claimed to rule over, and it could take a long time to deploy military and other resources in times of trouble. Even today, the phrase 'the mountains are high and the emperor is far away' (山高皇帝远) is regularly used to highlight the difficulty for the central government to impose its rule in provinces far from Beijing.

Fourth, the Yangtze (长江) and the Yellow Rivers, which provided irrigation to support China's agricultural backbone, changed course multiple times over the centuries, dramatically altering the productive viability of entire regions when this occurred, and exposed the surrounding areas to devastating floods.

Fifth, China's large population, which was the primary source of its military, economic and cultural strength for most of its history but which fluctuated significantly with wars, famine, disease and natural disasters, made governance complex and required huge and consistent administrative effort. Rises in population put a strain on resources, and the density of the urban centres fostered diseases and plagues that struck from time to time. It has also been argued that the sheer size of China's population makes consensual government difficult, if not impossible.

Finally, perhaps due to all the foregoing challenges, China has always been ruled autocratically, save for a historical instant following the fall of the Qing Dynasty. The country has been ruled by many enlightened rulers of outstanding ability, but it has also seen more than its fair share of tyrants and despots. Some rulers who were once brilliant leaders saw their faculties sapped by age or the aloofness that often comes from being too-long cocooned within imperial palaces and became ineffectual or even tyrannical in later life. Strong leaders came to be succeeded by weak ones, and dynasties were prone eventually to fall into decadence, spiritual decay, and moral corruption.

On several occasions, the fall of a dynasty resulted in the division of the country. Considering its large territory, diverse ethnic groups, multiple languages, and lack of a unified religion, it might have been expected that China would remain permanently splintered into multiple different states. Each time, however, the country was eventually reunited under a single ruler. Even when China was invaded from outside, it was the foreign invaders that adopted Chinese culture and governance systems, rather than the other way around.

Through wars and conquest, China's borders underwent substantial shifts. At the time of its unification under the Qin Dynasty (秦朝,

221–207 BC), China occupied less than a quarter of the territory that it does today. China's largest territorial acquisitions actually took place under foreign rule. It was through the conquest of China by the Mongols who founded the Yuan Dynasty (元朝, 1271–1368) that today's Inner Mongolia (内蒙古) became part of the empire. Similarly, Manchuria in the northeast became incorporated not by China's outward expansion, but through its invasion by the Manchurians who founded the Qing Dynasty and then went on to bring Xinjiang (新疆) and Tibet (西藏) under their dominion.

It is nevertheless a misperception that the Chinese had always been insular and inwardly focused before the country was prized open by the colonial powers in the 19th century. During the seventh century AD, the Buddhist monk Xuanzang (玄奘) undertook a journey lasting 17 years through Central Asia to India, from where he brought back the Buddhist scriptures and translated them from Sanskrit into Chinese. It was at around the same time that Islam first arrived in China and, in the same century, the first official Christian mission to the Tang imperial court was received by Emperor Taizong (太宗) who, after studying the Christian scriptures, declared the religion's principles to contain 'important truths' and to be 'advantageous to mankind', and permitted a church to be built in his capital.[7] Under the Tang Dynasty, Chinese literature and culture flourished and spread westward to the Middle East and eastward to Japan. These exchanges were facilitated through the channels of trade and commerce, by sea via the port city of Canton (*Guangzhou*, 广州) and over land via the Silk Road, at the eastern end of which lay the bustling Tang capital Chang'an (长安 – today's Xi'an, 西安).

This trade continued during the Song Dynasty (宋朝, 960–1279 AD), whose two capital cities, Kaifeng (开封) and Yangzhou (扬州), hosted Jewish and Italian communities, and under the Yuan Dynasty, during which Rabban Sawma, a Mongolian convert to Nestorian Christianity, became the first person known to have travelled from China to France, where he met Philippe IV and Edward I of England (who happened to be in France at the time). However, the most extraordinary overseas journeys by the Chinese during the pre-modern era were undertaken at the initial behest of the Ming Emperor Yongle.

Maritime Power

After he seized the throne from his nephew in a coup in 1402, the Emperor Yongle ordered the construction of an imperial fleet consisting of hundreds of trading ships, warships and support vessels. It has been claimed that the largest vessels in this fleet were 400 feet in length. Modern experts dispute this and, based on current knowledge of the construction techniques and materials available at the time, it is estimated that the fleet's largest ships were between 200 and 240 feet long. Even at this more modest size, however, they dwarfed the 85-foot *Santa María* in which Columbus crossed the Atlantic in 1492. Between 1405 and 1433, Yongle's 'treasure fleet' made seven voyages in Southeast Asia and across the Indian Ocean, reaching as far as the Persian Gulf and East Africa over half a century before the Portuguese explorer Bartolomeu Dias rounded the Cape of Good Hope.

There is still debate over what exactly the purpose of these voyages was. Unlike later European explorers, the Chinese treasure fleet did not colonise new lands. Instead, they appeared to have engaged extensively in scientific discovery. Further, they were engaged in putting down piracy, extending China's 'tributary' trade system and projecting regional power. There is evidence that, even then, China had employed the incentive of trade with its giant market as a lever to achieve its desired diplomatic goals.

Against a backdrop of encroachments by the Siamese and Javanese on the city-state of Malacca, the fleet was sent to bestow China's ritual recognition on Malacca's ruler in 1409. Though the Siamese continued to harass Malacca afterwards, this gesture seemed to have deterred them from an outright invasion, which might have endangered Siam's trade with China.[8]

The admiral who led the treasure fleet's voyages was a singular figure in Chinese history. Admiral Zheng He (郑和) was a Muslim eunuch from Yongle's court. He had been born in Yunnan (云南) province and was captured as a boy in 1382 by the Ming army, which was on a campaign to crush the remaining forces of the Mongol Yuan Dynasty after a peasant uprising had brought Zhu Yuanzhang (朱元璋), a poor farmer's son from Anhui (安徽), to power. Zheng He was castrated and placed in the household of Prince Zhu Di (朱棣), Zhu Yuanzhang's 25-year-old fourth son. Over the next decade, Zheng served Zhu Di as he undertook military campaigns on the fringes of the empire. Intelligent and courageous, the boy came to be highly regarded by his master and they developed a close friendship.

Zhu Yuanzhang was an absolute monarch, who was obsessive about centralising power. After his death in 1398, the throne passed to his grandson Zhu Yunwen (朱允文), who took the imperial name Jianwen (建文). After an attempted purge of potential rival claimants to the throne, Zhu Di, with assistance from eunuchs in the imperial court in Nanjing (南京), overthrew Jianwen and declared himself emperor, taking the reign name Yongle (meaning 'lasting joy').

Having assisted Yongle in seizing the throne, the eunuchs came to enjoy unprecedented power. Trade and prestige associated with the treasure ship voyages saw them grow further in wealth and influence. Not all within the court approved of the voyages, however. The conservative Confucian bureaucracy was critical about their expense and considered foreign travel to interfere with important familial obligations. The Confucians' later fight to regain political influence was to have a profound impact on the course of Chinese history.

During the final years of Yongle's reign, China was struck by a series of natural disasters and epidemics, as well as unrest in the outer reaches of the empire. Annam (now northern Vietnam) had been annexed in 1408 but, in a foreshadowing of America's experience in the 20th century, the Chinese imperial army became bogged down in struggles against Annamese guerrilla forces for the next 20 years. In the northern provinces, a Tartar and Mongol rebellion further stretched the empire's resources. After Yongle's death in 1424, the Confucians seized on these problems and succeeded in halting the costly treasure fleet voyages.

China's governance system, highly centralised on the person of the emperor, has tended to breed factional politics. In striking down China's naval capacity, the Confucians in the Ming court eliminated the primary source of the seafaring eunuchs' power and income. The imperial fleet gradually fell into decay. By 1500, it was a capital offence to build boats with more than two masts. An edict was issued in 1525 to destroy all oceangoing ships and arrest the merchants who sailed them. Thereafter, China's naval capabilities declined so dramatically that, by 1551, its coastal cities were regularly being harassed by piracy.

If this internal power struggle during the Ming Dynasty had turned out differently, the world may well have looked very different today. Notwithstanding China's huge head start in maritime technology, it was the Europeans who went on to colonise the Americas, from which they extracted vast wealth that helped propel their later scientific developments. It is arguable whether, even if they had maintained their maritime superiority, the Chinese were interested in colonising far flung territories. Nevertheless, as maritime commerce powered the beginnings of globalisation and naval power came to underpin European empires, China's lack of naval capabilities left it at an increasing disadvantage at the onset of this new era.

Encounters with the outside world did not cease altogether though. The Portuguese first arrived on China's shores in 1516 and established trading links. They were followed by the Spanish, the Dutch and the English. These foreign traders were mostly uncouth profiteers and adventurers, who were confined to the coastal regions. European missionaries, on the other hand, were welcomed at the imperial court in Beijing. The Jesuit priest Matteo Ricci, who presented himself to the court of Emperor Wanli (万历) in 1601 after having already spent 15 years in China studying its language, culture and philosophy, won many admirers in the Ming court for his scientific knowledge. During the early Qing Dynasty, the Portuguese priest Thomas Pereira played an important role in early diplomacy with the eastward-advancing Russians.[9] Notwithstanding the knowledge shared by the Jesuits, however, science and technology did not gain widespread popularity. The Jesuits' influence on the Qing court gradually waned during the 18th century due to a combination of power struggles within the imperial administration and attacks from within the Catholic Church itself by other orders that saw the Jesuits' tolerance of Chinese customs as a betrayal of Christian principles.

The very strengths that had allowed China to take an early lead began to hold it back. Although political unification had enabled China to efficiently mobilise its huge resources, its autocratic constitutional structure meant that one single decision during the Ming Dynasty to destroy the treasure fleet irreversibly held back its maritime development. In contrast, political fragmentation in Europe meant that the Italian Christopher Columbus was able to take advantage of competition between different rulers, first switching allegiance from his native Genoa to the Duc d'Anjou in France, then to the King of Portugal. When the Portuguese king refused to finance his westward exploration, he turned to other patrons and eventually won backing from Ferdinand and Isabella of Spain.[10]

Likewise, the strength of China's state and its bureaucracy restricted the role of private merchants and enterprise. Those who did acquire wealth tended to plough it into land and education, rather than investing in industrial development. Due to the imperial system's emphasis on classical scholarship for social and political advancement, printing was restricted to scholarly works and not employed to disseminate practical or scientific knowledge, let alone the social criticism that helped power the European Enlightenment.[11]

In 1644, the Ming Dynasty was toppled by Manchu invaders who founded the Qing Dynasty. However, the Manchu rulers not only maintained their Ming predecessors' autocratic system but actually reinforced it. As outside invaders, the Manchus harboured suspicions about Chinese officials, subjecting them to 'a tight net of regulations, restrictions, and checks' and threatened them with 'punishment for derelictions or offences even in matters beyond their individual control'.[12] Rather than facilitating efficient administration by delegating authority to local officials, decision making continued to be centralised with the emperor. Most officials therefore avoided taking initiative and focused on formal compliance with written rules rather than exercising judgement in order to reap wider benefits. Thus, the prosperity and development of the state were inhibited by the limitations of less resourceful rulers that succeeded after Qianlong's (乾隆) reign (1735–1796).

Essentially, excessive centralisation of power inhibited the proper functioning of competitive forces in China's marketplace of ideas, which held back technological and institutional development. This was at precisely the time when the West was making huge advances across the political, economic, scientific and social spheres, which ushered in the Industrial Revolution. By the 19th century, China had fallen so far behind the Europeans across so many fields that it was virtually defenceless against the onslaught of the colonial powers.

The Milk of Paradise

There is perhaps no flower that has had a greater influence on the course of history since the 18th century than the poppy – or, more precisely, the milky extract of its seed pod. Opium is credited with inspiring the work of romantic poets such as Thomas De Quincey, George Crabbe and Samuel Taylor Coleridge.[13] However, as the US opioid epidemic in recent years has borne witness, its addictive properties can lay waste to individual lives and entire communities. Deprived of the drug, addicts will suffer from chills, nausea, muscle pains and agitation, and would go to almost any lengths to satisfy their craving.

The opium poppy was first introduced to China for its pain relieving properties in the 7th or 8th century by the Arabs. Opium smoking for pleasure did not develop until the 1600s, when it became a pastime for the leisure classes. Disturbed by the spread of this habit, the Emperor Yongzheng (雍正) banned the sale and smoking of opium in 1729. Small amounts smuggled in by Portuguese traders continued to satisfy illicit demand. However, the defeat of the Nawab of Bengal by the British under Robert Clive in the Battle of Plassey in 1757 was to have a profound impact on China's history that continues to colour the country's contemporary relations with the West. The chain of events it set off also highlights starkly how, as the world was becoming ever more interconnected by commerce, financial imbalances in one part of the world, like the proverbial butterfly flapping its wings, can cause a mighty typhoon on the other side of the world.

Clive's victory led to the East India Company taking monopoly control over the cultivation of opium poppies around Patna in the Bihar region of Bengal, from which the opium most highly desired by Chinese opium smokers was made. Staffed mostly by rapacious men whose sole aim was short-term profits, the East India Company's administration of Bengal was exploitative and ruinous. What had been the wealthiest province of the Mughal Empire, rich in agriculture and with a vibrant economy, was reduced to what might today be described as a narco-state. In 1773, Parliament passed the India Act, which set up a council of five members to rule British India. As the British government became more involved in India's administration, the exigency of finding funds to pay for this became ever more acute.

The cost of administering India wasn't the only financial conundrum the British government faced, however. The phenomenal growth in demand for Chinese tea in Britain was creating a huge balance of payments deficit. The East India Company had first brought tea to England in 1684 and, gradually, tea drinking became fashionable in polite society. In the first quarter of the 18th century, tea imports rose to 400,000 pounds a year. By 1800, tea drinking had spread to the wider population and Britain's annual tea imports had grown to 23.3 million pounds.[14] In contrast, Chinese demand for British exports, such as woollens, lead, tin, copper and linen, remained low. In the late 18th century, gold and silver often comprised 90 percent or more of the East India Company's shipments to China.[15]

As tea consumption increased, the British government's dependence on related import duties also grew. Even after a reduction in the rate of tea import duty from 100 percent to 12.5 percent in 1784 to combat smuggling, Chinese tea still provided a tenth of British tax revenues.[16] The outbreak of war with France in 1793 in the wake of the French Revolution further increased pressure on Britain to preserve its reserves of bullion.[17] Therefore, the sale of opium, which was the only commodity for which the Chinese showed any enthusiasm, became all the more important to Britain's financial wellbeing.

Of course, given the Chinese ban on opium imports, the British government and the East India Company publicly distanced themselves from the trade. At the time, foreigners trading with China were restricted to the outskirts of the southern city of Canton. The 'Canton system' of trade was conducted under a monopolised structure through a small number of authorised 'hongs' (hang, 行), which organised themselves as a guild and fixed commodity prices. The hong merchants took on the task of collecting customs duties for the Chinese government and were responsible for the foreign traders. The British trade was monopolised by the East India Company, but the Company granted charters to private ships to sail between India and China under its license. The trade conducted by these ships was known as the 'country trade', which was distinguished from the 'Company trade'. This provided a veneer that allowed the Company to disclaim responsibility for Company opium imported to China, as the goods technically ceased to belong to it the moment they were bought and shipped by these private traders.

Foreign traders were subject to various taxes and fees. While the official customs dues ranged between two and four percent of the cargoes' value, poorly remunerated customs officials regularly extracted a 'squeeze' of up to three or four times this amount.[18] Indeed, it had become established practice under Qing rule that officials would supplement their meagre government salaries by extracting surtaxes to support lifestyles far beyond their regular remuneration. An official who levied a surtax of only 10 percent was considered conscientious and incorrupt. Notwithstanding the irregular levies and various restrictions, the monopolised trade system generally functioned well.

The East India Company operated a policy of keeping opium production low, so as to maintain high prices. The cost per chest to the Company was around $50, while the price rose from $100 in 1776 to around $1,400 per chest in 1803 before beginning to level out, thereby providing a profit margin of around 2,000 percent over the following decade.[19] Country traders carrying the opium would unload their cargoes in Portuguese-administered Macau, from where it was smuggled by smaller boats into other parts of the country. The local authorities, who made their living from the squeeze, the hong merchants and the Company's agents all had a common interest in maintaining the fiction that the Company had nothing to do with this illegal traffic.

The Canton system of trade avoided conflict between the vastly different customs and legal traditions of the Chinese and the Westerners. Trade disputes with the hong merchants were generally settled by negotiation or arbitration. An incident in 1784 involving a country ship called the *Lady Hughes*, however, upset the foreigners' feeling of security.

A ceremonial salute fired from this ship accidentally wounded three minor officials, two of whom later died. The Canton authorities demanded that the gunner be handed over to face justice and, when told that he had fled, seized the supercargo responsible for the ship, halted trade and besieged the factory. Looked at from the Chinese perspective, justice needed to be done for the killing of two of their citizens and the authorities were exerting pressure on the British to ensure that the fugitive was handed over to be punished. However, looked at from the perspective of British legal process, the matter of the accidental killing and trade were unrelated. Further, the Chinese authorities had imprisoned an innocent man. Making matters worse, the other supercargoes handed over the gunner following a private assurance that he would be acquitted at trial, only for him subsequently to be executed. The Europeans were horrified by the unfairness – by their standards – of Chinese justice and resented the coercive methods that had been employed. The foreigners' lack of trust in the Chinese legal system would later lead them to demand extraterritorial jurisdiction over their citizens in China.

With a view to expanding trade, the British government sought to establish formal diplomatic relations with Beijing. On the first attempt in 1787, the mission was aborted due to the death of the ambassador *en route*. It was not until 1792 that a second attempt was made under Lord Macartney, who was appointed 'Ambassador Extraordinary and Plenipotentiary from the King of Great Britain to the Emperor of China'.

George Macartney was one of the most experienced diplomats of his generation. His long and distinguished career at that point had already included appointments as ambassador to Russia, governor of the West Indies, and governor of Madras. He had turned down the post of governor-general of India to return to Britain, but was now recalled for a mission to try and establish direct diplomatic relations with Beijing, open up new ports to expand British commerce with China, and perhaps secure some territory near to centres of production and consumption, where British traders might be able to live under British jurisdiction.

The pretext for his mission, which was funded by the East India Company, was to present felicitations from the King of Great Britain on the occasion of Qianlong's 83rd birthday. Flattered at this first British 'tributary' mission, the Emperor welcomed the ambassador's visit. Ahead of his audience with Qianlong, lengthy negotiations took place over whether Macartney would perform the ritual *kowtow* (磕头, given by a series of three prostrations on both knees, each time touching the forehead to the floor three times). In the end, an elegant compromise was found, whereby the Chinese accepted a modified ritual with Macartney kneeling on one knee, as he would to his own sovereign.

Macartney presented many expensive gifts intended to display Britain's technological prowess and the benefits of trade. The mission spent well over a month in Beijing and at the Emperor's Manchurian summer retreat in Jehol (*Rehe*, 热河), and was treated with the utmost politeness and hospitality. However, in terms of achieving its objectives of either expanding trade or establishing permanent diplomatic representation in Beijing, the mission was an utter failure. The Emperor Qianlong famously wrote condescendingly to George III:

> As your Ambassador can see for himself, we possess all things. I set no value on objects strange or ingenious, and have no use for your country's manufactures. This then is my answer to your request to appoint a representative at my Court, a request contrary to our dynastic usage, which would only result in inconvenience to yourself. I have expounded my wishes in detail and have commanded your tribute Envoys to leave in peace on their homeward journey.[20]

The Emperor's haughty tone was calculated, however. He was well aware of the fact that, in 1790, customs duties from the Canton trade had contributed 1.1 million taels[21] of silver to state coffers. Against the imperial court's annual expenditure of 600,000 taels, this was a substantial amount.[22] From the Jesuits serving at his court, Qianlong had some idea of European scientific and military prowess, and knew that, having gained a foothold in India through trade, Britain had gone on to subjugate its people. What the British saw as the arrogant tone of his letter, therefore, stemmed at least in part from a sense of insecurity and was intended to keep Britain at arm's length. From a domestic perspective, Qianlong also understood that his control over his empire was founded on unquestioning submission to his authority over All Under Heaven. Opening China's population to Western ideas might have posed a risk to this blind obedience.

Notwithstanding Macartney's diplomatic failure, he did succeed in gathering valuable intelligence on the state of the Qing Empire. He discovered the backwardness of its army, widespread poverty and the corruption of its government, presciently observing that:

> The empire of China is an old, crazy, first-rate Man of War, which a succession of able and vigilant officers have contrived to keep afloat for these hundred and fifty years past, and to overawe their neighbours merely by her bulk and appearance. But whenever an insufficient man happens to have the command on deck, adieu to the discipline and safety of the ship. She may, perhaps, not sink outright; she may drift some time as a wreck, and will then be dashed to pieces on the shores; but she can never be rebuilt on the bottom.[23]

With the end of the Napoleonic Wars in Europe, Britain attempted again to pursue diplomatic relations with the Qing imperial court, sending former governor of India Lord Amherst as ambassador in 1816. However, Qianlong's successor Emperor Jiaqing (嘉庆) was less adept at the subtleties of the polite but firm diplomacy his father had employed to keep the British at bay. The Amherst mission was fraught with acrimony over ritual protocol and Amherst's refusal to perform the kowtow, so he never gained an audience with the Emperor. Meanwhile, a number of developments were dramatically altering the nature of the trade in Canton.

★★★

There had been a number of attempts to challenge the East India Company's monopoly over the opium supply to China. American merchants had tried to introduce Turkish opium, but consumers considered it to be of far inferior quality and it did not catch on. In time, however, Malwa opium produced in India's independent Maratha native states gained acceptance with Chinese opium smokers and started to compete with the Company's Patna product. Trafficked through the Portuguese possessions of Goa, Diu and Damaun, it bypassed export controls in British India. The Company initially tried to buy up all the Malwa opium in order to deprive the traffickers of their source of supply. However, it proved unworkable to restrict the production of Malwa and, eventually, the Company gave up its policy of limiting the opium supply to keep prices high. This led to a surge in the volume of opium imports to China.

Another factor driving a change in the opium trade was the rising power and boldness of the private merchants. Particularly influential was the firm Jardine Matheson, formed by two Scots traders in 1832. William Jardine was a former ship's physician, who had abandoned medicine for trade in 1817. Twelve years his junior, James Matheson was a young trader who had left his uncle's firm to seek his own fortune. The two men met in Bombay in 1820. Matheson began prospecting northwards along the coast towards Amoy (*Xiamen*, 厦门) and beyond in the 1820s in a bid to expand the market for his product. Through its consolidation of the coastal trade north of Canton, Jardine Matheson came to handle around a third of total opium imports to China.

After Parliament revoked the East India Company's monopoly on China trade in 1834, Jardine Matheson came to play a leading role among the private merchants. When the death of Emperor Daoguang's (道光) opium-addicted son and heir Yiwei (奕纬) precipitated a raid by the Canton authorities and the arrest of one of the hong merchants, the foreign traders began to lobby the British government to uphold their interests. William Jardine and James Matheson were at the forefront in orchestrating this campaign.

It was not just the death of Prince Yiwei that had brought about the Chinese authorities' tougher attitude towards the opium trade. In the early 19th century, addicts were mostly young men from rich families, but the growth in supply had seen the habit spread to people from other walks of life, including government officials, soldiers, women and even common labourers, monks and nuns. The opium scourge was infecting and corrupting all levels of Chinese society. However, it was the effects of the opium trade on China's monetary system that created the greatest exigency.

While China had previously enjoyed a strong positive trade balance, after 1826 the balance tipped the other way and the country began to experience rising outflows of silver. This was a particular problem since silver was the basis on which tax quotas were assessed, but copper coins were the medium of the rural marketplace and most workers' wages. In 1740, a tael of silver was exchanged for 800 copper coins; by 1830 though the exchange rate had reached 1,365 copper coins per tael of silver. In parts of the country, it had risen to as high as between 2,500 and 2,600 copper coins per tael. This meant that many Chinese peasants had suffered 40 to 50 percent increases in their effective tax burdens for reasons none really understood. Since the outflow of silver could be readily identified with foreign commerce, this generated calls to halt trade altogether.[24] The underlying reasons for the copper-silver exchange rate going haywire were more complex, however.

China's domestic silver currency, known in English as 'sycee', was unminted and traded in units of taels. Since it was illegal to export sycee, the currency of China's foreign trade came to be Spanish silver dollars. Between 1805 and 1834, fully one-third of Mexico's entire silver output was carried to China by American traders.[25] Two developments upended the balance in this arrangement. First, since most of this silver came from mines in Spanish Mexico and Peru, national revolutions in Latin America beginning in the 1810s, which caused a shutdown of those mines, choked off global supply of the metal. Second, a shift in US monetary policy made silver more expensive for American merchants, so they switched to using bills of exchange instead. This was acceptable to the hong merchants, but resulted in a substantial decline in tangible silver flowing into China.

The global silver shortage was exacerbated by China's own restrictions on the export of sycee silver. Sycee was accepted by foreign traders in the illicit opium trade. However, since they were unable to recycle the sycee into China in their legitimate trade, they simply began shipping it back to London, where it could be melted down and sold as bullion. These factors combined to create a one-way flow of silver *out* of China, leading to the domestic monetary problems that the country was experiencing.

The imperial court debated over how to deal with the opium problem. In the summer of 1838, the Emperor sought advice from a number of his officials about how to stamp out opium smoking. A report by Lin Zexu (林则徐) analysing the issue in great detail impressed him, and Lin was summoned to Beijing for further discussions. On New Year's Eve, the Emperor appointed him Special Commissioner to Canton with full authority to pursue whatever measures were necessary to bring an end to the opium trade.

Lin was a native of Fujian province. The second of three sons, he had distinguished himself in local examinations and ranked seventh out of 237 candidates for the final civil service examinations in Beijing in 1811. He rose rapidly and was appointed to the post of governor-general of Hubei (湖北) and Hunan (湖南) provinces while still in his forties. There, he had been successful in supressing opium smoking in China's interior. Extracts from his diaries paint an image of a humane and scholarly official, who was incorruptible and strove to carry out his duties to the best of his abilities.[26]

In Canton, Lin set out to address the opium problem at all levels, arresting dealers and instituting a collective responsibility system to discourage smokers. He also appealed to the foreigners' sense of morality. In a letter to Queen Victoria that apparently never reached her, he pointed out the fact that opium smoking was forbidden in Britain and exhorted her on legal and moral grounds to put a stop to the trade.[27] Matters came to a head, however, when Lin blockaded the foreign compound in Canton on 18 March, demanding that the traders hand over their opium.

A stand-off ensued until Captain Charles Elliot, the 37-year-old British Superintendent of Trade, assured the traders on 27 March that they would receive compensation. Elliot had no authority to give such a guarantee on behalf of the British government. However, the traders quickly made arrangements to hand over a total of 20,000 chests of opium and were allowed to depart to Macau. Jardine Matheson's consignment of over 7,000 chests was by far the largest.[28]

After the stocks had been handed over, Lin had the opium destroyed by mixing it with salt, lime and water, then flushed it out into sea. A tense situation persisted and minor incidents became overblown on both sides. After Lin put pressure on the Portuguese to expel the British from Macau, they retreated to the then barren island of Hong Kong on 29 August.

News of the blockade reached London in September. William Jardine, who had returned to live in Britain, arrived at around the same time. He met the Foreign Secretary Lord Palmerston and furnished the Foreign Office with company charts of the Chinese coast and intelligence gathered from their smuggling operations. With a fund of $20,000 raised from the Canton merchants, Jardine also aggressively stepped up public advocacy of the traders' cause through British newspapers.

Jardine Matheson exploited the situation to their maximum benefit. In fact, Lin's confiscation and destruction of their opium stocks had been a godsend for them. Lin's earlier moves to curtail opium smoking had already sunk demand and the price that traders could hope to get for their stocks would have been extremely low. Elliot's guarantee of compensation meant they would be made whole at much higher prices than they could obtain on the open market. Furthermore, news of the events in Canton had raised fears of a supply glut, depressing opium prices further. On learning that supply was building up in Singapore, James Matheson despatched 20 chests of opium to Singapore from Hong Kong, ostensibly for sale. Seeing that even the mighty Jardine Matheson could no longer sell opium in China, the market fell into a panic. Along with the chests of opium, however, Matheson had sent a secret letter to the company's Singapore agent instructing him to take advantage of the low prices to buy up stock. Disguising the source of the purchases, the agent bought up 700 chests at $250 per chest, which were 'readily disposed of at an average of $2,500 per chest'.[29]

On 18 October, without prior consultation with Parliament, Lord Palmerston wrote to Elliot to inform him that he planned to send an expeditionary force to Canton. Meanwhile, on 3 November a scuffle between the Chinese and British navies at Chuanbi (穿鼻), at the mouth of the Boca Tigris,[30] resulted in four Chinese war junks being sunk. These were the opening shots of the Opium War.

★★★

Chinese forces were no match for Britain's vastly superior naval and military power. The course of the war was punctuated with a series of tactical and diplomatic failures, with each side undermining their own negotiators' efforts to find a settlement. Part of this could be accounted for by the length of time it took to communicate between the front and the two capitals in an era before the telegraph. However, misreporting of battle outcomes on the Chinese side was also a significant factor and resulted in overconfidence that led Beijing to overplay its already weak hand.

When a British expeditionary force reached Baihe (白河) near Tianjin (天津), threatening the capital, the Emperor despatched the governor-general of the capital province of Zhili (直隸), Qishan (琦善), to negotiate them. A wily diplomat, Qishan recognised the superiority of British forces and pursued a tactic of mollifying them. Remarkably, he managed to persuade the British that it would be best to return to Canton to continue negotiations.

Both sides blamed Lin Zexu's actions for precipitating the conflict and Lin was exiled. On 20 January 1841, Qishan and Charles Elliot agreed to a draft settlement known as the Chuanbi Convention.[31] The settlement provided for the lease of Hong Kong to the British; the payment by the Chinese of an indemnity of $6 million; reopening of trade in Canton; and a principle of direct and equal dialogue between the two countries' officials going forward. Qishan did not seal the convention himself but agreed to send it to the Emperor for his approval.

When reported back, the terms of the agreement aroused ire on both sides. The Emperor was so enraged by the cession of any territory that Qishan was thrown in chains and sentenced to death, later commuted to exile in the far northeast. Lord Palmerston, who was more interested in opening further ports to expand the market for British goods, was furious with Elliot for not exploiting the British military upper hand to demand more. He derisively referred to Hong Kong as 'a barren island with hardly a house upon it'.[32] Although spared Qishan's fate, Elliot also found himself dismissed and replaced by Colonel Sir Henry Pottinger, who became the first British governor of Hong Kong.

The repudiation of the Chuanbi Convention by both sides ushered in renewed military engagement. After Chinese forces were overwhelmed, the Treaty of Nanjing[33] was signed aboard the *Cornwallis* on 29 August 1842. Hong Kong was ceded to the British in perpetuity. The treaty also opened the ports of Amoy, Fuzhou (福州), Ningbo (宁波) and Shanghai, and the British would be allowed to maintain consuls there. Further, the Chinese would pay an indemnity of $21 million. Going forward, the monopoly trading system would be abolished, and tariffs set at a fixed rate. It was an utter humiliation for the imperial regime.

The pretext on which the British had waged war against China was morally indefensible. Even in Britain, it was heavily criticised at the time. Much was blamed on the haughtiness of the Qing government, with former US President John Quincy Adams attributing the cause of war to the kowtow.[34] It is fair to say that the lack of diplomatic engagement between the two countries had meant that tensions were unable to be resolved through diplomacy. However, this problem was exacerbated by China's sclerotic and corrupt institutions, which had not only left it technologically and militarily backward, but also made it prone to miscalculations.

Not daring to report bad news, local officials delivered blatantly false reports to the Emperor throughout the course of the war. This can be a major challenge in highly centralised and hierarchical power structures, and there are parallels in China even today. In 2007, Premier Li Keqiang (李克强) reportedly told the US ambassador that he did not pay much heed to the GDP figures provincial officials fed him, but instead looked to statistics such as railway cargo volumes and electricity consumption as more reliable indicators of economic performance.[35]

Notwithstanding the military humiliation, the Qing regime did not immediately pursue modernisation or try to gain a better understanding of the foreign powers. Neither was the Chinese population shocked into realising the regime's backwardness. However, the consequences of the Opium War were far-reaching.

Wanting to avoid further conflicts, China entered into a series of 'unequal treaties' (不平等条约) with foreign powers that ceded control over tariffs and granted the foreigners jurisdiction over their own citizens on Chinese soil. Concessions granted under the treaties betrayed the Chinese negotiators' lack of understanding of international law. Tariff rates proposed by Britain were readily agreed to, since they were higher than the existing imperial tariffs. However, the fixed nature of these tariffs stripped China of future flexibility to impose protective tariffs to shield its own industries against the influx of foreign goods. This reduced many of China's industries to penury, particularly in Canton, which faced a loss of trade to other ports. The acquiescence to 'most favoured nation' (MFN) treatment to each counterparty also meant that the treaties with the different countries were mutually reinforcing, with each subsequent concession to any other country also benefiting the signatories to these agreements.

As the first 'trade war' in which China became embroiled, the Opium War is highly significant in the contemporary context, and it continues to colour Chinese attitudes towards the West today. For many Chinese, the lesson of the Opium War was that, irrespective of legal or moral rectitude, it was ultimately superior military strength that counted. Perhaps the more important lesson for us all, however, is that, left unaddressed, financial imbalances can lead to escalating conflict. Without open and positive diplomatic engagement, this can quickly spiral into war.

Having lost the war, the Chinese government dared not try to impose restraints on the opium traffic. As a result, imports rose rapidly, further exacerbating the outflow of silver. This, in turn, drove up the copper-to-silver exchange rate. Since copper was the currency of exchange for everyday goods, such as rice, this fuelled inflation. The cession to the British of Hong Kong as a base of operations and the opening of the treaty ports further laid China's entire coast open to expanding foreign influence. All of this laid the ground for rising social unrest.

Wars and Revolutions

Until well into the 20th century, China was predominantly an agrarian society. Social order depended to a very large degree on the distribution of land. China's so-called 'dynastic cycle' can therefore be viewed in terms of rises and falls in the population relative to the availability of arable land. During long periods of social order, the population would increase and the amount of arable land per capita would fall, causing a decrease in peasants' living standards, thus precipitating a rise in social discontent. As the philosopher Mencius (孟子) observed over two millennia ago, a period of disorder would follow, in which the population would be reduced, a new balance would be achieved and order was then restored.

In the period from 1741 to 1850, China's population trebled from 143 million to 430 million, while the amount of arable land increased by only 35 percent. As the demographic pressure increased, some peasants were forced to sell their small landholdings and become tenant farmers. Rich landowners who bought up their land would rarely sell it back unless at a very good price. This contributed to rising wealth inequality. Some 50 to 60 percent of all arable land came to be concentrated in the hands of rich families, while military officers and officials held roughly 10 percent. Some 60 to 90 percent of the population had no land at all. Combined with the moral and military degradation of the Qing Empire, as well as widespread political corruption, conditions were already ripe for revolution. The onslaught of the colonial powers only compounded the problems facing the government.[36]

In the mid 19th century, the internal uprising that came closest to toppling Qing rule was the Taiping Rebellion (1850–1864, 太平天国运动) led by Hong Xiuquan (洪秀全), the third son of a Hakka (*Kejia*, 客家) farming family from Guangdong (广东) province who had converted to Christianity and claimed to be Jesus' younger brother. This religiously inspired movement succeeded in capturing a large swathe of central and southern China, including Nanjing, and caused tens of millions of casualties before it was finally put down. Together with the Nian Rebellion (1853–1868, 捻乱) in the north of the country and Muslim rebellions in Yunnan (1855–1873, 云南回变) and several western provinces

(1862–1878, 同治回乱), it is estimated that the upheaval between 1850 and 1873 reduced China's population by some 60 million.[37]

Meanwhile, the foreign powers' encroachments continued. The treaty powers became insistent on establishing permanent diplomatic representation in Beijing, signifying that they were not tributary envoys but representatives of equal sovereign states. The Qing court, stuck with its authoritarian structure but lacking in strategic or visionary leadership, was unable to reconcile the realities of the new international order and its self-image as the ruler of All Under Heaven. It saw only vulnerability and humiliation in opening up to direct diplomatic relations with the West, so it employed delaying tactics. This created tensions with the foreign powers. When, in 1856, Chinese authorities boarded a Chinese-owned but Hong Kong-registered ship called the *Arrow* in search of a notorious pirate, the British flag was hauled down in the process. This desecration of their flag gave the British a pretext to attack Canton and then proceed northwards. The Arrow War[38] was settled via the Treaty of Tianjin,[39] the terms of which included the opening of ten additional ports,[40] greater freedom of travel for foreigners in China, and a monetary indemnity.

On their way to Beijing to exchange ratifications of the treaty, the British envoy and his party were attacked by Chinese forces at the Dagu Forts (大沽炮台). In response, Lord Palmerston sent Lord Elgin to lead a joint British and French march on Beijing. There, Lord Elgin ordered the burning of the Summer Palace. The Emperor fled the capital, leaving his younger brother Prince Gong (恭亲王) to negotiate a peace settlement. This settlement established an unequivocal right for the British to maintain diplomatic representation in Beijing, increased the size of the previous indemnity, and opened Tianjin to foreign trade and residence. It further ceded the Kowloon Peninsula opposite Hong Kong to the British.

Born in 1833, Prince Gong was the sixth son of the Emperor Daoguang. Noted for his brilliance from a young age, he was once considered a potential heir. However, upon Daoguang's death, the throne went to his older half-brother who took the reign name Xianfeng (咸丰). In the negotiations with the British and French in 1860, Prince Gong impressed them with his intelligence, fine manners and pragmatism.

He, in turn, came to respect and admire British power. The Anglo-French forces' prompt withdrawal from Beijing once the peace treaty was signed led him to conclude that the British had no territorial designs on China. So long as, he believed, China kept to its treaty obligations and treated the foreigners with goodwill, the British were predominantly interested in the expansion of trade. He also realised that the foreigners' continued enjoyment of their treaty rights was predicated on the continued existence of the government that had granted them, thereby giving the Westerners a powerful interest in the continuation of the Dynasty. This convinced him that China needed to chart a new course, pursuing diplomatic engagement with the foreign powers, while modernising and strengthening itself.

Even after the departure of the occupying forces, Emperor Xianfeng refused to return to Beijing. Prince Gong took charge of affairs in the capital and began to pursue a programme of reforms, most notably through the establishment of the Zongli Yamen (总理衙门), China's first foreign office. The Emperor eventually died in August 1861, naming his five-year-old son Zaichun (载淳) as heir on his deathbed. Before his death, he also appointed a Council of Regents dominated by conservative princes and officials to advise on state affairs during the boy emperor's minority. This threatened to derail Prince Gong's programme of modernisation.

Cooperating with the two Empress Dowagers, Cixi (慈禧太后) and Ci'an (慈安太后), he executed a coup to oust the Council of Regents and handed power to the Empress Dowagers, who would 'govern from behind a silk screen' (垂帘听政) on behalf of the boy emperor. The boy emperor took the reign name Tongzhi (同治), which can be translated literally as 'co-rule'.

Of the two Empress Dowagers, it was the mother of the boy emperor Cixi who took the more active role in matters of state. Until her death in 1908, Cixi loomed as a commanding presence over the imperial government. At times aligning herself with the reformers and at others with the conservatives, she balanced the power of the two factions to dominate them both. Thus, although Prince Gong's Self-strengthening Movement (自强运动) was able to make some important strides towards modernisation, including the establishment of foreign language and scientific education, military strengthening and the beginnings of industrial enterprise, reforms were too slow to reverse the decline of the Dynasty.

In truth, even without the conservative opposition, it is unclear that the Self-strengthening Movement would have been sufficient to change the final outcome. This is because the vision of even its most ardent proponents was limited in scope. Prince Gong's preoccupation was with military strengthening and he saw the opening to foreigners as a temporary means to an end. Li Hongzhang (李鸿章), who had risen to prominence as a military commander during the suppression of the Taiping Rebellion and was later appointed governor-general of Zhili, understood better that military weakness was only one aspect of the challenges China confronted. Having spent years travelling around the entire country dealing with one problem after another and serving as a key interlocutor with the foreign powers, Li understood that China had to address both economic and institutional weaknesses. As a key coordinator of the Self-strengthening Movement, Li sought to stimulate the development of industrial enterprises. However, although he drew in private capital to invest in 'government-sponsored merchant undertakings' (官督商办), the government retained tight control over the appointment of management. This meant that, in practice, the enterprises were racked with bureaucratic inefficiency, corruption and nepotism. The institutional modernisation needed to drive higher productivity and to secure the reforms was never pursued.

The failure of China's approach can be seen most starkly when it is compared with that of Japan. When confronted with the arrival of the American naval expedition under Commodore Matthew Perry in 1853, the Japanese recognised the need to modernise and not only threw open their doors to foreign technology, but also pursued extensive institutional reforms. By the mid-1890s, they were in a position to rout the Chinese navy in the First Sino-Japanese War (1894–1895). Elite corruption was a significant contributor to this humiliation. Funds originally raised for the modernisation of China's navy had been diverted pay for the reconstruction of the Summer Palace for the Empress Dowager Cixi, leaving the obsolescent Chinese fleet no match for the modern warships of the British-trained Japanese Imperial Navy. Under the Treaty of Shimonoseki (下关条约) that ended the war, China ceded to Japan Taiwan, the Penghu Islands (澎湖) and the Liaodong Peninsula (辽东半岛), setting the stage for further Japanese colonial advances that were only reversed by Japan's eventual defeat in WW2.

Following this defeat by Japan, the Emperor Guangxu (光绪), supported by reformers in his court, attempted – albeit belatedly – to drive through institutional and political modernisations. Their Hundred Days' Reform (戊戌变法) in 1898 included a bold set of objectives, including the transition towards a constitutional monarchy. However, they were thwarted by a *coup d'état* led by the Empress Dowager Cixi and conservative opponents. The reformist officials fled into exile and Guangxu was effectively put under house arrest.

In 1899, popular frustration at foreign domination and economic hardship boiled over in the Boxer Uprising (义和团运动) in northern China. Practicing a form of ancient mysticism and claiming invulnerability to foreign weapons, the Boxers carried out a violent campaign against foreigners and the symbols of Western presence, such as churches, Chinese Christians, railroads and telegraph lines. The Qing court was divided on how to respond and itself was vulnerable to the Boxers' campaign. Perhaps due to this vulnerability, the Empress Dowager decided to embrace the Boxers. After foreign embassies in Beijing came under siege, an allied force of eight foreign powers, including Japan, Russia, Britain, France, the US, Germany, Italy and Austria-Hungary, marched on the capital with anti-Boxer Chinese forces and put down the uprising. A further unequal treaty imposed on China included additional occupation rights and a huge indemnity of 450 million taels.[41] In a charitable gesture, the Americans eventually returned their share of the indemnity on condition that the funds be used for educational purposes, which led to the establishment of Tsinghua University (清华大学). Robert Hart, an Englishman who faithfully served the Qing court as head of China's customs service for almost half a century, negotiated with the foreign powers to increase China's customs duty rate from 3.17 percent or less to five percent, so as to help pay for the indemnity.[42] Nevertheless, the financial burden created further economic hardship and the prestige of the Qing Dynasty sank to a nadir.

Notwithstanding their efforts to reform and modernise China, Prince Gong and Li Hongzhang failed to set the country on a sustainable path of rejuvenation and growth. The forces of conservative opposition were too strong and they themselves were not necessarily willing to undertake the fundamental structural reforms needed. The short-lived Hundred Days' Reform was unable to reverse the tide. Li Hongzhang, who was forced to negotiate the Treaty of Shimonoseki and the settlement with foreign powers following the Boxer Uprising, has been reviled in Chinese history for signing those unequal treaties. However, against the backdrop of China's enfeebled position, internal conflicts and the advances of the colonial powers, Li and his fellow reformers could only delay the inevitable fall of the Qing Dynasty.

***

The toppling of the Manchus who had ruled China for over two and a half centuries had less to do with the strength of the revolutionaries that replaced them than with the fundamental weakness of the imperial regime itself. Following the negotiated abdication on 12 February 1912 of the six-year-old Puyi (溥仪), the twelfth and final emperor of the Qing Dynasty, it was not long before infighting among the revolutionaries saw the country descend into chaos and civil war.

Sun Yat-sen (孙中山), credited as the 'Father of (republican) China',[43] was born to a family of modest means in Xiangshan (香山) in Guangdong province in 1866, just two years after the Taiping Rebellion was quelled. Stories of that uprising inspired him as a child. At the age of 12, he was sent to live with his older brother in Honolulu, where he attended school for several years. However, concerned that he was embracing Christianity, his brother sent him home. After arousing local ire by breaking a statue in the village temple, he fled to Hong Kong where he made his way to the Diocesan Boys' School, which doubled as an orphanage run by the Anglican Church.

Sun continued his studies in the British colony, whose orderliness and relative modernity were a stark contrast to the backwardness of his home village, which lay just some 50 miles away. This had a strong influence on Sun. He came to see China's problems as stemming from the Qing government's weakness and corruption, which motivated him to become involved in revolutionary activities to seek its overthrow.

After instigating a failed uprising in Canton in 1895, Sun was forced to flee China and barred from Hong Kong. During his exile, he travelled the world, developing connections and rallying support from overseas Chinese communities. Funds he raised were channelled back to support the revolutionary movement in China. When the 1911 revolution began in Wuchang (武昌), he was abroad and was not even aware that it was happening. However, his status as the only Chinese revolutionary with any significant international reputation helped secure his election as Provisional President (临时大总统) of the new Republic in December 1911. Sun stepped down from this position in March 1912 in favour of Yuan Shikai (袁世凯).

As a young man, Yuan had fought under Li Hongzhang during the suppression of the Taiping Rebellion. After the rebellion was put down, he was posted as a military advisor to Korea – at the time a Chinese tributary – where Japan was vying for greater influence. He served as China's Imperial Resident in Seoul but was recalled just before the outbreak of the First Sino-Japanese War. Back in China, he played a significant role in the modernisation of the military under the Self-strengthening Movement. He was later promoted to the governor-generalship of Zhili and became Commissioner of North China Trade. Crucially, he commanded strong loyalty among the armed forces responsible for the defence of Beijing. This meant that, although he was forced to resign amidst a power struggle in 1908, the imperial court had few other people to turn to at the time of the Wuchang Uprising.

On being called back, Yuan was appointed Prime Minister and became the key negotiator between the Qing court and the revolutionaries. In return for securing the Emperor's abdication and a peaceful transfer of power, the revolutionaries promised to appoint him President of the Republic.

From the beginning, the Republic was little understood by most Chinese. Republicanism was a foreign import and, when the Qing Dynasty fell, from the Chinese historical perspective, many simply saw this as the Mandate of Heaven being passed from the Manchus to a new ruler. At the grass roots level, democracy was not necessarily trusted. One Confucian farmer in Shanxi (山西) made the following observation in his diary after witnessing China's first democratic election in December 1911:

They are using the method of election by ballot, so that all the rogues and villains intrigue for office by campaigning, and the ones who have the most money win. How can we possibly get decent officials from a selection process like this? Who says that elections are a fair method? All I see is people campaigning. They have no sense of modesty and no shame. When they tout for your vote they treat you like a god.[44]

Yuan Shikai, having served an emperor-state all his life, simply saw the president as some sort of non-hereditary emperor.[45] Once installed, he sought to subvert the power of the parliament so he could rule unimpeded. In 1913, he created a new constitution that eliminated presidential term limits. Still unsatisfied, he sought to reintroduce the monarchy in 1915 and had himself declared emperor. In the ensuing months, several provinces declared independence and went their own way. Yuan died suddenly of illness in June 1916 and the country fell into a period of disorder under regional warlords.

Sun Yat-sen established a military government in Canton in 1917 but lacked an army capable of unifying the country. This was a period of political transformation in many parts of the world and a large number of Chinese who had studied overseas were bringing new ideas back to the country. Sun himself married one such returnee after divorcing his wife in 1915. Soong Ching-ling (宋庆龄), 26 years his junior, was the American-educated daughter of a wealthy Shanghai businessman. Many of the young intelligentsia were much enamoured with the Western model of liberal democracy and saw China taking its place in the Western world order. However, for many, this idealist vision was shattered by the Treaty of Versailles. China had entered WW1 on the side of the Allies and had expected that Shandong, which had been colonised by the Germans, would be returned to China. Instead, Shandong was handed to Japan. This set off a huge demonstration by students, who protested against China's own weakness in Tiananmen Square on 4 May 1919. The so-called 'May Fourth Movement' (五四运动) that this inspired sought to sweep away China's old culture and embrace modernism. Equally importantly, the outcome of the Treaty of Versailles imprinted on China's political consciousness a certain cynicism about the nature of the 'rules-based' global order. Versailles reinforced the lesson of the Opium War and the unequal treaties that only by being powerful would China be treated fairly by the world powers.

China's treatment by the Western powers influenced many to embrace Communist ideas that were spreading at the time. The Soviet Union, keen to further the Communist movement internationally after the 1917 Bolshevik Revolution, courted Sun and his young bride. Attracted by Soviet financial and military support, Sun allied his Nationalist Party with the CCP. Following Sun's death in 1925, however, his party became divided between its right and left wings.

Eventually, it was a young superintendent of the Nationalists' military academy, Chiang Kai-shek (蔣介石), who seized power. Chiang split with the Communists and led a northward campaign against the warlords. By 1929, Chiang had successfully reunified the country and established Nanjing as his capital.

Unification of the country did little to improve the lot of the peasant class that made up over 80 percent of the population, however.[46] The former warlords and urban middle classes that were installed as the leadership of the Nationalist government had little interest in the welfare of the masses. Chiang married Soong May-ling (宋美齡), a sister of Sun's widow, in 1927 and appointed members of her family to key posts in his government. Her brother T.V. Soong (宋子文) was appointed Premier and H.H. Kung (孔祥熙), the banker husband of another Soong sister, served as Minister of Finance. Kung, a Yale-educated 75th-generation descendent of Confucius, would represent China at Bretton Woods in 1944. These Western-trained financiers were far removed from average Chinese citizens and understood little about their hardships. The Nationalist government was also beset by the twin challenges of the Communists and Japanese aggression. Thus, social and economic reforms were neglected.

War broke out with Japan in 1937. The exigencies of repelling the Japanese forced the Nationalists and the CCP into an uneasy alliance that lasted throughout WW2. However, once the Japanese had been defeated, civil war broke out between them. The eventual CCP victory was driven by a number of factors.

After eight years of war, the Nationalists were exhausted militarily, financially and spiritually. Meanwhile, the CCP had significantly expanded its support base during the war. The Communists were perceived as more attuned to the plight of the peasant class, who had been entirely neglected by the Nationalist government. This was compounded by widespread corruption in the Nationalist regime, in which the Soong and Kung families were implicated. H.H. Kung was eventually removed from the government after a corruption scandal in which he was alleged to have pocketed $3 million.[47]

The US had backed the Nationalists through WW2 and did not want to see China taken over by the Communists. However, the US too was weary of war and the Truman Administration was turned off by Chiang's arrogance and the corruption of his government. The CCP, on the other hand, continued to receive substantial financial and military support from Moscow.

Defeated, Chiang's Nationalist government retreated to Taiwan and, on 1 October 1949, overlooking Tiananmen Square, Mao Zedong proclaimed the founding of the People's Republic of China. The country had been ravaged by more than two decades of war. Industrial and food output had collapsed to 56 percent and 70–75 percent of their respective pre-war peaks, and inflation had rocketed out of control.[48] China's share of global GDP, which had peaked at around a third during Qianlong's reign, fell to just 1.3 percent by 1950.[49] However, the suffering of China's people was far from over yet.

A Leap into the Abyss

The band of revolutionaries who took power in 1949 had accomplished an incredible feat. Against improbable odds and through years of fearsome struggle, their determination to forge a new egalitarian path for China had won out. However, the skills they had honed in propaganda and guerrilla warfare, which had helped them emerge victorious from the civil war, were not the ones needed to govern the country. In fact, the CCP had a severe shortage of reliable and competent administrators when it came to power.[50]

To implement its agenda of reform and industrial modernisation, therefore, the new government relied on administrators who had served the Nationalist government and on continuing assistance from the Soviet Union. The amount of Soviet assistance received was astonishing. Between 1946 and 1960, aid provided by the USSR to China was equivalent to $25 billion at today's prices, or just under one percent of annual Soviet GDP over the period. And this does not account for the value of technology transfers, the salaries of Soviet experts sent to China, or the cost of hosting Chinese students in the USSR. The Soviet assistance programme for China, in fact, exceeded the size of America's Marshall aid plan for Europe.[51]

The Sino-Soviet relationship, however, was complex. The Marxist-Leninist doctrines that Mao and his fellow revolutionaries adopted had emerged from the Soviet Union. Many members of the CCP leadership had spent time in Russia, and Soviet assistance had been a key factor behind the CCP's eventual victory over the Nationalists. At the same time, Stalin had backed Chiang Kai-shek in the run-up to and during WW2, mainly due to his cold calculation that Chiang was the only credible leader who could resist the Japanese. This had allowed Soviet forces to avoid fighting a war on two fronts and focus on defeating the Nazis. Stalin was a realist in his dealings with the CCP and, even as Mao was completing his conquest of the Mainland, Stalin was encouraging Xinjiang to declare independence. And it was only with great reluctance – and after negotiating extensive mineral and port rights, and the maintenance of an independent Outer Mongolia – that the Soviets finally withdrew from Manchurian territories that they had occupied at the end of WW2. Thus, while Mao respected Stalin's power, the realities of China's historical relationship with Russia still coloured the overall Sino–Soviet alliance.

One of the 'costs' incurred for Stalin's assistance was the million troops that China sent to fight with Kim Il-sung in the Korean War.[52] Many of them died, including one of Mao's sons. A consequence of China's involvement in this conflict was to divert resources that could have been directed towards the country's reconstruction. The outbreak of the Korean War also heightened US concerns about Communist aggression in Asia, drawing the Americans into a commitment to defend Taiwan from Mainland Chinese attack.

On the domestic front, the new government set about repairing the badly damaged economy it had inherited. To stem inflation, it issued a new currency and reduced the amount of paper money in circulation, while banning the circulation of foreign currencies. The CCP also undertook administrative measures to stabilise wages and the prices of staple goods.[53] On land and industrial policy, two key initiatives were pursued. The first was to redistribute land from rich peasants and landlords to poor peasants. At first, this stopped short of full collectivisation and was popular with the majority of peasants. The second key initiative was the preparation of the First Five-Year Plan, which called for the construction of 694 industrial projects. Starting from a low base of development, this plan was highly successful and exceeded its original targets. In 1956, industrial output grew by 25 percent over the previous year.[54]

The success of the First Five-Year Plan encouraged the planners to pursue a more ambitious set of targets in the Second Five-Year Plan (1958–1962). However, that plan had barely gotten underway before the government announced the 'Great Leap Forward' (大跃进) in February 1958, calling for significant increases in the output of steel, coal and electricity.

The Great Leap Forward had its origins in Mao's impatience to hasten the Communist ideal of collectivisation and to accelerate China's industrialisation. In this lay an element of competition with the Soviet Union. After Stalin's death in 1953, Mao saw himself as the Communist world's elder statesman. When, in 1956, Nikita Khrushchev denounced Stalin's policies (in particular, the purges he carried out within the Soviet leadership), it posed an ideological threat to Mao, who had advocated a Stalinist agenda within the CCP, and marked the beginning of the souring of Sino-Soviet relations. Mao became preoccupied with demonstrating the CCP's superior growth model, boasting in 1957 that 'we can overtake Britain . . . in 15 years or slightly more'.[55] Neither economically trained or ever much involved in the implementation of economic and industrial policies, Mao believed that this growth could be achieved through sheer force of will. The Great Leap Forward turned out to be one of the greatest ever human disasters.

The output quota for steel was raised in May from 6.2 million to 8–8.5 million tons. In August, it was raised again to 10.7 million tons. To meet these targets, the government pursued a campaign of mass mobilisation, encouraging all citizens to get involved in the production. The campaign was accompanied by land collectivisation and the organisation of the population into communes, which controlled the agricultural and industrial resources in each area. In villages and communes across the country, people had set up an estimated 600,000 small-scale backyard furnaces by the autumn of 1958. Although steel production volumes did increase as a consequence, this was highly inefficient, and the output was of low quality. In August 1959, it was pronounced that

3 million of the 11 million tons of steel produced in 1958 was unfit for industrial use.[56]

Inevitably, these inefficient activities involved a diversion of resources from other areas, notably food production. Nevertheless, eager to demonstrate strong performance, party cadres overreported output on a mass scale. As reported output of grain increased, central planners demanded that more be handed over to the government. Instead of benefiting from higher output, farmers who produced more crops just had more taken away from them, discouraging them from producing more. In many cases, when output was below expectations, overzealous local officials would still insist – by use of force if necessary – that enough food was sent to the central government to meet their quotas. The massive misreporting of output meant that, as famine gripped the country in 1959, China actually *exported* 4.74 million tons of grain, worth $935 million.[57] By the time the Great Leap Forward was discontinued in 1961, at least 40 million people had died.[58] Amidst the starvation, some in Anhui and Gansu (甘肃) province resorted to cannibalism, including a couple who strangled and ate their eight-year-old son.[59]

Such a disastrously misguided policy had not gone completely unopposed within the ranks of the CCP. Many of the leadership understood that the peasants had supported them in the civil war because of the promise of land redistribution. To the agrarian backbone of the population, the transition to CCP rule was no different from China's age-old transfers of power from one dynasty to the next. The Communists' concept of collectivisation was not what they had sought or supported. At the same time, the intellectual elite of the Party were not uniformly in favour of Mao's policies. In 1956, Mao had invited criticism of the government's policies and alternative views, declaring 'let a hundred flowers bloom' (百花齐放).[60] For a brief period, citizens from all walks of life freely shared their opinions but, stunned by the vehemence of the criticisms received, Mao launched a brutal purge of those who had come forward. This experience made people fearful of voicing any opposition to the Great Leap Forward. Mao had also fostered the creation of a personality cult around himself,[61] adding to the difficulty of challenging him. Finally, at a conference of top party leaders in Lushan (庐山) in the summer of 1959, Defence Minister Peng Dehuai (彭德怀), a veteran of the Long March[62] and commander of Chinese forces in the

Korean War, spoke out in opposition to Mao's policies. For his criticisms, Peng was purged. However, Mao was forced to cede day-to-day power to President Liu Shaoqi (刘少奇), Premier Zhou Enlai and Party Secretary Deng Xiaoping.

Meanwhile, Mao's vocal ideological opposition to Khrushchev's reversal of Stalinist policies was worsening relations with the USSR. Moscow eventually withdrew all Soviet advisors from China in 1960. This precipitated a worldwide struggle for influence in the Communist world. To demonstrate the superiority of its model, China instituted a generous programme of international aid. Poverty stricken and in the midst of a severe famine, China dramatically increased the amount of aid it was giving to Africa in 1960. To Algeria alone that year, China increased its aid to 50.6 million yuan, up from just 600,000 yuan the previous year. One Beijing-based diplomat from Albania – a particular battleground for influence with the Soviets – later recalled that, although the famine in China was clearly apparent to him, 'The Chinese gave us everything'. China was supplying the Balkan country with one-fifth of its grain needs, even as millions of its own citizens were starving.[63]

Although Mao had ceded administrative power after the Great Leap Forward, he continued to wield strong influence behind the scenes and ensured he maintained control over the propaganda functions of the party. Gradually, he used this influence to purge opponents within the Party and the military. In 1966, under the pretext of eliminating the remnants of capitalist and traditionalist thought from Chinese society, he launched the Cultural Revolution to purge the moderate elements of the CCP leadership. Liu Shaoqi and Deng Xiaoping were removed from power. Radicals in the party mobilised a mass student-led paramilitary movement known as the 'Red Guards'(红卫兵), which waged violent class struggle against traditional sources of authority that did not conform to Mao Zedong Thought. Intellectuals, 'class enemies' and counter-revolutionaries were persecuted, with many of them brutalised or even killed. Traditional Chinese culture was attacked, and many historical and religious sites were vandalised or destroyed. Society almost broke down entirely; schools and universities were closed down and millions of urban intellectual youths were sent down to the countryside to be reformed through hard labour.[64]

By the time the Cultural Revolution was ended in 1976, China had hit the bottom of the abyss. The CCP's leadership had been so thoroughly purged of capable officials that, after Zhou Enlai was diagnosed with cancer, Mao had no choice but to bring Deng Xiaoping back from exile to help administer state affairs.

The Cultural Revolution marked one of the darkest periods of modern Chinese history. Its causes and much of what happened defy rational explanation. Some writers have attributed it largely to Mao's megalomania and determination to stay in power, irrespective of the consequences for the country.[65] This explanation is not entirely satisfactory, as it stretches credulity that one man alone was responsible for the brutality that took place across the entire country. The struggle for power between different factions of the CCP leadership under Mao played a major role, as did underlying tensions across society.

In China's foreign relations, it has been argued that Mao's antagonism towards the Soviets was designed to keep its northern neighbour at bay.[66] This was costly though, as it required enormous resources to be diverted towards defence, instead of development. Eventually, as the threat of Soviet aggression became greater, Mao pursued rapprochement with the US to provide a strategic counterbalance.

Whatever the motivations behind Mao's policies, however, it was of little relevance to the Chinese people. For them, his period in office plunged the country to a new low and the chaos of the Cultural Revolution continues to haunt the generation that lived through it (which includes many of the country's current leadership). Not only had China fallen further behind the West economically and technologically, but an entire generation had been denied access to education and the country struggled to feed itself. From there, it would take a leader of exceptional determination and skill to resurrect it.

Herding Cats

Immediately after Chairman Mao's death in September 1976, notwithstanding the depths to which it had sunk, there was no guarantee that China would embark on the eventual path of reform that it pursued. Led by Mao's widow Jiang Qing (江青), radical elements of the leadership known as the 'Gang of Four' (四人帮),[67] who had propagated the Cultural Revolution, still held significant sway. Moreover, Mao's hand-picked successor Hua Guofeng (华国锋) had been chosen in large part because he was not expected to overturn Mao's policies. Therefore, it was a surprise to many when, scarcely a month after Mao's death, Hua had the Gang of Four arrested and denounced for their part in the Cultural Revolution. Thus, Hua made a decisive break from the Mao era and took the first step on China's path to recovery. However, Hua lacked charisma as a leader and his only source of legitimacy was that he had been chosen by Mao, which would ultimately inhibit him from straying too far away from Mao's ideology. Instead, the party leadership put its support behind the seasoned and disciplined Deng Xiaoping.

Deng was already 72 years of age when Mao died. He had joined the CCP as a student in France in the 1920s. It was there that he first got to know Zhou Enlai and others who went on to become prominent revolutionaries. Before returning to China in 1927, he spent a year studying in the Soviet Union, where Chiang Kai-shek's son Chiang Ching-kuo (蒋经国) was one of his classmates. Later, Deng proved an adept organiser and military commander, playing important roles during the war against Japan and the civil war. In 1952, he was appointed vice premier, a position in which he worked directly under Mao and Zhou Enlai. He served Mao loyally, helping to manage the campaign against intellectuals who had spoken out during the Hundred Flowers Campaign. He later expressed regret to his daughter for not doing more to restrain Mao during the Great Leap Forward. However, it was his push to change course after those policies had proven disastrous that led to the first of two purges he suffered at Mao's hands.

At the height of the Cultural Revolution, Deng was accused of being a 'capitalist roader' (走资派) and removed from all positions. He was sent down to Jiangxi, where he was put to work as a manual labourer in a tractor factory. Unlike Liu Shaoqi, Mao did not expel him from the Party. However, he and his family suffered greatly. His eldest son Deng Pufang (邓朴方) was left a paraplegic after being tortured by Red Guards and thrown from the window of a building at Peking University (北京大学).

Deng was rehabilitated in 1974 and, as Zhou Enlai's cancer drained his strength, Deng began to take over many of Zhou's responsibilities for foreign affairs. However, Deng's attempts to steer the country away from continuous revolution put him at odds with Mao again, and he was purged for a second time after Zhou Enlai's death in early 1976. In the wake of Mao's death and the arrest of the Gang of Four, Deng was again brought back to serve the country. This time, notwithstanding everything he and his family had been through, he was determined to do whatever was necessary to improve the lives of China's people. And, in view of his already advanced age, he was a man in a hurry.

By the end of 1978, although Hua Guofeng would remain Party Chairman until June 1981, Deng's promise of reform and opening up had won him sufficient backing to emerge as paramount leader. Notwithstanding popular support for steering the country away from the mistakes of the Mao years, however, Deng never enjoyed the unquestioning support that Mao had commanded. For one, the Party – and Deng himself – recognised the dangers of unchecked power. Deng would never attempt to recreate Mao's cult of personality around himself and, had he tried to do so, it is unlikely that other leaders would have tolerated it. For another, years of isolation and ideological indoctrination had left many in the Party and the population at large with a deeply ingrained mistrust of market forces and the outside world. Indeed, Communism has been likened to a religion[68] and, as much as Deng implored his countrymen to 'seek truth from the facts', letting go of long-held beliefs would not be easy and the road to reform was strewn with many obstacles.

The first of these was a shortage of talent. During the Cultural Revolution, formal education had been almost entirely halted and many qualified officials had been purged. In their place, poorly qualified officials had been elevated solely for having the 'right' class backgrounds. To implement reforms, Deng had to rehabilitate many older, more experienced officials and replace the unqualified ones. This had to be done without opening the door to mass retribution by returning cadres for all the injustices meted out during the strife of the prior decade. Those who had been denounced and abused would have to work alongside their accusers. At the same time, removing unqualified officials risked fierce resistance from those who stood to lose out. Successful reform required not only skilful implementation of new policies, but also the maintenance of general social order.

Second, China had fallen drastically behind technologically. Close neighbours such as Japan, South Korea, Taiwan and Singapore had relied heavily on US science, technology and education to modernise after WW2. By the late 1970s, these countries were setting a strong pace of economic growth. To catch up, China would have to rely on outside help, which in turn would require it to improve relations with countries that not long ago it had treated as enemies. And it was not sufficient just to open markets and import new technologies; for modernisation to take root, new institutions would have to be built and this could only be done gradually.

Third, China was desperately poor. At the time, even North Korea's industrial development made up a higher share of GDP than China's did.[69] The country still wasn't producing enough food to feed its population adequately. To pay for its modernisation, China would need to raise capital from overseas and begin to generate surpluses for investment.

Fourth, the country continued to face physical threats along its vast land borders. Relations with the Soviet Union remained hostile. Meanwhile, the Soviet-backed Vietnamese regime appeared to have hegemonic designs in Southeast Asia. So long as its territorial security remained threatened, military expenditures would continue to tie up considerable resources that were badly needed elsewhere.

Deng's approach to dealing with these challenges is best captured in his own words: 'it doesn't matter if the cat is black or white as long as it catches the mouse'.[70] He was a pragmatist first and foremost and had little time for ideology if it stood in the way of achieving his desired outcomes.

When Deng was brought back from exile in Jiangxi, he had enjoyed access to better information on the outside world, met with other world leaders and travelled to the US to address the UN General Assembly in 1974. This had given him a realistic insight into where China stood relative to other countries. Having been cut off from the rest of the world and subjected to constant propaganda, many in China, including its leadership, had little appreciation of how far behind the country had fallen. Deng encouraged members of the leadership to undertake study trips abroad to see for themselves and to bring back new ideas. Between the end of 1977 and early 1979, Deng himself made five overseas trips. The purpose of these was primarily diplomatic, but media coverage of

Deng's visits to places like Japan and the US gave China's population a glimpse of life in more advanced nations. This and trips undertaken by other officials helped bring home the need for China to pursue modernisation and reduced resistance to reforms.

In his posthumously published memoir, Zhao Ziyang (赵紫阳), then serving as Party Secretary of Sichuan (四川), recalled the profound impact that a visit to Europe in 1979 had on him. Maoist economic policy had emphasised 'self-reliance' at both the national and local levels. As a result, farmers in many areas had been forced to cultivate crops that were not suited to local conditions. In addition, huge resources had been expended on irrigation projects to render certain crops feasible. Visiting southern France, Zhao noticed that local conditions were dry and that almost no rain fell in summer, but local farmers had become wealthy by developing the wine industry. Similarly, in Greece he witnessed hills covered in olive trees and a flourishing olive oil industry. Zhao observed:

> *The farmers' living standards were high. Why were they able to do this? Because they were not living in an autarky, but instead relied on trade with the outside world and utilised their strengths to export their goods in exchange for what they needed.*[71]

Zhao became one of the most enthusiastic reformers. In Sichuan, he relaxed strict collectivisation in agriculture and allowed rural households to sell any surplus crops they produced. This incentivised farmers to produce more crops. Zhao's policy became widely adopted across the country and, by 1984, annual grain production had surpassed 400 million tons, compared to just 300 million tons in 1977. Per capita grain consumption over that period rose from 195 kilograms to 250 kilograms, while consumption of meat and eggs rose even more sharply.[72] For the first time in decades, China was able to feed itself adequately. Later, as premier, Zhao would champion even more far-reaching economic and political reforms.

Deng's overseas visits also generated goodwill and foreign commitments of support. Japan, in particular, offered enormous assistance to China. Between 1979 and 2007, the Japanese Overseas Economic Cooperation Fund gave grants to China of 2.54 trillion yen (around $25 billion), more than it allocated to any other country.[73] More importantly, it transferred significant technology and modern manufacturing methods, which allowed China to leap forward in heavy industries such as steel production. Of course, many countries offering support to China had calculated motives for doing so. China provided a counterbalance against the Soviet Union and, over time, promised a giant market for exports. However, Japan's assistance to China stretched far beyond such considerations and, to a great extent, were also a practical means of apologising for the harm it had inflicted over years of occupation and war.

Normalisation of relations with the US in 1979 provided a greater sense of security against the Soviet threat. Shortly afterwards, Deng launched a pre-emptive strike against Vietnam to check its territorial aspirations in the region. PLA forces invaded Vietnam and occupied five provincial capitals before declaring victory and withdrawing after 29 days. This military action was financially costly, and it is estimated that around 25,000 Chinese were killed and a further 37,000 wounded in the campaign.[74] However, the Singaporean statesman Lee Kuan Yew (李光耀) would later argue that 'it changed the history of East Asia. The Vietnamese learned that China would attack if they went beyond Cambodia on to Thailand. The Soviet Union did not want to be caught in a long drawn-out war in a remote corner of Asia'.[75] Having thus bolstered China's national security, Deng was able to divert greater resources towards domestic modernisation and development. According to official figures, China's military expenditures fell from 4.6 percent of gross national product (GNP) in 1979 to 1.4 percent of GNP by 1991.[76]

Notwithstanding the more favourable external conditions he had engineered, however, domestic reforms would continue to be contentious, and Deng would constantly need to balance the demands of the 'reformer cats' among his leadership with those of the 'conservative cats'.

★★★

As Deng Xiaoping was making his case for reforms to the Party leadership in 1978, a 34-year-old entrepreneur named Cheng Ho-ming (郑可明) crossed from Hong Kong's New Territories over to Shenzhen, a small Guangdong fishing village just bordering the British colony. Cheng had been running his own handbag factory in Hong Kong for a decade and had come to negotiate a deal with a state-run wig factory.

He found himself in a rural backwater. Local officials didn't have a car, so had arranged for him to travel to their office by bus.

The small factory in the Luohu (罗湖) district was reached by a single concrete road. To convert it into a production line suitable for making handbags for export around the world, Cheng would not only have to import manufacturing machinery, but also install power generators, as there was no steady supply of electricity at that time. Workers allocated by the government were paid a fixed monthly salary of 26 yuan (around $39 at the time), much lower than prevailing wages in Hong Kong. However, since the Shenzhen workers were paid the same irrespective of their performance, they had little incentive to work hard. For the first couple of years, most of them would disappear in the autumn to go and harvest crops, just as Cheng was rushing to meet production deadlines to deliver goods to overseas buyers.

When Cheng tried to raise productivity by introducing a new system to pay each worker based on how many pieces he or she produced, his government-appointed factory manager worried that this 'capitalist idea' may contravene the law. Undeterred, Cheng eventually convinced him by promising to go to jail with him if the authorities took action against the factory. Once the workers saw their wages could rise substantially if they worked harder, their attitudes changed. Suddenly, they were rushing to resume work straight after lunch and productivity rose rapidly.[77]

In certain ways, the challenges Cheng faced reflected conflicts within China's leadership. At a meeting with military leaders in Guangdong in November 1977, Deng was briefed on the problem of young men trying to escape across the border from Mainland China into Hong Kong. To deter them, a barbed-wire fence was erected along the 20-mile land border and troops were deployed to patrol the area. Those caught were sent to detention centres. Still, tens of thousands were risking their lives each year by attempting to run or swim across the border. After listening to the briefing, Deng said frankly that the problem had arisen because of the gulf between living standards on either side of the border; the way to solve it was to improve the livelihoods of those on the Chinese side.[78] Deng had no fixed view as to how this should be achieved and was open to experimenting with market mechanisms. However, this challenged the deeply held views of conservative state planners.

Chief among these was Party elder Chen Yun (陈云). Chen had joined the CCP in the 1920s in Shanghai, where he played a prominent role as a labour unionist. Although a year younger than Deng, for more than two decades from when he was appointed a member of the Central Committee, he had ranked much higher in the Party than Deng. In the 1950s, he took on a leading role in economic planning and was responsible for the First Five-Year Plan, which had seen successful results. After Mao derailed the planning apparatus during the Great Leap Forward and destroyed the economy, Chen led the recovery effort in the early 1960s. Chen was therefore held in high esteem and his experience in economic policy far outweighed that of Deng, whose experience was primarily in foreign policy and military affairs.

Chen had no apparent leadership aspirations and had been a key supporter of Deng's elevation to paramount leader in 1978. However, the two men held very different views as to the approach to and extent of reforms. Where Deng was bold, Chen tended to be cautious. In Chen's view, the market should operate like a bird in a cage; a balance should be found between setting the bird free and choking it with an overly restrictive central plan. As a member of the Standing Committee of the Politburo, Chen acted to restrain the pace of reforms and continued to exert a strong influence on policy after his official retirement.

Deng tended to avoid direct confrontation and sought to counterbalance the influence of Chen Yun and other conservatives by bringing two committed reformers – Hu Yaobang (胡耀邦) and Zhao Ziyang – into the core leadership.

Hu Yaobang had been one of the youngest participants in the Long March. His career had followed that of Deng, who became a mentor to him. Hu served as the first secretary of the Communist Youth League from 1952 until 1966. He was purged during the Cultural Revolution and then brought back to Beijing when Deng first returned to power. Hu took on the task of rallying support from scientists and intellectuals, who were needed for China's modernisation, and was tireless in his efforts to rehabilitate those who had been falsely accused during the Cultural Revolution. This earned him the admiration and loyalty of many. Purged again along with Deng in 1976, he was brought back once more after Mao's death and elevated by Deng to become General Secretary of the Party in 1982.

Zhao Ziyang had risen up as a provincial leader. After the civil war, he had served in Guangdong province, where he rose to become provincial secretary in 1965. Since Communist organisations operating in Hong Kong reported into Guangdong, he became familiar with the market climate in Hong Kong and gained a deep understanding of foreign business. In 1975, Deng selected Zhao to be party secretary of Sichuan, China's most populous province from which Deng himself hailed. There, Zhao applied his keen analytic abilities and grasp of economics to experiment with new approaches to industrial and agricultural issues. Seeing the success of his reforms, Deng persuaded him to come to Beijing to serve as premier.

The reformers clashed with the conservatives on a wide range of issues, over which most came to be fought out in the battleground of Guangdong. To modernise, the province needed capital, which China was short of. To attract foreign investment, Guangdong needed greater autonomy and flexibility than the rigid central planning system allowed. The introduction of foreign capital itself was a controversial issue, since foreign capitalists were closely associated with the imperialist oppression to which China had been subjected over the century prior to 1949. Central planners also worried that freedoms granted to Guangdong would interfere with overall national plans. At a party work conference in Beijing in 1979, then provincial party secretary Xi Zhongxun (习仲勋, father of President Xi Jinping) argued pointedly against China's excessive centralisation of authority and – quite likely touching a nerve – went so far as to say that, if Guangdong were a separate country, its economy could take off within several years.[79] The elder Xi succeeded in getting greater flexibility.

Guangdong, along with neighbouring Fujian province, was granted special powers to adopt measures to attract foreign capital, technology and management practices to produce goods for export. In particular, four areas were designated for additional government support, which Deng suggested should be named 'special zones' (特区). Three were located in Guangdong – Shenzhen, Zhuhai (珠海) across the border from Macau, and Shantou (汕头) – and one – Xiamen – was located in Fujian. Later, at Chen Yun's insistence, the term 'special zones' was changed to 'special economic zones' (SEZ, 经济特区) to make clear that political experiments were not to be carried out.

Although the conservatives were willing to accept some degree of experimentation with market forces, they remained on guard against the wholesale introduction of capitalism. One other prime candidate to be designated an SEZ was Shanghai, which had been Asia's most cosmopolitan financial centre in the 1930s. However, Chen Yun, remembering his time there in the 1920s, opposed this on the basis that the Shanghainese were too susceptible to the 'spiritual pollution' of foreign capitalists.[80] Shanghai was not opened to foreign investment until 1984, when China opened up a further 14 coastal cities. The conservatives were also instrumental in preventing China from becoming overly dependent on foreign finance. While China received numerous offers of foreign loans that could have helped accelerate its development in the 1980s, Chen cautioned that the country should avoid getting into debt and should accumulate capital before undertaking projects.[81] Deng deferred to Chen on these points.

Nevertheless, investment poured into Guangdong from Chinese living overseas. Around two-thirds of foreign direct investment (FDI) into China between 1979 and 1995 came from, or at least via, Hong Kong.[82] More than money, however, Hong Kong businessmen like Cheng Ho-ming and other overseas Chinese brought technology, management expertise and a new way of thinking that powered Guangdong's modernisation. Foreign investment was matched by the inflow of migrant labour. While there is no exact figure available, it has been estimated that, by 1992, as many as 100 million migrants had made their way from rural villages all over the country to work in the factories that sprang up in Guangdong's coastal regions.[83] As Xi Zhongxun had predicted, with greater decentralisation and freedom to adopt market mechanisms, the province took off. Within three decades of opening up, China's exports had grown from less than $10 billion per annum in 1978 to over $1 trillion.[84] Guangdong's share of these exports during this period rose from 12 percent in 1979 to over one-third.[85]

Liberalisations brought problems as well. The requirement for foreign investors to obtain multiple licenses and approvals opened the door to corruption by poorly paid local officials. To a certain extent, market forces served to check some corrupt practices, as localities that set up a 'one-stop shop' system to simplify approvals for investors were favoured over ones with complex bureaucratic processes. Nevertheless, corruption was not eliminated and reformers, more focused on the overall direction of modernisations, did not aggressively clamp down. As Guangdong and Fujian grew faster, they could afford to pay higher prices. Goods intended for other provinces therefore began to be diverted there instead. Not only did this cause envy among officials elsewhere and attract the ire of the planners, it also threatened inflation.

In the rush to pursue modernisation after 1978, the reformers often neglected the realities of China's financial circumstances. Contracts were signed with foreign companies to supply technology without concern for China's ability to pay. In 1980, the budget deficit stood at 11.7 percent of revenue.[86] Chen Yun feared a repeat of the mistakes of the Great Leap Forward and emphasised the need for balanced development and to give priority to feeding China's huge population. He succeeded in pushing for 'readjustment' (调整) in economic policies to restrain uncontrolled growth. By 1982, the budget deficit had fallen to 2.6 percent of revenues and foreign currency reserves had more than tripled to $14 billion. That year, the grain harvest also rose 9 percent to 354 million tons.[87] Now Deng grew impatient and pushed for higher growth, but the planners opposed this.

Seeking to avoid an open split, Deng preferred not to debate the issue and simply leaned on Hu and Zhao to push ahead regardless. Zhao established a number of think tanks to study industrial and economic issues and consulted widely with foreign experts. He was careful to consult with Chen Yun on policy matters and, through analysis and experimentation, made progress on expanding the role of private enterprise. It was difficult for the planners to resist this, given the need to generate employment for young people moving back to urban areas from the countryside. By 1994, 'township and village enterprises' (TVEs, 乡镇企业) had captured 42 percent of industrial production and were employing well over 100 million people. Meanwhile, Hu toured the country offering encouragement to local officials, who frequently proved adept at finding ways to circumvent the central planners' restrictions.

Economic growth and the changes that accompanied it were on the whole beneficial, but they also created tensions. As the role of private enterprise increased, a class of newly wealthy businesspeople began to emerge. Their conspicuous consumption irked government workers and others on fixed salaries, who lost out as the prices of staple goods rose. Profiteering officials parlayed their positions and personal contacts to line their own pockets or those of their family members. Meanwhile, market forces were threatening the 'iron rice bowls' of employees of SOEs, which provided not only employment, but housing, medical care and schooling for workers' children. Without a national social security system, to lose a job was to lose everything.

When Deng took the decision in 1988 to push ahead with further market reforms by rolling back price controls on more goods, he unintentionally unleashed a spike in inflation that caused a general panic. In July, following the removal of price controls on alcohol and tobacco, prices on those products jumped by over 200 percent.[88] Official figures, which most likely understate the actual changes, showed consumer prices in Beijing rising by more than 30 percent between 1987 and 1988. Families who had saved for their children's education and old age saw the value of those savings drastically eroded. A bank run ensued, as the anticipation of further rollbacks of price controls caused people to withdraw their money to buy commodities before prices went up even more. This compounded the inflationary problem.[89] The stage was thus set for a wave of unrest that would threaten to topple the entire regime.

Crackdown

The underlying causes and series of events that led up to the bloody crackdown on student demonstrators in Tiananmen Square on 4 June 1989 were not just rooted in economic issues. Ideological and political factors played a major role. The personal histories of, and relationships between, the group of men at the centre of China's power structure were also critical factors. The protests that erupted following Hu Yaobang's death on 15 April forced the crystallisation of fundamental differences within the leadership.

Hu had long attracted the ire of the conservatives due to his embrace of liberalism. His dedication to the country and the CCP was unquestioned, but he had been appalled by the Cultural Revolution. When asked which of Mao Zedong's thoughts had application to China's efforts to modernise its economy, he was reported to have answered: 'I think, none'.[90] After he rehabilitated many intellectuals who had been purged during Mao's lifetime, he encouraged them to speak out on controversial issues and, in return, enjoyed their fierce and loyal support. Having had little experience in implementing policy, he was seen by some as lacking in pragmatism, and detractors considered his popularity to derive from his excessive permissiveness towards intellectuals. Eventually, his tolerance for critics of the regime and failure to crack down on student protests that broke out in Hefei (合肥), Shanghai and Nanjing in 1986 led even Deng to question his judgement and he was side-lined and forced to stand down as Party Secretary in 1987. Fearful that Hu's ouster might cause a backlash due to his popularity, however, it was deemed insufficient just to remove him from power; he was also subjected to attacks in the media and harsh criticisms at a series of 'party life meetings' from 10 to 15 January. Unprepared for such public humiliation after having toiled selflessly for the Party for so many years, Hu ended his career utterly dejected. He was permitted to remain on the Politburo but died two years later after suffering a heart attack during a Politburo meeting.

Zhao Ziyang was elevated to Party Secretary to replace Hu. Li Peng (李鹏), an engineer who had been raised by Zhou Enlai and his wife after his father had been executed by the Nationalists, was promoted to Premier. In this position, Li Peng had power over economic policy and, in this, he was aligned with Chen Yun. The relationship between Li and Zhao, the committed reformer, was therefore not an easy one. Meanwhile, though these two men were nominally in charge, Party elders continued to exert a high degree of influence behind the scenes.

As Zhao pursued economic reforms during his premiership, he became increasingly convinced of the need for deeper political reforms. He understood that, as the old planned economy system weakened and disintegrated, excessive centralisation of power created greater structural opportunities for corruption. In his memoirs, he recorded:

> *Take power-money exchanges as an example. Now that the economy is freer, with commodities and markets, many enterprises and entities are subject to market competition. But power is still monopolised in the hands of government agencies. In other words, economic reform has not completed the shift to free markets. Many residual elements from the era of the planned economy still exist. If certain participants in the market competition get favours from*

agencies with power, they can gain huge profits. . . Under these conditions, power and money are linked and exchanged so that some businesses profit from unequal competitive conditions. . . The only solution for resolving this issue is continued deepening of reform to separate government and enterprise, to hand down powers currently held by the government to administrators of the industries, and to resolve the issue of monopolies or the overconcentration of power. Doing this limits the environment for power-money exchanges.[91]

Zhao's extensive studies of other countries' systems, including those of many emerging markets in Asia, also convinced him that, to rein in official corruption and sustain the country's development over the long term, there needed to be an effective check on the power of the Party:

Another important issue – in fact the most essential – is the independence of the judiciary and rule of law. If there is no independent enforcement of law, and the political party in power is able to intervene, then corruption can never effectively be resolved.[92]

Deng tasked Zhao Ziyang with undertaking a study on political reforms in 1986. Zhao formed a study group on the matter and, following a year-long review, he presented Deng with a draft report, which called for broader freedoms and democratic practices. However, Deng rejected the study group's conclusions. Like Prince Gong and Li Hongzhang in the late 19th century, Deng's focus was on economic and technological modernisation and he was willing to concede political reforms only to the extent that they served those objectives. Deng was particularly opposed to a multi-party political system and the separation of powers, seeing the CCP's monopoly on power as a key advantage, since it avoided the need for extensive debate and process, and decisions could be implemented more efficiently than in a democratic system.[93]

Zhao did not push further. Having spearheaded economic reforms, even though he had taken care to consult with Chen Yun on policy, Zhao had eventually alienated Chen and the conservatives. Further, as he had risen up through provincial government, he had not previously been immersed in the intricate world of Beijing politics. His children had not grown up playing with the children of other high officials and attending the same schools. Not being a member of the Beijing 'old-boy club' and without Deng's support, he would have struggled to get support from other key political decision makers whose hold on power would have been threatened by democratic reforms. In any case, it would not be long before events took over.

★★★

A day after Hu Yaobang's death, Peking University students marched from their campus to lay wreaths at the foot of the Monument to the People's Heroes in the centre of Tiananmen Square. Over the following days, the mourning evolved into protests calling for greater freedom and democracy, and denouncing corruption by party leaders and their families. More than democratic government, they were fighting for greater freedoms for themselves, hopes for which had seemed to be dashed with Hu Yaobang's removal from power. In 1989, graduates were not even free to choose their own careers. Given a shortage of trained graduates in the government and key industries, the government still assigned jobs to graduates based on reports written on each of them by 'political guides' who lived on campus. These political guides, who were often far less educated than the students, thus had enormous influence over their futures. Some political guides flaunted their authority and students generally resented having to worry constantly about pleasing them.

Zhao left on a scheduled trip to North Korea on 23 April, the day after Hu Yaobang's funeral. During his absence, at Li Peng's urging Deng Xiaoping authorised the publication of a stern editorial in the *People's Daily* on 26 April warning the students of the dangers if they did not cease the protests. This was a grave miscalculation. The editorial only served to further inflame the students. On his return from North Korea, Zhao could see that the editorial made it harder to de-escalate the situation and tried to have it retracted, even offering to take the blame for it himself. Over the following weeks, senior leaders felt besieged and were in serious disagreement among themselves about how to deal with the protests. On a visit by Mikhail Gorbachev to Beijing from 15 to 18 May for a long-awaited normalisation in Sino-Soviet relations, the students' occupation of Tiananmen Square meant that a welcoming ceremony at the Great Hall of the People had to be moved to the airport. During the visit, some students also decided to begin a hunger strike. This was a serious humiliation for the leadership.

As soon as Gorbachev had departed, Deng took the decision to impose martial law in the city. Zhao, unwilling to carry this out, tendered his resignation. In the early morning of 18 May, Zhao made his way to Tiananmen Square, where he tearfully tried to persuade the students to give up their strike. That was the last time he was seen in public. Zhao would spend the rest of his life under house arrest. The following day, 50,000 PLA troops were sent into the city.

For a nail-biting fortnight, it was unclear what the outcome would be, as sympathetic Beijing residents and even some of the soldiers rallied around the students. However, in the afternoon on 3 June, Deng gave the order to crack down. Tiananmen Square was cleared in the early hours of 4 June. Members of the student movement who survived were rounded up and imprisoned or escaped into exile.

There is no doubt that the Party leadership had made a long series of missteps in the run-up to the tragedy of 4 June 1989. In retrospect, Chen Yun's caution over the transition from government-set prices to market pricing had been justified, as high inflation brought about by the sudden withdrawal of price controls contributed significantly to underlying social tensions. Failure to rein in corruption by high officials and their families also generated popular dissatisfaction with the government. Once the protests started, the leadership's unwillingness to brook dissent had made rapprochement with the students impossible. As much as Deng ordered the crackdown to maintain the Party's hold on power though, he also had a genuine fear that the CCP's collapse would plunge the country back into the sort of chaos and disorder experienced during the Cultural Revolution.

It is unknowable what would have transpired if Deng had chosen a different course; however, the disintegration of the Soviet Union two years later perhaps offers some clues. In the years that followed, Russia and its former republics experienced economic turmoil, lawlessness and dangerous instability, the reverberations of which persist to this day.

Wrapped up in the excitement of their movement, the students did not really have a full appreciation of the consequences of their actions on the country more broadly. By posing a challenge to the Party's authority, they inadvertently played into the hands of those in the leadership who opposed the trend towards liberalisation. Moreover, they forced a showdown between those in the leadership who supported further political reforms and those who stood against them. The reformers ultimately lost out, thereby halting the gradual trend towards greater political freedoms in its tracks.

The images of the harsh suppression by the PLA of unarmed students broadcast around the world by the international media, who had descended on Beijing to cover Gorbachev's momentous visit, ensured that China was ostracised in the international community and subjected to a range of sanctions. However, the setback domestically was far more significant. In the aftermath of the Tiananmen incident, the ranks of the reformers in the leadership were decimated and the conservatives gained the upper hand. Political liberalisations would be reversed and even the fate of economic reforms teetered on the brink.

Journeys to the South

When student demonstrations convulsed Shanghai in 1986, the city's then little known mayor visited his *alma mater*, Jiaotong University (交通大学). There, he saw wallposters quoting Abraham Lincoln's words: 'All men are created equal'. He stood up in front of the students and began to speak. The crowd paid little attention and some began to heckle him, so instead he invited some of the students to come up to the podium to express their views. He listened, then proceeded to recite Lincoln's Gettysburg Address in full, from memory, and in English. The students were impressed. Having captured their attention, he went on to tell them that they only knew Lincoln's speech 'in words', but not its historical context. He explained that Chinese society was very different to that of America; Lincoln's address was about abolishing black slavery, whereas the Chinese revolution was intended to end class exploitation.

The students returned to their studies and, over the following days, the Shanghai municipal authorities decreed that, going forward, all public demonstrations would require a permit. The student demonstrations gradually petered out without incident. The mayor, Jiang Zemin (江泽民), earned admiration among top leaders in Beijing for his ability to quell the demonstrations without conflict and, in 1987, was elevated to Party Secretary of Shanghai and appointed to the CCP's Politburo.

Following Zhao Ziyang's ouster in 1989, Jiang emerged as the compromise candidate between Deng Xiaoping and Chen Yun to lead the Party. Having graduated with a degree in electrical engineering in 1947, Jiang had climbed slowly through the industrial bureaucracy. Although he would later exceed all early expectations as a leader, at the time he succeeded Zhao as Party Secretary Jiang lacked any significant power base. He was therefore obligated to hew closely to a compromise path between the reformers and the central planners.

International outrage at the Tiananmen crackdown further complicated matters. Immediately following the incident, the US suspended high-level government exchanges; halted military cooperation; banned the sale of any military or dual-use technologies to China; and announced its opposition to the PRC joining the World Bank and other international institutions. Similar sanctions were imposed by the European Community, Japan, Australia and New Zealand. However, President George H.W. Bush, who had first met Deng Xiaoping in 1975 when he headed America's Liaison Office in China, understood that, notwithstanding domestic political pressures for tough action, good Sino-US relations were important to America's broader strategic interests. Therefore, he wrote to Deng on 21 June to explain the US response:

> I ask you as well to remember the principles on which my young country was founded. Those principles are democracy and freedom — freedom of speech, freedom of assemblage, freedom from arbitrary authority. It is reverence for those principles which inevitably affects the way Americans view and react to events in other countries. It is not a reaction of arrogance or of a desire to force others to our beliefs but of simple faith in the enduring value of those principles and their universal applicability.[94]

Bush worked hard to keep open channels of diplomatic communication at considerable political risk to himself. When the question of international sanctions on China was discussed at a G-7 meeting in France a month after the Tiananmen incident, Bush and Japanese prime minister Sōsuke Uno argued for milder sanctions. Still, international confidence in China was badly damaged. That year, its GDP growth rate fell from 11.2 percent the year prior to 4.2 percent.[95]

As Communist regimes across Eastern Europe began to collapse one after another, it was not entirely clear that the CCP would survive.

In the face of continuing high inflation, the government pursued fiscal austerity. Planners attributed the social unrest to the excessive opening of markets and a loss of discipline. Greater controls were therefore introduced over local governments and enterprises.

Deng saw things differently. He believed that, unless high economic growth was maintained, the Party's rule would be in danger. He shared this view with Jiang and Li Peng, but the conservative economic policies prevailed. Having resigned all of his official posts in the autumn of 1989, Deng's influence was waning. However, fearing that the new leadership's direction was likely to put the fruits of earlier reforms in jeopardy, he was determined to change their course. To do so, he needed to rally political support.

The wealthier coastal regions were the prime losers in the central government's drive to rein in growth and it was to these provinces that Deng turned. He was aware that Shanghai officials, proud of the city's history as Asia's preeminent financial centre in the 1930s, had fumed at being held back in the early 1980s, when Guangdong and Fujian were allowed to open up. He also knew that they were eager to develop Pudong (浦东), the 188 square mile area across the Huangpu River (黄浦江) from the grand buildings erected by foreign merchants in the early 19th century along the city's famous Bund (外滩). In early 1991, Deng took a 'holiday' to Shanghai, where he met with Zhu Rongji, Jiang's successor as local party secretary, and toured the city's factories. During the visit, he was vocal in emphasising the importance of developing Pudong and turning Shanghai into an international financial centre once again.

However, conservative control of the Central Propaganda Department meant that his comments were not reported in the media. Frustrated, Deng took to penning a series of editorials under a pseudonym, which Zhu Rongji arranged to be published in the *Liberation Daily* (解放日报), Shanghai's main newspaper. Discarding his usual restraint, Deng's editorials attacked the conservatives directly, stating that 'we must prevent lapsing into certain "new thought rigidity"' and urging officials to 'abandon any conservative, rigid, and isolated perspectives'. Officials in Guangdong, Tianjin, Hebei (河北) and Jiangxi swiftly had their local newspapers echo the ideas expressed in these editorials.[96] Deng also began to make clear that, unless Jiang Zemin promoted more rapid growth and opening up, he would back other party leaders at the 14th Party Congress in 1992.

Zhu Rongji had taken a gamble in having Deng's editorials published, but his bravery paid off. Recognising his talent and commitment to reform, Deng ordered Li Peng to bring Zhu to Beijing as a vice premier. From there, he would have a meteoric rise, eventually replacing Li as premier in 1997.

Deng was not done yet, however. On 17 January 1992, he and his family – 17 people in all – set off from Beijing by train on a 'family holiday'. Arrangements for the trip had been made by the PLA and none of the central leadership were informed. His first stop was in Wuhan (武汉), where the revolution that toppled Qing rule had begun in 1911. Deng was greeted by local officials on the platform of the Wuchang train station. During his 20-minute stop there, he told officials that 'You should do more and talk less' and warned that 'Whoever is against reform must leave office'.[97] Jiang appeared to get the message. Two days later, he told fellow officials that China should speed up reforms and revive the open-door policy.

On the morning of 19 January, Deng arrived in Guangzhou, where local officials joined him for an 11-day inspection of Shenzhen and Zhuhai, two of the original and most vibrant SEZs. Everywhere in Guangdong, Deng was greeted by adoring crowds, who were grateful for the improved livelihoods that his reforms had delivered to them. Throughout his tour, Deng lavished praise on local officials for their achievements and, in private conversations with them, railed against conservative and leftist policies.

Word got out and journalists from Hong Kong poured across the border to cover Deng's trip. Media around the country were also eager to report on his journey and it became impossible for Beijing propaganda officials to stop the news getting out. Popular support for continued reforms piled pressure on Jiang and the rest of the leadership.

Deng's Southern Tour marked a key turning point. Even before Deng had returned to Beijing, Jiang began publicly stating his support for Deng's call for further reforms. By April, even Chen Yun had offered his backing for Shanghai officials' plan to develop Pudong. By the summer, local officials were permitted to increase their rates of investment and expand foreign trade. Further, the coastal experiments were extended inland. At the 14th Party Congress in October, Jiang set a course for China to build a 'socialist market economy' and substantially raised the target for economic growth.

Deng's last major political act had rescued his reforms and perhaps even the fate of the CCP. Thereafter, age and failing health forced him to retreat from public life. However, the path of growth and reform carved out by China's next generation of leaders would be radically different to that which Hu Yaobang and Zhao Ziyang had pursued during the 1980s.

A New Path

When reformers embarked upon the path of reform and opening up in 1978, they followed two broad strategies. First, they decentralised authority for economic decision making; initially to provincial officials, then to TVEs and, finally, down to the level of the individual. Second, they relied on fiscal and monetary expansion to invest in new technologies and industrial development. By and large, these strategies were highly successful in unleashing market forces, creating financial incentives and generating economic growth. However, they also generated high inflation that threatened social stability.

Throughout the 1980s, whenever inflation jumped, the conservatives gained the upper hand and called for retrenchment. When inflation declined, the reformers were back in the driving seat. The planners saw greater decentralisation as a particular threat, since the provincial governments, ever eager to accelerate growth in their own regions, were constantly finding new ways of raising capital for investment. This, in turn, weakened the planners' ability to regulate inflation through control over the supply of capital. Even though planners had sought to restrict economic liberalisation to designated provinces and SEZs, within a large national economy it was impossible to prevent inflation 'leaking out' from those regions into others. By increasing regional disparities and opening up avenues for corruption, the two-tier system exacerbated social tensions.

Zhao Ziyang had publicly identified the need to drive greater efficiency in China's economy as early as 1981.[98] To generate *real* economic growth – in other words, growth in excess of inflation – China needed to raise its productivity. However, in 1994, the country still had over 100,000 SOEs,[99] whose chronic inefficiency was a huge drag on the system. As mayor of Shanghai from 1988 until his appointment as vice premier in 1991, Zhu Rongji had extensive experience of the SOE problem and he had shown a steely determination in trying to tackle it.

Hailing from Changsha (长沙) in Hunan province, Zhu was born into a family of wealthy landowners descended directly from the founder of the Ming Dynasty Zhu Yuanzhang. He graduated from Tsinghua University in electrical engineering in 1949 and joined the CCP the same year. During the Hundred Flowers Campaign, he had criticised Mao's economic policies, for which he was prosecuted and thrown out of the Party. During the Cultural Revolution, he was exiled to the countryside and worked as a manual labourer. He was eventually rehabilitated under policies initiated by Deng Xiaoping and, in 1980, volunteered to accompany World Bank experts who Deng had invited in to study the Chinese economy. This exposed him to Western economic thinking and policies. As he rose slowly through the bureaucracy, Zhu was notable for his bluntness and willingness to speak his mind. This did not always endear him to his colleagues, but he ultimately earned respect for delivering results. Considered by Deng to be the only person among the top leadership who 'understands economics',[100] Zhu would come to be dubbed by foreign media as China's 'Economic Czar'.

When he arrived in Beijing in 1991, Zhu was handed one of the toughest financial challenges at the time to solve: that of the triangular debt problem. Fierce competition with TVEs, combined with their own latent inefficiency, was driving mounting losses at large and medium-sized SOEs. Interconnected relationships between the SOEs meant that, as failing players were forced to delay payments to suppliers, SOEs' debts to each other, or 'triangular debts', were ballooning. By 1991, the total triangular debt outstanding had reached 300 billion yuan, or 16 percent of GDP.[101] This enormous debt load meant that the entire SOE sector was facing chronic cash shortages and remittances to the central coffer were falling.

Others had tried and failed to solve the problem. However, Zhu grasped that, given the state's ownership of all these companies and the banks, the debt was ultimately all owed by the state to itself. The issue that he had to address therefore was how to unentangle the debts between the SOEs, so that the failing ones would not drag down the viable enterprises with them.

Zhu mandated that the state banks inject a whopping 80 billion yuan of loans into the largest debtors, then ordered the recipients of those funds to repay debts they owed to other SOEs. The capital injected into the SOEs allowed not only the direct recipients of those funds to repay money that they owed, but also enabled their creditors to repay other SOEs down the chain to which they owed money. This meant that, by 1992, the 80 billion yuan injected had helped clear 380 billion yuan in triangular debt, or 4.75 times the actual amount of capital injected.[102] This result impressed other top leaders. However, Zhu was only just getting started.

Naturally, forcing the banks to lend money to over-indebted SOEs created a lot of bad loans. In 1991 alone, the bad debt in the state banks jumped by 42 percent from 70 billion yuan to 100 billion yuan.[103] It was therefore to the banking sector and control over monetary policy that Zhu turned next.

Li Peng suffered a heart attack and was hospitalised in April 1993. This made Zhu acting premier, giving him significantly more leeway than he had enjoyed previously. At a meeting of economic policymakers in the middle of that year, he stunned attendees by removing the Governor of the PBOC Li Guixian (李贵鲜) and replacing him with himself, thereby making Zhu simultaneously vice premier and governor of the central bank. He then introduced 'Sixteen Measures' (十六条) as macroeconomic levers to control the economy.[104] Flying in the face of both market and socialist economic theory, these included a range of monetary, fiscal and administrative measures, including the reintroduction of selective price controls, to control inflation and regulate economic development.

As opposed to the decentralisation policies of Hu Yaobang and Zhao Ziyang, what this amounted to was a massive *recentralisation* of economic policy control. Tax reforms were introduced to increase the government's tax receipts, which had fallen from around 30 percent of GDP in 1978 to just 10 percent.[105] The reforms unified and simplified the tax system. Responsibility for the collection of taxes was transferred to the central government and, in return, local governments were granted a higher share of revenues. Notwithstanding the lower share taken by Beijing, improved efficiency in tax collection resulted in a substantial increase in total tax revenues and the absolute amount received by the central government. Further, control over local branches of the state banks and the PBOC, which had hitherto rested with local Party committees, was transferred to the central government. Predictably, Zhu's Sixteen Measures were met with stiff local resistance. In 1994, inflation shot up to 22 percent, even higher than the previous peak in 1988 of 19 percent. However, over time, the Sixteen Measures proved successful in reining in inflation, which fell to 8.3 percent in 1996 and further down to 2.8 percent in 1997.[106]

When the Asian Financial Crisis struck in 1997, China was relatively unscathed. Part of the credit for this goes to Chen Yun's resistance to incurring large foreign debts at the outset of economic reforms in the 1980s, which meant that China did not find itself at the mercy of foreign creditors. It also reflected the fact that China's capital markets were relatively undeveloped and, thus, foreign investment had largely taken the form of FDI. In contrast to the massive capital flight from securities markets in countries around the region, China suffered no major withdrawal of foreign investment. Zhu Rongji also resisted devaluing the renminbi, earning China substantial credit for helping prevent further regional financial instability.

After his appointment as premier in 1997, Zhu further accelerated the pace of SOE and banking reforms. This is discussed in further detail in Chapter 5. However, it was negotiations over China's accession to the WTO that took primacy in Sino–US diplomatic dialogue.

★★★

In his 1992 election campaign against George H. W. Bush, Bill Clinton lambasted the President for maintaining cooperative relations with Beijing after Tiananmen and vowed that, if elected, he would never 'coddle the butchers of Beijing'.[107] However, after stumbling over human rights issues during his first few years in office, the Clinton Administration ultimately concluded that it was in both countries' interests to deepen engagement. The mechanism through which that would take place was via Chinese membership of the new WTO.

China had, in fact, been a founder member of the WTO's predecessor, the GATT. However, the Nationalist government took the membership with it when it retreated to Taiwan in 1949. Although Taiwan was later forced to give this up, China had to apply to re-join. It did so formally in 1986. At that time though, it was considered that China's domestic market reforms had not gone far enough to be compatible with the GATT. Following Tiananmen, the US had imposed further obstacles to China joining and began requiring an annual renewal of its MFN clause for China. Had China already been a member of the GATT, it would have been difficult for the US to continue with the annual MFN pressures on China, since this would have been against the principle of reciprocity and non-discrimination of the multilateral agreement. Therefore, Zhu was able to persuade others in the leadership of the importance of participation in such international bodies. Zhu also realised that the membership requirements of the GATT and other international institutions could be used to help overcome domestic opposition to further reform and development.[108]

In 1995, the GATT was replaced by the WTO. By that time, China's case for membership was also looking a lot stronger. Between 1980 and 1995, the government's control of production and trade had fallen significantly. The share of industrial output under state control fell from 80 percent to 47 percent, state-controlled exports fell from 100 percent to 57 percent, and state-controlled imports fell from 99.8 percent to 44.8 percent.[109]

Negotiations over China's entry into the WTO were primarily conducted with the US Trade Representative and did not always proceed smoothly, not least because of political conflicts that arose over the span of the discussions. A US decision to allow Taiwanese President Lee Teng-hui (李登辉) to give a commencement speech at Cornell University in 1995 drew anger from China, which responded by conducting military exercises in the Taiwan Strait that year and in early 1996. The US bombing of the Chinese embassy in Belgrade in May 1999 caused further tensions.

At stake in the negotiations were also significant national economic interests. While China represented a potentially huge market for US companies, it was still far from being a market-oriented economy and its size meant that its greater integration into global trade threatened considerable impact on the economies of existing WTO members. Protesters against the WTO caused violent disruption at the organisation's

December 1999 meeting in Seattle. Union leaders argued fiercely against China's accession on labour and human rights grounds. The US therefore pushed for China's market to be opened as wide as possible. Meanwhile, China's relatively underdeveloped and uncompetitive domestic enterprises risked being overwhelmed by foreign competition. China's official urban unemployment rate in 1997 was 3.1 percent (counting 'registered unemployed' only), but the true figure was closer to 7 percent[110] and mass displacement of Chinese workers by an influx of foreign goods and services would have threatened social stability. In fact, Zhu Rongji found himself heavily criticised for making too many concessions to join the WTO.

Ultimately, a deal was reached under which China agreed to eliminate or heavily reduce tariffs on imported goods. Restrictions on foreign companies offering services in China were gradually phased out. In financial services, for example, foreign institutions were immediately allowed to begin offering foreign currency services in China upon its accession; local currency services to institutions were subsequently opened up in 2003, followed by an opening of local currency services to all Chinese clients in 2006. Export subsidies were curtailed and protections for intellectual property were introduced. Safeguards for China's trading partners were also agreed to, including anti-dumping provisions and rights for countries to impose import restrictions where it could be demonstrated that serious injury might be caused to domestic firms producing similar products.

Even before China's formal entry to the WTO in 2001, FDI surged on anticipation of accession. When Zhu Rongji handed over to his successor in 2003, the country was boasting double-digit GDP growth that continued until the GFC in 2008. Exports also surged. Having fluctuated at between -2 to +2 percent of GDP in the 20 years prior to accession, exports reached 10 percent of GDP by 2007, aided by an undervalued currency.[111] This imbalance has, however, gradually fallen back in subsequent years, as the currency has been allowed to appreciate and China's economy has matured. Also noteworthy is that, while China's exports in goods surged, its trade deficit in services ballooned from $6.4 billion in 2001 to $107 billion in 2020.[112]

Regarding accusations of China having manipulated the WTO's rules to drive growth at the expense of other countries, there is certainly some merit in these. For example, in December 2002, the PBOC issued a regulation that limited banks' borrowing in the interbank market to 40 percent of domestic deposits. While this applied to all banks equally, whether domestic or foreign, foreign banks in China have much lower local deposits than domestic banks. Thus, this rule gave Chinese banks a significant competitive advantage over foreign banks operating in the country while being perfectly in accordance with WTO rules.[113] Ironically, China had learned from its experience of the unequal treaties and was now making use of international laws and regulations to its advantage. Nevertheless, to a great degree, China's growth following WTO accession can be attributed to the reforms that it underwent in order to gain entry.

Zhu Rongji's path of reform was pioneering. Drawing on elements of both a market and a planned economy, he pursued a highly pragmatic approach that was tailored for China's stage of development at the time. However, he was also required to face down enormous conservative opposition and vested interests. Referring to his fight against systemic corruption and rent-seeking activities, he famously said: 'Prepare for me 100 coffins, 99 of them for corrupt officials and the last one for myself'.[114] As discussed in Chapter 5, notwithstanding his considerable achievements, he also left behind a lot of unfinished business when he stepped down at the end of his term. The job of carrying forward his reforms was therefore left for China's next generation of leaders.

The Bird's Nest

The crowds were hushed and the lights in the vast stadium were darkened. At precisely eight minutes after eight o'clock in the evening on 8 August 2008 – the number eight being considered auspicious in China for its association with prosperity – 2,008 drummers broke the silence with one sonorous beat and continued playing for 10 minutes. The stadium, designed to resemble a bird's nest, was filled to its 91,000 capacity. Among the spectators were over 100 heads of state and government from around the world, the largest ever gathering of world leaders for a sporting event. The opening ceremony of the Beijing Summer Olympics was rich in symbolism, harking back to the celebration of Yongle's completion of the Forbidden City almost 600 years earlier. The cost of hosting the Games was $43 billion, then a record in Olympic history.[115] The audience was treated to an extravaganza showcasing thousands of years of Chinese civilisation in which Confucius, once vilified under Chairman Mao, featured prominently. As the GFC was just beginning to convulse Western markets, China was announcing – in dramatic style – its return to the front of the world stage.

In a little over a decade, China had successfully managed the return of sovereignty of Hong Kong and Macau from under colonial rule, and had enjoyed compound annual GDP growth of 10 percent.[116] Hundreds of millions of Chinese citizens had been lifted out of poverty. In 2010, China would overtake Japan to become the second largest economy in the world in nominal terms and, by 2014, it would overtake the US to become the world's largest economy on the basis of purchasing power parity.

China's leaders from the time that Deng Xiaoping took the first step on the path to reform and opening up can, with ample justification, claim to have delivered nothing short of an economic miracle. In the process, China has embraced technology and significantly closed the gap between itself and other leading nations. In fact, in many areas of technology, such as telecommunications, renewable energy and electrical transmission, China can now claim to be the world leader.

Nevertheless, incentive structures that drove government officials to focus single-mindedly on economic growth had many adverse consequences. In 2007, the World Bank estimated that pollution was costing China 5.8 percent of GDP and causing 750,000 premature deaths each year. Explosive growth in energy demand and the number of road vehicles saw carbon dioxide emissions double between 2000 and 2007.[117] Of course, all countries that have industrialised have paid an environmental price; however, the size of China's population and its speed of development have meant that the environmental costs of its growth have been unprecedented. Belatedly, the Chinese government is focusing on these issues but, even where the damage can be repaired, it is likely to take many decades.

There remain questions about other aspects of the sustainability of China's development model as well. Deng Xiaoping's younger son, Deng Zhifang (邓质方), once told an acquaintance that 'My father thinks

Gorbachev is an idiot'. Deng considered it a mistake for Gorbachev to have set out to change the USSR's political system first because 'he won't have the power to fix the economic problems and the people will remove him'.[118] History has vindicated Deng's view. However, now that China has reached a certain level of prosperity, is the current governance system still suitable for driving the country's next stage of development?

The path of economic growth carved out by Zhu Rongji has succeeded far beyond the expectations of almost all observers at the time. Nevertheless, as with China's ancient imperial system, the highly centralised nature of the country's governance model today depends on consistently selecting strong and competent leaders. History has demonstrated that such a system is eventually crippled when weak leaders come to power or when even strong leaders hold onto power for too long.

China has a large and increasingly well-educated population from which to draw its future leaders. However, the development of private enterprise in recent decades means that China's best talent is ever more likely to be lured away from government service by the greater rewards on offer in the private sector. The concentration of power within the state bureaucracy also creates structural opportunities and incentives for corruption and nepotism. Not only does this risk sapping economic vibrancy over time; it also fundamentally undermines the legitimacy of the government. Periodic anti-corruption campaigns may act as a short-term deterrent; however, these are unlikely to be as effective as greater transparency in government and an ability for local communities to properly hold their leaders to account.

Much of this comes down to whether the Party is able – or, more importantly, willing – to make itself subject to the rule of law. Deng Xiaoping had recognised the need to impose a check on the Party's excesses and, given the abuses that he himself suffered, stressed the need for the rule of law.[119] As he drove ahead with economic reforms and modernisation though, he found that the lack of encumbrance by legal due process was convenient. More recently, it has been argued that China's one-party system, with fewer pressures to pander to voters' short-term whims, is a source of advantage and, certainly, the country's recent performance on many measures appears to support this view.[120] Nevertheless, by continuing to place the Party above the law, China's legal system lacks the clarity and objectivity that give confidence to entrepreneurs and investors, thereby potentially discouraging greater contributions from the private sector. This places greater reliance on the CCP continuing to 'get it right' over the long term – a big gamble, in light of China's historical experience.

Given China's turbulent history, the instinct to prioritise social order and stability is understandable. In some ways, however, the breakdown of some of China's old strictures precipitated by Deng's reforms have actually reinforced national cohesiveness and stability. For example, the mass migration of labour from rural areas into the SEZs that powered the country's export boom brought together a huge number of people from different parts of China who spoke different dialects. This has reinforced the use of Putonghua, meaning that disparate regional and ethnic groups now speak one common language. Improved technology and financial resources have also improved the state's ability to cope with natural disasters. In May 2008, when the worst earthquake the country had experienced in over 30 years struck Sichuan province, over 69,000 people lost their lives, many more were injured, and more than 4.8 million were left homeless. Notwithstanding the enormous human tragedy, it might have been a lot worse had China not been able to rapidly deploy a huge relief effort and invest close to $150 billion in the subsequent reconstruction of the affected areas. Subsequent to the disaster, it has further improved its earthquake prediction technologies. Thus, China today is less vulnerable to a number of the challenges that it has faced historically and less susceptible to the splits that have followed dislocations in the past.

There is also the question of China's interactions with the rest of the world. China's opening to international trade and investment was a critical driver of its economic resurgence. Today, cross-border trade and investment are vital to maintaining China's continued prosperity. The level of integration between China and the global economy also means that China now has a greater stake in the stability and prosperity of other countries, and *vice versa*.

Deng Xiaoping avoided foreign entanglements in order to focus China's resources on domestic development, advising other leaders that in foreign policy China should 'avoid the limelight, never take the lead, and try to accomplish something' (韬光养晦、决不当头、有所作为).[121] However, as China's international presence has grown, so have its foreign policy interests. How China pursues its interests internationally has a huge bearing not only on domestic Chinese welfare, but on the livelihoods and prosperity of people around the world. Here, the importance of fostering an atmosphere of goodwill runs well beyond purely economic calculations.

As China has become more prosperous, growth is now slowing rapidly from the rates seen in the heady earlier years. As discussed in Chapter 5, a rapidly aging population is adding to China's social burdens, while wealth inequalities are on the rise. Notwithstanding the CCP's enviable track record of improving people's livelihoods, future economic growth is going to depend on much-harder-to-deliver productivity gains. The risks and challenges that China faces are substantial. Are China's governance system and economic model today capable of coping with these over the long run, or will it fall back into the trap of its age-old dynastic cycles? To make a judgement on this, it is necessary to examine in greater detail the challenges that China now faces.

Chapter 5

Two Steps Forward, One Step Back

中国经济存在着巨大问题，依然是不稳定、不平衡、不协调、不可持续的结构性的问题。

– 温家宝

There are huge structural problems in China's economy which are still causing unsteady, unbalanced, uncoordinated and unsustainable development.

– Wen Jiabao

As much as the CCP leadership deserves credit for overseeing China's economic transformation over the past four decades, the true heroes of the tale are the Chinese people. When Deng Xiaoping initiated reform and opening up, he was simply removing some of the constraints that had been placed on the people's creativity and commercial spirit. This greater economic freedom coincided with underlying demographic forces to create what has been termed a 'growth miracle'. This is defined as when an economy's GDP grows at a minimum of 7.5 percent for 25 years or more. In the period following WW2, eight or nine economies have experienced growth miracles, including Japan, South Korea, Brazil, Taiwan, Hong Kong and Singapore. A common feature among them has been the harnessing of a substantial one-time jump in working age population to drive rapid development, enabling the economy to undergo a complete transformation in a period of 30 to 40 years.[1]

Following the end of the civil war, China experienced a baby boom in the 1950s and 1960s. The result of that boom, coupled with the one-child policy introduced in 1979, was to raise the working age share of China's expanding population by around 20 percentage points between the early 1970s and mid-2000s.[2] By any measure, this was an enormous increase in labour supply but, in China's case, actually understates its demographic gains. This is because, during the 1980s, organic growth in the working age population was accentuated by the return to the cities of millions of youths who had been sent down to the countryside, and the return to work of millions who had been politically marginalised.[3] As market reforms began to raise agricultural productivity and generate food surpluses, rural labourers were further freed up to go and work in factories, thereby enabling a manufacturing boom.

Many economies, of course, have featured favourable demographics but have not experienced growth miracles, often because they have not reinvested their surpluses to drive further growth. China has undergone the most dramatic growth miracle of any economy in history in terms of its scale, speed and duration in large part because the government has been able to turbocharge investment by suppressing domestic consumption growth. It has done this in a number of ways.

The first was just to keep wages low. In this, the government didn't really need to do much. The sheer size of China's working age population meant that there was more than enough supply to suppress real increases in labour costs. If anything, the problem the government confronted was ensuring sufficient new job creation to prevent unemployment from spiking up. However, its preservation of the Mao era *hukou* (户口) household registration system helped keep wages for rural migrants low. This system was designed in the 1950s to prevent a mass influx of rural migrants into cities by tying citizenship rights – most importantly at that time, grain rations – to the location of their *hukou*. Not only did this deny rural migrants access to employment benefits offered to urban workers, but it has also left them under constant threat of eviction. In practice, business needs meant that local governments did not rigorously enforce laws preventing rural migrants from holding jobs in cities. Nevertheless, the constant risk of being sent back to the countryside made for a relatively compliant workforce. This has contributed to the fact that Chinese workers at non-financial corporations are paid only around 40 percent of the value of what they produce, compared with close to 70 percent for workers in most other countries, providing a significant boost to business profitability.[4]

The second constraint on consumption was the government's land policy. By maintaining collective ownership of land even when collective agriculture was abolished, the huge gains in land value arising from increased farmland productivity did not accrue to the peasant families who farmed the land. Peasants had the right to use the land and sell the surplus that they produced from it, but they did not have the right to sell the land.

Although urban housing began to be privatised in 1998, the ownership of rural land remains in the hands of local governments to this day. This has led to further iniquities for the rural peasant class as Zhu Rongji's 1994 tax reforms squeezed local government budgets. The sale of land became one of the few ways in which stretched local governments could raise funds. Consequently, as urbanisation dramatically increased the value of land in the periphery of growing towns and cities, many were evicted from their homes without adequate compensation so that the land could be sold for development.

Local governments' ability to expropriate land without having to engage in extensive negotiations or to pay market value for it allowed them to rapidly develop modern cities and infrastructure. However, this system was rife with corruption and abuses, which bred considerable resentment. Moreover, it meant that the benefit of the increases in land value accrued mostly to the government and well-connected elites, rather than being widely distributed among the population to increase its spending power.

The third means of keeping consumption down was through financial repression. This is most widely understood as the suppression of interest rates paid by the state-controlled banking sector to depositors and the channelling of loans to fund enterprises or projects supported by the government. However, that is just one of many forms of financial repression and, even in that manifestation, there is more to it than immediately meets the eye. The failure to replace the *hukou* system with comprehensive national social security has meant that Chinese citizens are forced to maintain higher savings as a form of self-insurance. A higher savings cushion is not a bad thing *per se* and it would be hard to argue that Americans, with much lower levels of household savings, are better protected. However, when viewed in conjunction with the limited options available to Chinese citizens to optimise their returns on those savings, it may reasonably be argued that China's population is getting the worst of both worlds.

Like the US, China's tax system has become increasingly regressive, favouring the relatively wealthy. Personal income taxes collected amount to around one percent of GDP, while social security and consumption taxes, which make up a disproportionate share of lower-wage earners' incomes, together amount to 14 percent of GDP.[5]

Perhaps the most controversial form of financial repression though (at least internationally) has been China's currency policy. Between mid-1995 and mid-2005, China maintained a hard peg of 8.27 renminbi per US dollar, notwithstanding the fact that China experienced far higher productivity growth than the US.[6] As discussed in Chapter 3, the resulting undervaluation of the renminbi contributed to a huge jump in China's exports and foreign currency reserves. For Chinese workers, however, the effect was to hold down their capacity to purchase imports. According to BIS estimates, China's inflation-adjusted exchange rate depreciated by around 20 percent between 1998 and the end of 2007 – a huge benefit for exporters at the expense of workers.[7]

Taking all these factors into account, while the incomes of Chinese households grew rapidly during the 1990s and 2000s, their share of consumption as a portion of China's GDP declined continually, falling by 15 percentage points between the late 1980s and the bottom in 2010. As of 2018, Chinese households consumed less than 40 percent of China's output – a far lower share than every other major economy in the world.[8]

In contrast, the government's spending capacity has soared. Reported budget revenues as a share of GDP doubled from less than 11 percent in

1996 to 22 percent in 2015. However, this significantly understates the actual increase in the Chinese government's revenues due to new revenue sources. Unlike almost all other countries, China does not include social insurance receipts in government revenues. These jumped from essentially zero to 8 percent of GDP by 2018. Further, local government revenues from land sales, which amounted to more than 7 percent of GDP in 2018, are not included in the earlier figures. Taking these three sources of income into account, Chinese government revenues roughly tripled from 12 percent of GDP in 1996 to around 35 to 36 percent in 2017–2018. This compares with the budgets of developed countries, but with the crucial difference that China does not yet have major social security outlays, which typically take up 10 percent of government spending in developed countries.[9] This has put a huge amount of money at the Chinese government's disposal.

Looked at from the perspective of society as a whole, the burden borne by Chinese households is not necessarily negative. Indeed, a major enabler of social and technological progress throughout the history of human civilisations have been the surpluses generated by the masses. Social hierarchies freed an elite of administrators, philosophers, scientists and inventors to devote their time and energies to coordinating the population and striving for breakthroughs that have raised our collective quality of life. Absolute equality across society is a utopian dream that has never been achieved, and the 20th century experiments in communism that claimed such a goal generally had disastrous consequences. However, history has also shown that excessive inequality has, over time, been similarly disastrous. In China, given the gains in living standards over the past 40 years, this is not yet an acute issue, but it is now apparent that a number of aspects of the Chinese development model are unsustainable if domestic stability is be to maintained in the long run.

Further, given China's integration into the global system through international trade and investment (and the huge size of its economy today), it can no longer look at its domestic policies in isolation of their impact on the rest of the world. Distortions in the Chinese market have had significant consequences for other countries and territories. The challenges facing China are, therefore, global challenges and the Chinese government must anticipate that its policies, whether domestic or overseas, will draw international responses.

Under Zhu Rongji, China carved out a unique new path of development. Although this path contributed to China's rapid economic growth, it has also left a number of domestic dilemmas that have not yet been resolved by subsequent leaders. As Chinese businesses and investment have gone global, these have contributed to global imbalances and tensions with other countries. Among the most challenging to resolve has been the outsized role the Chinese state continues to play in enterprise and financial markets.

Going Public

Close to dusk on 25 February 1997, two cars passed by the Xinhua Gate (新华门) of Yongle's Forbidden City and turned north onto Fuyou Street (府右街). Deng Xiaoping had died just a week before and Beijing's streets were unusually quiet. The cars drove along the Forbidden City's vermillion walls to the northwest entrance of Zhongnanhai (中南海), the compound where China's top leaders work and live. There, a guard checked the passengers, then waved them through with a salute.

The passengers of the two vehicles were investment bankers from the Wall Street firm Goldman Sachs, led by Chief Operating Officer Hank Paulson. They were there to make a pitch to advise on the IPO of China Telecom (中国电信) to Vice Premier Zhu Rongji. Zhu, accompanied by China Construction Bank (CCB, 中国建设银行) chairman Wang Qishan (王岐山), received the bankers in the Purple Light Pavilion (紫光阁), where Chinese emperors had once received foreign tributaries. Paulson talked about Goldman's role on the privatisation and IPO of the German telecommunications operator Deutsche Telekom, which was completed the previous year. The meeting went well. Eight months later, China Telecom[10] debuted on the Stock Exchange of Hong Kong (SEHK, now a subsidiary of HKEX) and the NYSE, raising $4.22 billion. It was a remarkable achievement for both Zhu and the Goldman bankers – not least because, at the time of their February meeting, the company China Telecom didn't actually exist.

Given ideological opposition to capitalism within the Party, market reforms often proceeded before appropriate legal or regulatory frameworks could be put in place. When, in late 1984, the Shanghai audio equipment maker Feile Acoustics (飞乐音响) proposed the novel concept of raising capital by issuing shares to the public, local bureaucrats had no idea what legal category the entity fell into. *Was it a collective or was it an SOE?* Eventually, a new category was created, and the company sold 10,000 shares at 50 yuan each. Since there was no stock exchange, the shares were traded OTC through the Shanghai branch of the Industrial and Commercial Bank of China (ICBC, 中国工商银行).

The promulgation of a Company Law (公司法) in 1994, followed by a Securities Law (证券法) in 1999, helped clarify the legal status of companies selling shares to the public. However, the SOEs that still dominated the economy at the time were nothing like what investors might recognise as commercial enterprises, let alone publicly listed companies. These entities had grown out of various ministries that had overseen both commercial activity and social provision across the entire economy. SOEs quite literally provided for the cradle-to-grave needs of workers and their families, maintaining everything from hospitals, schools and restaurants to cemeteries. Making matters worse, as businesses, most of these SOEs were essentially defunct, laden with debt that their unprofitable operations were unable to service.

To carve out companies that were capable of being sold to international investors, investment bankers started out by grouping all of an SOE's productive assets into a subsidiary company, then listing the subsidiary. However, this left the parent company unable to meet its obligations to redundant workers and retirees. Following Shanghai Petrochemical's (上海石油化工) 1993 listing in Hong Kong, the Shanghai government found itself compelled under duress to assume responsibility for the parent company's social obligations. After that, local governments weren't about to get caught out again. The same year, Ma'anshan Steel (马鞍山钢铁) also listed its profitable operations in Hong Kong. However, after the IPO, redundant workers began to be migrated back into what had now become the listed company, driving it into losses.

Learning from these experiences, bankers realised that the assets left behind in the parent entity had to produce sufficient cash flow to meet the parent's obligations. Unfortunately, that didn't leave many candidates capable of being listed. There followed in the mid-1990s a wave of infrastructure company IPOs. These included assets such as toll roads and power utilities, the scope of which was limited to collecting fees based on tariff formulas pre-agreed with municipal governments and paying out a predictable stream of dividends to investors. They were hardly the most exciting investments in a rapidly growing economy.

Another innovation of the era were 'Red Chips'. The brainchild of Hong Kong investment banker Francis Leung (梁伯韬), who left Citibank to found the investment company Peregrine in 1988, Red Chips were offshore companies into which Chinese assets were injected. They are still common today but, after a brief heyday in the 1990s, Chinese authorities lost enthusiasm for them, since this structure put the listed entity out of the reach of Mainland Chinese regulators.

The China Telecom IPO was a radical breakthrough compared with what had gone before because it was the first time an entire industry in China had been packaged up and sold to investors. Run by the military during the Cultural Revolution, the telecommunications network had been under the purview of the Ministry of Posts and Telecommunications (MPT, 邮电部) since 1973. By the end of the 1980s, China still had just one telephone line per 200 citizens. Beginning in the early 1990s, China embarked on a huge investment programme to build out its telecommunications infrastructure, spending more than \$35 billion between 1992 and 1996. That resulted in a significant jump in coverage. Fixed line subscribers grew from 11.5 million to 55 million and mobile subscribers leapt from 177,000 to 7 million. However, that meant that still just 4.5 percent of the population had fixed line access and only 0.6 percent had a mobile phone.[11] A large amount of additional capital was needed to continue the infrastructure build-out, but the growth prospects of the business were enormous.

The holding company China Telecom (Hong Kong) was set up a month after the meeting in the Purple Light Pavilion, and the bankers worked with the MPT to identify what of the ministry's sprawling telecoms assets had the revenues and growth potential to meet Hong Kong's listing requirements and to attract investors. This task involved more than 350 full-time accountants from the audit firm KPMG in a massive due diligence exercise. Meanwhile, the MPT battled provincial officials, who were reluctant to give up control of their local telecom assets.

Eventually, it was determined that the listing vehicle would focus on mobile telecoms and would initially just include the networks of

Guangdong and Zhejiang provinces, which accounted for close to 30 percent of China's mobile subscribers.[12] It was further determined that the company would acquire the mobile assets of Jiangsu and additional provinces later on. This meant that the listed entity would have two attractive sources of growth: organic subscriber growth in the first two provinces; and inorganic growth from rolling up the mobile assets of other provinces.

By the summer, preparations were proceeding smoothly towards a September listing. However, on 2 July, one day after the return of Hong Kong's sovereignty to China, the Thai baht plummeted 20 percent against the dollar, kicking off the Asian Financial Crisis. Market volatility soon spread to Hong Kong and the IPO date was pushed back to October. At this point, the bankers conceived another innovation that would become a common feature in large Hong Kong IPOs: cornerstone investors. A dozen Hong Kong tycoons and the offshore arms of various Mainland enterprises were persuaded to commit to purchasing 10 percent of China Telecom, nearly half of the shares being floated, and holding them for at least a year. This not only ensured that there would be buyers for a large tranche of the offering, but also signalled confidence in the company's prospects to other potential investors.

Notwithstanding the crisis unfurling in global markets, strong demand for China Telecom's shares allowed the bookrunners to raise the IPO's indicative price range during the investor roadshow. Markets were extremely volatile though. On 23 October, when the shares began trading, the Hong Kong market plunged 10 percent and China Telecom opened down sharply from its offering price. Nevertheless, by the year's end, the stock had rebounded 26 percent from its first day closing price to trade 13 percent above the offer price.[13]

Over the following years, one by one, China's major SOEs across power, natural resources, airlines, insurance and banking were packaged up and sold to investors, creating giant players that dominated the domestic market and, as they began to go global, would become major players in international markets.

Initially, it was felt that, due to the size of the offerings, shares needed to be listed in New York as well as Hong Kong; however, within a few years it had become apparent that the Hong Kong market was capable of attracting sufficient capital from international investors to make a

New York listing unnecessary. After all, in an era when huge sums of money could be moved around the world at the touch of a computer key, capital could easily flow anywhere. That begs the question: why did the Chinese government choose Hong Kong and not Shanghai, or another Mainland financial centre?

★★★

There are many answers to that question, but the first thing that needs to be understood is what Zhu Rongji and his fellow reformers were trying to achieve. Like major privatisation programmes in other countries, such as that pursued by Margaret Thatcher in Great Britain, the objective was not just to raise capital for the companies or the government, but to transform the entire economy by forcing deep (and often painful) reforms on the SOEs. Zhu had clearly recognised capitalism was the most efficient system for organising production. However, he had to contend with significant resistance to change from vested interests and numerous practical problems.

For all the SOEs' inefficiencies, they kept a huge number of people employed. When Zhu started on the path of SOE reform in 1994, there were over 100,000 of them. Through restructurings that had taken place by 1997, 12 million state sector workers had already effectively been laid off under the euphemistic term *xiagang* (下岗, or 'off post'), where they continued to receive minimum benefits while searching for new employment. Further large scale lay-offs would have posed a serious threat to social stability.

After battling to win support for further SOE reforms at the 15th Party Congress in September 1997, Zhu proposed an approach of *zhuada fangxiao* (抓大放小, holding onto the large strategic SOEs and letting the smaller ones go).[14] This allowed the government to control the entities that employed large numbers of SOE workers and reduced opposition from within the Party. Therefore, the sale of shares in the major SOEs were not true 'privatisations' (in terms of ceding government control) and only minority stakes were floated on public markets.

Another reason for eschewing the 'big bang' approach to privatisation was the lesson Chinese leaders had drawn from the Russian experience. Following the collapse of the USSR, Boris Yeltsin's government had rapidly sold off state assets for significantly less than their true market value, spawning an oligarch class and a legacy of deep social problems.

However, if the government wasn't ceding control, then *how would the impetus for the necessary reforms be generated?* The answer to this question was to list the companies on international markets. By forcing the large SOEs to meet listing requirements in Hong Kong and New York, they would be forced to raise their governance standards and improve transparency. They would also need to contend with scrutiny of their businesses by sophisticated international investors.

By and large, this strategy was highly successful. However, could the listing standards of domestic exchanges not have been raised to similar levels as Hong Kong and New York? And could international investors not have been allowed to participate in IPOs on the Shanghai and Shenzhen bourses?

In practice, there were many factors that precluded these options. One glaring obstacle was the lack of convertibility of China's currency, the renminbi. Currency reform has been a goal of the PBOC for many years, but the currency crises and market volatility experienced by neighbouring countries during the Asian Financial Crisis imprinted on Chinese leaders' minds the advantages of maintaining capital controls. The Hong Kong dollar, on the other hand, was freely convertible and had maintained a stable exchange rate to the US dollar since 1983, when it was pegged to the greenback.

Hong Kong's attractions were not just limited to its currency though. Its legacy as a British colony left it with an English common law legal system and a robust judiciary in which international investors could be confident. The Securities and Futures Commission (SFC), established in 1989 to regulate the territory's securities industry, further upholds the highest international standards of regulation. Under the Scotsman John Cowperthwaite, who served as Financial Secretary of the colonial government from 1961 until 1971, Hong Kong had also resisted Keynesianism at the height of its influence in the West and stuck firmly to *laissez faire* economic policies that ensured low taxation. Capital gains, dividends and interest income on securities investment in the territory are not subject to any tax by the Hong Kong authorities. All of this, coupled with the entrepreneurial spirit and work ethic of the millions of migrants who fled Communist rule in China in the

1950s and 1960s, helped Hong Kong emerge as one of the wealthiest places on Earth and a highly attractive centre for international capital. Under the One Country Two Systems (一国两制) formula devised by Deng Xiaoping, these features of the Hong Kong system were guaranteed to be upheld for at least 50 years following the return of sovereignty to China.

In contrast, the Mainland capital markets remain racked with legal, regulatory and fiscal uncertainties that the central government has found difficult to resolve. Many of these problems trace back to the evolution of China's financial markets.

***

China's first stock exchange was founded in Shanghai in 1891 and, in pre-revolutionary times, Beijing and Tianjin had both hosted securities exchanges. These were closed down in the early 1950s and it was not until Deng Xiaoping's reforms got underway in the 1980s that consideration was again given to establishing securities exchanges. Initially, shares in nascent private enterprises and TVEs were traded OTC. By the end of the decade, however, there were various state-sponsored and private attempts to set up electronic trading venues. The events of June 1989 briefly set back developments, but the Shanghai Stock Exchange (SSE, 上海证券交易所) officially opened in December 1990, followed by the Shenzhen Stock Exchange (SZSE, 深圳证券交易所) in July 1991.[15] The creation of an effective regulatory structure around the nascent securities industry was, however, a bit of an afterthought.

At inception, the central bank was nominally responsible for supervising the equity and debt markets, but actual oversight fell to the PBOC's local branches, the staffing and control of which was in the hands of provincial governments. Given the overwhelming focus at the local level was on raising capital for development, concepts like investor protection took a back seat. Further, the PBOC was involved in sponsoring the establishment of securities companies all around the country, creating a fundamental conflict with its role as the industry regulator. In October 1990, the PBOC issued national regulations governing the establishment of securities companies, including the stipulation that new securities firms could only be set up with the approval of PBOC

Beijing. However, its local branches were allowed to retain ownership of securities companies that they had already established and continued to reap the profits that they generated. Predictably, supervision was lax, and abuses were rife.

The Chinese population, unfamiliar with capital markets, was slow to awaken to the concept of investment in shares. However, by the beginning of the 1990s, a fever had taken hold. Unsurprisingly, Shenzhen, neighbouring fiercely capitalist Hong Kong, led the way. It was an incident here in 1992 that precipitated a restructuring of the regulatory framework around China's securities industry.

In August of that year, around 700,000 would-be investors from far and wide packed into the town to subscribe to a new issue. They lined up for three days and nights to obtain a form that gave them the right to subscribe for the shares, but on 10 August, when the prescribed five million forms were due to be handed out, there were far fewer available than advertised and they rapidly ran out. It turned out that the local branch of the PBOC had already distributed most of them 'internally'. This set off a violent riot by the frustrated public, who vented their anger at the corrupted process. This became known as the '810 Incident' and led to the establishment of the China Securities Regulatory Commission (CSRC, 中国证监会) in October of that year.

The CSRC was initially chaired by Liu Hongru (刘鸿儒), a respected and committed reformer, who had a PhD in economics from Moscow University. Liu set out to build a high-quality regulatory body and recruited a professional staff, many of whom were internationally educated. However, like the struggles for influence between the eunuchs and the Confucians in the Ming court, China's financial markets have often been plagued by factional infighting between different regulatory agencies.

The CSRC's progress was stymied for a long time by a struggle with the PBOC over control of the industry. In this, the CSRC was at a disadvantage as, unlike the PBOC, it was only granted vice-ministerial status. Further, it only had a small office in Beijing and provincial securities *bureaux* continued to be controlled by local governments. With no independent enforcement authority to crack down where it uncovered violations, the fledgling regulator was dependent on the cooperation of other agencies, such as the Ministry of Law, the Ministry of Finance (MOF), and the State Asset Management Bureau. Faced with such obstacles, Liu bided his time and focused on areas where the CSRC could have some influence. Here, Hong Kong offered considerable help.

In the early 1990s, the SEHK was just a small regional exchange. However, seeing the long-term opportunity in capital raising by Mainland companies, the SEHK suggested that the Chinese government consider listing Chinese enterprises in Hong Kong. In December 1991, Liu led a small team of specialists to Hong Kong to study the feasibility of the proposal. The team's report weighed the pros and cons carefully. Among the downsides of Chinese companies listing in Hong Kong was that they would have to give up a share of their profits to overseas investors, and it might conflict with the government's efforts to develop the exchanges in Shanghai and Shenzhen. However, the practical need to raise much needed capital, coupled with a desire to promote the internationalisation of Chinese companies, ultimately led Liu's team to come down in favour of promoting listings in Hong Kong.

In April 1992, the SEHK's chairman Charles Y.K. Lee (李业广)[16] visited Beijing to lobby Zhu Rongji to allow Mainland Chinese companies to list in Hong Kong. During their meeting, Zhu suggested that they select 10 potential listing candidates and set up a working group to study how these IPOs could be accomplished in practice. Support on the Mainland side was certainly not unequivocal, but the 810 Incident later that year may have increased the attraction of listing companies in Hong Kong, since it allowed the government to export the problem of social unrest.[17]

Following a year of work on legal, accounting and technical issues, a Memorandum of Understanding (MOU) was signed in June 1993 and the first Hong Kong IPO of a Mainland Chinese company took place the same month. The listing of beer maker Tsingtao Brewery (青岛啤酒) raised $115 million. It was a modest sum, but in subsequent years capital raising in the territory by Mainland companies would see exponential growth, transforming Hong Kong into a global financial centre rivalling London and New York.

Offshore listings marked the beginning of the CSRC's consolidation of power over China's securities industry. Its sole authority to select candidates for listing in Hong Kong gave it influence that it hadn't hitherto enjoyed and enabled it to elicit compliance by SOEs with its regulations. Put simply, without CSRC approval, there was no overseas listing and, hence, no money.

In 1993, the CSRC assumed authority over the SSE and SZSE via control over the appointment of their senior management. Then, in 1995, a scandal in the bond futures market allowed it to further extend control over the domestic market.

What became known as the '327 Incident' involved the Shanghai government-controlled Shanghai Wanguo Securities (上海万国证券), which had learned of an impending government bond issue. Anticipating the additional supply would cause prices to fall, it tried to corner the market by shorting government bond futures trading on the SSE. The MOF, displeased when it learned of this attempt to manipulate the market, decided to teach Wanguo a lesson. It cancelled the bond issue and began building a corresponding long position through a trust company it controlled. Oblivious to this, Wanguo continued to build a massive short position. The losses bankrupted Wanguo and its CEO was thrown into jail. The firm was later merged with Shenyin Securities (申银证券) but the fallout was considerable.

Although it was hardly his fault, Liu Hongru shouldered the responsibility and resigned as chairman of the CSRC, though his reputation remained intact. Unfortunately, it also led to a closure of the Chinese bond futures market for the next 18 years.[18] However, the PBOC was finally forced to divest its investments in 43 brokerage firms and transfer the staff supervising them to the CSRC. The CSRC was elevated to full ministerial status in 1998 and took over control of the provincial securities regulatory offices from local governments. The passage of the Securities Law in 1999 further set out clearly delineated responsibilities of the CSRC and a documented process for new listings. China finally had a securities regulator with teeth.

The Protection Racket

In the early days of China's securities markets, retail investors dominated. As is common in immature markets, unsophisticated investors tended to speculate rather than invest, often causing wild swings in share prices.

Market manipulators took advantage of this to profit, while numerous cases surfaced where unscrupulous brokers had misappropriated client funds. All of this highlighted a need for better investor protection.

In April 2000, Zhou Xiaochuan was appointed chairman of the CSRC. Zhou was the son of two central planners who had studied in the Soviet Union in the 1950s. During the Cultural Revolution, his family had been scattered and he was sent to work on a farm in Heilongjiang (黑龙江) province, bordering Siberia. During the long frigid winters, he had taken solace in books and classical music. In the 1980s, he earned a PhD in automation and system engineering at Tsinghua University, then went on to work at the Institute of Chinese Economic Reform Research. He emerged as one of a group of energetic young reformers and worked with Zhu Rongji on pricing, trade and foreign exchange issues. From 1991, he served in a series of roles in the state-owned banking sector and at the central bank, becoming an influential voice on banking reforms. A deep thinker, Zhou undertook a number of important initiatives at the CSRC before he moved on to become governor of the PBOC in December 2002.

Most of these steps were targeted at raising overall market standards, including training and certification of industry professionals; improving company disclosure; and raising the bar for corporate governance standards. These efforts were significantly bolstered through the bringing on board of personnel with international experience. For example, Laura Cha (史美伦), a former regulator from the SFC in Hong Kong,[19] was appointed a vice chairman and played a prominent role in raising corporate governance standards for listed companies. During this time, the CSRC also stepped up its enforcement activities and prosecution of market manipulation, and championed minority investor rights.[20]

In the regulation of any market, there is a line between appropriate investor protection and excessive interference that stifles the proper functioning of the market. Zhou Xiaochuan struck a fair balance. However, the concentration of power vested in the CSRC posed a risk when less exceptional leaders took the helm. Three traps that the CSRC has regularly fallen into include the abuse of its power; succumbing to political interference; and intervening to try to bail out investors when the market falls.

While the law and regulations governing listings lay out a clear and transparent process, in practice the CSRC retains a high degree of discretion over the approval of listing applications. Over the years, a number of senior CSRC officials have been implicated in corrupt practices relating to listings, including the sale of information and influence, and preferential access for their family members to subscribe for hot IPOs.[21] However, it is not just individual cases of corruption that have been a problem. Control over listing approvals has also been used as a tool of macroeconomic and macro-market control. When share prices have performed poorly, the CSRC has been known to slow down or even completely halt listings to limit the supply of new stock to the market. SOEs and large well-connected companies have also been favoured over smaller private companies in listing approvals.

The most persistent problems in Chinese markets have stemmed from a focus on protecting retail investors from the consequences of market volatility and their own poor investment decisions. In January 2020, the number of registered share trading accounts in China surpassed 160 million,[22] so in light of the government's focus on social stability this is perhaps understandable. However, many of the measures pursued have themselves generated dangerous distortions. Moreover, it has been argued that headline figures vastly overstate the actual level of retail participation in China's markets, resulting in misguided policies.[23]

There is certainly plenty of evidence to support this argument. Many share trading accounts are inactive and there is significant double counting, as the headline figure includes accounts opened at both the SSE and the SZSE by an individual investor. Further, most account sizes are very small. It has also surfaced that stock manipulators have opened accounts in multiple different names (sometimes numbering in the thousands) to conceal their activities.[24] Holdings in many companies are, in any case, concentrated in the hands of the state or of company founders. Therefore, looking just at the number of stock trading accounts certainly gives a rather exaggerated view of retail investors' *share* of the Chinese market. Nonetheless, it is undeniable that the Chinese stock market features a large number of small investors.

Whether it comes from retail investors themselves or other vested interests behind the scenes, the CSRC and the government have been highly susceptible to pressure to step in to pump up stock prices when investors have suffered steep losses. For example, when the overheated Chinese stock market crashed in the summer of 2015, a so-called 'national team' (国家队) of state-affiliated investors spent a reported $234 billion in an effort to 'support the market'.[25] This has led to an entrenched market psychology that the government will always step forward to bail investors out of losses, creating significant moral hazard.

The futility and, indeed, counterproductivity of the authorities' efforts to manage market price levels were aptly demonstrated when the CSRC briefly introduced so-called 'circuit breakers' in January 2016.

In response to the 2015 stock market crash, the CSRC decided to introduce a mechanism to limit market volatility. Circuit breakers, which were launched on 1 January, were intended to provide a break to allow the market to cool off when there was a sharp fall. The mechanism had two elements: (i) if the CSI 300 index, which tracks the Shanghai and Shenzhen markets, fell five percent during the trading day, trading would be halted for 15 minutes; and (ii) if the index fell seven percent, trading would be halted for the rest of the day. Circuit breakers exist in a number of other markets to manage the risk of faulty computerised trading algorithms or human error; however, they generally have much higher tolerances for volatility. For example, in the US, if the benchmark S&P 500 index falls by seven percent, trading is halted for 15 minutes, and a 20 percent fall triggers a halt in trading for the rest of the day.

In the face of an already-nervous market in early 2016, the very tight levels of the Chinese circuit breakers actually exacerbated selling pressure, as traders were incentivised to dump stocks when the index fell close to the trigger levels in order not to be locked into their positions. Within the circuit breakers' first week of operation, the market had been closed twice, and the CSRC was forced to scrap the mechanism. Six weeks later, CSRC chairman Xiao Gang (肖钢) lost his job. However, the CSRC's direct attempts to manage stock movements are far from the only means by which pricing in the Mainland securities markets has been distorted.

Concentrated shareholdings in many companies have limited the supply of 'free floating' shares available to trade, which has had the effect of pushing up share prices. Because of capital controls and the limited availability of investment products relative to the amount of savings, prices not just in equities but also other Chinese asset classes – notably residential property – have been prone to bubbles. This is evidenced clearly by the significant premium at which Mainland-listed 'A-shares' often trade at over the Hong Kong-listed 'H-shares' of the same companies.[26] However, even when stock prices are clearly wildly overinflated, investors have been restricted from shorting stocks to profit from price declines.

The CSRC began to permit short selling in 2008 on a trial basis, then gradually increased the number of shares designated as permissible to sell short to around 900 by 2015, but again tightened restrictions on short selling in response to the 2015 market crash. At the same time, it effectively closed down the already narrowly-based equity derivatives market. This has removed natural demand that comes from short sellers who profit by buying shares to close out their positions when the market falls. Thus, the Mainland stock markets are structurally biased to be mono-directional, making them highly prone to wild swings on the way up and on the way down.

And it is not just in secondary trading where stock prices don't reflect fundamental value. In order to avoid state assets being sold off on the cheap, the State-owned Asset Supervision and Administration Commission (SASAC) has stipulated that SOE shares may not be sold at less than their reported net asset value (NAV). On the surface, this does not seem unreasonable. However, companies in difficulty needing to raise capital often generate returns below their cost of capital or even losses. There have also been many instances where SOEs' balance sheets have harboured unrecognised losses, meaning that NAV is overstated. In such circumstances, the requirement not to sell shares at a price below NAV makes it difficult to raise capital from *bona fides* investors.

More damaging for the Mainland exchanges as listing venues, however, has been the valuation cap on IPO pricing. Since 2014, CSRC guidelines restricted the IPO price of issuers to a maximum of 23 times earnings. Ostensibly, the IPO price cap was designed to protect investors from sponsor firms overinflating valuations of new share offerings. As a result, investors in Mainland IPOs often see prices shoot up on the first day of trading. In 2017, all 432 companies that listed on Mainland stock exchanges saw their share prices jump by 43 to 44 percent on the first day of trading (the Mainland bourses cap first day price rises at 44 percent).[27] This means that companies raising capital in China's domestic markets are effectively leaving a lot of money on the table that could otherwise be used to invest in their operations. While the price cap has now been relaxed for high tech companies listing on the STAR Market (科创板) of the SSE, it remains highly distortive to pricing in the overall Mainland IPO market.[28]

It is difficult to see who actually benefits from government and regulatory interference in the price discovery mechanism in China's stock markets. For retail investors, it has turned the markets into a casino instead of a place where they can invest their savings to meet long-term needs, such as building a nest egg for retirement. It has also inhibited the development of China's financial services industry. Restrictive price bands for IPOs means that IPO sponsors have had little need to train up professionals with sound valuation skills. The impression that the regulators can pressure fund managers to buy – or at least not sell – shares in the face of a falling market has likely held back the development of China's professional asset management industry.

Regulatory aversion to allowing the development of a healthy derivatives market has meant that Chinese corporations, financial institutions and investors with legitimate needs to hedge market prices for commodities or interest rates have few efficient means of doing so, exposing them to operational and financial risks.

For private enterprises, the uncertainties of the IPO process make it difficult to rely on the Mainland equity markets for their capital needs. Even where they are able to get the CSRC's green light to list, the IPO valuation cap has made it unattractive for many growth enterprises (whose shares command high price-to-earnings multiples) to proceed. The launch of Shanghai's STAR Market has removed this barrier for high tech issuers, but there remain many other attractions for Chinese companies to list offshore. Funds raised in Hong Kong can be deployed in their international operations without having to worry about capital controls. Entrepreneurs and large private shareholders have the further incentive of using an overseas listing to move part of their wealth offshore, where they have greater freedom and investment choices. Reflecting their concerns about weak protections for private property rights and the absence of the rule of law in Mainland China, one Chinese billionaire entrepreneur remarked that 'If you are rich in China, you are not really rich. The money all belongs to the government'.[29]

Even for Hong Kong, which has grown to become one of the leading IPO markets in the world as a result of capital raising by Mainland Chinese companies, it can be argued that more robust competition from Mainland financial centres would have forced it to innovate more and raise its market standards further.

By the time Zhu Rongji stood down as Premier in 2003, China's state-owned sector had been dramatically trimmed down, with its main focus confined to 120 large-scale centrally-owned enterprises.[30] Undoubtedly, pushing them to list on international markets has improved transparency, raised corporate governance standards and made them far more market-oriented and internationally competitive. Nevertheless, if it had been Zhu's intention to further shrink the state's role in the economy, the results have been mixed. The state continues to hold majority stakes in the industry giants that have been created. Further, the structure of China's capital markets has put small private enterprises at a distinct disadvantage in terms of access to funding, contributing to monopoly and oligopoly dominance of major industries. However, the structural problems in China's stock market are merely the tip of the iceberg.

The Price of Money

Scaling up and improving the efficiency of moribund SOEs was one important aspect of raising China's industrial productivity. However, without better risk-based mechanisms for allocating capital, the economy would still be weighed down by poor investment decisions on a massive scale. The key role in intermediating the allocation of capital in most economies is played by the banking sector. By the 1990s, China's banks were riddled with bad loans arising from state-directed lending and were themselves technically bankrupt. Zhu Rongji's solution to the triangular debt problem in 1992 had exacerbated this situation and, facing the additional threat of the Asian Financial Crisis in 1997, Zhu tasked Zhou Xiaochuan – then chairman of CCB – to come up with a plan for banking reform.

It was a gargantuanly complex assignment. The banks not only did not meet minimum capital requirements set down by the BIS, but also had vast amounts of NPLs on their balance sheets that had not been recognised. In 1997, the PBOC estimated that 20 percent of the state-owned banks' outstanding loans were non-performing, an amount totalling RMB1.2 trillion ($143 billion), or 15.6 percent of China's GDP.[31] New capital would need to be introduced and the banks' accounting and risk monitoring systems would need to be upgraded. However, if the lenders simply went back to their old ways of state-directed lending after they were recapitalised, then wouldn't they just be doomed to a repeat of their predicament at a future date? Further, new capital infusions risked enabling a lending spree that could spark runaway inflation. And who would pick up the tab for the sector's bail-out? China's bureaucratic intrigues are dangerous territory at the best of times, but major changes to a sector that had served as the 'piggy banks' of the SOEs, provincial governments and other powerful actors risked upsetting a whole cabal of vested interests.

The first step was a recapitalisation of the 'Big Four' banks – Agricultural Bank of China (ABC, 中国农业银行), Bank of China (BOC, 中国银行), CCB and ICBC – which in 1997 together held 91 percent of the country's loans and 89 percent of its deposits.[32] To bring them up to a minimum capital adequacy standard of 8 percent of total assets, it was deemed that a sum of RMB270 billion ($35 billion) in new capital was required. This was a huge amount of money for China at the time, equivalent to around 4 percent of GDP. To put it into more vivid context, this was equal to China's entire government bond issuance for the year and around 25 percent of its foreign exchange reserves.[33] To come up with this sum, the MOF effectively nationalised the deposits of the Chinese people.

The PBOC reduced the minimum ratio of deposit-reserves, which banks were required to hold with the central bank, from 13 to 8 percent, freeing up some RMB377 billion in bank liquidity. The MOF then raised RMB270 billion by issuing bonds that were bought by the banks themselves. The proceeds were injected into the banks as new capital. It was a good deal for the banks, since it not only provided for their recapitalisation but, whereas they received no interest on reserves held with the central bank, they *would* receive interest on the bonds bought from the MOF. The aggregate interest on these bonds came to around RMB24 billion per year, almost as much as their combined estimated profits of RMB27 billion in 1997.[34]

The next step was to reduce the NPLs on the banks' balance sheets. This is where things started to get *really* creative. The obvious thing to do might have been for the banks to realise the losses and write off the value of the bad loans. However, since the loans had been made to SOEs, which were owned by the state, this would have implied that the state was unable to meet its obligations – a position that offended the sensibilities of Party ideologues. More practically, an immediate write-down would have required further funds to recapitalise the banks. It was not the first time a government facing an insolvent banking sector chose to 'kick the can down the road' and it certainly wasn't the last.[35] In the event, Zhou and his colleagues modelled their solution on the Resolution Trust Corporation, which had been set up in 1989 to deal with banks' NPLs during the American Savings and Loans Crisis.[36] This involved setting up four asset management companies (AMCs), each designated to purchase the NPLs from one of the Big Four banks' balance sheets.[37] The intention was for the AMCs to try to recover what they could or sell off portfolios of NPLs to third parties.

The peculiarity of the Chinese solution was that it left the banks and the AMCs fully intertwined, rather than providing for the cleaned-up banks to move on unencumbered. The reason for this ultimately came down to funding: *where were the AMCs to get the money to purchase the NPLs from?* The answer was again: the banks themselves.

In 1999, the MOF capitalised the AMCs by purchasing a total of RMB40 billion in Special AMC Bonds (roughly $1 billion for each bank), which had a 10-year maturity. This was consistent with the intention that the AMCs were to be wound down after 10 years. The AMCs then raised a further RMB858 billion ($105 billion) by issuing 10-year bonds to the banks. By that point, it had been determined that the banks' NPLs amounted to 39 percent of total loans – almost double the PBOC's estimate in 1997.[38] The following year, the AMCs made their first purchase of NPLs from the banks. NPLs of RMB1.4 trillion ($170 billion) were transferred at full face value, *without any discount* to reflect the likelihood of losses, from the banks to the AMCs. This required the PBOC to extend the AMCs a further RMB634 billion ($75 billion) in loans.[39] By the time of the final transfer from ABC when it was restructured in 2007, $480 billion in NPLs had been spun off from the Big Four banks.[40]

The third step was to bring in strategic investors to support the banks' operational modernisation and for them to pursue international listings. In June 2005, Bank of America announced a $3 billion investment in CCB in return for a stake of 8.5 percent. As part of the deal, the American lender would also get an option to purchase additional shares to take its ownership up to 19.9 percent. This was followed by an investment of a similar amount by the Scottish bank RBS to acquire a 9.6 percent holding in BOC, and an investment of $3.8 billion by a consortium including Goldman Sachs, American Express and the German insurer Allianz to acquire an 8.5 percent stake in ICBC.[41] Given these state-owned banks had been pariahs just a short time before, those investments were not without substantial risk. The fact that these major international financial institutions had been willing to invest such large sums, however, was a major endorsement of the reforms that the Chinese banks had undergone. It was further expected that the strategic investors would support the banks in upgrading their corporate governance, risk management and product development. This paved the way for the highly successful IPOs of BOC, CCB and ICBC on the Hong Kong market in 2005 and 2006, which yielded substantial paper gains for their strategic investors. ABC, the weakest of the Big Four, was eventually listed in 2010.

Notwithstanding the successful international IPOs, however, there remained a host of unresolved issues. Many of these traced back to the mechanism of NPL transfers during the banks' restructuring.

Given the loss-making nature of the loans that they had bought at full face value, *how were the AMCs supposed to repay the funding from the banks and the PBOC?* It was an impossible mission. It can only be surmised that, as China's economy continued to grow rapidly, the expectation was that, by delaying the reckoning, the eventual write-offs would become easier for the government to absorb. However, in the meantime, the AMCs still had to service the interest on the bonds they had issued to the banks. *Where was the cash flow for this to come from?* By this time, it will hardly be surprising that the answer was again: the banks themselves.

Dividends paid out by the banks were funnelled back into servicing the interest on the AMC bonds. This circularity meant that, in order for the AMCs to meet their obligations to the banks, the banks were compelled to pay out sufficient dividends in order for the AMCs to service the bond coupons. The dividends may not have been a problem, except that the banks' loan books were growing very rapidly, which required more and more capital to support new lending. This meant that they would constantly need to come back to the market to raise new capital. Indeed, notwithstanding record profits the previous year, BOC, CCB and ICBC all announced plans to raise an aggregate of $25 billion in new equity capital in 2010. When the original AMC bonds were due to mature in 2009, instead of winding down the AMCs as the PBOC had originally intended, the bonds were extended and, in fact, the AMCs have gone on to expand into various diverse investment operations.

To be sure, there was an important macroeconomic purpose served by the banks' purchase of the AMC bonds. The bonds soaked up liquidity released from the recapitalisations and NPL disposals. Without them, the banks would have seen a surge in their lending capacity. A sudden increase in liquidity would have sparked heavy inflationary pressures and would very likely have resulted in a large number of bad loans – precisely the problem that the restructurings were supposed to remedy. However, the government's interest in ensuring the banks' profitability in order that they keep paying their dividends worked against Zhou's objective of introducing market-based interest rates corresponding to lending risks.

A further blow to Zhou's drive for comprehensive banking reforms came in 2005. His campaign to extricate China's banking sector from the hazards of state planning control was ruffling a lot of feathers. In his original proposal to Zhu Rongji in 1998, Zhou had advocated that the state sell down its stake in the banks to just a minority shareholding. Even Zhu had balked at this as being politically unfeasible. However, but for this one point, he had backed Zhou's reforms to the hilt. After Zhu stepped down as premier in 2003, Zhou's principal political sponsor was Vice Premier Huang Ju (黃菊), a *protégé* of Jiang Zemin who inherited responsibility for the financial sector. Huang fell ill with terminal cancer in early 2005 and was forced to step aside. Premier Wen Jiabao took over his responsibilities for the sector and pursued a more consensus-driven approach. As a result, the PBOC lost influence and, through a series of machinations, control over the banks was transferred to the MOF. That fateful decision proved to be a huge setback for China's banking reforms.

After the collapse of Lehman Brothers in 2008, the Western banking model became widely discredited, allowing those opposed to market-based reforms to gain an upper hand. The fall in international demand for Chinese exports also threatened the economy and social stability. In response, the government rolled out a massive economic stimulus package. Some of the programmes pursued were certainly a positive step. For example, in April 2009, Beijing announced that it would extend health insurance cover from 30 to 90 percent of the population, and that it would pay for the construction of 2,000 county hospitals and 5,000 clinical centres across the country. It was the largest ever expansion in national healthcare provision in world history. However, much of this spending spree would be funded by the banks. The banks' lending targets for 2009 were doubled from RMB4.7 trillion to RMB10 trillion and, given the political cover of economic stimulus, loan underwriting standards were cast aside. Local governments used all manner of financing vehicles to raise funds for various pet projects and, between 2008 and 2010, local government debt ballooned from RMB1 trillion ($146 billion) to an estimated RMB10 trillion ($1.7 trillion).

Thus, China reverted to its earlier state-directed lending model and capital misallocation on a massive scale. In Hubei province alone, with its population of 57 million and a regional GDP of $225 billion in 2009, projects under construction in 2010 were notionally costed at $363 billion, with a further $840 billion planned over the following two years. To put this into perspective, this meant that a single Chinese province with a population the size of the UK and a GDP the size of Greece was spending more on stimulus than any programme ever attempted in the *entire* US until the Covid-19 pandemic struck in 2020.[42]

In the wake of the GFC, the straitened circumstances of the strategic investors in China's Big Four banks forced them to sell their holdings to bolster their own capital positions. This generated much consternation amongst the Chinese authorities, who were irked by the profits the foreign investors had reaped. However, the tragedy of the GFC for the PBOC's reformers was the giant step backward in China's financial sector modernisation. This was seen not just in banking sector practices, but also in the stymied development of the country's bond market.

★★★

The initial impetus for establishing a bond market in the 1980s was to raise badly needed funds for Deng Xiaoping's modernisation programme. The government had suspended bond issuance in 1958 and, for the next 23 years, no bonds were issued at all. When the MOF began to issue treasury bills in 1981, it was considered a patriotic duty to purchase them and they were primarily sold to SOEs. There was no secondary trading and no market rate by which prices were set. Interest rates were differentiated based not on the risk of the borrower, but on the type of investor. For example, in the early 1980s the coupon on bonds issued to SOEs was 4 percent, whereas individual investors received a coupon of 8 percent on the *same bonds*.[43]

A private bond market began to develop with the growth of small enterprises in the 1980s, with two-thirds of all bonds being sold to household investors.[44] When banks were ordered to stop lending due to an inflation spike in 1987, an unregulated OTC secondary market developed spontaneously for cash-strapped investors who needed to sell their bonds – generally at a steep loss. That was China's first *real* – albeit short-lived – experience of market-determined bond pricing. After the dust settled from the Tiananmen incident, bond trading began to be regularised within the confined walls of the SSE and SZSE and pricing once again became managed.

The MOF introduced syndication for government bond sales in 1991, with 70 intermediaries participating in an underwriting syndicate. However, interest rates continued to be set by fiat, rather than by the market. When, in 1993, interest rates rose as high as 20 to 30 percent, the rate offered on the three-year government bond was only 9.5 percent and the five-year bond paid only 10.5 percent. In the face of a guaranteed loss, few underwriters would participate willingly. The state banks forced to buy the bonds simply held them on their own books to maturity in order to avoid recognising losses.

At a difficult tendering meeting at Shanghai's Jinjiang Hotel (锦江饭店) in 1995, the MOF's representative Gao Jian (高坚) could see that, notwithstanding a fixed quota they were obligated to buy, underwriters were reluctant to underwrite the RMB10 billion worth of government bonds on offer, and there was a serious risk of a failed tender. Gao stepped out of the meeting and called the vice minister in charge, suggesting that the underwriting incentives be improved. The vice minister agreed to increase the underwriting fee by 0.1 percent and to extend the settlement date by which the firms had to deliver the cash by 10 days. Returning to the meeting room, Gao decided to try running a Dutch auction[45] by asking each underwriter to write their offer down on a piece of paper and place it into an empty *Hongtashan* (红塔山) cigarette carton. He told them that those who didn't bid would simply be allocated their quota on the worst terms available. Seeing they would be disadvantaged if they did not submit an offer, some 40 underwriters placed their bids in the cigarette carton. The competitive dynamic that Gao introduced had a positive effect on demand and the MOF ended up selling RMB11 billion worth of bonds, RMB1 billion more than it had originally sought, and Chinese government bond (CGB) auctions were born.[46]

Notwithstanding Gao Jian's innovation, this was still a far cry from a real bond 'market'. There was hardly any secondary trading and the lack of liquidity meant that there was no true 'price discovery' – the process by which a market value is established through purchases and sales. The prospect of true market-determined interest rates was put even further out of reach by the cessation of nascent trading in bond futures after the 327 Incident.

The manipulation of bond prices to keep funding costs low for the state and the SOEs made the market unattractive for real investors searching for a market rate of return. There is a story of an angry Shanghainese housewife whose complaints about the banks' *de facto* monopoly over trading in government bonds reached the ears of Zhu Rongji. As the story goes, Zhu reacted decisively and, in June 1997, kicked the banks and most government bond issuance out of the stock exchanges onto the then small and inactive interbank bond market.[47]

The development of the Chinese bond market then languished for some time, but few really cared. For SOEs, it was far easier just to borrow from the permissive state-owned banks, rather than dealing with bondholders. The exchanges and the CSRC viewed corporate bonds as competing directly with equity listings, which were their primary focus. Oversight of corporate debt issuance was vested in the National Development and Reform Commission (NDRC, 国家发展和改革委员会), a successor to the State Planning Commission, which could reliably obtain funding for its projects from local government budgets or state banks. The drive to develop the corporate debt market eventually came from the PBOC.

Zhou Xiaochuan understood well the risks of the command economy model and the systematic mispricing of capital. In the midst of a stock market collapse in 2005, the PBOC opportunistically exploited a regulatory loophole that defined 'corporate bonds' (企业债) as securities with a maturity of longer than one year in order to create a short-term commercial paper (短期融资债券) market. That year, SOEs struggling to raise money in the equity market issued more than RMB142 billion ($17 billion) in commercial paper in the interbank market. The key attraction of the commercial paper market was that the PBOC did not require issuers to seek regulatory approval before issuance. The process was modelled on international practice, with issuers required to seek a credit rating, work with an underwriter to prepare a prospectus, then just simply register the issue with the PBOC. To minimise government interference in this market, the PBOC authorised a non-governmental industry association, the National Association of Financial Markets Institutional Investors (NAFMII, 中国银行间市场交易商协会), to oversee it. By 2008, commercial paper issuance volumes had trebled from 2005.

Further stepping into the NDRC's domain, in April 2008, working through NAFMII, the PBOC created a medium-term note (MTN, 中期票据) instrument with maturities of between three and five years. A regulatory dust up with the NDRC, which claimed oversight over corporate bonds exceeding one year's duration, delayed the launch by four months. However, the State Council (国务院) ultimately supported the PBOC's assertion of the need to develop this market and, in just the first three months, corporate issuers raised RMB174 billion ($26 billion) through MTNs. These new products attracted non-state investors, such as mutual funds and foreign banks, helping to drive forward market-based credit pricing.

The PBOC's opening up of this market came just in time for local governments seeking to take advantage of Beijing's post-GFC stimulus programme. The terms of the RMB4 trillion ($486 billion) stimulus package required local governments to come up with two-thirds of the funding for the projects they identified. Without ready cash on hand, most provinces turned to the bond market. By June 2009, local governments had set up 8,221 corporate entities as financing platforms (融资平台). During the course of that year, these entities raised RMB650 billion ($95 billion) via bond issues, accounting for

48 percent of total commercial paper and MTN issuance. By the end of 2009, together with unrestrained bank lending that accounted for 90 percent of funding for stimulus projects, it was estimated that local government debt had ballooned to RMB7.8 trillion ($1.14 trillion). By the end of 2010, this figure had grown further to RMB10.7 trillion, raising the spectre of a huge spike in bad debts.[48]

Notwithstanding the PBOC's drive to develop the bond market, by 2009 Chinese banks still held more than 70 percent of all bonds outstanding by value and, in aggregate, state-controlled entities accounted for 92 percent of total bond investment. Chinese households held just one percent of total bonds issued by value.[49] Nevertheless, if the government wants to use the state-owned banks to fund state enterprises – in effect, lending money to itself – *what's the problem?*

Herein lies the fundamental risk to China's future prosperity caused by the structural mispricing of capital, and a major underlying source of tensions with other countries. To understand why, it is necessary first to better understand China's economic growth model, the power dynamics between the political elite and private enterprise, and the demographic challenges the country faces.

Still Building, But Will They Come?

Today, China's economy remains highly dependent on investment spending for growth. This traces back to the 1990s, when the country embarked upon a massive infrastructure spending programme. At the time, many could not imagine all those huge new airports and expressways would ever be filled up and criticised the projects as wasteful. As it turned out, in light of the country's very high rate of growth, the Chinese government's 'build-it-and-they-will-come' model of anticipatory development proved the critics wrong. In fact, it can well be argued that the new infrastructure *enabled* China's growth miracle. However, top-down targets, which largely focus on GDP growth, have created incentives for provincial and local leaders to over-rely on investment, often financed with borrowed money, to deliver the results needed for them to advance professionally. The low quality growth driven by this model and its environmental costs were discussed in

Chapter 4. Economists debate over what China's sustainable rate of GDP growth is, but pretty much all agree that it will fall, with many arguing that the long-term rate is likely to be in the range of 3 to 4 percent, in line with more developed countries.[50] As China's economy slows, this continued addiction to investment-led growth runs an ever greater risk of serious capital misallocation and growing bad debts.

Rapid increases in debt levels give some cause for concern. Since 2008, domestic debt has been growing at around 20 percent per year, far higher than overall GDP growth. The credit intensity of China's growth has increased significantly. In 2007–2008, RMB6.5 trillion ($1 trillion) of new borrowing was needed to increase nominal GDP by RMB5 trillion ($769 billion). In 2015–2016, it required RMB20 trillion in new borrowing to generate the same nominal GDP growth.[51] A surge in residential property investment has also added to household debt levels. In 2011, residential investment accounted for roughly 14 percent of GDP, three times the 2003 level.[52] At the end of 2020, China's household debt-to-GDP ratio stood at 62.2 percent, up around 35 percentage points versus a decade ago.[53]

A lack of transparency about the extent of domestic debt makes it difficult to fully gauge the level of risk. Given the difficulties many borrowers face in obtaining bank loans and the systemic mispricing of interest rates, China has also seen rapid growth in shadow banking activities that take place outside the formal banking system.[54] In part, this has been actively encouraged by the government, which tacitly promoted the development of so-called 'wealth management products' (理财产品, saving instruments paying higher interest rates) as a means of indirectly liberalising deposit rates against the opposition of the big banks. Shadow banking assets in China were estimated to be 29 percent of China's total banking assets in 2019, or 86 percent of GDP.[55] Based on an IMF study in 2014, US shadow banking assets exceeded 150 percent of GDP,[56] so China does not compare unfavourably. However, shadow banking's inherent lack of transparency makes it difficult to monitor and control.[57] Local governments have further obscured the full extent of their borrowing through the use of financing platforms. While China's National Institution for Finance and Development (国家金融与发展实验室) put the country's overall debt at 270 percent of GDP in the third quarter of 2020, the Washington-based Institute of

International Finance estimated that figure was actually as high as 335 percent of GDP.[58]

It must be emphasised that the current government has placed greater emphasis on the quality of growth and stated that environmental protection is an 'urgent priority'.[59] Further, compared with the 1990s, there is no doubt that Chinese banks have made significant improvements in their operations and service quality. Financial sector reforms have also continued, notably with the liberalisation of interest rates. In July 2013, the floor on bank lending rates was removed, while caps on deposit rates were scrapped in October 2015.[60] Nevertheless, 54 percent of the Chinese domestic bond market continues to be held by domestic banks[61] and heavy state intervention during the 2015 stock market crash shows that China is still far from allowing market forces to drive the cost and allocation of capital.

For a number of years now, economists and observers have been warning that China faces an imminent debt crisis and financial collapse. So far, this has not materialised. As we saw in the case of the US subprime mortgage crisis, financial imbalances can persist for years or even decades without blowing up and it is extremely difficult to predict the timing of when financial crises might occur. However, in China's case, there is further reason to be sceptical about such doomsday predictions.

Thanks to Chen Yun and the state planners' aversion to foreign debt when China began opening up its economy in the 1980s, China's external borrowings remain relatively low. FDI accounts for 52 percent of its external liabilities and portfolio equity investments make up 15 percent. This means that portfolio debt and other liabilities (typically trade credit and bank debt) make up only 33 percent of the rest of the world's claims on China. Further, China's external assets of $8.2 trillion significantly exceed its external liabilities of $6.0 trillion.[62] Unlike stocks and bonds, which can be quickly sold, FDI typically represents investments in production plants and machinery. In practice, this means that China is insulated from the type of financial crisis that its Asian neighbours experienced in the late 1990s, when rapid withdrawal of foreign capital precipitated simultaneous debt and currency crises.

Of course, excessive *domestic* borrowing can still lead to a credit crisis. However, China's closed capital account and state control over the banking sector make such an eventuality much easier to manage within the system. In any banking crisis, the key issue comes down to the allocation of losses between investors, depositors and taxpayers. In the 2008 GFC, US policymakers' highest priority was to protect depositors and losses were primarily borne by investors. The Chinese government's fixation on social stability would no doubt dictate that depositors' funds be absolutely protected in the event of a bank failure. The Chinese state is ultimately the largest shareholder in (and creditor to) the banks, so there is no question that the government would ultimately bear the brunt of any losses. Since the vast majority of debts in the system are denominated in renminbi and the government controls the central bank, in the worst case the PBOC could simply be ordered to print more money to pay for a bail-out. Eventually, this might lead to higher inflation, but China's closed capital account affords the PBOC a great degree of flexibility to manage this through both monetary policy and administrative measures. Thus, China's failure to push through further banking reforms and develop a fully market-oriented bond market has become a major inhibitor to fully liberalising cross-border capital flows.

Nevertheless, steps towards liberalising China's capital account since the mid-2000s have eroded the government's ability to prevent capital flight. These have been pursued by the PBOC primarily in response to practical needs, as international trade has grown and Chinese citizens increasingly travel overseas for tourism, studies and work. However, reformers within the PBOC have also used the rallying cry of 'renminbi internationalisation' (人民币国际化) to help overcome opposition to further domestic financial reforms. Liberalisations of outbound capital flows included the Qualified Domestic Institutional Investor (QDII) scheme, which allowed approved Chinese asset managers to gather funds from domestic investors for investment overseas. The scheme is subject to an overall quota, which has been gradually raised over time. As of January 2021, the overall quota that had been approved by State Administration of Foreign Exchange (SAFE, 国家外汇管理局) was around $126 billion.[63] In 2015, the State Council announced the Qualified Domestic Individual Investor (QDII2) scheme to allow individuals from six pilot cities[64] with at least one million renminbi in assets (roughly $160,000) to invest directly in overseas securities and real estate.

From January 2010, individual Chinese citizens have been allowed to convert up to $50,000 worth of renminbi into foreign currency per year.

These officially sanctioned channels have added to other non-sanctioned ones. Trade mis-invoicing has long been a method by which Chinese business owners have shifted assets offshore. This involves importers or exporters agreeing with an overseas counterparty to deliberately over- or under-invoice for the goods or services transacted, enabling the Chinese party to move money out of the country. Other channels include laundering money through Macau casinos, underground banking networks, or even buying luxury collectibles (such as high-value wristwatches) in Mainland China for renminbi then reselling them offshore for foreign currency. These illicit capital flows are included in official statistics as 'net errors and omissions' (NEOs), which capture the residual movement in the balance of payments not recorded in capital or current account transactions.

In 2014, NEO outflows from China amounted to $108 billion, then suddenly, in 2015, they jumped to $188 billion.[65] This event highlights the PBOC's waning power to control the renminbi's exchange rate.

Through the 2000s, China's growing current account surplus saw the country draw growing international criticism for holding down the value of the renminbi. The US, which was experiencing growing trade deficits, was the most vocal critic. In June 2005, the PBOC moved the renminbi from a hard peg against the dollar to a managed float against a basket of currencies. During the GFC, China reverted to managing the renminbi's value against the dollar. However, from mid-2005 up to mid-2014, the Chinese currency appreciated by almost 25 percent versus the dollar. By then, trade with the US only accounted for around 14 percent of China's total merchandise trade – significant, no doubt, but small relative to trade with the rest of the world.[66] Since, owing to the euro crisis and a slow Japanese recovery, the dollar had appreciated against other major currencies, the renminbi's appreciation on a *trade-weighted* basis was even higher – around 30 percent.

As the dollar continued to rise between July 2014 and July 2015, the renminbi fell a modest 0.8 percent against the dollar but *increased* by 14 percent against the currencies of China's other major trading partners. From their peak of $3.99 trillion in June 2014, China's foreign currency reserves fell by $350 billion over the following year. The PBOC appeared to be selling foreign currencies to *hold up* the value of China's currency. In the face of a slowing Chinese economy at the time, the IMF declared in May 2015 that the renminbi was no longer undervalued.[67]

The PBOC could not indefinitely keep selling down its foreign exchange reserves to prop up the renminbi. The Chinese stock market had been on a bull run but, having peaked at 5,166 on 12 June, the Shanghai composite index fell by a third over the next month.[68] On 11 August, the PBOC announced a change that US policymakers had long been calling for. In conjunction with a 1.9 percent devaluation of the renminbi against the dollar, it announced that it was moving towards a more market-driven mechanism for setting its exchange rate.[69] Specifically, although the renminbi had been allowed to trade freely within a daily limit of +/− 2.0 percent, the PBOC had been setting the opening reference rate for the renminbi each day somewhat arbitrarily (though, unlike President Roosevelt in the 1930s, it is doubtful that President Xi was calling the shots from his bed). This meant that the previous day's movement could just be ignored. Henceforth, the PBOC committed that the opening reference rate would tightly track the previous day's closing rate.

Rather than viewing this as a positive step towards further financial reform, the markets panicked. The PBOC had historically been opaque and currency traders did not know how to interpret the move. They assumed the worst and began dumping the renminbi. The offshore yuan (CNH), which floated more freely, traded at a large discount to the onshore yuan (CNY), which still traded within the two percent daily band. Using the official and unofficial channels now open to them, Chinese citizens began to move funds offshore, either to preserve the value of their savings in foreign currency terms or to profit from continued renminbi depreciation. In August alone, China's foreign exchange reserves fell by $94 billion, as the PBOC tried to stabilise its currency. Between July and December 2015, reserves fell by a total of $415 billion.[70]

If the PBOC's actions had misfired with the market, US policymakers' reactions were hardly any better. It seems that their calls for China to move to a more market-oriented exchange rate mechanism only applied if it meant that the renminbi's value went up. Rather than commending China on the move, which the US had long called for, American politicians heaped on further criticisms.

On the day of the PBOC's announcement, Donald Trump, then the leading candidate for the Republican presidential nomination, told his supporters:

> [*China*] *continuously cuts their currency, they devalue their currency. They've been doing it for years; this isn't just starting.*

The head of the Senate Finance Committee, Charles Grassley, who might have been expected to be better informed, said in a statement:

> *China has manipulated its currency for a long time. This is just the latest example, and it's past time to do something about it.*[71]

The key lesson for the PBOC though – other than the need to improve its communications with the market – was that the liberalisations that it had undertaken to date had already made it much harder to maintain currency stability than in the past. And, given that reforms tend to have a momentum of their own, there was no going back. Notwithstanding the extraordinary circumstances relating to the Covid-19 pandemic in 2020–2021, in the longer run, Chinese citizens are unlikely to accept curtailments in the freedoms to travel and study abroad that they have now been granted. Chinese businessmen are looking ever more to expand their companies' footprints internationally.

In some ways, the 'limbo' territory that the PBOC finds itself in today is more dangerous than moving swiftly ahead with further reforms. Although it has blunted its own administrative measures to control capital flows, it still cannot rely on normal market adjustment mechanisms. Thus, if speculators see any sign of economic weakness, they have a substantial incentive to test the limits to which the central bank will go to maintain a particular exchange rate level for the renminbi.

Full exchange rate liberalisation means opening up the country's capital account. In this, China's policymakers find themselves prisoners of the fear of sudden destabilising capital flight were they to do so. To mitigate this risk, China would need to move away from its state-directed investment-led economic model and allow market forces to drive the pricing of capital, so that Chinese depositors and investors are not incentivised to seek better risk-adjusted returns overseas. However, it is not just rates of return on their capital that might drive Chinese citizens to move their wealth offshore.

Notwithstanding the fact that access to funding is still skewed towards relatively less efficient SOEs, private enterprises have started an economic insurgency. This has created a new class of wealthy businesspeople who are now just as concerned to protect their wealth from the risk of arbitrary exercise of state power.

Alien Attack

In June 2013, a 14-year-old Hangzhou-based business specialising in matching buyers and sellers online for everything from diapers to fake eyelashes and power tools launched a revolution in China's financial services sector. It began accepting cash deposits. Savers could deposit anything from as little as 0.1 yuan (around 1.5 US cents), which the company would combine into pools of around $1.5 million or more and auction to the banks, obtaining for its customers a higher interest rate than they could on their individual bank savings accounts. This service, named *Yu'ebao* (余额宝), was effectively bringing MMFs to China's masses. By May the following year, it had pulled in an astonishing $93 billion in deposits from over 80 million Chinese savers who had long been used to derisory rates of interest and non-existent customer service from their banks.[72] The banks were furious but, if they didn't want to lose deposits, they had no choice but to pay up.

Yu'ebao was the latest in a series of services offered by Alipay, the payments business linked to Chinese internet giant Alibaba, founded by the charismatic and outspoken Jack Ma (马云). A former teacher who used to practice his English by offering free tour guide services to foreign visitors to his hometown, Ma is the poster child for the Chinese entrepreneurial spirit unleashed by Deng Xiaoping's reform and opening up. Some in China refer to the diminutive entrepreneur as 'E.T.' due to his supposed resemblance to the loveable outer space creature from Steven Spielberg's 1982 movie, while Ma's friend and fellow Chinese billionaire Guo Guangchang (郭广昌) has called him an 'alien', in apparent reference to his extra-terrestrial intellect.[73]

Started in 1999 in a small apartment that Ma shared with his wife, Alibaba had begun as a business-to-business (B2B) platform connecting China's growing number of small manufacturers with overseas buyers. Ma's timing was fortuitous. Until March 1999, Chinese citizens had faced high barriers to accessing the internet. Getting a phone connection could take months and cost up to $600. However, the China Telecom IPO had accelerated investment in telecoms infrastructure to catch up to more advanced countries and, that month, the installation fee for a second phone line was scrapped. The monthly connection fee also fell from an average of $70 per month in 1997 to just $9 by the end of 1999.[74] Falling costs led to a rapid rise in the number of Chinese internet users.

In the early days of the Chinese internet, trust – or, rather, the absence of it – was a major inhibitor to the growth of online commerce. When they sent their payment, buyers had no way to ensure they would receive the product they had purchased. To resolve this trust issue, Alibaba set up Alipay as an escrow service to give buyers and sellers greater confidence to transact. Riding on the explosive growth in Chinese internet users and the surge in exports catalysed by the country's WTO accession, Alibaba's business boomed, and it soon diversified into business-to-consumer (B2C) and other services. The company's trajectory was further boosted by the launch of Apple's iPhone in 2008, which set off the vast expansion of online commerce via smartphones. Alipay (subsequently spun off into Ant Group, 蚂蚁集团) became a ubiquitous mobile payment tool, with over a billion users and handling more than RMB118 trillion ($17 trillion) in Chinese payments in the year to June 2020.[75] Today, mobile payment usage in China is so developed that it has overtaken cash in most urban centres, with even street vendors and buskers accepting payment through Alipay or its rival WeChat Pay. Alibaba was listed on the NYSE in September 2014 at a valuation of $168 billion, one of the largest ever IPOs, and the company's stock has surged further since.[76]

From virtually nothing in 1978, the private sector has grown to account for around 80 percent of China's GDP, while the share of the workforce employed by SOEs and collectively owned enterprises has fallen to just nine percent. Many of these private firms are now very large. The share of private companies in the top one percent of firms ranked by total value added rose from roughly 40 percent in 1998 to 65 percent in 2007.[77] Commercial competition has been a big factor behind this, but the Chinese private sector has also been supported through fiscal policy. To incentivise rapid adoption of foreign technology and business methods, firms funded through FDI paid only 15 percent income tax versus 33 percent for domestically funded firms.[78] Unlike SOEs, private firms have not been saddled with heavy social obligations. The phenomenal growth of China's high tech and internet sectors in particular was also boosted by other factors.

The technology boom and the growth of internet-based businesses have been a global phenomenon. However, in most places, US internet giants – such as Amazon, Apple, Facebook and Google – have dominated. China is one of the few countries that has generated a large stable of home-grown companies to rival them. Protection from foreign competition has certainly helped to a degree. Many of China's biggest internet companies do not have unique business models and have copied from the West. The search giant Baidu (百度) is a Chinese version of Google, which has benefited from Chinese censors' blocking of Google's website in the country. The Shenzhen-based internet conglomerate Tencent's (腾讯) ubiquitous messaging service WeChat originally mimicked Facebook's WhatsApp messenger application. Alibaba's business model effectively amalgamates those of Amazon, eBay and PayPal, though it has made many key changes and improvements to adapt these services to the local market. Nevertheless, it would be unfair to say that these companies have succeeded only through imitation or protectionist policies. Cutthroat competition, a superior understanding of Chinese consumer needs, and the sheer scale of China's market have been key drivers behind their success.[79]

Also critical was the fact that these industries were almost entirely new. There were no incumbent players against which they had to compete, which meant that they were not in constant battle against vested interests. The capital-light nature of internet businesses relative to industrial enterprises also meant they were not heavily dependent on bank financing, which was heavily skewed towards supporting SOEs. And, given the Chinese government recognised the need to support the development of China's high tech sector, it did not rush to erect the regulatory or bureaucratic barriers that exist in more developed industries. Thus, emerging Chinese technology players were freer to experiment than companies operating in many other sectors. By the time that they began seriously upsetting vested interest groups, the major Chinese internet players already had the scale to look after themselves, and the popularity of their services made it difficult to curtail them.

The significance of the development of Chinese private sector champions like Alibaba goes way beyond their direct economic contribution. They potentially threaten to upend a social order and power structures that have remained largely unchanged since 1989.

China's one-party state system effectively entrenches the rule of a small elite. On the one hand, as Deng Xiaoping had intended, this has enabled a meritocratic technocracy to push through China's rapid modernisation and economic development. On the other, it is a system that lends itself to endemic corruption and, as the original ideological constraint of communism has been lifted and capitalist practices openly drive the country's growth, this has enabled the political elite and their families to amass enormous wealth through their positions and connections. This has blurred the lines between where the state bureaucracy ends and business begins, since individuals can play a dual role, or family members can be dispersed across the political and commercial spheres. The 'politico-entrepreneurial clans' thus created rely on and benefit from the CCP's continuity.

While Deng's resistance to political reforms in the 1980s was justified by the need to focus on economic growth and raising living standards, China is now the second largest economy in the world and its citizens enjoy a far higher degree of prosperity. The continuing lack of an independent judiciary and the arbitrary application of the law now appear largely to benefit a small group of the Party elite.[80]

For much of Chinese history, the merchant class was kept out of the political system. From the time of the Song Dynasty, notwithstanding the wealth that merchants accumulated, they never succeeded in establishing themselves as a political force, as the state was always vigilant to prevent the emergence of a rival source of power.[81] This changed after the fall of the Qing Dynasty and money politics ran rampant in the Nationalist regime. Chiang Kai-shek's failure to restrain corruption was a key factor contributing to the CCP's rise to power. However, reform and opening up in the 1980s and 1990s made it once again easier for private business interests to exert political influence, initially in a limited way and at the local level. Under Jiang Zemin, the CCP began to embrace private entrepreneurs more enthusiastically and to admit them into the Party. A 2015 survey showed that China had 1,271 billionaires, of which 203 were members of the National People's Congress (NPC, 全国人民代表大会) or the People's Political Consultative Conference (人民政治协商会议).[82]

While wealthy and business interests' influence on state policy is nowhere near as strong or as institutionalised as in the US, the emergence of the politico-entrepreneur class had begun to seriously undermine the legitimacy of the CCP during the Hu Jintao (胡锦涛) Administration (2003–2013). One Chinese government advisor has estimated that 'rent-seeking' activities, or corruption, accounted for 20–30 percent of GDP.[83] Political influence peddling was highlighted in 2013, when a scandal broke out over foreign investment banks' hiring of 'princelings' (太子族, children of politically connected individuals) without requisite professional qualifications in return for lucrative advisory business from Chinese SOEs. This, in fact, had been common practice for some time, which JPMorgan Chase had even institutionalised as its 'Sons and Daughters Programme', under which it hired close to 100 individuals referred by officials at Chinese state-owned firms between 2006 and 2013. For this, JPMorgan ultimately paid $264 million to resolve civil and criminal charges relating to violations of the US Foreign Corrupt Practices Act.[84] However, such episodes have stoked anger and deep resentment amongst the Chinese population.

The rise of the politico-entrepreneur class has also been accompanied by a rise in wealth inequality. Driven primarily by the large-scale privatisation of housing, private wealth increased from 100 percent of national income in the 1980s to 450 percent in 2015. One 2012 study found that capital income[85] as a share of total income for the bottom 95 percent of urban households was zero but, between the 95th and 99th percentile, hovered around five percent. For the top one percent of urban householders, it reached one-third of their total income. Naturally, the Chinese government is highly sensitive about the publication of data showing rising levels of wealth disparity,[86] but studies show that, by some measures, Chinese wealth inequality is now comparable to, or even exceeds, that of America.[87]

When he came to power in 2012, Xi Jinping was faced with burgeoning popular dissatisfaction about official corruption, rising inequality and environmental pollution, and a growing sense that factional infighting and vested interests within the CCP were preventing the government from pursuing pressing reforms. At the same time, the GFC and increasingly fractious politics in the US and Europe had undermined faith in the Western capitalist model, giving greater voice to nationalist sentiment that China should pursue a different path.

Xi is the son of a veteran Communist leader, who was purged during the Cultural Revolution. Following his father's fall from grace, the young Xi was exiled to the northeast of Shaanxi province, where he lived in a cave home in a small village. He became the village party secretary and, when universities were re-opened to people with the right class backgrounds, was admitted to study chemical engineering at Tsinghua as a 'worker-soldier-peasant student' (工农兵学员). He rose up the Party ranks through the coastal provinces, serving as governor of Fujian province from 1999 to 2002, then as governor and party secretary of neighbouring Zhejiang province (home to Alibaba) from 2002 until 2007. He was appointed to the Standing Committee of the CCP's Politburo in 2007 and, pursuant to China's opaque succession process, rose to become Party General Secretary and President at the end of Hu Jintao's term.

Once in power, Xi initiated a far-reaching anti-corruption campaign that promised not only to prosecute the 'flies' but also the 'tigers' holding high office. Within a few years, over a million members of the CCP, around one percent of the total membership, had been disciplined for varying levels of corruption. True to his word, the campaign reached the top echelons of the Party, with 20 out of the 205 Central Committee members elected at the 2012 Party Congress indicted.

The cases uncovered shocking levels of embezzlement and graft. At the time of his arrest in 2014, it was discovered that the entire basement of Central Military Commission (中央军事委员会) vice chairman Xu Caihou's (徐才厚) 20,000-square-foot residence was stacked with dollar, euro and renminbi banknotes weighing more than a ton.[88] Just a month after Xu was expelled from the Party, former Standing Committee member Zhou Yongkang (周永康) was formally placed under investigation. Zhou had risen up through the oil industry to become Minister of Land and Resources in 1998. He later served as party secretary of Sichuan and Minister of Public Security. Charged in December 2014 for corruption, leaking state secrets and adultery, Zhou was the highest-ranking member of the CCP to be toppled by Xi's campaign. It was estimated that $14.5 billion in family-related assets were seized during the investigation into his network.

The anti-corruption campaign was popular but has drawn varying interpretations. Critics see it as a purge to remove political opposition and consolidate power, while supporters have pointed to the need to stamp out corrupt practices and restore public confidence in the CCP. The respected and highly accomplished Wang Qishan, who as Secretary of the CCP's Central Commission for Discipline Inspection (中央纪律检查委员会) spearheaded the campaign, told former US Treasury Secretary Hank Paulson in November 2013 that 'There is no chance for economic reform without this'.[89]

Wang's comment was highly revealing about the motives behind the anti-corruption campaign. Given the historic difficulty of pushing through major reforms against vested opposition within the Party and wider society, it can be understood why the leadership has sought to eliminate opposition and concentrate power. The administration's highly controversial move in 2018 to abolish presidential term limits might be viewed in this context. Nevertheless, it has generated a deep sense of unease both inside China and internationally, and there remain questions over the precise nature of the reforms Xi is looking to pursue.

Since 2012, China has seen rising censorship and greater limitations on the activities of civil society elements, such as human rights lawyers, non-governmental organisations (NGOs) and religious groups.[90] Xi's administration has also rejected a number of aspects of the US political and social model, such as free market ideology and constitutional democracy, which it sees as opening the door to the capture of the political system by moneyed interests. Recalling the East India Company and Jardine Matheson's roles in the outbreak of the Opium War, as well as the rising influence of wealth in US politics, it is easy to see why Chinese leaders fear reforms that might open the door to private enterprises dictating the policies of the state. However, there is a risk that their fear might stifle China's own further development and stoke greater international conflict.

In the commercial sphere, the Xi Administration has extended the Party's influence over private enterprise, including enhancing the presence of CCP branches within private companies.[91] In the first half of 2018, SOEs acquired stakes in 46 private companies listed on the SSE, with more than half of those investments representing a controlling interest.[92] The longer-term effects of the state's resurgent role in enterprise on China's innovative capacity and productivity growth remain to be seen but, given the enormous contribution of private enterprise to the country's economic revival, great care needs to be taken to balance the interests of the private sector and the state.

★★★

On the morning of 24 October 2020, Jack Ma stood before an audience at the Bund Financial Summit in Shanghai and spoke for 21 minutes on the role of innovation in the financial sector. Referring back to the Bretton Woods Agreement and the development of the Basel bank capital adequacy rules, he questioned whether financial regulators were now so fixated on risk that they were ignoring the need for development. The night before, Ant Group, the parent company of Alipay, had just priced its upcoming IPO, valuing the company at $315 billion. By 2020, the company had expanded well beyond mobile payments into distributing mutual funds, insurance and personal loans. In the year to June, it had handled $17 trillion in digital payments and its public floatation was due to raise $34.4 billion, the largest IPO in history.[93] Speaking of the needs of young people, small entrepreneurs and developing countries, Ma criticised the 'pawnshop mentality' of China's banking system as not meeting modern needs.

The entrepreneur's message contrasted sharply with a speech two hours earlier by Wang Qishan, who had emphasised the need to 'place emphasis on financial innovation and the strengthening of supervision'.[94] Ma's words caused a stir in the media at the time, but little did journalists know about the storm that was brewing.

By 2 November, Ant's shares, which were due to begin trading in Hong Kong and Shanghai on 5 November, were trading in the unofficial 'grey market' at a 50 percent premium to their IPO price, reflecting frenzied demand. Investors had submitted orders totalling $3 trillion to try and get an allocation for the offering.[95] Then on 3 November, the SSE issued an announcement suspending Ant's offering, citing a 'material event' and indicating that impending new regulations might disqualify Ant from listing. The company announced the following day that it was freezing its Hong Kong IPO. The market was devastated. The exchanges in both Hong Kong and Shanghai had worked hard to position themselves to host the offering. For the SSE in particular, it had been seen as a huge coup for its new tech-focused STAR Market, which had been set up specifically to attract companies like Ant. Investment bankers, who had been expecting to share in almost $400 million in bookrunner fees, also saw their fat anticipated bonuses go up in smoke.

In the days that followed, media speculated that China's leaders had taken umbrage at Jack Ma's speech in Shanghai and decided to cut him down to size. Perhaps there was some element of truth in the speculation. However, observing events at face value, it appears that there were two fundamental issues. The first was that Ant had expanded at lightning speed into multiple categories of financial services before a full regulatory framework had been put in place and, in particular, regulators were concerned about its low capital levels compared to bank lenders. Higher capital requirements would clearly negatively impact the company's valuation. Therefore, the second regulatory issue at stake was the protection of investors who had subscribed to Ant's IPO. These regulatory concerns were not unreasonable, but the decision to act just 48 hours before the company's shares were due to begin trading reinforced perceptions about the arbitrariness of the application of China's laws and regulations.[96] Those perceptions were further compounded when, on Christmas Eve, Chinese regulators announced a probe into alleged monopolistic practices at Alibaba.

The rapid rise of internet behemoths that gather massive amounts of user data and wield enormous – and often monopolistic – power has not just been a problem for China. Governments and regulators around the world have been grappling with how to deal with the emerging issues. However, in China there is an additional underlying question about the relative roles of the Party, private enterprise and the state. Businesspeople are increasingly demanding legal clarity and due process.

Since Deng Xiaoping's rejection of Zhao Ziyang's 1987 proposals for political reform, the Party has resisted submitting to a separation of powers under the rule of law, which would reduce the state's flexibility and check the power of the CCP leadership. However, if the private sector is to continue to serve as China's growth engine, it is inevitable that private wealth holders will demand greater legal security for their property rights, setting them and the Party on course for conflict. Further, notwithstanding the success of President Xi's anti-corruption campaign, without impartial application of the rule of law, corrupt practices in China's political system are likely to remain endemic.

Who Will Look After Grandma?

Notwithstanding tensions over rising inequality and other social issues, the Chinese people have generally experienced a steady improvement in overall prosperity and living standards over the past 40 years. Such conditions do not suggest any imminent threat to social stability. However, were economic growth to slow significantly, things could change radically. Here, China's demographic profile poses the most serious risk.

China's population in 1949 was around 540 million. As it recovered from the civil war and early CCP economic policies yielded successes, the country's fertility rate reached as high as 6.4 children per woman in 1957. Devastating famine and malnutrition during the Great Leap Forward saw this collapse to 3.3 children per woman in 1961. However, fertility recovered to 5.8 children between 1963 and the early 1970s, as the country experienced a baby boom. By 1976, sharp falls in infant mortality and longer life expectancy had seen the population grow to 940 million.[97]

China was far from the only country that had seen a population surge during this period. Post-WW2 baby booms had also led to large population increases in Europe and the US, and policy and environmental organisations such as the Club of Rome and the Sierra Club began to worry about an overpopulation crisis. A 1972 book commissioned by the Club of Rome entitled *The Limits to Growth*, which warned of impending ecological and economic collapse if the world failed to constrain population growth, sold 30 million copies worldwide. As Chinese scientists began to have greater contact with the outside world following Chairman Mao's death, they became heavily influenced by these

Malthusian arguments. One of these scientists was Song Jian (宋健), an aerospace engineer who read *The Limits to Growth* during a study trip to Europe in 1978.

Song was born in Shandong province in 1931 and enlisted in the Communist army during the civil war aged just 14. After the Communist victory, he went on to study at the Harbin Institute of Technology (哈尔滨工业大学). A gifted student in the fields of cybernetics and military science, in 1953 he was sent for further education in Moscow, where he earned his PhD. Back in China in the 1960s, he became one of the country's foremost experts in missile guidance systems. As such, he was given special protection during the Cultural Revolution, during which he continued his research at a missile base in Inner Mongolia.

Gripped by the population question, Song and his associates employed newly available computer technology to construct a mathematical model to forecast future population growth. Based on their calculations, if China maintained its 1975 fertility rate of 3.0 children per woman, the population would reach 4.26 billion by 2080.[98] Song's group presented their findings at a symposium on population held in Chengdu (成都) in December 1979. Academics and government officials in the audience were stunned. Even without an understanding of China's dynastic cycles, the implications for social stability were clear. Coming on the heels of the turbulence of the Cultural Revolution, it is not hard to see why Song's forecasts elicited a strong response.

The Chinese government had already been encouraging couples to have no more than one child since 1978. However, this was on a voluntary basis. When news of Song's findings reached Chen Yun, it set in motion a hardening of state policy. The resulting one-child policy, which lasted until 2013, was the largest-scale implementation ever of national population control. The policy was controversial, and the government was forced to concede to numerous exceptions. For example, if the family's first child suffered from a disability, couples were allowed to have more than one child. In the case of rural communities, parents were permitted to have a second child if their first-born was a daughter. Thus, in practice, China's fertility rate remained above one child per woman but, in the early 1990s, it fell to 1.45 children, far below the 2.07 level required to maintain a stable population.

The consequences of China's one-child policy have been far-reaching. One result, given a traditional cultural preference for boys, has been a huge gender imbalance. Compared to a global average of 107–108 boys per 100 girls, China produced over 121 boys per 100 girls in 2004.[99] Some two million girls were abandoned or given up for adoption.[100] Beyond the heart-wrenching human stories, however, the one-child policy has left troubling social and economic legacies that are only just beginning to be felt.

Population controls forced down China's birth rate just as its baby boomers were hitting working age. The surge in the labour supply, coupled with a fall in the number of children that each working age person had to support, significantly accelerated China's demographic dividend. However, the result is that China now has one of the most rapidly aging populations on Earth. In advanced countries, the cohort of citizens aged over 60 approximately doubled between 1950 and 2015 to 24 percent of the population. In China, this process will take place in just 20 years, or less than one-third of the time. By 2030, those aged over 65 will account for 25 percent of the population.[101] China's working age population fell by 3.45 million people in 2012, the first decline since the Great Leap Forward. This decline is now accelerating, with the working age population to decline by around 7 million a year between 2025 and 2035. By 2050, China's working age population is forecast to fall from the current level of around one billion to just 213 million.

At the same time, China's population of old people is continuing to grow. Those aged over 60 numbered 209 million in 2015 (just over 15 percent of the population). By 2050 the number of over-60s is expected to reach 490 million (36.5 percent of the population). In 2017, there were 7.7 workers to support each older citizen. By 2050, this ratio is predicted to fall to just 2.1 workers.[102] This will place considerable strain on China's financial resources.

For a long time, China had resisted increasing entitlements. If anything, reforms under Zhu Rongji had sought to move away from the cradle-to-grave care offered to workers by SOEs. However, Hu Jintao's extension of national healthcare coverage in 2009 was followed by the 2011 Social Insurance Law (社会保险法), which extended social security, especially pension rights, to previously uncovered citizens, including farmers and migrant workers. These moves reflect the government's recognition that it can no longer rely on traditional family support structures to provide for the elderly. Rural-to-urban migration means that children now often live far from their parents, and the bonds of traditional family structures are weakening. More importantly, the sheer size of the senior population relative to younger people makes it impossible to rely solely on family support. After two generations of the one-child policy, a single working age person might have to support not only his or her parents, but also two sets of grandparents!

Similar to many other countries, most of China's pension schemes are unfunded. As the population ages therefore, these entitlements will weigh heavily on national finances. Healthcare and pension expenditures, which currently account for 7 percent of GDP are forecast to rise to around 20 percent. This is likely an underestimate, since it is predicated on a fertility rate of 1.85 children and current rates of life expectancy. If births fall short of this or people live longer, or if rates of welfare provision are increased to the higher levels offered in America and the EU, the burden will rise further.[103]

The indirect impact on China's economy and finances will also be considerable. Not only do older people generally consume less but, as they draw down their savings over their retirements, the level of deposits in China's banking system will fall. This will reduce banks' capacity to lend and lower the country's investment firepower.

Shrinkage in the labour force will also whittle away what has thus far been China's greatest competitive advantage in manufacturing and trade. In fact, rising Chinese wages have already seen lower-value manufacturing move to cheaper countries, such as Vietnam and Cambodia.

To remain competitive, Chinese firms have been trying to boost productivity. Since 2013, China has been the largest market for industrial robots.[104] However, as manufacturing becomes more automated, China's cost advantage over other countries is likely to dissipate further, and it is quite conceivable that production will move closer to consumption centres to save on shipping costs and speed time-to-market.

China's demographic challenges also pose a significant threat to social stability. Quite apart from the financial strains on the working age population, the one-child policy's legacy of a huge gender imbalance means that, over the next few decades, China will have around 30 million 'surplus' men of marriageable age, who will have trouble finding wives.[105] Large numbers of unmarried young men have historically been associated with higher levels of violence in society.[106]

Given the multi-dimensional challenges posed by China's aging population, the government has been scrambling to find solutions. One means of reducing the burden of old-age pensioners is to raise the retirement age to extend their working lives and reduce the number of years of dependence on the state. China's retirement age has remained unchanged for four decades at 60 for men and 55 for female white-collar workers. Given increases in life expectancy, there is certainly room to require workers to work for longer. However, like governments elsewhere, the Chinese government has faced resistance to reforms. A proposal to raise the pension eligibility age in 2012 was derailed by a fierce public backlash. The government announced plans in March 2021 to pursue a gradual increase in the pension age[107] but this will not be sufficient on its own.

China is also trying to increase family sizes. The one-child policy was relaxed in 2009 and again in 2013 to allow more couples to have a second child, then the one-child policy was abolished altogether in 2015 and all couples were allowed to have a second child. The impact was an immediate jump in the number of births, but this didn't last long. In 2016, 17.9 million babies were born, around a million more than the year before. However, births fell back quickly to 14.6 million in 2019, the lowest since 1961. The fertility rate remains at 1.7 children per women, far below what is needed to keep the population stable.[108] In May 2021, family planning restrictions were further relaxed to allow couples to have three children. However, it is unclear whether this will be successful in boosting the birth rate. The reasons why Chinese couples nowadays are having fewer children are the same as those in other modern societies: rising income levels, access to better social security, higher levels of female education, and urbanisation.

An alternative solution would be to boost inward migration. However, due to social and cultural factors, China does not seem likely to accept immigration on any substantial scale. It is therefore hard to see how China can avoid its demographic fate.

Without being able to materially alter the country's demographic profile, the government will have to look to other means. From a macroeconomic perspective, it will need to continuously raise productivity to cushion the fall in labour supply. From a financial perspective, to help fund their post-retirement lifestyles, Chinese savers will need to generate a better return on their financial assets. Today, the Chinese population holds around $33 trillion of its savings in cash deposits at banks,[109] while their stock and bond holdings stand at just $17 trillion and $11 trillion, respectively.[110] In contrast, Americans hold $21 trillion in cash deposits, but hold much more in stocks and bonds – around $57 trillion and $58 trillion, respectively.[111] Given the effects of inflation and the relatively low returns on cash versus stock and bond investments over the long run, Chinese savers' conservatism is likely to place a greater burden on the state. A key component of Chinese government policy therefore is to increase its savers' exposure to capital markets.

China's still relatively underdeveloped capital markets will struggle to absorb any significant portion of the country's huge deposit base without stoking serious price bubbles. In any event, it is desirable for long-term savings to be diversified, in order to reduce the risks of concentration in any individual market or asset class. This is why the Chinese government has had no choice but to expand its investors' access to overseas markets.

Connecting China and the World

In late 2012, SSE chairman Gui Minjie (桂敏杰) approached HKEX with an intriguing proposal: *how about linking trading between the two exchanges to allow investors in each market to invest in the other?*

This was not the first attempt to allow greater capital flows between Mainland China and international securities markets. The QDII programme, which allowed Mainlanders to subscribe to funds investing overseas, had been around since 2006. The Qualified Foreign Institutional Investor (QFII) programme allowing foreign funds to invest in domestic Chinese securities had been around for even longer, since 2002. This was supplemented in 2011 by the Renminbi Qualified Foreign Institutional Investor (RQFII) programme, which laid out clearer eligibility guidance and allowed foreign fund managers to use renminbi raised offshore to invest in Mainland stocks and bonds. However, these channels were cumbersome at that time, since they were subject to quotas and fund managers were required to go through a lengthy – and often opaque – approvals process. Moreover, individual investors were restricted to investing in funds, rather than being able to select specific companies to invest in.

A 'Through Train' (直通车) scheme, which would have allowed Mainland Chinese investors to open accounts in Hong Kong directly to buy shares, had been touted in August 2007. However, this led to an investment frenzy in the Hong Kong market, which inflated a big stock price bubble, and the scheme was quickly shelved. In any event, the Through Train proposal had failed to address many issues. For example, since Hong Kong operates an open capital market, how could Mainland authorities ensure that Chinese investors only invested in Hong Kong shares, and not in other assets like real estate or overseas shares? And how could China's tax authorities keep track of investors' financial dealings to ensure they paid any Chinese taxes due? There were many other such unresolved questions, mostly to do with practical problems relating to opening up China's closed capital account. As the spike in the Hong Kong market demonstrated, this was not just a problem for Mainland China but, given the huge potential flood of Chinese capital, also for the markets receiving this investment.

Shanghai had long been thinking about how to internationalise its market and the concept for linking the two markets had emerged from the work of the SSE's Global Business Development Department, headed by Fu Hao (傅浩). 'Harry' to his Western friends, Fu Hao is a veteran who has spent more than 20 years at the exchange. Bald, stout and jocular, he has the appearance of bespectacled smiling Buddha. However, underneath his unfailing bonhomie lies a passionate determination to transform Shanghai into the world's leading financial centre.

The idea was brilliant in its simplicity. The two exchanges would create an electronic link to allow orders from investors in each market to be routed to the other. Thus, using a broker in Hong Kong connected to the SEHK, an investor could purchase shares listed on the SSE, and *vice versa*. Clearing and settlement would be underpinned by a similar link between the clearing houses in the two markets. Each market would maintain its own rules and regulations, with enforcement of any cross-border regulatory issues undertaken by the local regulator in each jurisdiction, based on an MOU between Hong Kong's SFC and the CSRC. The beauty of the proposal was that it allowed the Chinese authorities to have full transparency over cross-border investors' trading activity and holdings. Thus, they could monitor traders' profits and losses to track any taxes due and set specific parameters around what securities they were allowed to purchase. Because of the clearing and settlement link's 'closed loop', there was no risk that funds could 'leak out' of the system to purchase assets that the regulators had not approved, thereby maintaining the integrity of China's closed capital account.

Over the next couple of years, the SSE and HKEX worked with a large number of agencies on both sides of the border to bring the idea to reality. Parties involved included ChinaClear (中国结算), the CSRC, the Financial Services and Treasury Bureau (FSTB) of the Hong Kong Government, and the SFC. Guo Shuqing (郭树清), the seasoned and energetic reformer who headed the CSRC until his appointment as governor of Shandong March 2013, played a lynchpin role in getting the ball rolling. Although the PBOC was not directly involved in negotiations, given the proposal involved potentially large cross-border capital flows, Governor Zhou and Deputy Governor Yi Gang (易纲), who then headed SAFE and succeeded Zhou in 2018, lent critical behind-the-scenes support and coordinated with the Hong Kong Monetary Authority (HKMA) on monetary matters. The most challenging issues, however, related to market regulation, given the gulf between Hong Kong's rules-based free market philosophy and the tightly controlled – and sometimes arbitrary – regulatory system in the Mainland. The SFC, headed by Ashley Alder, an English lawyer, negotiated intensely with the CSRC over a raft of fine details to ensure the workability of the cross-border regulatory framework. Nevertheless, as with any major pioneering cross-border investment programme, it was ultimately still a big leap of faith.

To mitigate the risk of over-exuberant investors unleashing unconstrained flows into either market, a number of controls were imposed. While all 'Northbound' investors (based in Hong Kong or overseas) were allowed to buy Shanghai stocks, Mainland (or 'Southbound') investment into Hong Kong would be restricted to institutional investors and qualified private individuals (with a minimum asset value of RMB500,000 in their securities accounts). Initially, only large- and mid-cap stocks in both markets were eligible for trading.[112] Further, daily and aggregate quotas were introduced to limit both the net amount of money crossing the border each day, and the absolute total under the programme. At launch, the daily and aggregate quotas for Northbound investment were set at RMB13 billion ($2.1 billion) and RMB300 billion ($49 billion), respectively, and the corresponding quotas for Southbound investment were RMB10.5 billion ($1.7 billion) and RMB250 billion ($41 billion). These restrictions have been gradually relaxed over time, with the aggregate quotas being abolished entirely in August 2016.

The programme, which came to be known as 'Shanghai-Hong Kong Stock Connect' (沪港通, or just 'Stock Connect'), was announced by Premier Li Keqiang at the Bo'ao Forum (博鳌亚洲论坛) on Hainan Island (海南岛) on 11 April 2014. This created a rush of excitement in the media and among the global investment community, and the working teams from all parties prepared for an early autumn launch. However, this was to be delayed by the eruption of a political crisis in Hong Kong in September.

★★★

On the afternoon of 28 September 2014, motorists on Gloucester Road, the artery that links Hong Kong's Cross-Harbour Tunnel and the Central business district, found traffic brought to a virtual standstill, as protesters streamed across to surround the government offices in the Admiralty district. This was the beginning of the so-called 'Umbrella Movement' (雨伞运动), which saw students and pro-democracy activists set up camps that blocked roads in and around Hong Kong's financial centre for the following two months. The movement took its name from the yellow umbrellas that protesters used to defend themselves from the pepper spray used by police to disperse the crowds.

The proximate cause of the protests was a perceived rescission by the Chinese Government of a commitment to transition towards universal suffrage in the territory. The British colonial administration had never offered Hong Kong people the right to vote for their leader. However, in the evolving political climate between the 1984 Sino-British Joint Declaration[113] and 1997, this commitment had apparently been enshrined in Article 45 of the Basic Law, the mini constitution that has governed Hong Kong's affairs since the return of sovereignty to China, which states:

> The chief executive of the Hong Kong Special Administrative Region shall be selected by election or through consultations held locally and be appointed by the Central People's Government.
>
> The method for selecting the chief executive shall be specified in light of the actual situation of the Hong Kong Special Administrative Region and in accordance with the principle of gradual and orderly progress. The ultimate aim is the selection of the Chief Executive by universal suffrage upon nomination by a broadly representative nominating committee in accordance with democratic procedures.[114]

This article is, of course, rather vague, reflecting a tenuous compromise between the outgoing British colonists, the Chinese Government and local representatives who had overseen the drafting of the document in the run-up to the return of Hong Kong's sovereignty to China. However, in the years following 1997, the call for universal suffrage by Hong Kong's pro-democracy parties grew louder. In December 2007, the Standing Committee of the NPC appeared to rule in favour of a transition to universal suffrage in 2017:

> The Session is of the view that . . . the election of the fifth Chief Executive of the Hong Kong Special Administrative Region in the year 2017 may be implemented by the method of universal suffrage; that after the Chief Executive is selected by universal suffrage, the election of the Legislative Council of the Hong Kong Special Administrative Region may be implemented by the method of electing all the members by universal suffrage.[115]

However, consultations on electoral reform in 2010 and 2014 ended in a stalemate between the Hong Kong Government and pro-democratic parties over two issues. The first was over the Government's proposal that the candidates for chief executive would be nominated by a 1,200-person Nominating Committee appointed by Beijing. This committee was seen as undemocratic and, moreover, was stacked with people representing business interests. The second was over the composition of Hong Kong's parliament, the Legislative Council (Legco). Out of 70 seats on Legco, 40 were geographic constituencies elected based on proportional representation in local elections. The remaining 30 were 'functional constituencies', elected by special interest groups, made up largely of professional or industry representatives.[116] The government proposals took a highly gradualist approach to reforms, which did not fundamentally alter the balance of power.

After the pro-democracy camp opposed the Government's proposals, the Standing Committee of the NPC issued a ruling on 31 August, which stipulated that the chief executive must 'love the Country and love Hong Kong', a statement taken to mean that pro-democracy candidates would be ruled out. This was the trigger that set off the demonstrations, which took the form of civil disobedience and peaceful protest. Foreign media correspondents covering the protests were somewhat bemused to find student protesters hunched over homework assignments in the camps they had set up.

The underlying causes of the protest movement, and Hong Kong's political challenges more broadly, are far more complex and are rooted in a long history. It is not the purpose of this volume to provide a detailed analysis of these causes (which, in any case, would take up at least an entire volume in their own right), nor to pass judgement on the positions of the various opposing factions. However, at the core of the problems is the failure of Hong Kong's political system to deliver for its people.

For a quarter of a century, the Heritage Foundation, a conservative American think tank, ranked Hong Kong as the freest economy in the world.[117] The late economist Milton Friedman regularly lauded Hong Kong's *laissez faire* free market model, saying in a 1990 interview:

> *If you want to see how the free market really works, Hong Kong is the place to go. The power of the free market has enabled the industrious people of Hong Kong to transform what was once a barren rock into one of the most thriving and successful places in Asia.*[118]

Friedman also expressed admiration for the chief architect of that model, John Cowperthwaite, who famously refused even to allow economic performance statistics to be compiled, for fear that they would be used for central planning.[119]

Hong Kong's low-tax system certainly helped propel the territory to become one of the wealthiest places in the world. However, the territory is also one of the places with the highest level of wealth inequality on Earth and the gap has been widening. In 2006, the income of the top decile of earners was 33.9 times the income of the lowest decile. By 2016, this ratio had grown to 43.9 times.[120] To maintain low taxation, Cowperthwaite blocked attempts by the liberal minded governor Sir David Trench to introduce healthcare and retirement benefits in the 1960s.[121] He also refused to provide for universal primary education, which was not introduced until 1971.[122] The impact of this was later seen during the recession in the wake of the Asian Financial Crisis, when workers who'd had no or limited access to full-time education in the 1970s accounted for a high proportion of the unemployed.[123]

The Heritage Foundation's annual accolade has long been seen as a joke by anyone with any familiarity with how Hong Kong's economy actually works. The system is rampant with monopolies, oligopolies and a raft of cosseted sinecures. Housing supply failures driven by the government's abetting of a property cartel have resulted in one of the most expensive property markets in the world, in which low earners have been reduced to living in 'cage homes' within subdivided apartments, with poor sanitary conditions and little privacy. More pernicious have been successive failures in education policy, which have created a 'Balkanised' educational system in which the children of the wealthy have access to world class schooling, but children from poor backgrounds are condemned to an education that does not adequately prepare them for the modern international workplace. Thus, the most traditional vehicle of social mobility has simply not functioned, further entrenching Hong Kong's social stratification.[124]

When Guangdong opened up to foreign investment, Hong Kong businesspeople were among the first to transfer their manufacturing operations to the Mainland. As a result, many manufacturing workers became unemployed and local wages have stagnated. More recently, even higher skilled white-collar workers are being displaced by better educated Mainland Chinese who have migrated to Hong Kong. In addition, newly wealthy Mainlanders have been buying up everything from formula milk to luxury goods and apartments in the territory, driving up the cost of living.[125] In the face of these livelihood issues faced by most Hong Kong people, the government's continued *laissez faire* policies have stoked popular resentment. Hong Kong's administrative system is structured to favour the rich and politically well-connected. It is hardly surprising, therefore, that so many have been calling for political change.

The Umbrella Movement divided Hong Kong society. On the one hand, many supported the fight for political reforms; on the other, the protesters were getting in the way of business, not just for large commercial enterprises, but also for taxi drivers and restauranteurs, whose livelihoods were impacted. The protesters themselves eventually grew weary and their camps were finally cleared out by the authorities in early December.

★★★

Shanghai-Hong Kong Stock Connect launched before the end of the protests on 17 November 2014. Expectedly, there were a few teething troubles.[126] It was not until the eleventh hour before launch that the Chinese State Administration of Taxation (SAT, 国家税务总局) provided clarity over the tax treatment of foreign investors' capital gains and dividends on Mainland shares.[127] The CSRC, the SSE and HKEX all despatched teams all over the world to explain how this new cross-border investment channel worked, and to liaise with regulators in key jurisdictions on investor protection issues.[128] It was hectic work. However, by and large, the programme was a huge success.

The operational robustness of the programme was tested early on. Seeing a rising stock market as a means of helping over-indebted SOEs to recapitalise, Chinese regulators fanned the flames of a stock price boom through public comments and turned a blind eye to the proliferation of peer-to-peer margin lending. In an October 2014 interview with *Xinhua*, a CSRC official sought to justify the rising market, saying:

> [T]he macroeconomy has been good, liquidity is ample and other factors such as reforms have been put into effect, all of which are boosting the market confidence and laying a solid foundation for future reforms . . . financing costs are expected to go down further. The stock market is only reflecting all these positive developments.[129]

Stock prices rose by around 150 percent between July 2014 and June 2015 before crashing. During this time, trading volumes shot up. However, cross-border trading through Stock Connect continued without a glitch.

More importantly, notwithstanding various extraordinary actions by the CSRC to stem the crash once it began – including suspending trading in around 1,300 listed companies, representing around 45 percent of the market[130] – Mainland regulators did not interfere directly with trading between Shanghai and Hong Kong. This was a critical test in the eyes of major foreign institutional investors, who still harboured doubts about investing in Chinese A-shares through the Stock Connect link.

Sovereign wealth funds (SWFs), which make investments on behalf of their governments, were particularly concerned about Chinese political interference in their Mainland investments in the event of diplomatic rows. For instance, there was a risk that their funds could be frozen on the Mainland and that they would not be able to get their money out. In fact, investing through Stock Connect significantly alleviated this risk. This is because, unlike the QFII or RQFII channels, the investor's account remains in Hong Kong.

When investors sell their Mainland A-shares, the obligation to deliver back their cash falls on the Hong Kong Securities Clearing Company (HKSCC), a subsidiary of HKEX, which is subject to Hong Kong's laws and regulations. Of course, there is theoretically a risk that the Mainland Chinese clearing house ChinaClear does not deliver back the cash to HKSCC to meet its obligation. However, in practice, the chances of this happening are extremely remote, since HKSCC holds all Chinese Southbound investors' Hong Kong securities on ChinaClear's behalf. If China-Clear were to prevent HKSCC from meeting its obligations to international investors, this could cause it to be unable to meet its obligations to Mainland Chinese investors. In effect, therefore, international investors investing in China through Stock Connect are availing themselves of the legal and regulatory protections of Hong Kong's English common law system. This key advantage has led at least one major SWF to exit all Chinese securities holdings held via the QFII and RQFII channels where the securities could be bought through the Stock Connect channel instead.[131]

The success of the link with Shanghai allowed HKEX to pursue a similar link with the SZSE, and the Shenzhen-Hong Kong Stock Connect (深港通) programme was launched in December 2016. This was followed in July 2017 by the launch of Bond Connect (债券通), which allows international investors to invest in the Chinese interbank bond market.[132]

Bond Connect differs from the Stock Connect programme structurally in a number of ways. Bonds are far less standardised than equities, with a single issuer able to issue multiple types of bonds with different maturities, seniority or coupon rates. The vast majority of bonds are traded OTC bilaterally between the buyer and the seller, rather than via an exchange. For this reason, they are not centrally cleared (whereby the clearing house steps in immediately after the trade to guarantee that each party will receive what they agreed upon). Bonds are generally just settled, and each party continues to bear a risk that the counterparty might default on the deal until the cash or bonds are transferred. HKEX did not have a suitable platform to handle the specific trading mechanisms that these differences dictated. Moreover, given the dominance of the electronic bond trading platforms Bloomberg, Tradeweb and MarketAxess, HKEX faced high barriers to breaking into bond trading. It had therefore instead been focusing on rolling out fixed income and currency derivatives related to the renminbi and on providing clearing services for the interest rate and currency swaps markets. Unbeknownst to HKEX though, the major bond trading platforms were facing their own challenges in breaking into China.

A Tradeweb executive named Andrew Bernard arrived in Hong Kong in early 2014 to head the company's Asian business. A tall Englishman who looked far more like an army officer than a bond salesman, Bernard had a keen sense of the potential of the Mainland Chinese bond market. He immediately began courting the PBOC and the China Foreign Exchange Trading System (CFETS), the operator of China's interbank bond market. However, by mid-2015 he had concluded that Tradeweb needed a partner who had better credibility with Chinese policymakers. He discussed his problem with Goldman Sachs' Head of Principal Strategic Investments in Asia Pacific, Alokik Advani, who suggested HKEX might be a good partner and arranged a meeting.

The economics of the bond trading business aren't particularly attractive for exchanges. However, there were several good reasons for HKEX to get involved. Firstly, until and unless there was greater international investment in China's bond market, there would be limited demand for the fixed income and currency derivatives that HKEX was working on. Second, given the demographic pressures China faces, it was easy to see that it would have to expand international demand for its government debt and that the market could become very large. Thirdly, HKEX was about the only organisation that had the necessary relationships to coordinate all the disparate parties that would need to be involved. Helping China open up its bond market would reinforce Hong Kong as a strategic gateway for Chinese capital markets, thereby reinforcing HKEX's core business.

Tradeweb was not HKEX's first choice as a partner though. Bloomberg was the platform with the greatest reach in international bond markets. Shortly after Tradeweb's approach, HKEX approached Bloomberg to propose partnering to set up a cross-border bond trading link. However, the overture was rebuffed. Bloomberg had already initiated its own discussions with CFETS and did not feel that HKEX brought much to the table. Further, HKEX's proposal, which firmly cemented CFETS' role as the primary interface to Chinese bond dealers, conflicted with Bloomberg's strategy to expand the use of its iconic terminals in China.[133] HKEX therefore agreed to work with Tradeweb. Bloomberg later regretted its decision and eventually joined Bond Connect as a second international interface in 2019.

The third member of the partnership on the Hong Kong side was the Central Moneymarkets Unit (CMU) of the HKMA, which handles settlements in the Hong Kong bond market. Working together, this trio put together a detailed proposal for the PBOC. The idea was met with enthusiasm by Vice Governor Pan Gongsheng (潘功胜), a veteran of the Big Four bank IPOs, who championed the proposal through the labyrinthine Chinese approvals process. Meanwhile, the three partners kicked off the detailed technical work with CFETS and the two Mainland bond settlement infrastructures, China Central Depository and Clearing (CCDC) and the Shanghai Clearing House (SCH).

The resulting structure involved a trading link between Tradeweb and CFETS. Cross-border settlements were handled between CMU on the Hong Kong side, and CCDC and SCH on the Mainland side. Like Stock Connect, the scheme was underpinned by a regulatory enforcement agreement, in this case between the PBOC and the HKMA. Given the bilateral credit risk between parties trading through Bond Connect, however, the programme was not open to all, but limited to institutions and subject to individual approvals. To handle approvals of investors, dealers and offshore trading platforms, HKEX and CFETS set up a joint venture in Hong Kong called Bond Connect Company Limited (BCCL), which was licensed by the SFC.

Stock Connect and Bond Connect have played a critical role in internationalising China's domestic capital markets. When the SSE first approached HKEX in 2012, it was not only looking to attract more foreign investment into its market. What the SSE team hoped was that, by bringing in more foreign institutional investors, they would be able to improve the quality of the domestic securities markets as rational price discovery venues. A key aspect of this was to persuade major international index providers to include Chinese securities in their benchmarks, which had hitherto excluded them due to the barriers to foreign investors in accessing the Mainland markets.

Over the past two decades, index providers have emerged from the financial pages of newspapers and back rooms of stock exchanges to become a major force in the investment world. This has been driven by many factors, including computerisation, greater demand for performance benchmarking, the invention of exchange-traded funds (ETFs) in 1993, and the subsequent popularisation and growth of passive investing.[134] In the 12 years to 2019, passive investing had grown from 9 percent of funds invested globally to 27 percent,[135] representing $11.4 trillion in assets under management.[136] Given inclusion in major indices can drive huge flows of passive index tracking funds into particular securities and markets, index companies such as S&P Dow Jones, MSCI and FTSE Russell have come to wield huge power and to be wooed by major corporations and governments alike.

During 2014 and 2015, MSCI consulted its users about including Chinese A-shares in its Emerging Markets Index, to which funds in excess of $1.6 trillion were benchmarked.[137] However, inclusion was rejected on both occasions due to various market access constraints. From that point, the CSRC appeared to make it its mission to win A-shares' inclusion within the index. Following the opening of the Shenzhen Stock Connect link, it was felt that Mainland Chinese shares were sufficiently accessible to warrant inclusion. MSCI consulted again in 2017 and finally agreed to include A-shares in the index at a 5 percent weighting from 2018. This weighting was further increased to 20 percent over three stages during 2019. Other index companies quickly followed suit in adding Chinese stocks and bonds to key global benchmark indices.

These inclusions have drawn hundreds of billions of dollars of foreign capital into China's securities markets. The latest such inclusion is into FTSE Russell's World Government Bond Index, which is beginning to phase in CGBs from October 2021. It is estimated that this could draw in a further $140 billion in foreign capital.[138]

Stock Connect and Bond Connect have not just helped achieve Chinese securities' inclusion in international stock and bond indices. The IMF's decision to begin including the renminbi in the basket of reserve currencies that back its SDRs from October 2016 was influenced by the launch of the Stock Connect programme. While the renminbi's weighting in that basket of 10.9 percent remains low compared with the US dollar (41.7 percent) and the euro (30.9 percent), this was a huge symbolic step towards the renminbi taking on a greater global role.[139]

Since the launch of Stock Connect in 2014, foreign investment as a share of China's stock markets has increased from 1.5 percent to 4.3 percent.[140] Over 70 percent of all foreign investment in the Chinese domestic stock markets is now held via HKEX's clearing subsidiary. Similarly, Mainland Chinese investment in Hong Kong has shot up. In March 2021, Southbound holdings via Stock Connect made up 4.9 percent of the Hong Kong market.[141] Since the launch of Bond Connect, foreign holdings in China's bond market had grown 284 percent from RMB952 billion to more than RMB3.6 trillion by March 2021.[142] By serving as a conduit for these investments, Hong Kong has further increased in importance to both China and the foreign investment community. Thus, the risks associated with any instability in Hong Kong have also grown commensurately.

★★★

At the height of the Cultural Revolution in 1967, a series of industrial disputes broke out in Hong Kong. During a clash between police and picketing workers at an artificial flower factory in San Po Kong (新蒲崗) on 6 May, 21 workers were arrested. The next day, mass street demonstrations erupted, fomented by pro-Communist sympathisers. More arrests followed and the colony was placed under curfew. Violence in the form of bombings and murders continued for months.

During the 1967 riots, the radical commander of the Guangzhou Military Region, Huang Yongsheng (黃永勝), proposed to invade the colony, but was vetoed by Zhou Enlai.[143] In October, Zhou ordered left-wing groups in Hong Kong to cease the bombings and, gradually, order was restored. Hong Kong was China's main source of hard currency and a vital channel for acquiring Western technology, which had been under a strict US embargo. The territory was simply too important to Beijing for it to allow the unrest to continue.

At the time of the transfer from British to Chinese rule, Hong Kong accounted for 18.4 percent of China's economy. By 2019, China's explosive growth meant that Hong Kong's share had fallen to just 2.7 percent. Notwithstanding the fall in its share of GDP, Hong Kong continues to play an outsized role in China's economy. It remains the largest conduit for FDI into China and, in 2018, Chinese banks held $1.1 trillion of assets in the territory, equivalent to 9 percent of China's GDP.[144] Of course, most of that investment neither originates from nor is made in Hong Kong. The territory serves as a conduit for investment between China and the rest of the world, which, owing to its unique combination of being a part of China but operating under a rule-of-law-based common law legal system, is acceptable to both Chinese and international parties as a venue to transact commercial contracts.

Notwithstanding Hong Kong's importance to China between 1949 and 1978 as its principal window to the world, the Chinese leadership's understanding of Hong Kong people was extremely poor when it began to increase its engagement with the territory in the 1980s. The CCP had maintained a number of organisations in Hong Kong. These included the *Xinhua* News Agency, which issued various publications and housed officials from the Ministry of Foreign Affairs (外交部); a branch of the Bank of China, which managed financial interests; and China Resources (华润), which conducted external trade on behalf of government agencies. It also had links to left-wing schools and labour unions. However, all these organisations had exaggerated the level of local support for the Communists.[145] In fact, a large proportion of Hong Kong's population had fled Communist rule in the Mainland. The leftist violence in 1967 had outraged most of the city's population and, as the horrors of the Cultural Revolution came to be known, Hong Kong people began to feel fortunate. Social welfare reforms that followed the 1967 unrest further transformed their lives for the better.

Nevertheless, local Communist officials and even Hong Kong businesspeople, keen to win Beijing's favour, tended to just tell the leadership what it wanted to hear. Therefore, as Deng Xiaoping entered into negotiations with the British for the return of territory, he had little idea of the depth of mistrust Hong Kong people had for the CCP.

It was not until Deng appointed former Jiangsu party secretary Xu Jiatun (许家屯) in 1983 to head the *Xinhua* News Agency, making him China's *de facto* representative in Hong Kong, that the Beijing leadership began to receive a more accurate picture. Xu made the effort to visit schools, businesses, sporting events and poorer neighbourhoods and became popular with locals for his openness and genuine desire to understand Hong Kong. He was also brave in reporting the unvarnished truth about Hong Kongers' views to the Party leadership.

As China sought to attract foreign capital for its modernisation, Beijing's efforts to woo Hong Kong people focused on the business community. When the country's efforts to liberalise and open up became clearer during the 1980s, fears in Hong Kong that had been sparked by the Sino-British Joint Declaration began to subside. However, the Tiananmen crackdown provoked widespread outrage and an outpouring of sympathy for the student protesters by Hong Kong people, who worried also about their own fates. Many emigrated to places like Canada and Australia, which were only too eager to take in Hong Kong's skilled middle-class professionals. A sympathiser of the student protests, Xu Jiatun himself fled to the US, where he lived in exile until his death in 2016 at the age of 100.

The Jiang Administration continued to court Hong Kong's leading businesspeople as it focused on driving economic reforms. As the territory's first chief executive following the return of sovereignty, China appointed Tung Chee-hwa (董建华), the scion of a wealthy shipping family. Tung was well meaning, but his administration was overwhelmingly focused on business interests and maintaining the *status quo*. Hong Kong people came to believe that he was not accurately reflecting the views of the majority to Beijing and his close ties to local tycoons lent themselves to accusations of cronyism.[146] Tung was also confronted with the twin challenges of the Asian Financial Crisis and the 2003 SARS epidemic. The nadir of the Tung Administration, however, was when it attempted to introduce national security legislation, as it was required to do under Article 23 of the Basic Law, which stipulates:

> *The Hong Kong Special Administrative Region shall enact laws on its own to prohibit any act of treason, secession, sedition, subversion against the Central People's Government, or theft of state secrets, to prohibit foreign political organisations or bodies from conducting political activities in the Region, and to prohibit political organisations or bodies of the Region from establishing ties with foreign political organisations or bodies.*

Although such legislation exists in other countries,[147] the move elicited strong opposition from pro-democracy politicians, journalists, lawyers, human rights organisations and religious groups, for whom the Tiananmen incident was a recent memory. The proposed legislation was dropped after roughly half a million of Hong Kong's seven million residents took to the streets to protest against it on 1 July 2003. Tung stood down in March 2005, ahead of the end of his term, citing 'health reasons' and no serious attempt was made by subsequent Hong Kong leaders to revive the Article 23 legislation.

The end of the 2014 Umbrella Movement brought only a short and uneasy period of respite. Filibustering and general obstructionism by pro-democracy politicians in Legco impeded the functions of government. Meanwhile, the imprisonment of activists who had taken part in the Umbrella Movement and the disqualification of six elected pro-democracy lawmakers in 2017 heightened the feeling that Hong Kong's freedoms were being curtailed. Things eventually came to a head in 2019 when the Hong Kong Government under Carrie Lam (林郑月娥), a career civil servant who was installed as Chief Executive in 2017, tried to pass a law that would have allowed Hong Kong residents and visitors wanted in Mainland China to be extradited there.

Ostensibly, the Fugitive Offenders and Mutual Legal Assistance in Criminal Matters Legislation (Amendment) Bill was introduced in response to the murder of a young Hong Kong woman by her boyfriend while the couple were on holiday in Taiwan. The fugitive fled home to Hong Kong and, since there was no extradition treaty between the territory and Taiwan, there was no way to send him back to face justice. However, the proposed bill would have also allowed suspects wanted by Chinese authorities to be extradited to the Mainland. Given Hong Kong people's lack of confidence in the Mainland justice system, this aroused serious concerns.

These concerns were not unfounded. In 2015, five staff of a Hong Kong bookseller involved in the dissemination of publications critical of the Chinese leadership went missing. It later emerged that two of them had been detained outside Mainland China and transferred there, one from Thailand and one from Hong Kong. In 2017, the late night abduction by Mainland security agents of Chinese-Canadian businessman Xiao Jianhua (肖建华) from his room at Hong Kong's Four Seasons Hotel caused further furore. There was a general unease that Xi Jinping's administration was taking a more authoritarian approach on matters of freedom of expression and civil liberties, and that the extradition law would expose Hong Kongers to politically-motivated prosecutions.

Several minor peaceful protests against the proposed law took place in the spring and pro-democracy lawmakers launched a filibustering campaign in Legco. However, the Hong Kong Government did not back down and, instead, announced that it would press ahead by bypassing the legislative body's Bills Committee, which had responsibility for scrutinising the bill. A large protest against the law was held on 9 June. When the Government still paid no heed to popular concerns, protesters surrounded the Legco building on 12 June to prevent a second reading of the bill. Protesters clashed with police in what was declared a 'riot' by the authorities.

Carrie Lam suspended the bill on 15 June, but her refusal to withdraw it completely inflamed protesters, who began calling for her resignation. Radical protesters stormed the Legco building on 15 June and vandalised government offices. Violent protests and clashes with police spread throughout the territory over the summer. An occupation of the airport by protesters on 5 August forced the cancellation of more than 200 flights. Carrie Lam eventually formally withdrew the bill on 4 September, but by that time it was too late. Protesters were calling for a full inquiry into alleged police brutality, the release of arrested protesters, Lam's resignation and the implementation of universal suffrage. A small number of people also began calling for independence from Mainland China.

Elections for the District Council on 24 November saw record turnout and a rout of pro-Beijing lawmakers. Meanwhile, protests continued into early 2020 and only subsided after the onset of the Covid-19 pandemic.

Throughout the protests, Mainland and Hong Kong officials have accused the US and other countries of 'fanning the flames' of unrest in the city and of masterminding the pro-democracy movement.[148] China's *Global Times* also published an editorial stating that 'It is an open secret in Hong Kong that the forces protesting the extradition bill have been sponsored by the US'.[149] So far, little concrete evidence of this has been presented. However, the Chinese leadership has been incensed by US politicians' public criticisms about developments in Hong Kong and expressions of sympathy with the pro-democracy movement, which has actively sought American support for their cause.[150] Irrespective of whether US politicians' concerns were genuine or if they were trying to score political points at home, amidst Donald Trump's trade war, this further elevated tensions with China. It may also have goaded the Chinese leadership into dramatic steps to assert its authority over Hong Kong, which may ultimately prove to weaken the territory's ability to serve China's strategic financial interests.

As the pandemic engulfed governments around the world, police arrested 15 veteran pro-democracy activists on 18 April 2020. On 21 May, the Standing Committee of the NPC announced that it was drafting a new security law that would be annexed to the Basic Law, bypassing Hong Kong's local legislative process. Against a backdrop of international condemnation, the National Security Law (NSL) was passed on 30 June.

It will be some time before the full implications of the NSL are known. There have been claims that the Hong Kong Government may be using the new law to target political opponents and critics of Beijing.[151] However, the focus of the present analysis is on the potential financial dimensions in which the NSL could impact China, the US and relations between the two countries.

First to consider is the impact on relations with other countries. The NSL has already drawn negative reactions from various governments. These range from the suspension of extradition arrangements with Hong Kong[152] to the US Congress' passing of the Hong Kong Autonomy Act, under which sanctions have been imposed on Hong Kong and

Mainland Chinese officials considered to have undermined Hong Kong's autonomy. Further escalations in sanctions, particularly limiting trade and capital flows between China, Hong Kong and other countries and territories, could severely damage China's economy and would likely also negatively impact global growth.

Second, it will need to be seen how international investors' willingness to use Hong Kong as a conduit for investment in China is impacted. If the NSL is applied extremely judiciously, then international apprehension may subside, and its impact can be limited. In fact, if the NSL contributes to an improvement in Hong Kong's social stability, business confidence that had been dented by violent protests in 2019 may improve. However, the critical factor will be whether international confidence in Hong Kong's rule of law and the integrity of its judicial system can be maintained. In this regard, a case brought by the Hong Kong Government against the pro-democracy and anti-CCP proprietor of the now-defunct *Apple Daily* newspaper Jimmy Lai (黎智英) highlights several causes for concern.[153]

At the time of writing, Lai stands accused of violating the NSL by requesting that a foreign power impose sanctions on China or Hong Kong. In a review of a bail application that went all the way up to Hong Kong's Court of Final Appeal (CFA) in February 2021, a five-judge panel issued a clear but subtly worded explanation of the impact of the NSL on the way in which bail applications must now be reviewed. Faithfully adhering to the terms of the legislation, the CFA effectively held that the NSL imposed a presumption against a person charged under the law being granted bail pending trial, as opposed to the common law tradition of a presumption in favour of bail. The panel further ruled that the NSL is not subject to constitutional review under the Basic Law. This means that this presumption against bail in NSL cases cannot be challenged under the International Covenant on Civil and Political Rights, which stipulates certain protections, including a presumption in favour of bail.[154]

A person accused of breaching the NSL, therefore, can potentially be incarcerated for an extended period before a case comes to trial, creating considerable scope for abuses by the authorities. Other criticisms of the NSL include the stipulation that judges in NSL cases be selected by Hong Kong's Chief Executive.[155] This potentially calls into question the judges' independence and whether individuals prosecuted under the law can receive a fair trial.

Of course, it may be argued that the NSL does not affect the standing of Hong Kong's legal system in so far as commercial cases are concerned. However, there are already signs that international investors and corporations are exercising greater caution about designating Hong Kong as a jurisdiction for striking commercial contracts.[156]

In addition to the question about Hong Kong's rule of law, there is a question about whether the NSL might impact the territory's ability to serve as a global financial centre in other ways. There are signs that the law might be spurring a 'brain drain' of local professional talent. The British government has offered a fast-track process for 5.4 million Hong Kong people entitled to British National (Overseas) passports to gain right of abode in the UK.[157] In August 2021, local newspapers reported that almost 90,000 Hong Kong people had emigrated in the past year.[158] Further, a perception that Hong Kong is a less open and free society would likely make it harder to attract and retain foreign professional talent. Given the importance of free information flows to the efficient functioning of financial markets, any significant form of censorship in Hong Kong may also prove commercially damaging.

It is regrettable that Hong Kong has now become a front in the Sino-US confrontation, since it has served such a vital role for both sides. If international investors cease to view Hong Kong as a distinct jurisdiction within China, they may simply opt to bypass Hong Kong to transact directly with counterparties in the Mainland. However, absent the legal and regulatory protections that Hong Kong has traditionally offered, it is quite likely that some foreign investors will choose to invest elsewhere. A reduced willingness by international investors to transact in Hong Kong also poses greater risks to Chinese businesses and individuals seeking to invest internationally. Hong Kong's One Country Two Systems model has offered valuable protections for Chinese investment overseas, since contracts struck in the territory also benefit from a degree of protection from international sanctions or interference by foreign governments. If contracts for Chinese outbound investment must be struck in overseas jurisdictions, then the Chinese parties will lose this protection. This would further complicate the Chinese government's task of increasing outward investment.

Can't Buy Me Love

In a pair of speeches given in Astana and Jakarta in the autumn of 2013, President Xi launched the concept of a 'Silk Road Economic Belt' and a '21st Century Maritime Silk Road'. Evoking the voyages of Zheng He, Ibn Battuta and Marco Polo centuries ago, the Belt and Road Initiative is considered to be the centrepiece of Xi's foreign policy. At its core is the promise of very substantial investment in infrastructure development in more than 130 target countries to enhance their transport, communications and commercial links with China. This investment is being underwritten through a $40 billion Silk Road Fund Xi announced in 2014, and the Chinese-led multilateral development bank the Asian Infrastructure Investment Bank (AIIB), launched the same year with initial capital of $100 billion. Taking into account debt raising capacity, this implies potential total investment of more than $1 trillion.

The BRI has been compared to the US Marshall Plan for post-WW2 European reconstruction. Given the need for infrastructure enhancements in the targeted countries, they have generally welcomed it. However, the strategic purpose of the initiative has been subject to varying interpretations[159] and numerous criticisms.[160] It has also been seen as a strategic challenge to US interests.[161] Beyond the grandiose vision and China's declaration of benevolent intent, there are four key objectives underlying the BRI.

First, the large-scale infrastructure projects provide a partial solution to China's excess production.[162] Investment-led growth in recent decades has resulted in significant industrial overcapacity. BRI projects are largely undertaken by Chinese SOEs. Thus, the building of roads, railway lines, ports, power plants and other infrastructure abroad helps dispose of China's problem of excess domestic capacity. That most of these projects employ Chinese labour also helps to stave off the risk of large-scale unemployment.

Second, by supporting the development of neighbouring economies, China hopes to open up new markets for its exports. The GFC highlighted the risk of China's overdependence on highly indebted Western economies with low growth. To diversify its risk and maintain the country's export-led growth model, Chinese leaders have quite sensibly recognised the need to help create new sources of demand.

Third, the BRI is a way for China to diversify its foreign reserves into higher-yielding assets. As a result of its years of large balance of payments surpluses, at the end of 2019 China was a net creditor to the rest of the world to the tune of $2.3 trillion. However, since around 41 percent of its foreign assets were comprised of central bank reserves (of which the vast majority were invested in low-yielding government securities such as US Treasuries), China actually earned a net *negative* return of $106 billion on its net external holdings in 2020.[163] In other words, foreigners' investments in China were yielding a significantly higher return than China's investments abroad. This contrasts with Japan, which at the end of 2019 had net foreign assets of $3.3 trillion and had net *positive* investment income of $195 billion in 2020.[164] More remarkable is the comparison with the US, which had net foreign *liabilities* of $11.2 trillion at the beginning of 2020 (in other words, foreigners held far more American assets than the US holds in overseas investments) but saw *positive* net investment income of $196 billion that year.[165]

That was not an unusual year for the US. Because foreigners have been willing to hold large amounts of low-yielding US Treasuries, whereas US holdings overseas comprise 62 percent FDI and portfolio equity investments, the US consistently generated positive returns on its net foreign holdings in the decade to 2020, despite having just $29 trillion in foreign assets versus $40 trillion in foreign liabilities.[166]

China's national wealth has been built up in recent decades on the back of a huge demographic dividend. In this sense, it might be viewed as similar to the natural resources-based wealth of oil-producing nations, such as Abu Dhabi and Norway. These countries' foreign investments are a store of wealth that will be needed to maintain their peoples' standard of living when their natural endowments are finally exhausted. While China's labour force is not exactly a finite resource, the country's falling working age share of population means that it may soon have greater calls on its national savings. It is therefore imperative that it begins to generate better returns on those savings. Infrastructure investments through the BRI are potentially a means of achieving that.

The BRI's fourth purpose is to serve as part of China's overall drive to increase its global influence. *But to what end?*

America's influence over multilateral institutions has certainly been used to protect and further US interests, as seen in the IMF rescues of Mexico and South Korea (discussed in Chapter 3). However, while China has increased its participation in multilateral institutions such as the World Bank and the IMF in the wake of the GFC, it does not enjoy the same degree of influence as the US in driving their agendas. Viewed from the Chinese perspective, there are many ways in which these institutions can be improved. For example, the IMF's bureaucratic governance processes mean that it can be slow to act, and China does not always agree with the conditionality that its support often comes with, particularly concerning human rights. Through the BRI and by sponsoring alternative multilateral organisations such as the AIIB, China can circumvent the sometimes-glacial process of changing existing institutions and present itself as more attuned to the needs of developing nations.[167]

Another aspect of China's quest for greater international influence is that the associated outward prestige confers greater legitimacy on the CCP's rule at home. Through taking a lead in global institutions, the Chinese leadership can provide a counterbalance against the dominance of the liberal-based international order, which it sees as a threat to its own position.[168] It is not hard to understand why America has greeted Chinese multilateral institutions with wariness, since, as discussed further in Chapter 6, the US has substantial interests at stake in maintaining the *status quo*.

The BRI is not China's first drive to increase its outbound investment. At the Fourth Plenum of the 15th National Party Congress in 1999, Jiang Zemin encouraged Chinese firms to internationalise through his 'Going Out strategy' (走出去战略). However, Chinese FDI in other countries has often been controversial. The controversy goes beyond the nationalistic passions that were stirred by Japanese corporations' overseas acquisitions in the 1980s. Given the level of control the government is seen to exercise over Chinese enterprises, both state-owned and private, there is great sensitivity about perceived political and military agendas underlying Chinese outbound investment. To counter any potential strategic threat, both the US and the EU have tightened up restrictions on Chinese firms investing in critical infrastructure and in technology sectors, ranging from energy, water, transport and communications to data, media, biotechnology and food security.[169]

However, developing nations are less well placed to turn down the offer of Chinese capital. Here, China has been accused of engaging in 'debt-trap diplomacy' to coerce strategic concessions. An oft-cited example of this is in Sri Lanka, where a Chinese SOE took a 99-year lease over Hambantota Port in 2015 to settle a $1 billion debt that the Sri Lankan government could not afford to pay. In 2018, Malaysian Prime Minister Mahathir Mohamad cancelled two rail projects worth $20 billion agreed with China by the previous Malaysian government under Najib Razak, who was later prosecuted on charges of corruption over the 1MDB scandal.[170] In doing so, Mahathir pointedly warned Beijing against engaging in a 'new form of colonialism'.[171]

Diplomatic controversies aside, the BRI's record of improving returns on its foreign investments appears to have been spectacularly unsuccessful. This is a direct result of the state-directed nature of those investments. Chinese companies have lost billions of dollars in contracts and capital through investments in politically unstable countries, including Libya, South Sudan and Venezuela.[172] One study has found that China has renegotiated and refinanced $50 billion in loans over the past decade, with debt write-offs in 14 instances.[173] Far from being 'guileless dupes or helpless victims', incumbent elites in a number of recipient countries have exploited China's eagerness to extend its influence and its governance weaknesses to extract substantial kickbacks.[174]

In 2016, loans by the two major Chinese development banks[175] exceeded the $700 billion in outstanding loans of all six Western-backed development banks combined, raising the spectre of more write-offs to come. Even Chinese analysts have criticised the initiative, warning that it will further saddle the country's fragile banking sector with large foreign NPLs and strain relations with both developing countries and the West.[176]

A combination of diplomatic blowback and poor returns appears to have driven a re-think in China's BRI strategy. During 2019, new loans by the two major Chinese development banks fell to $4 billion from $75 billion in 2016.[177] In addition, mega projects exceeding $1 billion, many of which were viewed as 'white elephants', were reduced to just 20 in 2020, the lowest level to date.[178] During 2020, President Xi also unveiled a new 'dual circulation' (双循环) economic strategy, which places a greater focus on reinforcing China's domestic production and consumption, while maintaining its focus on international trade.

While not a total repudiation of the BRI, the dual circulation strategy appears to be an acknowledgement of the shortcomings of China's state-driven investment-led approach. However, to succeed, it will require a huge transfer of wealth from the state to China's households – a process that is not likely to be accomplished easily.

★★★

In recent years, China's progress on further market-oriented reforms has not stalled entirely. However, it has been a case of 'two steps forward, one step back'. Underlying this has been a struggle for power at the heart of Chinese society between the interests of the political elite and other competing forces.

Deng Xiaoping chose to crack down on student demonstrators in 1989 because he determined that the continued leadership of the CCP was the best means of improving the lives of the Chinese people. Similarly, when Jiang Zemin looked to be retreating from economic reforms in the wake of Tiananmen, Deng brought to bear all the influence he could and undertook his Southern Tour to reignite the economic modernisation agenda because that was in the best interests of the Chinese people.

In the 1990s and early 2000s, Zhu Rongji had – like Deng in the 1980s – to deal with social and political realities, which constrained his freedom to act, and he was forced to navigate carefully between various competing interest groups in pursuing SOE and financial sector reforms. His achievements were considerable, but he left the job uncompleted. Further, the private sector reforms and economic growth that his policies unleashed created three additional complications.

First, the greater economic opportunities available, coupled with China's highly centralised power structure, allowed the politico-entrepreneur class to flourish. This has exacerbated conflicts in China's governance structure between the interests of this elite and those of the state and its people as a whole. This politico-entrepreneur class benefits directly from the CCP's position above the law. This has entrenched opposition against further political reforms, and a transition towards the rule of law and a separation of powers. At the same time, abuses and widespread corruption by this group have undermined the legitimacy of CCP rule.

Second, Zhu's economic reforms also enabled the rise of a new class of private entrepreneurs whose interests are not necessarily affiliated with those of the Party. The political establishment has vacillated in its treatment of this group. On the one hand, it has sought to bring these private businesspeople into the fold; on the other, it has been wary of allowing them to gain too much power. Fundamentally, however, it is in the overall interests of the private entrepreneur class to see greater checks and balances on the power of the CCP, as this would provide them with greater property right protections. Thus, the interests of this class ultimately put them in conflict with the Party.

Third, China's huge economic growth has heavily integrated it with the rest of the world through trade and, increasingly, through cross-border investment. This means that China's domestic policies – be they in the financial, economic, environmental or other spheres – now have a major impact on other countries, giving them a far greater direct interest in how China is governed – not dissimilar to the interest that people around the world take in American presidential elections.

Given the wide range of interests involved for the Party elite, the preservation of CCP rule has become an overriding objective in and of itself, with potential risks for China's overall economic development and growth going forward. Since a major pillar of the CCP's power is its control over the major SOEs and the financial sector, this has stymied progress on further reforms in China's state-owned sector, financial markets and currency policy. While the huge economic stimulus package undertaken in the wake of the GFC helped speed economic recovery both in China and globally, the reversion to large-scale state-directed lending was a regressive step that exacerbated domestic and global imbalances. An attempt to 'export' part of the problem through the BRI further precipitated tensions with other major countries, which perceived the initiative as a strategic threat.

Meanwhile, China's demographic clock is continuing to tick. From its position of abject poverty immediately before the start of Deng Xiaoping's economic reforms, China has rapidly risen to become one of the largest capital exporters in the world. However, the rising burden that its rapidly aging population will place on the state could swiftly reverse this position again. If China is to maintain and increase the level of economic prosperity it has attained for its citizens, it will need to confront a number of major financial challenges.

First, it will need to continue to raise economic productivity. To a degree, it is a matter of subjective opinion as to the best way to achieve this. During its initial stages of development, the top-down state-directed model had a number of advantages that enabled rapid growth. However, from its much higher base today, future productivity improvements are likely to be incrementally more difficult to achieve. In recent years, it is the private sector that has been the main driver of both innovation and economic growth. In practice, a combination of public and private sector initiatives can be used to drive future development. Nevertheless, where the state is endowed with excessive powers, these powers can be used to subvert the private sector to entrench political elites, thereby harming the country's overall development. This is discussed in greater detail in Chapter 7. Further, while state-led initiatives have contributed to China's remarkable economic growth, the roles of both the country's one-time demographic dividend and huge international support must be acknowledged. Therefore, it is imperative that Chinese leaders reflect fully on the balance of the parts played by the public and private sectors going forward, and allow for an institutional framework that adequately protects the interests of the private sector.

Second, in order to minimise the burden its aging population will place on the state, China needs to offer its citizens the ability to pursue greater investment diversification and better returns on their capital. This will include further steps towards true market-based risk-returns domestically, and access to a wider range of investment choices internationally. This will require further relaxation of China's capital controls. Allowing Chinese citizens greater freedom of choice in their international investments would also alleviate concerns harboured by recipients of Chinese outbound investment. Unlike FDI and corporate takeovers, 'portfolio' investments such as the purchase of a few shares by a Chinese individual for his or her pension pot raises no questions over Chinese control, technology transfer or government influence.

Third, China must further improve its own access to international capital markets. In particular, to meet increased social welfare demands, China will need to widen the market for its sovereign debt. If China is perceived as a strategic threat to other nations, it is likely that its access to foreign capital will be further curtailed. Therefore, the country must make every effort to foster harmonious international relations. In addition, there remains significant wariness over private investor protections under the Chinese legal system. China will need to further improve its rule of law and regulatory framework to attract international investors in larger numbers, and will need to grant them greater efficiency in their holdings of Chinese securities. This would include the development of derivative instruments to allow investors to hedge their exposures, and an offshore repo market to allow them to pledge their Chinese securities holdings in return for short-term liquidity.

All of these steps would entail some cession of the CCP's absolute control over the Chinese judicial and financial systems. This will require significant courage and long-term vision on the part of the political leadership. Nevertheless, much remains outside the control of the Chinese government and regulators.

The cost of having maintained heavy government control over renminbi interest rates, exchange rates and domestic capital allocation is that China remains highly dependent on the US dollar system. The US could apply its influence over the rules and regulations governing this system to constrain China's financial rise. This is discussed further in Chapter 6.

China's rise over the past four decades has been built on greater commercial and financial engagement with the rest of the world, and its continued prosperity will depend on maintaining and deepening that engagement. However, doing so will require deft navigation of conflicts that have arisen as a result of its rise, and a thorough examination of whether China's institutional frameworks need to be further reformed both to smooth its further financial integration with the rest of the world, and to foster its own long-term prosperity. Differences with the West – and America in particular – have tended to be cast in ideological terms. However, what will ultimately determine the trajectory of Sino-US relations will be whether and how the two countries can find a way to accommodate each other's material interests.

PART THREE

THE FINANCIAL COLD WAR

Chapter 6

A New Cold War?

Monetary policy is foreign policy and world politics.
— Helmut Schmidt

In his famous elaboration on the *realpolitik* underlying Britain's 19th century foreign policy, Lord Palmerston told the House of Commons in 1848 that 'We have no eternal allies, and we have no perpetual enemies. Our interests are eternal and perpetual, and those interests it is our duty to follow'. Indeed, from the Treaty of Westphalia (1648) until the Treaty of Versailles (1919), European nation states had collectively pursued a 'balance of power' in order to prevent any one state from establishing hegemony over a substantial part of the continent. Ultimately, the shifting set of alliances that this balancing necessitated was what drew all of Europe into a war precipitated by the assassination of the heir to the Austro-Hungarian throne by the Serbian nationalist Gavrilo Princip in June 1914. Seventy years after Palmerston spoke those words, total war had devasted Europe, leaving some 20 million dead.

The expression 'national interest' takes its origins in the work of the Italian political thinkers Niccolò Machiavelli and Giovanni Botero. However, it was the Cardinal de Richelieu who, as France's chief minister from 1624 to 1642, first established the concept of the state as an abstract entity in its own right, with interests distinct from its ruler's personal interests or religious leanings. This is what allowed France, a Catholic kingdom, to align with the Protestant princes of Northern and Central Europe in the Thirty Years' War (1618–1648), against the interests of the Catholic Church, in order to check the power of the Habsburg Empire. Yet, in spite of the delineation between the interests of national leaders and the state as a whole, national interests remain primarily influenced by the interests of the ruling elite. Their interests not only fashion the external policies of nation states, but also their internal governance.

Of course, leaders' powers are circumscribed by what their people are willing to endure. A population pushed beyond its point of endurance is likely to overturn the incumbent regime. During the Thirty Years' War, Central Europe's population declined by as much as 40 percent in rural areas and one-third in the cities, as famine, epidemics and emigration added to direct battle losses.[1] Faced with physical and economic exhaustion, European rulers sued for peace under the Treaty of Westphalia, thereby keeping most of the prevailing elite in power. In contrast, when WW1 had tipped the Russian people past their breaking point in 1917, centuries of repressive Tsarist rule were overturned, eventually bringing the Bolsheviks to power. The balance of the social compact between the elite and the wider population is intricately linked to both stability within the state and its foreign policy.

Politics are also heavily influenced by history and national experience. This is why leaders often look to history to find justifications for their actions. Recognising the rhythms of history is helpful. Nevertheless, leaders (like all of us) are susceptible to cognitive biases and conditioning. It is therefore critical for each successive generation of leaders to evaluate the differences in circumstance between the present era and the past.

Between 1862 and 1870, the Prussian statesman Otto von Bismarck managed to steer the establishment of a unified German state, creating a central European power capable of dominating its neighbours. Emerging military technology had also vastly magnified the destructive power of war. Conditioned to pay heed to subtle changes in the balance of power, European leaders had thoroughly grasped the significance of the former development. However, they had not fully appreciated the consequences of the latter. This contributed to their disastrous miscalculation in 1914. As the diplomatic machinery was set into motion by Archduke Franz Ferdinand's assassination, political leaders lost control of their own tactics and became locked into a rigid path leading to a war that shattered a century of relative peace and order.

Today, we are confronted by a set of circumstances that has brought China and America into conflict. There is no inevitability that this should lead to a continual ratcheting-up of tensions resulting in war. Neither is there any guarantee that it will not. Much will come down to many individual decisions taken by political leaders.

Reflecting a human tendency to hew to our most recent historic anchors, many view current Sino-US tensions as a 'New Cold War'. The parallels with the 20th century US-Soviet conflict are obvious: 'capitalism' versus 'communism'; and 'liberal democracy' versus 'authoritarianism'. Nevertheless, while the Cold War provides many lessons from which contemporary leaders can learn, it would be highly risky to blindly follow the playbook of the past. Today's circumstances differ from the Cold War in certain important ways.

A key assumption made by American hawks advocating a New Cold War is that the US would win. At the end of WW2, America's economy was far larger than that of the USSR and its military predominance was backed by a nuclear monopoly. Today, the Chinese economy is already larger than America's on the basis of purchasing power parity and, in sharp contrast to the Soviet Union's sclerotic economic model, China has harnessed major elements of both private enterprise and state planning to drive rapid growth. Chinese citizens have enjoyed rising prosperity and living standards for several decades. Economic strength has also enabled it to modernise militarily and to invest in cutting edge technologies. Meanwhile, America's domestic infrastructure is aging and the country has been riven by deep social division. Even if there could be said to be a 'winner' from a conflict, it is not guaranteed that it would be the US.

Equally, there is a risk that China's extraordinary success over the past four decades has generated overconfidence among Chinese leaders and a sense that the country's continued economic ascendency is pre-ordained. This risks blinding them to the limitations of the Chinese development model. Rapid economic growth was only achieved through deep reforms and with the support of other nations. China's structural and institutional challenges are considerable. Unless the country continues to adapt to changes in its internal and external environments, there is no guarantee that China's economic success can be continued.

Further, trade and financial investment have created deep linkages between the Chinese and American economies that never existed between the US and the USSR. In his famous 'Long Telegram' despatched from Moscow in early 1946, the American diplomat George Kennan observed of the US–Soviet relationship:

> Our stake in this country, even coming on the heels of tremendous demonstrations of our friendship for Russian people, is remarkably small. We have here no investments to guard, no actual trade to lose, virtually no citizens to protect, few cultural contacts to preserve. Our only stake lies in what we hope rather than what we have. . .[2]

In contrast, given their tight economic links, a decoupling between China and the US would be highly damaging economically to both sides. That is no reason for complacency, however.

In the early 20th century, economic links between European countries were tight too. Germany and Britain were major trading partners and the City of London provided extensive services to German businesses. Indeed, much of the German merchant marine fleet was insured through Lloyds of London. At a hearing conducted by the British Committee on Imperial Defence in February 1912, the chairman of Lloyds testified that, in the event of war, were German ships to be sunk by the Royal Navy, Lloyds would be legally and morally obliged to cover the German losses.[3]

Just months before war broke out in 1914, the writer and later Nobel Peace Prize winner Norman Angell told a reporter: 'There will never be another war between European powers.' In his bestselling 1910 book *The Great Illusion*, he argued that the commercial and financial linkages between countries had become so extensive that no rational country would even *think* about starting a war. The book was popular with many statesmen of the time and even Kaiser Wilhelm was said to have read it 'with keen interest'.[4] In the end, none of that mattered. Mutual economic dependency is not a guarantee that nations will not go to war; all it guarantees is that war will be all the more damaging.

One narrative that has emerged is that the US could leverage Great Power competition to drive much needed domestic reforms. There are certainly historical precedents for this. However, as the historian Adam Tooze has pointed out, to pursue this line of thinking is 'to put the cart before the horse'.[5] That some seem to look back on the US-Soviet Cold War with rose-tinted spectacles is in large part because it ended without the eruption of a large-scale war between the main protagonists, but it is also because they have drawn the wrong lessons from it. Let us be clear: the costs of the Cold War were horrific and we continue to pay the price to this day.

A Close Call

In the early hours of 26 September 1983, Lieutenant Colonel Stanislav Petrov faced a life or death decision. Petrov was the officer on duty at the Serpukhov-15 bunker near Moscow, which housed the command centre for the Soviet Union's nuclear early-warning system. The computer he was looking at had just sounded an alarm that an intercontinental ballistic missile was heading towards Russia from the US. Protocol dictated that, on detecting an inbound missile, he was to notify his superiors, who in turn would follow their compulsory protocols under the USSR's nuclear strategy – namely, to launch an immediate counterattack against the US and its NATO allies under the doctrine of mutually assured destruction (MAD).

The MAD concept had come about in the years following the 1962 Cuban Missile Crisis, which had brought the Soviet Union and America within a whisker of all-out nuclear war. The doctrine had been formally acknowledged under the 1972 Anti-Ballistic Missile Treaty, which had banned *defences* against long-range missiles on the logic that, due to the *fear* of total destruction of life on the planet, a nuclear war would never occur and that, in order to maintain that fear, the only means of defence should be a counterattack.[6] However, in March 1983, Ronald Reagan upended that delicate balance with the announcement of his Strategic

Defence Initiative (nicknamed the 'Star Wars Programme'), under which he proposed a missile defence system to protect the US from ballistic strategic nuclear weapons.

The tense atmosphere was compounded when, at the beginning of September, the Soviet military shot down a South Korean passenger jet that had strayed into Soviet airspace, killing all 269 passengers and crew on board, including a US Congressman.[7]

Petrov hesitated. He knew the stakes if he were to report what he had seen, but something didn't feel right. If the US was going to launch a first-strike, *why would it only launch one missile?* Surely an attack of that sort would involve hundreds of simultaneous missile launches in order to disable any means of a Soviet counterattack? He had other reasons to doubt the accuracy of the system, so even when it reported that four further missiles were on their way, he decided to wait for further confirmation of a nuclear attack. That never came. Thus, one man's cool-headed gamble averted a nuclear war.[8]

Shocking as it was, that incident was just one of more than a dozen nuclear close calls during the Cold War, any of which could have resulted in mass annihilation.[9] And just because the US and USSR managed to avoid a direct all-out military confrontation, that didn't mean that the conflict wasn't deadly. Millions were killed in proxy wars across Korea, Indochina, Central Asia, Africa and Latin America. Many of those proxy wars also left a lasting legacy of civil strife in the countries where they played out.

During the Soviet-Afghan War in the 1980s, China and America cooperated in providing support to Mujahideen forces against the USSR.[10] Although they eventually succeeded in forcing a Soviet withdrawal, the nine-year war left a legacy of destruction and social displacement, leading to a civil war that brought the Islamic fundamentalist Taliban regime to power in 1996. Young Afghan refugees displaced by war were ripe for radicalisation by Osama bin Laden's Al Qaeda, which plotted the September 2001 attacks on the US from the failed state. China's problem with radical Islam in Xinjiang can also be traced to its involvement in the Cold War era conflict in Afghanistan.[11]

Even where there was no military engagement, the arms race between the Cold War protagonists consumed enormous financial resources that could otherwise have been spent on education, healthcare, or domestic infrastructure improvements. In China, the Cold War context also added to pressure to speed up industrialisation through the Great Leap Forward, which resulted in one of the worst famines in modern times. It is estimated that the USSR spent 15–17 percent of its GDP on defence in 1977 – an enormous drain on public resources that ultimately contributed to its collapse. US military spending that year consumed 4.9 percent of its much larger GDP.[12] That was roughly the same as total US public spending on education,[13] while federal outlays on health programmes that year were just 2.1 percent of GDP.[14]

Even victory had its dangers. In the chaos that ensued after the fall of the Soviet regime, the Russian military became a major source of weapons for organised crime groups around the world.[15] There was also a material risk that parts of the country's massive nuclear arsenal would fall into the hands of terrorist groups or a rogue regime.

Given all the manifest horrors of the Cold War, *why would anyone welcome the idea of a New Cold War?*

Fly Me to the Moon

'We choose to go to the Moon!' declared President John F. Kennedy before a 40,000-strong crowd at the Rice University Stadium in Houston, Texas on 12 September 1962. That launched the $25.4 billion Apollo space programme.[16] In its peak funding year, Apollo consumed a whopping 2.2 percent of GDP.[17] The context in which Congress approved such a large expenditure was a technology race against the Soviet Union.

After two atomic bombs dropped on Hiroshima and Nagasaki ended WW2, the US had expected its nuclear monopoly to last six to eight years. It came as a great shock when the USSR carried out its successful atom bomb test in the Kazakhstan desert in August 1949. The Soviets continued to advance their military capabilities, testing their first air-dropped thermonuclear bomb in 1955. In August 1957, they launched the world's first intercontinental ballistic missile. However, it was Russia's launch on 4 October 1957 of the first artificial satellite *Sputnik* that sparked the greatest reaction from the American public.

Sputnik orbited the Earth for three weeks until its batteries died, then fell back into the atmosphere two months later. President

Eisenhower had been forewarned about *Sputnik's* launch and had not appeared overly concerned. Nevertheless, coupled with the televised failure of America's own attempt to launch a satellite in December the same year, American politicians and the wider public suddenly became gripped with concern that the US was falling behind technologically. The technology race against the Soviet Union became a major issue in the 1960 presidential election campaign. When the USSR stole the march again in April 1961 by becoming the first country to successfully launch a human into space, the Kennedy Administration felt compelled to respond.

Kennedy never lived to see it, but by the end of the decade the American astronaut Neil Armstrong had become the first man to set foot on the Moon, declaring: 'That's one small step for man, one giant leap for mankind'. He was watched by audiences in homes around the world, many families having bought their first television set in order to witness the historical event.

Our collective memory of the Cold War today conjures up a more sinister era, be it in the grey imagery of John Le Carré spy novels, or in the real-life horrors of McCarthyism,[18] the Vietnam War and the constant threat of nuclear annihilation. However, for populations in the liberal democracies of the West, it was on the whole a period of rapid growth in opportunity and prosperity. Indeed, the Cold War itself was a major contributing factor to post-WW2 economic growth, broader distribution of prosperity, technological advancement, and more consensual politics. This was owed to the fact that this was a war primarily of competing ideologies, in which the focus was as much on winning hearts and minds domestically as it was on external rivalry.

All too aware of the mutually assured destruction that a direct military confrontation might entail, the fields of battle between the US and the USSR were transposed to the terrain of the Space Race, Olympic sports, and even the drama of the World Chess Championship title match between Boris Spassky and Bobby Fischer in 1972. However, the most profound impact of US-Soviet competition was seen in the creation of a far more egalitarian social order, both *between* different nations and *within* them.

In the immediate aftermath of WW2, the Communist threat in Europe was a major factor underlying America's European Recovery Plan, better known as the Marshall Plan. Between 1947 and 1952,

America transferred $17 billion, or roughly 1.1 percent of its GDP, in the form of reconstruction aid to 16 Western European countries. In contemporary terms, an equivalent proportion of US GDP from 2012 to 2016 would have amounted to a transfer of $800 billion. Never before had one country voluntarily transferred such a sizeable amount of its financial wealth for the assistance of others. Over the plan's duration, this aid accounted for 2.6 percent of the output of the recipient countries. Assistance also included the provision of fuel and machinery, and support for the continent's industrial and agricultural modernisation, transport renewal and trade revival. This helped increase the recipients' aggregate output by 60 percent, putting Western Europe firmly back on the path to self-reliance.[19]

Technological competition with the Soviet Union led to a renewed focus on science and technology education in American schools, and spurred Congress to enact the 1958 National Defence Education Act, which provided subsidies for college students majoring in science and mathematics. The need to remain competitive meant that a premium was placed on higher education and, between 1955 and 1970, enrolments in US colleges and universities tripled, with much of the increase financed by the federal government.[20] It also led to a surge in research and development (R&D) spending.

To run its space programme and wider Cold War military industrial complex, the US invested eight percent of its national income on research, a figure that no European country came remotely close to. The Apollo programme led to the development of many crucial technologies of modern life, such as the Global Positioning System (GPS) for navigation, home insulation, water filtration systems and solar energy cells.[21] In computer technologies, the US spent five times the amount invested by *all* of Western Europe.[22] These investments put America in pole position for the dawn of the Information Age and laid the foundation for Silicon Valley's global dominance today. From a social perspective, however, increased educational access also opened the door to greater social mobility.

The late Marxist historian Eric Hobsbawm wrote that 'Whatever Stalin did to the Russians, he was good for the common people of the West'.[23] In many ways, he was right. Fearing that the appeal of Soviet communism to the less advantaged segments of their own societies might overturn established political orders, Western democracies significantly expanded social security and workers' rights. The German Social Democrat Ludwig Preller reflected Western European governments' thinking in 1953, when he stated that the 'battalions' mobilised by a generous welfare state would be decisive in securing victory in the Cold War.[24]

Even in America, where social welfare has been less generous than in European countries, Lyndon Johnson introduced the Great Society programme 1964, under which the Medicare and Medicaid programmes were created to provide healthcare for the elderly and the uninsured. In wage bargaining, the Cold War context was also influential in securing significantly enhanced worker pay and rights.[25] In all, across 18 long-term members of the Organisation for Economic Cooperation and Development (OECD), total public social spending as a proportion of GDP rose from 10.6 percent in 1960 to 21.5 percent in 1990.[26]

Pressure to create a fairer society was not just limited to increased spending on welfare and worker protections. The Cold War also contributed to advances achieved by the American Civil Rights Movement. In its struggle against the oppressive dictatorship of Soviet communism overseas, America's continued denial of civil liberties to the African American minority at home was a glaring inconsistency. Not only did it put a strain on foreign relations, particularly with countries comprised of non-white populations, but it also left the US open to Soviet propaganda attacks. Leaders of the Civil Rights Movement exploited this by appealing to America's international audience, where the struggle became intertwined with anti-colonial movements. This added pressure on the US government to deliver on the substance, rather than just the veneer, of civil rights.[27]

The advancement in state social policies was not only a Western phenomenon. If Cold War competition drove democratic countries to improve the social bargain for the previously downtrodden and neglected in their societies, the need for governments of communist countries to enhance legitimacy was all the more compelling. Civil rights and liberal reforms would not come until Mikhail Gorbachev's *glasnost*, but in the more politically repressive period prior to that, pressure to improve social welfare became a key target. After economic scarcity contributed to social unrest and uprisings in East Germany (1953), Hungary (1956) and Czechoslovakia (1968), the USSR called on its Eastern European satellites to enhance their social provision to shore up their legitimacy at the Soviet Communist Party's 14th congress in 1971.[28]

Expansions in social welfare and education spending were underpinned by more progressive and, specifically, more *redistributive* tax systems.

★★★

The era the French call the *Belle Époque* (1880–1914) was characterised by a high degree of wealth and income inequality. The share of private property owned by the wealthiest 10 percent was around 90 percent in Europe and roughly 80 percent in the US. Wealth was even more concentrated at the very top. The wealthiest one percent held 60 percent of all private property in Western Europe and around 45 percent in the US.[29]

Governments' tax philosophy throughout the 19th century had revolved around specific spending needs, such as paying for wars, with no consideration about creating more egalitarian societies. Social attitudes began to change a little before WW1. In Britain, David Lloyd George's Liberal Party forced a showdown with the House of Lords in 1911 in order to implement a 'People's Budget' aimed at enhancing social welfare. However, it was the period from the Great Depression until 1980 that saw a shift to much higher and more steeply progressive levels of taxation.

In the period from 1900 to 1932, the top marginal rates of income tax in the US, the UK and Germany were 23 percent, 30 percent and 18 percent, respectively. These rose sharply. Between 1932 and 1980, the top marginal income tax rate averaged 81 percent in the US, 89 percent in the UK and 58 percent in Germany. High income taxes were accompanied by high taxation on the largest inheritances as well. Between 1932 and 1980, the top rate of inheritance tax averaged 75 percent in the US, 72 percent in the UK and 23 percent in Germany.[30] These tax rates were fundamentally aimed at redistributing wealth.

By the 1980s, this had resulted in far more egalitarian societies. The share of private property held by the top 10 percent had fallen to 50–55 percent in Western Europe, and to below 65 percent in the US. The top centile saw an even larger fall in their share. The proportion of private property held by the wealthiest one percent in Western Europe had fallen to 20 percent, while their American counterparts' share of private wealth fell to below 25 percent.[31]

Notwithstanding high taxation, the post-WW2 period was one in which the West enjoyed high levels of economic growth. The Cold War was no doubt one catalyst for the wealth redistribution and higher public spending on education and technology. Other influences on that generation of political leaders included their experiences of the Great Depression and of WW2. However, to conclude that international conflict or a New Cold War is necessary to achieve greater social equality and spur technological advancement would be to draw the wrong lesson. What enabled these developments were political vision, a progressive and redistributive tax system, and well-targeted public investment.

That political vision began to fade in the 1970s. Beset by oil price shocks, rising competition from emerging markets and bureaucratic inefficiency, growth in the West began to stagnate. This opened the door to the rise of free market ideology, a fundamental reassessment of the role of government, and radically different fiscal policies.

Tax Me If You Can

Steven Spielberg's 2002 movie *Catch Me If You Can* tells the story of Frank Abagnale, who, as a teenager, successfully perpetrated cheque fraud worth millions of dollars while posing as an airline pilot, a doctor and a litigator. Abagnale's character, played by Leonardo DiCaprio, is pursued through the movie by FBI agent Carl Hanratty, played by Tom Hanks. As the charming Abagnale moves on from one con to another, the hapless Hanratty is always just one step behind.

To viewers enthralled by Abagnale's capers, his financial misdemeanours can appear to be 'victimless crimes'. In that sense, this light-hearted movie serves as an apt analogy for tax avoidance by international corporations and the global rich. Their tax minimisation strategies have long been an accepted feature of the global financial system and, in their quest to capture a fair contribution to state coffers from this group, national tax authorities have often appeared a little like Agent Hanratty.

The power of any state is inseparable from its fiscal strength. European military dominance in the 19th and early 20th centuries was owed in large part to the unprecedented levels of fiscal and administrative capacity they developed during the 17th and 18th centuries. In the period from 1500 to 1600, tax rates across Europe, the Ottoman Empire and China were all roughly equivalent. However, wars in the 1600s drove significant increases in European taxation, while tax rates in the Ottoman Empire and China remained broadly constant. European states' increased fiscal capacity enabled them to develop sophisticated administrative bureaucracies and substantial militaries. By the mid-1800s, European tax receipts stood at 8–10 percent of national income versus just 1–2 percent in the Chinese and Ottoman states. By comparison with modern times, European tax levels in the 19th century were still very modest. They were enough to finance police forces and courts to maintain order at home and a military capable of projecting force abroad, but insufficient to pay for the elaborate educational, health and welfare systems that developed in the 20th century. Such greater provision typically consumed 30–50 percent of national income. However, with their *much lower* incomes, the 19th century Chinese and Ottoman states were unable even to fulfil the task of maintaining minimum order and fell into precipitous decline.[32]

Political and economic power in the 19th and early 20th centuries was concentrated in the hands of local elites. *Laissez faire* capitalism reigned supreme and international financial investment grew rapidly. As agricultural societies gave way to industrial societies, however, better educated workforces were needed and formerly scattered rural populations congregated in urban centres. This made glaring inequalities harder to justify. It was at around this time that Karl Marx and Friedrich Engels developed their socioeconomic theories. Political shifts were also reflected in financial policies.

While financial capital has always been highly mobile, capital shortages in the post-WW2 era drove governments to impose certain restrictions. The Bretton Woods system specifically provided for capital controls where severe distortions in the balance of payments arose. As economic recovery in Europe and Japan took hold, however, savings were rebuilt and capital once again became plentiful. Under the influence of the Washington free market consensus, restrictions on international capital flows began to be removed. One of the first acts of the Thatcher Government that came to power in Britain in 1979 was to eliminate capital controls. During the 1980s, the French socialist government reversed its previous stance and followed suit, leading to a European directive that enshrined the free movement of capital in 1988.[33] These moves opened the door to an ever more global market for capital. This went hand in hand with an acceleration in globalisation and fiscal developments.

The invention of container shipping in the 1950s facilitated the rapid growth of international trade, and the global outsourcing of production. This created the ideal conditions for international corporate tax planning to take off. As the leading economy by far, the US led the way.

★★★

When the US corporate income tax was first introduced in 1913, no taxes were assessed on overseas earnings. This went largely unnoticed until US companies started aggressively relocating parts of their businesses to other countries to exploit lower tax rates. As this started to have a meaningful impact on government revenues, the Kennedy Administration sought to eliminate fiscal incentives for US companies to relocate jobs and factories abroad. There were differences in opinion on how this should be done, however. In one camp were the proponents of 'capital export neutrality', who favoured levying US taxes on American companies' overseas profits, subject to a credit against foreign taxes that had already been paid. In other words, companies would be subject to US levels of profits taxes wherever they made those profits, but would not be taxed twice. In the other camp were those who argued that every country's tax code should treat foreign and domestic companies alike. The proponents of this 'capital import neutrality' worried that US companies would be uncompetitive in foreign markets if they were subject to higher taxes than domestic companies. The Revenue Act of 1962 was a compromise between these two positions. Drawing a difference between 'active business' and 'passive' income, profits made from operations located abroad would not be subject to US tax, so long as they were reinvested in the foreign operations. American companies would only pay taxes on profits repatriated in the form of dividends, buybacks or acquisitions.

Patents and royalties, like dividends and interest from overseas, were treated as passive income. This meant that income earned on this intellectual property would be subject to the US corporate tax rate wherever the patents were claimed to be located. However, all this changed in 1996 with a Treasury Decision that was supposed to simplify the tax filing process.[34] Inadvertently, the decision altered the treatment of income from patents and royalties to put it on the same footing as income from active business. Although the Internal Revenue Service (IRS) quickly realised the implications of this and tried to amend the rule, political interference blocked any fix. This led to a surge in tax shifting manoeuvres by US multinationals to move income into lower-tax jurisdictions.

To illustrate how this works in practice, the parent company might sell the right to licence a patent to a subsidiary in a low-tax jurisdiction. In return, the parent company gets a regular payment from the subsidiary to cover a portion of total R&D costs, while the subsidiary gets a large share of the group's worldwide sales. Done correctly, this can allow multinational corporations to dramatically cut their tax burdens in a perfectly legal manner.

Around 40 percent of all profits earned by multinational corporations are shifted from high-tax jurisdictions, such as the US, China, Germany and Japan, to low-tax ones. Through the shifting of profits into lower-tax jurisdictions, large US companies managed to reduce their effective tax rate from over 35 percent in the mid-1990s to around 26 percent in the mid-2010s, before the Trump tax reforms in 2017 lowered effective US corporate tax rates to below 20 percent.[35]

The Trump tax reforms, much as they were touted as a means of restoring US economic growth, were in reality a capitulation to widespread global fiscal competition. In their desire to attract multinational corporations, countries around the world have engaged in a 'race to the bottom' on corporate taxation. Small countries with limited natural endowments have been particularly prone to engaging in this sort of competition.

Luxembourg had long been a tax haven for Belgian dentists holding bearer bonds. In 2014, it came to light that it had also been siphoning off corporate tax revenues from its neighbours on a very large scale. Through a series of confidential agreements entered into with private companies from 2000, the tiny principality had been allowing them to pay taxes below the already low official rates. The so-called LuxLeaks scandal broke just as former Luxembourg prime minister Jean-Claude Juncker was taking office as president of the European Commission. Notwithstanding popular approbrium, the leading parties of the European Parliament chose not to demand his resignation after he defended the policy as being perfectly legal under Luxembourg's tax laws and promised to desist going forward.[36]

It should not be surprising that such fiscal competition has led to international tensions. Ireland, which had previously been dependent largely on agriculture and fishing, decided in the 1980s to focus on high value industries such as software and pharmaceuticals to develop its economy. In addition to offering grants for employee training, the country pursued a low-tax strategy. With one of the lowest headline corporate tax rates in the world at just 12.5 percent, Ireland was highly successful in attracting multinational corporations to set up there. Geographically well situated between North America and Continental Europe, it has been home to Apple's European headquarters since 1980, and hosts operations of major US companies, including Pfizer, Johnson & Johnson, Microsoft, Google and Facebook. In 2002, however, the UK listed Ireland as a tax haven for the purposes of its Controlled Foreign Corporation legislation.[37] Following an investigation by the EU's Competition Commissioner, the European Commission found in 2016 that Ireland had allowed Apple to pay an effective corporate tax rate of one percent on its European profits from 2003, falling to just 0.005 percent in 2014. The Commission ordered Apple to repay €13 billion in illegal state aid plus interest.[38] At the time of writing, this penalty remains the subject of a process of appeal and counter-appeal.[39]

It is sometimes argued that international fiscal competition is healthy, as it forces countries to become more efficient and avoid wasteful public expenditure. There is some merit to this argument. However, taken to excessive levels, it can leave a state without sufficient fiscal capacity to provide for the needs of its population as a whole. In practice, fiscal competition has led to increasingly regressive forms of taxation on labour, simply because it is less mobile than capital.[40] Examples of this include value added taxes, which disproportionately impact those on lower incomes because they generally have to spend a higher portion of what they earn; and property taxes, which are levied on immovable property but do not affect those with large amounts of wealth stored in financial assets. Fiscal competition to attract and retain corporates has effectively eroded the autonomy of nation states.

Countries that attract businesses by offering tax incentives may actually benefit very little if the companies pay little or no taxes to the local community and can easily relocate when another country offers a better incentive. There is also a fundamental question of fairness, since many companies rely on their home state's historic investments in areas such as infrastructure and education in order to generate their profits. If they have benefited from those historic investments but then structure themselves in such a way as to avoid paying taxes at home, the state may eventually no longer have sufficient income to provide the opportunities from which those companies originally benefited.

The simple fact is that the greatest beneficiaries of this fiscal race to the bottom have been the wealthy, who hold large stock portfolios. And it is not just through corporate tax avoidance that they have benefited. Fears that the wealthy might move either themselves (or at least their capital) elsewhere has been a major factor in driving tax cuts for higher-income earners and the rich in many countries.[41]

Even countries not under pressure to attract foreign capital have adjusted their tax systems to favour the wealthy. The justification for this generally revolves around the idea that lower taxes will stimulate greater entrepreneurship and investment, leading to 'trickle down' benefits to the rest of the economy. Individuals at the top end of the wealth and income curves often enjoy significantly lower total tax rates than lower-income earners through reduced rates of taxation on earnings on capital compared with labour income. The line between the different types of income has frequently been blurred. In the US, private equity and venture capital executives have long benefited from the treatment of their earnings tied to the returns on the funds they manage (known as 'carried interest') as capital gains instead of salary income. This allows them to reduce their tax rate on this income from the individual income tax rate of 37 percent to the long-term capital gains tax rate of 20 percent, notwithstanding the fact that carried interest is clearly a form of employment income.[42] In China, no taxes are levied on capital gains and inheritances, and individual income taxes on interest and dividends are taxed at a proportional rate of 20 percent, far below the 45 percent top marginal rate of tax on salaries.

Tax policies that have favoured the wealthy have contributed directly to rising levels of wealth and income inequality. They have also contributed to the increased financialisation of the global economy (discussed further in Chapter 7). America's reduced fiscal capacity as a result of lower taxes on the wealthy has contributed to soaring government deficits and has curtailed public spending on social welfare, education and infrastructure. Meanwhile, although China's fiscal position today is relatively strong, its rapidly aging demographic profile is likely to lead to severe fiscal strains in the future. Personal income taxes currently only make up around 6.5 percent of China's total tax revenues.[43] If the country is to meet its future needs, it will inevitably need to broaden its tax base and capture a greater contribution from the wealthy.

Highly unequal wealth distribution can sap a nation's economic vibrancy and undermine its social fabric. It may be argued that current levels of wealth and income inequality in both China and America are nowhere near as severe as during the *Belle Époque* or even earlier periods. This is true. However, this argument is not a justification for complacency over this issue. There are important differences between contemporary circumstances and those at the turn of the 20th century. Today, both countries' populations have become accustomed to much higher living standards, and it is the level of wealth, income and opportunity *relative to recent decades* that most affects *perceptions* of inequality. It is therefore the *trend* towards greater inequality that has driven social tensions. In today's world, this is further compounded by the proliferation of modern communications, which has increased awareness of wealth and income disparities.

Rising inequality has been linked to the recent surge in populist nationalism. Economic insecurity is linked to breakdowns in social cohesion and rising perceptions of threat. Under these conditions, people tend to become distracted from looking at the systemic explanations for inequality and instead focus on the security of local and national identities. These allegiances have, in turn, driven protectionism, anti-immigrant feelings and intolerance of cultural diversity. Opportunistic politicians have been ever ready to exploit these sentiments, further accentuating divisions with emotive and nationalistic rhetoric.[44]

A War of Words?

'We can't continue to allow China to rape our country', railed the Republican presidential front-runner Donald Trump on the campaign trail in Indiana in May 2016, accusing the Chinese of the 'greatest theft' of US jobs and intellectual property 'in the history of the world'.[45]

This deeply emotive narrative portrays America's relationship with China as a one-sided deal that has led to the loss of millions of American jobs and a steady erosion of the American Dream. To be sure, outsourcing of production to China has led to a loss of manufacturing jobs in the US. However, this has not been the only factor behind the decline of American manufacturing. Estimates vary, but it appears reasonable to attribute roughly half of the reduction in US manufacturing jobs since the early 1990s to industrial automation.[46] Further, to the extent that American job losses have been attributable to outsourcing to China, this was in large part a consequence of conscious US government policy.

American corporate profits benefited significantly from leveraging cheap Chinese labour to lower production costs. A plentiful supply of low-cost consumer goods contributed to lower inflation, allowing US interest rates to fall. This, in turn, reduced the cost of servicing mortgages and other loans, boosting consumption. China has now also become a big market for US companies. It is notable, therefore, that no American corporate leaders spoke up in defence of China when Trump launched his trade war.[47]

American businesses operating in China have long complained about an unlevel playing field and unfair trade policies, including forced technology transfer, intellectual property theft and non-tariff barriers. As they have moved up the production value chain, Chinese companies have now begun to challenge American technological dominance and compete with US businesses in international markets. Chinese companies operating overseas often enjoy privileged access to cheap funding and other forms of state backing, which private US enterprises can find hard to compete with. In addition, China's growing international presence is altering the global business environment in more subtle ways.

Since WW2, the US and Western European countries have conditioned assistance to developing countries on improvements in democratic governance, including citizen participation, media independence, transparency and accountability. Alongside this, they have promoted open markets with minimal tariffs and free capital flows, which have been difficult for poor countries to resist, irrespective of whether this was appropriate for those countries' stages of development.[48] These policies benefited US businesses by enabling them to access new markets and enjoy greater property protections overseas. Chinese development assistance offers developing countries an alternative to Western assistance and comes with no such conditions.

China's own economic success has also enhanced the appeal of its development model, which the Chinese government has increasingly sought to promote. In 2013, it launched CCTV Africa, based in Nairobi, and CCTV America, based in Washington DC. These channels present an alternative to Western viewpoints. By the end of 2017, it had also set up 525 Confucian Institutes in 146 countries to promote Chinese language and cultural education. Concurrently, democracy around the world has seen setbacks. The *Freedom in the World Survey* for 2017 registered 71 countries that saw a decline in political rights and civil liberties versus 35 that had seen improvements.[49] This challenge to its 'soft power' is making it more difficult for the US to shape international policies in favour of American interests.

It is perhaps no coincidence that the growing threat to American business interests has been accompanied by a hardening of political attitudes. Recent events have compounded the already tense atmosphere precipitated by Trump's trade war. As the world became engulfed in the Covid-19 pandemic, fierce criticisms were levelled at China over its lack of transparency and media freedoms, which were considered to have contributed to the virus' global spread. The imposition of the NSL in Hong Kong has further drawn expressions of outrage over curtailments of human rights and civil liberties. In response, China's so-called 'wolf warrior' diplomats have issued shrill denouncements of US interference in what they consider to be China's internal affairs and have sharply criticised America's handling of the pandemic.[50]

To a large degree, both sides play to their domestic audiences. The American people's sensibilities over human rights are deeply rooted in their national history and identity. However, American leaders also have a long history of overlooking such issues where it suits the country's interests to do so.[51] Meanwhile, China's political elite see liberal democratic ideals as a threat to their rule – as demonstrated by the 1989 student protests. This gives them a strong incentive to seek to discredit America's political model.

Chinese and Americans both have a strong belief in their own national exceptionalism. Founded on the principle that 'all men are created equal' with 'unalienable Rights' to 'Life, Liberty and the pursuit of Happiness', the US views its values as universal. Based on this view, Americans see it as an obligation to spread them to all parts of the world with an almost missionary zeal. China's sense of exceptionalism is based on its culture and long history. It has historically avoided proselytising its values. Following the 1989 student movement, however, the Chinese leadership saw a need to focus on civic and moral education to help preserve domestic stability.

With the collapse of communism in Eastern Europe and the USSR, Party elders realised that political training in Marxism-Leninism or Maoism was unlikely to appeal to China's youth. Instead, therefore, they focused on patriotism as an alternative. Patriotic education in China has tended to focus on the country's century of humiliation at the hands of the colonial powers, which has incubated and exacerbated a sense of China's victimisation and anti-foreign sentiment. This at least partly accounts for Chinese officials' sometimes vitriolic reactions to criticisms by foreigners. Nationalistic rhetoric can easily get out of hand though.

On 6 January 2021, people around the world were shocked by images of rioters storming the US Capitol. The occupation and vandalising of the legislative complex came after Donald Trump had falsely claimed that the 2020 presidential election had been 'stolen' from him and called on his supporters to overturn the election result. Xenophobic comments by Trump, such as referring to Covid-19 as the 'kung flu', have also been attributed to a rise in hate crimes against Asian Americans.[52]

For Chinese leaders, these episodes are seen as evidence to their people that the US system is broken, reinforcing their claim that only the CCP's unitary rule can deliver stability and growth. However, this is clearly self-serving. And China is by no means immune to violent outpourings of nationalist sentiment itself – as seen in the aftermath of the 1999 bombing of the Chinese embassy in Belgrade, when tens of thousands of rock-throwing protesters kept the American ambassador trapped in the US embassy in Beijing for several days.

Much of the recent war of words between Chinese and US officials has taken place over social media. Given these platforms' tendency to reinforce human beings' natural confirmation biases by showing users more content related to items they have viewed in the past, social media 'echo chambers' have contributed to greater polarisation of opinions.[53] The danger is that, when leaders employ nationalistic rhetoric and engage in the politics of hate, the populist nationalism that they provoke can easily get out of control and can limit their ability to de-escalate conflicts. And it is not just in words that Sino-US differences are being fought out. Troublingly, the conflict has been heating up in the financial sphere.

Geo-economic Warfare

America has a unique ability to impose its will on foreign countries, institutions and individuals through economic pressure. Its geo-economic arsenal includes four key components. First is its ability to deploy a large amount of capital in pursuit of diplomatic or strategic goals. Perhaps the best example of this was the use of Marshall Plan aid in post-WW2 Europe to counter the influence of Communist Russia. Second, it has a large and attractive domestic consumer market on which many other countries depend for export revenues. Third, through its own large natural endowment of energy and other commodities, as well as its ability to project power over key transit arteries such as the Panama Canal, the Malacca Strait and the Strait of Hormuz, it has a high degree of influence over global energy and commodity flows. Finally, and most importantly in this analysis, is its centrality in the global financial system. Through the dollar and control over key global financial infrastructure, the US has unparalleled power to impose and enforce sanctions, and to exert other forms of financial pressure on its rivals.[54]

America's employment of geo-economic tools in statecraft dates back to its very earliest days. The fledgling nation's first Secretary of the Treasury, Alexander Hamilton, had the federal government assume the war debts of the initial 13 states in order to bind them and their elites to the success of the union. Hamilton also saw commerce as a means of tying the interests of the various European powers to the US.[55] After WW2, its emergence as by far the leading economic power gave America unprecedented financial resources with which to pursue international diplomacy. The threat posed by the Soviet Union further gave it the incentive to do so, and it was ultimately Reagan's exploitation of America's strength in capital markets that helped bring about victory in the Cold War.

From the 1970s, the US pressured international financial institutions to improve transparency and disclosure in pursuit of its 'war on drugs'. It introduced laws and regulations that required banks and other intermediaries to report large financial transactions and suspicious activity. Financial institutions were required to gather information on their customers in order to help identify money laundering. In these efforts, the US enlisted the support of other countries through the G-7 and other similar fora. Generally, other nations shared an interest in thwarting drug trafficking, tax evasion and money laundering and were happy to collaborate on these initiatives. Following the 11 September 2001 attacks, the US significantly extended the scope of these measures to prevent the financing of terrorist activities.

Measures to combat financial crime, money laundering and terrorism have imposed a high cost on the financial sector around the world and on the US itself. It has been estimated that federal and state expenditures on enhanced rules introduced after 9/11 total around $3 billion per annum, while direct costs to the general public are estimated at another $1 billion per annum. The costs to the financial sector significantly exceed this. By comparison, a truck bomb used to carry out a terrorist attack in New York in 1993 cost $400, while the whole operation of carrying out the 9/11 attacks on the US was estimated to be just $500,000. As the late former Defence Secretary Donald Rumsfeld admitted privately in 2003, 'The cost-benefit ratio is against us!'.[56]

The debate about the efficacy of these measures relative to their cost notwithstanding, the use of America's geo-economic clout to detect and stamp out crime and terrorism still enjoys the broad support of other major nations. However, it is where geo-economic tools appear to be deployed to unfairly coerce other nations on diplomatic or strategic matters that raises concerns.

★★★

China's economic rise in recent decades has bestowed it with expanding geo-economic clout of its own, which its government has been quick to exploit. The two primary levers it has at its disposal are its control over access to its vast domestic market and its ability to direct or withhold Chinese outbound capital flows. By 2018, China was already the primary trading partner of 124 countries and this dependency has made many of them susceptible to Chinese coercion.

In response to the Norwegian parliament awarding Chinese dissident Liu Xiaobo (刘晓波) the Nobel Peace Prize in 2010, Beijing froze relations with Norway and reduced imports of Norwegian salmon by 60 percent, dealing a heavy blow to the country's aquaculture industry.[57] To appease China, the Norwegian prime minister refused to meet with the Dalai Lama when the religious leader visited Oslo in May 2014.

The late statesman Lee Kuan Yew highlighted the particularly strong pressure faced by China's Asian neighbours:

> China is sucking the Southeast Asian countries into its economic system because of its vast market and growing purchasing power. Japan and South Korea will inevitably be sucked in as well. It just absorbs countries without having to use force.[58]

China has brought this economic pressure to bear on smaller neighbours over territorial disputes. China claims 'indisputable sovereignty' over around 90 percent of the South China Sea, based on certain 'historic rights' it has asserted over various islands, shoals and land features spread across a vast area.[59] These territorial claims are disputed by Brunei, Malaysia, the Philippines, and Japan. The islands and land features themselves don't amount to much. What is really at stake, however, are the potential natural resources that might be extracted from under the seabed, fishing rights and, critically, maritime security. It is through these waters that two-thirds of China's maritime trade and 80 percent of its oil imports pass. Nevertheless, the South China Sea is vital to other nations too. Both Japan and South Korea are dependent on these waters for their energy security, and around 30 percent of total world trade passes through them.[60]

In 2012, Chinese customs left 150 containers of Filipino bananas to rot in port after the Philippines arrested Chinese fishermen working off the Scarborough Shoal, which both countries lay claim to. Since more than 30 percent of the Philippines' fruit production goes to China, this dealt a substantial blow to the country's exporters. That same year, China pledged $2.7 billion in loans and grants to Cambodia. As chair of the Association of Southeast Asian Nations (ASEAN) summit, Cambodia then used its power to block a joint statement by the regional grouping to criticise China's approach to territorial disputes in the South China Sea – the first time in 45 years that the ASEAN countries had failed to agree on a joint *communiqué*.[61]

More recently, China has used tariffs to target Australian wine exports amidst souring relations between the two countries. In April 2020, Australia had called for a global inquiry into the origins of the Covid-19 pandemic, specifically singling out China. In apparent retaliation, China launched an anti-dumping investigation into Australian wine in August that year. This resulted in the imposition of tariffs of up to 218 percent on Australian wine imports, dealing a huge blow to Australia's wine industry, for which China was the largest market, making up almost $800 million (or 37 percent) of its total wine exports in 2019.[62]

One observer has remarked that 'Beijing has been playing the new economic game at a maestro level'.[63] However, far from reflecting strength, China's readiness to deploy its geo-economic endowments may in fact stem from the weakness of its other forms of influence. Although China has significantly increased its military capabilities in the past two decades,[64] the PLA is still seen as lagging behind the US military in its overall capabilities.[65] And notwithstanding its investments in promoting the Chinese world view overseas, its soft power influence does not come close to matching that of the US.

In fact, China's influence efforts have often backfired. Many of China's close neighbours are wary of China's rise. This traces back to the CCP's legacy of supporting communist revolutionary movements around the region under Chairman Mao, and to the existence of large ethnic Chinese populations in a number of Southeast Asian countries. Chinese diplomats' increasingly bellicose nationalistic rhetoric and claims to defend the region's Chinese diaspora, many of whom have been settled in their host countries for several generations, has heightened fears about China's strategic intentions.[66] It is notable that diplomatic failures have pushed even Vietnam's communist leaders to pursue closer relations with the US.[67]

Nevertheless, China's size and continuing rapid economic growth mean that its geo-economic capabilities are likely to go on expanding.

★★★

America's use of its geo-economic endowments has by no means been entirely benign either. However, given its influence over international financial institutions and market infrastructures, as well as its control over the dollar-based global financial system, the US can access a far broader arsenal than China and has developed far more sophisticated means of geo-economic coercion. This does not mean that its actions have escaped controversy though.

In 2006, when it came to light that US intelligence services had been monitoring international money transfers through the Brussels-based SWIFT network, concerns were raised about the threat to civil liberties.[68] Just as the US would have problems with the intelligence services of other countries, such as Russia or China, having access to sensitive personal information on its citizens,[69] other countries have legitimate cause for concern over such privacy infringements by the US. Exploiting international financial infrastructures for espionage purposes is just one aspect of America's progressively refined use of its geo-economic endowments, however.

In its campaign to end apartheid in South Africa in the 1980s, the US instituted a country-wide embargo as a means of pressuring the ruling regime. However, this had the effect of hurting the entire South African population, including the victims of apartheid. Following Russia's actions in Crimea in 2014, the US, together with the EU, employed more targeted measures against specific Russian companies and individuals perceived as being close to the Russian leadership.[70] More recently, in response to Russian cyber-attacks on the US, the Biden Administration has prohibited US financial institutions from investing in newly-issued

Russian sovereign debt, thereby restricting the Russian government's access to capital.[71]

Usually, for financial sanctions to be effective, the country imposing them needs the support of allies. Without this, targeted countries or companies can circumvent the sanctions by turning to other countries and their financial institutions.[72] However, America's central position in the global financial system gives it a unique ability to enforce sanctions unilaterally. Recently, it has exhibited an increasing propensity to exploit this position, sometimes alienating traditional allies and undermining its own rules-based international order.

Under the Obama Administration, the US entered into a Joint Comprehensive Plan of Action (JCPOA) alongside the other permanent members of UN Security Council, Germany, and Iran. Under the JCPOA, Iran agreed to eliminate its stockpile of medium-enriched uranium and to submit to international inspections of its nuclear facilities. In return, Iran would receive relief from US, EU and UN nuclear-related sanctions. The agreement was hailed at the time as a major step forward in preventing nuclear weapons proliferation. To the consternation of the other signatories to the agreement, the US under President Trump unilaterally withdrew from the JCPOA in May 2018. Not only did it withdraw from the agreement, but it also announced fresh sanctions on countries that trade with Iran on the basis of the JCPOA. Given the binding nature of the agreement, America's withdrawal was, in fact, a violation of international law. The other UN Security Council members and Germany have stuck to the JCPOA, though fresh US sanctions have made this difficult. Quite apart from the potential step back in the fight against nuclear non-proliferation taken by the Trump Administration, this episode showed the US to be a fickle partner in international agreements that is willing to override international laws.

When Donald Trump launched his trade war against China in 2018, it seemed that the core of US demands was to address a chronic balance of payments deficit between the two countries. However, given the relatively miniscule role of the trade in goods and services today as a proportion of international monetary flows, trade may have been the wrong place to focus if the balance of payments was really what the US was seeking to address. Given the uncoordinated nature of the pronouncements that emanated from the US on the trade war, it was often unclear as to what the Trump Administration was actually seeking. However, taken together with other developments, it would be easy to develop a cynical view about US intentions.

On 1 December 2018, Meng Wanzhou (孟晚舟), the Chief Financial Officer of Huawei (华为), the Chinese telecoms giant, was detained upon arrival in Canada at the request of US authorities and became the subject of lengthy extradition proceedings. Huawei is the acknowledged global leader in 5G telecoms technology and Meng also happens to be the daughter of the company's founder, Ren Zhengfei (任正非). The charges alleged that Meng engaged in a conspiracy to defraud multiple financial institutions, diverting funds raised for Huawei to a subsidiary that had been dealing with Iran, in contravention of US sanctions. China reacted angrily and, in an apparent tit-for-tat, detained two Canadian citizens on espionage charges. Since then, the US has engaged in a campaign to pressure other countries to remove Huawei equipment from their telecommunications networks on the basis of vaguely specified security concerns.

In October 2019, the US further imposed sanctions on eight Chinese high technology companies,[73] citing human rights concerns, including their supply of surveillance technology to the Chinese government for use to suppress ethnic minorities in its north-western Xinjiang province. Given atrocities committed by the US during its War on Terror, the US stance on Chinese counter-terrorism policies in Xinjiang lends itself to accusations of hypocrisy. Viewed in conjunction with the trade war and attacks on Huawei, however, it gives rise to suspicions that America's true intention is to contain China's technological development, calling into question the moral and legal legitimacy of US actions.

Nor did this all start with Donald Trump. When China led the creation of the multinational development organisation the AIIB in 2015, the Obama Administration sought to prevent other countries from joining the initiative. The fact that even staunch US ally Britain broke ranks to sign on to China's AIIB initiative demonstrates that US attempts to curtail Chinese development aid do not enjoy international legitimacy.

In a parting shot of his presidency, Donald Trump issued an Executive Order banning US persons from investing in a range of Chinese companies, and requiring them to be delisted from US exchanges.[74]

Instead of trying to improve frayed relations, the Biden Administration has stepped up the geo-economic campaign against China, extending Trump's ban to cover 59 Chinese companies and giving investors one year to divest their holdings.[75]

In practice, the biggest threat that the US has at its disposal is the denial of access to the dollar and dollar payment systems. In recent years, the US wielded this forcefully in the pursuit of uni-lateralist agendas. In 2012, the British bank Standard Chartered was fined $340 million by New York regulators for using the US dollar to finance a trade transaction with Iran.[76] Standard Chartered had broken no British laws, nor had it violated any sanctions imposed by the UN Security Council. The US fine, therefore, was a clear application of extraterritorial US jurisdiction through exploitation of the dollar's international role, without widespread international support. Even more startlingly, in 2014 BNP Paribas was forced to pay a settlement of almost $9 billion after pleading guilty in a case brought by US prosecutors over violations of US sanctions on Sudan, Iran and Cuba between 2004 and 2012.[77]

Given America's ability to apply extraterritorial jurisdiction over foreign institutions through the dollar and international payment sys-tems, other countries are increasingly looking to sidestep these. In response to Trump's withdrawal from the JCPOA, Britain, France and Germany decided to set up the Instrument in Support of Trade Exchanges (INSTEX) to provide a non-dollar channel for international companies to trade with Iran. In practice, given the importance of the US market, many global companies still avoid dealing with Iran in order not to raise the ire of US authorities. However, the coordinated effort by long-standing US allies to create a means of circumventing the US stranglehold on international payments highlights the level of interna-tional exasperation at America's abuse of the dollar's global role.

Eventually, if the US continues to abuse its geo-economic endow-ments, it could well precipitate its own downfall by forcing other countries to extract themselves from the dollar-based system. Russia has already sold off US Treasury holdings and sought to de-dollarise its economy.[78] Asked about this at a conference in Moscow in 2018, President Vladimir Putin responded: 'We are not leaving the dollar, the dollar is leaving us'. In contrast to his predecessor, President Biden appears to grasp the need for international alliances. The future of the dollar, however, will hinge significantly on what path China chooses.

★★★

Today, China remains highly exposed to the dollar. This is not just because of its $1.1 trillion in US Treasury holdings, but also due to the effects of US monetary policy on the global economy and consumption around the world. Although their contribution to the Chinese economy has almost halved since their 2010 peak, exports still accounted for 18.5 percent of China's GDP in 2019.[79] Moreover, export manufacturing remains a major source of employment.

China is also heavily dependent on the dollar in other ways. Despite the US only accounting for 14 percent of its total merchandise trade,[80] China's exports and FDI are largely invoiced in US dollars.[81] In other words, China relies on the dollar in its financial dealings, not just with the US, but also with the rest of the world. As discussed in Chapter 5, the main reason for this lies in the stunted development of China's own financial markets. America is able pay for goods and services overseas in dollars primarily because of its highly developed financial system. Instead of being able to invoice all of its trade in renminbi, China receives dollars in return for most of its exports and, due to its capital controls, is required to re-export those dollars overseas – mostly through the purchase of low-yielding US Treasury debt.

Even absent geopolitical considerations and concerns over the long-term stability of the dollar, there are compelling reasons for China to seek a more international role for the renminbi. The ability to invoice and settle trade in their home currency would remove significant risks for Chinese businesses transacting with overseas counterparties. Wider international circulation of the renminbi would also allow China to reap the benefits of seigniorage (the difference between the value of the currency in circulation and the cost of producing it).

The major factor preventing the renminbi becoming more widely accepted in global trade is the difficulty international investors have in investing the renminbi proceeds.[82] The pool of renminbi-denominated securities issued offshore remains very small. Capital controls and lack of confidence in the impartiality of the legal system inhibit international investors' appetite for investing directly in China's onshore securities markets. Programmes that have channelled investment through Hong Kong have helped increase international appetite for Chinese domestic securities. However, to truly internationalise the renminbi, it will be necessary to massively expand the pool of renminbi securities offshore, and to give international investors similar levels of security and efficiency to those which they enjoy when holding other international securities.

Notwithstanding the many benefits of further developing China's financial markets and internationalising the renminbi, there are reasons why the Chinese government is proceeding cautiously.

First, there is a risk that too-rapid liberalisation of capital flows would lead to greater volatility in China's exchange rate and domestic financial markets. Numerous emerging markets crises in recent decades have highlighted the potential social and political consequences of financial crises brought on by sudden large cross-border capital flows. Chinese policymakers are also acutely aware of the enormous costs that the dollar's global role has imposed on the US. It is most likely for this reason that, in a *Financial Times* article published in mid-2020, Governor Yi Gang of the PBOC echoed his predecessor in calling for a greater international role for the IMF's SDRs, rather than pushing for a more prominent role for the renminbi.[83] To the Chinese government, stability and control are paramount.

Second, there is a significant risk that greater freedoms for Chinese citizens to invest overseas would be accompanied by a rise in tax evasion. Unlike the US, which has been able to impose US financial laws and regulations internationally,[84] China has limited ability to enforce its anti-tax evasion laws overseas.[85]

A third concern relates to China's national financial security. As things stand, Chinese outbound securities investment would be highly dependent on international payments systems[86] and depository infrastructures[87] over which the US government has a high degree of influence. This dependence means that greater outbound investment would expose Chinese corporations and individuals to greater potential US sanctions risks, such as those that have been applied against Russia.[88]

To reduce its vulnerability, China has been setting up alternative international financial infrastructures such as the Cross-Border Interbank Payment System (CIPS, 跨境银行间支付清算有限责任公司).[89]

However, given the central role of the dollar in international trade and investment, the US continues to have a stranglehold over major parts of the global financial system.

Even without explicit sanctions, the US can leverage its influence over global financial market infrastructures to pursue financial containment of China. It is notable, for instance, that the London Clearing House (LCH, a subsidiary of the London Stock Exchange Group), which enjoys over 90 percent market share in the clearing of interest rate swaps globally,[90] does not accept CGBs as good collateral. This structurally inhibits global demand for CGBs, thereby limiting the Chinese government's access to funding from international investors.

Any US campaign to limit China's financial integration with the rest of the world, however, would significantly harm the US itself. This is primarily because, without the renminbi taking on a more international role, the US will be condemned to continue shouldering the burden of the dollar's global role on its own and suffering the imbalances which that entails. Moreover, financial markets are not, in aggregate, a zero-sum game. By curtailing China's growth and ability to consume, the US would reduce its own economic prospects. Decoupling altogether, given the level of Sino–US economic integration that already exists, would simply leave both countries the poorer. Besides, rather than trying to slow down China's economic development, it would likely be more fruitful for the US to pursue policy reforms to better drive productivity growth at home.

For China's part, while it is understandable for it to pursue policies aimed at preserving domestic stability, its leaders must recognise that this has implications for other countries also. When its top-down industrial policies create surplus capacity at home and the government responds with programmes to export its surplus production, it is spreading its own domestic imbalances elsewhere. Tight management of its exchange rate to preserve currency stability might be viewed similarly. This may not have been such a problem when China's economy was still relatively small and less integrated with the global trade and financial systems but, given its scale today, these policies now pose significant risks to other countries. Moreover, reforms that have allowed the private sector to play a greater role have unleashed enormous creative energies that have helped drive China's recent successes. It is in the country's overall self-interest to uphold those gains and to pursue further liberalisations to increase the efficiency with which Chinese capital is allocated. However, given that government control over the domestic financial system and the pricing and allocation of capital are key pillars of the CCP's power, reforms are unlikely to be straight forward.

★★★

As tensions between China and the US have heightened, it has been tempting to cast these in the ideological terms of the 20th century Cold War. However, this ignores the significant role played by an accumulation of financial imbalances over many decades. Ideological differences between the two countries do exist, but underlying them are a host of elite interests, many of which have little do with the interests of the wider population.

The Chinese people and the American people are not each other's enemies. Rather, the main conflict in both countries is that between the elites and their wider populations. This has been driven by the fiscal, industrial and monetary policies that have pushed widening income and wealth disparities *within* both countries and led to significant imbalances in the commercial and financial relationship *between* them.

One of the most fundamental factors underlying these imbalances has been the role played by the US dollar in the global financial system. While the dollar's role as a global utility has had significant benefits for both America and other countries, this has undermined the US currency's ability to adjust to new economic realities. This has not only hurt US workers, but has also contributed to significant financial shocks that have had a devastating impact on the affected countries. These imbalances have been compounded by fiscal, industrial and other policies that have favoured corporate and wealthy interests at the expense of everyone else. Further, as fiscal competition between states has escalated, this has undermined both the long-term economic vibrancy of nations and their very sovereignty. This has been a *Financial Cold War*.

Troublingly, the Financial Cold War has now spilled over into both a rise in populist nationalism around the world, and a geo-economic conflict of growing dimensions between China and the US.

History has taught us that we cannot afford to be complacent amid these escalating tensions. In any conflict, leaders can easily lose control of their own tactics, and fanning the flames of populist nationalism is particularly dangerous, since it can ultimately reduce governments' flexibility to de-escalate diplomatic tensions. It is therefore incumbent on responsible leaders to address the root causes of the problems in the global financial system before they are allowed to metastasise further.

Before addressing possible remedies, however, it is important to remind ourselves of the fundamental purposes that financial markets were originally designed to serve. While their size and complexity can sometimes appear daunting, and they often seem to operate on a logic of their own, financial markets are ultimately man-made. They operate within institutional frameworks and are driven by the incentives that those create. It should, therefore, be up to society to determine the objectives that markets should serve, and to establish the policies that will help meet those objectives.

Chapter 7

The Role of Markets in the 21st Century

Phew! That's a nasty leak. Thank goodness it's not at our end
of the boat.
    – David Low, caption to his famous Great Depression era cartoon

From social science literature[1] to the surge in popularity of the paleo diet,[2] it has become fashionable in recent years to idealise the lifestyles of early hunter-gatherers. However, as Thomas Hobbes noted, life for our primordial forebears was, in reality, 'solitary, poor, nasty, brutish, and short'. A major reason for that was that, without the organising frame-works of the state and of trade, the only means for primitive peoples to obtain coveted resources (such as food and fertile women) from each other was by plunder. The evolution of trade has therefore had a major civilising effect on humankind.[3]

Trade has not only contributed to a reduction in violence, but also to the spread of ideas and technologies through the routes of commerce, and to social mobility by rewarding enterprise.[4] It further catalysed the division of labour – or specialisation – on a much greater scale, leading to significant increases in economic productivity.[5] Commercial competition has spurred innovation and technological progress, raising our collective quality of life. Indeed, it is notable that two of the worst famines in modern history – the Soviet Union in 1929–1933 and China in 1958–1962 – occurred under regimes that had largely cut themselves off from commercial intercourse with the rest of the world and eschewed private enterprise.[6]

Closely associated with the development of trade was the creation of money. Money has taken many forms. From around 3000 BC, people in ancient Mesopotamia used clay tokens as a medium of exchange. For around 4,000 years, cowry shells were used as money all over Africa, South Asia, East Asia and Oceania. Coins were first struck in around 640 BC in western Anatolia.[7] Paper money was later invented in China during the Han Dynasty (206 BC–220 AD).[8] Money facilitated trade by introducing a standard unit of exchange to replace the system of barter for goods. Not only did money increase the efficiency with which commercial exchange could be conducted, its relative portability also extended the geographic range over which trade could take place. By the first century AD, trust in the money system had developed to the extent that Roman coins were an accepted medium of exchange in the marketplaces of India.[9]

The development of finance followed closely behind the creation of money currencies. Mathematical records evidence the calculation of compound interest on long-term loans as far back as during the reign of the Babylonian King Hammurabi (1792–1750 BC). Through the adoption of Hindu-Arabic numerals and the innovation of double-entry bookkeeping, the foundations of the modern banking system were laid in the Italian city-states between the 13th and 16th centuries.[10] It was there also that bond markets first developed, as the feuding city-states raised loans from their citizens to finance their wars. Those loans could be sold on to other citizens if the holder needed to raise ready money, with secondary market prices reflecting the perceived likelihood of repayment. Unlike loans to European sovereigns, however, the purchasers of these loans tended to be local elites who held political power, creating a strong incentive for the state not to default.[11]

The Portuguese discovery of the sea route to Asia via the Cape of Good Hope expanded trade with the East. The hazards involved, and the size and timescales of the capital investment required, necessitated the sharing of risk between a large number of investors. These risks were initially shared on a voyage-by-voyage basis. However, in 1602 the Dutch pioneered the joint-stock company to share risks over multiple voyages with the founding of the Dutch East India Company. The same year, the world's first stock market was born when traders began to buy and sell the company's shares on Amsterdam's Warmoesstraat, next to the *Oude Kerk* ('old church'). Financial markets have continued to evolve ever since, spurred by the discovery of new technologies and other innovations.

From the perspective of society as a whole, financial markets serve two fundamental purposes. First, they are the avenue via which capital can be channelled to its most productive use within the economy. By providing a means of pricing and allocating capital, those who are able to make the best use of it might be able to obtain it; in return, those with a surplus of it are given the opportunity to generate better returns. The resulting increase in economic activity should, in theory, benefit all. Second, financial markets provide a forum in which economic risks can be shared or transferred to those most able to bear it. This allows larger or riskier ventures to be undertaken. The mutualisation or transfer of risk also enables the release of capital (that may otherwise be held back to cover the possibility of unforeseen financial exposures) for more productive use.

So are financial markets unequivocally a force for good? The answer is: well, it depends. . . Financial markets cannot be divorced from the political frameworks within which they operate. These dictate the incentive structures that drive financial activity. Further, markets ultimately reflect the collective beliefs of their participants at any given point in time. Those beliefs are shaped by individual interests, as well as human psychology. For financial markets to benefit society, they must be structured in a way that ensures they operate efficiently to meet society's objectives. *Can it be claimed that global financial markets today operate efficiently?* The answer to that question is: yes. . . And no.

Selective Efficiency

The debate about whether markets are efficient or not is often an exercise in talking at crossed purposes, since there is no generally accepted definition of what 'market efficiency' really is. The term could refer to how closely the price of an individual security reflects its fundamental value, or how closely the aggregate market reflects the fundamental value of all the securities in it. It could also be understood as a reflection of demand and supply at any given point in time (which is distinct from value). Alternatively, it could be taken to mean the achievement of desired macroeconomic outcomes.

The efficient-market hypothesis is most closely associated with the University of Chicago academic Eugene Fama, who was awarded a Nobel Prize in economics in 2013 for his work on asset prices.[12] This hypothesis postulates that asset prices always reflect all available information, implying that it is not possible to consistently outperform the market, since market prices should only react to new information. Along with the free market ideology espoused by Chicago school economists, the efficient-market hypothesis has been highly influential on economic policy since the 1970s. It has also contributed to the huge rise in popularity of index tracker funds, which seek to replicate the performance of the overall market and charge lower fees than traditional active asset managers. If markets are perfectly efficient and no fund manager can consistently outperform the average, there seems little point in paying more to invest in a fund that aims to beat the market. The only problem is that, as the highly successful track records of investors such as Warren Buffett and Edward Thorp attest, the idea that markets are *always* perfectly efficient is patently wrong.

One fatal flaw in the efficient-market hypothesis is that it assumes investors will always behave rationally. In the real world, investors oscillate between greed and fear, throwing caution to the wind in periods of market euphoria (driving prices irrationally upward) and becoming excessively pessimistic when gripped by market depressions (driving prices to irrationally low levels). Studies in behavioural finance have identified multiple psychological biases and cognitive traps that make human beings prone to miscalculations and irrational behaviour.

An example of human irrationality in financial decision making is loss aversion. It has been shown that most human beings would turn down a gamble offering a 50 percent chance of losing $100 and a 50 percent chance of winning $200 – notwithstanding mathematical probability implying a risk of a $50 loss ($100 x 50 percent) versus a chance of a $100 gain ($200 x 50 percent). In financial markets, this means that investors avoid cutting their losses on poor investments, even where it is the most rational thing to do. This bias creates a bizarre asymmetry: risk aversion in the face of positive prospects, and risk-seeking behaviour in the face of negative ones. Experiments suggest that a loss has 1.5 to 2.5 times the impact of a gain of the same magnitude.

Other cognitive biases that affect investors include 'confirmation bias' (the tendency to weight information that confirms what we already believe more heavily than information that refutes it) and the 'availability heuristic' (which causes us to make judgements based on our most readily available memories, rather than more relevant information).[13] Human irrationality and selective memories are not the only reasons why market inefficiencies arise, however.

The late American economist Paul Samuelson argued that modern markets are 'micro efficient' but 'macro inefficient'.[14] What he meant was that it is easier to spot price anomalies in an individual security and eliminate them than to do so for the market as a whole. However, Samuelson's dictum is perhaps true on more levels than the late economist had in mind.

There is no single issue that better illustrates the macro inefficiency of markets than the climate crisis the world faces. Since the world started to industrialise, increasing carbon and other greenhouse gas emissions have been causing the Earth's temperature to rise. So far, the global mean temperature has risen by at least one degree Celsius compared with pre-industrial times. Already, this has resulted in more frequent extreme weather events and a rise in sea levels, which have caused property destruction, population displacement and deaths. Unless we reduce emissions, it is estimated that we will have between 1.5 and 3 degrees Celsius of warming by the middle of this century, and between 4 and 8 degrees by the end of the century. Research suggests that a rise of just 2 degrees Celsius would cut the geographic range of vertebrates by 8 percent, plants by 16 percent and insects by 18 percent.[15] This would be accompanied by droughts, famines and mass extinctions. This is therefore a problem that must be tackled urgently. And yet we continue to drag our feet. Notwithstanding substantial progress in developing renewable technologies, over 80 percent of the energy the world uses today still comes from burning fossil fuels.[16]

The climate change problem exhibits three classic characteristics that tend to lead to a breakdown in market efficiency: (i) it is a long-term issue; (ii) its financial impact is uncertain and many associated costs cannot be measured in monetary terms; and (iii) those most responsible are not the ones who bear the highest cost.

Financial markets are notoriously short-term in their outlook. Investors often focus excessively on quarterly earnings and pay insufficient attention to strategy, fundamentals and long-term value creation. At the macro level, this can drag down long-term economic growth by creating pressures to reduce expenditures on R&D or to forego projects with strong potential but a long payback period. Reducing carbon emissions would involve substantial costs today to replace existing infrastructure, such as coal-fired power plants and petrol engine vehicles, whereas the near-term benefits are far less tangible. As we delay, the problem only grows worse.

Part of the obstacle lies in the fact that markets only value things in monetary terms. A decision making framework that relies solely on quantifiable financial metrics is ill-suited to tackling environmental and social issues, the costs of which are often difficult to quantify. This is why carbon pricing and charging mechanisms, if widely adopted, could help meaningfully reduce emissions. However, not all functions of the state and society can be performed through the mechanisms of the market. Governments' increasing reliance on the market for the provision of public services has, in many cases, led to a decline in public accountability for outcomes, particularly on matters of social equity.[17] Indeed, the Covid-19 pandemic has highlighted the extent to which the effectiveness of public services in many developed countries has been eroded.[18]

Further challenges arise from the fact that, left to themselves, markets are generally unsuited to arbitrate in instances where the costs of an activity or policy are borne by one group while the benefits derived from it accrue to another. Such situations frequently result in deep inequities. In ancient Athens, citizens took an oath to 'transmit this city not only not less, but greater, better and more beautiful' onto the next generation.[19] Unfortunately, there is scant evidence of adherence to this ideal in our contemporary world. Intergenerational conflicts of interest present major barriers to badly needed policy reforms. As a result, today's younger generation will inherit not only worsening climate related problems, but also in many countries unsustainable social welfare burdens tied to aging populations, and a mountain of public debt.

The same problem arises where what separates those reaping the benefits from those paying the costs is not age, but geographic or socio-economic distance. Many who suffer the worst consequences of global warming live in coastal areas, particularly in poor countries ill-equipped to deal with rising sea levels and extreme weather. Due to cyclones, storm surges and river floods, 20 to 30 percent of Bangladesh, one of the world's poorest nations, is now commonly under water, wiping out crops, destroying homes and killing people throughout the country.[20] Bangladeshis have little hope of relief unless China, the US and the other largest greenhouse gas emitters agree to cut down their polluting activities.

Ultimately, the efficient functioning of markets relies on incentives. Properly structured, markets are highly efficient at expanding economic growth and opportunity. Where they are structured in a way that improperly aligns incentives, however, markets are unlikely to deliver efficient outcomes. Markets themselves create incentives that spur human enterprise and innovation, but they can also pose challenges to incumbent vested interests. For this reason, history has witnessed time and again the subversion of the proper functioning of markets by political elites.

What Happens When Competition Dies

In the Middle Ages, Venice was one of the richest places in the world. Having gained its independence in 810 AD, the city went on to build a fortune based on maritime trade. Between 1050 and 1330, its population grew from 45,000 to 110,000, making it as large as Paris and around three times the size of London.

Venice's rise owed much to its geographic location in the Adriatic, which meant a shorter sailing time from the East compared with the competing city-states of Pisa and Genoa. This advantage was further reinforced by canny use of economic diplomacy and force.[21] However, most crucially, Venice's success was underpinned by a set of innovative and pluralistic economic institutions. Key among these was the *comenda*, an early forerunner of the joint-stock company, formed for the duration of a single trading mission.

A *comenda* brought together two partners, one 'sedentary' and one who travelled with the cargo. Typically, the sedentary partner contributed most of the investment. Young traders who lacked sufficient capital were thereby able to share in the profits by travelling with the goods. If a mission was successful, profits were shared based on two forms of *comenda* contract. One form involved the sedentary partner putting up 100 percent of the capital and taking 75 percent of the profits. Another form required the travelling partner to put up one third of the capital in return for a 50 percent share of the gains. Given the huge potential profits to be reaped, the *comenda* system became a major driver of upward social mobility for enterprising young traders.

The broadening of economic prosperity was accompanied by a drive towards a more inclusive political system. After 1032, the Doge, who governed Venice under a life tenure, was elected along with a Ducal Council, whose function was to ensure that the Doge did not acquire absolute power. Over time, further institutions were created to circumscribe the power of the city's leadership. These included independent magistrates, courts, a court of appeals, and private contract and bankruptcy laws. Strong legal institutions fostered financial innovations, including the beginnings of modern banking. However, not all were enamoured with the type of inclusive economic growth that this brought about. Efficient markets tend to generate – and are reinforced by – what the economist Joseph Schumpeter called 'creative destruction'. The new rich created by these institutions and the *comenda* system challenged the power and economic status of Venice's established elites.

Beginning in 1286, a series of manoeuvres by Venice's leading families wrested control over the city's political institutions and established a system of hereditary control. Gradually, the inclusive economic institutions that had made Venice rich were rolled back, and the *comenda* system was abolished. From 1314, trade began to be nationalised and long-distance trade became the preserve of the nobility. The city fell into economic malaise and, even as Europe's population expanded rapidly in the late 17th and 18th centuries, that of Venice contracted. Of course, there were other factors that contributed to Venice's decline, including the advance of the Ottoman Empire in the Eastern Mediterranean from the 15th century and the discovery of a sea route to the Far East. However, following the political coup by its elite in the late 13th and early 14th century, the city would never regain its former economic dynamism.[22]

The history of Venice's rise and decline provides a salutary lesson for our own time. Markets always operate within institutional frameworks. When the institutions of the state create a favourable environment, markets can provide powerful incentives for enterprise and innovation, allowing society to prosper as a whole. However, the market, the state and communities are in a constant struggle for power.[23] Balancing these constituencies to protect the proper functioning of competitive forces requires constant vigilance.

Where threatened, incumbent elites often seek to subvert the proper functioning of markets in order to entrench their own political and economic power. This does not imply that elites necessarily have malign intent. Like most people, members of the elite simply strive to improve their own lot in life, and to give their children the best educational and other opportunities. Better educated and blessed with useful social connections, the offspring of the elite enjoy significant competitive advantages in the jobs market and thus earn higher incomes. Further, well-educated elites often intermarry and, in their turn, seek to provide the best opportunities for their own offspring. Over multiple generations, this can lead to the creation of hereditary meritocracies that stifle social mobility and lead to societal decay. In other words, in the process of rewarding and reinforcing success, the natural forces of markets can themselves undermine fair competition. It is therefore not always sufficient simply to rely on markets to preserve proper competition on their own. Strong competition laws and enforcement thereof are vital to ensure that markets continue to allow creative destruction to take place.

★★★

In China, reforms since the late 1970s have actually spurred competitive forces within the economy, yielding highly beneficial results, but (as discussed in Chapter 5) the state's continued reluctance to relinquish control makes the future trajectory somewhat uncertain. Nevertheless, free market fundamentalism in the US has not resulted in perfectly competitive markets either. Far from it. This is because laws, regulations and the unchecked forces of markets themselves have created vastly unlevel playing fields that have frustrated competition.[24] This is manifested clearly in the monopolisation or oligopalisation of most US industries over recent decades.

Companies with greater scale tend to enjoy higher profit margins and better access to finance, giving them significant competitive advantages. This creates a strong incentive to scale up by acquiring or merging with competing businesses. Over time, smaller competitors are often left with the option of getting acquired or being squeezed out of business. Even where a company starts out as an innovator with a superior offering, as it eliminates the competition, it tends to exploit its market dominance to charge higher prices and reduce investment in developing new products. Far from being interference in the proper functioning of the economy – as Milton Friedman considered them to be – strong antitrust laws and enforcement of them are therefore essential to the efficient operation of markets.

At one time, it was well recognised that competitive markets lay at the very heart of preserving social order. President Kennedy's antitrust chief Lee Loevinger articulated this succinctly when he testified to Congress:

> *The problems with which the antitrust laws are concerned – the problems of distribution of power within society – are second only to the questions of survival in the face of threats of nuclear weapons.*[25]

The positive effects of regulatory intervention to protect competition can be observed in one of the most consequential cases in the history of antitrust law. In 1974, AT&T was the largest company in the world, employing over a million people. A regulated 'super monopolist' with deep ties to the government, it controlled local and long distance telephone services, physical telephones, all related attachments, business phone services, and even markets that were just emerging, such as online services. The company brooked no possibility of competition, swallowing up or undermining any potential rivals, even to the point of subverting national policy. When the Federal Communications Commission (FCC) tried to introduce competition in long distance services and equipment in the 1970s, AT&T did everything it could to frustrate the initiative. This galvanised Nixon's Justice Department to launch a decade-long legal process to bring the company to heel.

The case was eventually resolved out of court in the early 1980s, when AT&T agreed to a dramatic break-up that carved out seven regional entities (the so-called 'Baby Bells'), leaving the company with its long distance services, Bell Labs, and Western Electric, its equipment manufacturer. Although the Baby Bells remained local monopolies, each was required to accept long distance connections from any company, and they were all explicitly excluded from new markets such as cable and online services.

The impact of the break-up of AT&T was not merely to lower consumer prices. The more important result was to unleash a huge wave of innovation that the prior monopoly system had held back. The ability for other companies to sell products that plugged into consumers' telephone jacks yielded devices such as the answering machine and the modem, which led to the launch of online service providers and the internet revolution. The weakening of AT&T's political power also prevented it from blocking the entrance of rivals such as Sprint and T-Mobile into the mobile telecoms market.

The benefits of the AT&T break-up were further highlighted by the failure of Europe and Japan to break up their monopoly telecoms providers. The Europeans have since never managed to compete in the computer industry in any significant way. Japan, which had been seen as a serious rival in computing and online services in the 1980s, saw its independent telecoms and internet firms severely limited by the country's telephone monopoly. By the 2000s, the Asian challenger had fallen well behind the US in the technology race.[26]

AT&T was, however, the last major break-up of a monopoly in the US. By the 2000s, a shift in regulatory philosophy had significantly weakened antitrust enforcement. In eight years, George W. Bush's Justice Department did not bring a single anti-monopoly case and blocked no corporate mergers.[27] While the early years of the Internet Age were characterised by frenzied competition, where once seemingly unassailable players like AOL were rapidly toppled, this new industry eventually saw the emergence of a number of giants that, as time went on, have exploited their scale to see off competitors.

In response to the threat from Instagram in the 2010s, Facebook simply pulled out its cheque book and acquired its social networking rival for $1 billion. The company later spent $19 billion to acquire another potential challenger WhatsApp. Between its founding in 2004 and the end of 2020, Facebook made a total of 89 acquisitions. Nevertheless, this figure seems modest compared to the number of acquisitions made by fellow technology giants Google (104) and Amazon (240).[28] It was only after scandals emerged over failures to protect user data and its alleged role in election interference in 2016 that the Federal Trade Commission finally launched an anti-monopoly case against Facebook in December 2020.[29]

The erosion in competition is at least in part responsible for slowing US productivity growth in recent years. Instead of reinvesting profits to drive innovation and enhance their competitiveness, major US corporations have poured money into share buybacks. Here, short-term financial incentives have exacerbated the problem, undermining the country's long-term economic growth.

Wrong Incentives

Financial markets have always been riddled with principal-agent problems. Ever since the invention of the modern limited liability company and secondary markets for trading corporate stock, conflicts of interest have arisen between shareholders and management, and between long-term and short-term stakeholders. Widely distributed ownership can make it difficult for individual shareholders to exercise influence over company managers. Most often, public company shareholders express their evaluation of management teams and corporate strategy simply by buying or selling a company's shares, which has the effect of pushing the share price up or down. Recent decades have seen a sharp trend towards paying executives in company stock to better align their interests with shareholders. This sounds good in theory but, in practice, it has often created incentives for corporate managements to focus excessively on short-term strategies

such as share buybacks to boost the stock price, instead of on generating long-term value. Perverse incentives are compounded when
the size of executives' annual bonuses is directly linked to share price
performance.

Since the GFC, S&P 500 constituent companies have spent $2.8
trillion on share buybacks.[30] Although buybacks boost earnings per share
in the short term by reducing a company's total number of outstanding
shares, money spent on buybacks could otherwise have gone to R&D
and capital expenditures to boost long-term earnings growth. More per-
niciously, debt funded share buybacks can sometimes saddle companies
with high financial leverage that threatens their long-term survival.

Stock buybacks were actually outlawed in the US following the
1929 stock market crash, as they were considered to be a form of stock
manipulation. That law was, however, rescinded in 1982. Between 1959
and 2001, reinvestment into the workforce, R&D and capital projects
averaged 20 percent of US corporate revenues. Between 2002 and 2015,
the level of reinvestment had fallen to 10 percent.[31] This has been a
factor sapping America's long-term economic growth. In the context of
growing American paranoia about losing its technology lead to China,
it is also noteworthy to contrast the $129 billion US networking giant
Cisco Systems spent on share buybacks between 2002 and 2019 – more
than its entire spending on R&D – against the 'retain-and-reinvest'
model of Chinese telecoms leader Huawei.[32]

Meanwhile, as stock-based compensation has grown, executive
compensation has soared. In the 1970s, the ratio of CEO-to-worker
compensation in America was roughly 30:1; today it is 361:1.[33] Strong
performance should be rewarded, but it is hard to believe that CEOs are
now more than 12 times more valuable relative to the average worker
than they were in the 1970s.

If management have the wrong incentives, it should be asked why
company boards, shareholders or even governments haven't intervened.
Merely a cursory glance at the incentives at each of these levels will
answer that question.

Independent directors who serve on public company boards are,
by and large, a well remunerated bunch. They tend also to be drawn
from a relatively small social circle. Often, independent directors serve
on multiple company boards and, if an individual director were to gain a

reputation for 'rocking the boat', this might jeopardise his or her chances for future appointments.

The prevalent use of remuneration consultants to advise on executive compensation has also contributed to rising pay levels. Consultants' advice is usually based on benchmarking against compensation at other companies in the same industry. Boards wanting to attract and retain the 'top talent' generally look to pay executives in the top quartile of their peers. Remuneration consultants rarely have any incentive to recommend a reduction in executive pay, leading to a ratcheting-up effect on compensation.

The top shareholders of large public companies are generally institutional asset managers, who invest the pension savings of millions of small investors. Portfolio managers tend to be well paid themselves, and have few incentives to criticise high executive compensation. Quarterly or annual benchmarking of their investment performance creates pressure for them to focus on short-term returns, rather than building long-term company value. In the specific case of share buybacks, shareholders are also influenced by tax incentives, since capital gains from share price increases are often taxed at lower rates than dividend income.

If the market is failing to create the right incentives, it might be expected that governments should intervene. In some countries, they have done so. German public companies have a two-tier board structure whereby, in addition to a management board (*Vorstand*), there is a supervisory board (*Aufsichtsrat*) on which employees and other stakeholders are represented. This structure can slow decision making, but it does force companies to give consideration to their wider social responsibilities and helps encourage longer-term thinking. However, in America, shareholder capitalism still rules and the predominance of free market ideology in recent decades has discouraged any significant state interference in how companies are governed. Corporate lobbying and campaign contributions, as well as the revolving door between public office and private business, create further disincentives for politicians and officials from looking to impose constraints on areas such as executive pay.[34]

To be fair, a great many public servants are well intentioned and highly dedicated. However, as we saw in the subprime mortgage debacle that sparked the GFC (see Chapter 3), good intentions are no match for financial incentives. In principle, the goal of widespread home ownership was admirable, but comprehending the risks of the policies followed in its pursuit required second and third order thinking that was demonstrably absent. In many cases, regulators and policymakers are simply outgunned by the capabilities of the private sector. Nowhere is this more apparent than in financial services.

The financial services sector has played both handmaiden and instigator in many highly consequential developments. It has reaped huge rewards from the growth in corporate M&A, debt issuance and a multitude of financial innovations. Along the way, it has attracted some of the best and brightest talent. Entry level wages in financial services are almost three times the salaries earned by Ivy League graduates in other sectors, and those sitting at the top of the industry can receive gigantic pay packages. Just before the GFC, almost 50 percent of Harvard seniors took jobs on Wall Street, compared to just 3.5 percent who went into government.[35] It is worth pausing to imagine what the collective energies of all those bright young people might have accomplished had they chosen to go into other fields, such as engineering, ecological conservation or medical research. . .

In 1947, the financial sector accounted for 2.3 percent of the US economy;[36] by 2020, its share had grown to 8.3 percent of GDP.[37] Given the fundamental purposes of the financial sector are to allocate capital to its most productive uses and to manage risk, the fact that $1 out of every $11 earned in the US goes to people in financial services begs the question: *has the economy become excessively financialised?*

Bubbles and Cycles

In the past decade and a half, we have experienced the two worst financial downturns since the Great Depression: the 2008 GFC and the Covid-19 recession. Over the past 30 years, financial crises have also occurred with greater frequency than ever before.[38] Generally, such crises are precipitated by the bursting of financial bubbles, when prices in a given market or asset class have become overinflated then suffer a rapid drop. In the aftermath, there is usually a rapid drying up of liquidity, generally brought on by a fall in the value of collateral backing bank loans, resulting in rising defaults and a reduction in banks' willingness to lend. In the worst cases, this can lead to banking crises, where governments face the invidious decision of either allowing depositors to bear losses – inevitably compounding the economic turmoil – or bailing out banks with taxpayers' money, with consequent political implications.

Financial crises can be astonishingly destructive. Losses in economic output that they cause directly impact livelihoods, often leading to social conflict. The bursting of the Mississippi Bubble in the 1720s – credited as the first ever stock market bubble – crippled France's state finances, contributing to the French Revolution seven decades later.[39] The Great Depression precipitated by the 1929 Wall Street crash was a major factor in the rise of Nazism and the outbreak of WW2.[40] More recently, following the 2008 GFC, we have witnessed a corresponding rise in populist nationalism and Sino-US tensions. Nevertheless, not all financial bubbles have such disastrous consequences and some can even result in positive developments.

Bubbles have benefited society in at least three ways. First, they have provided capital for the development of technology and infrastructure that might not have been developed otherwise. Second, speculative technologies developed by bubble companies have stimulated later innovations. In the late 1990s, fuelled by excessive optimism about demand growth, US telecom companies poured more than $500 billion into laying new fibre optic cables and building related network infrastructure, much of which was funded by debt. When it became apparent that capacity growth had massively exceeded the increase in demand, stock prices crashed, wiping out $2 trillion for shareholders and driving many companies into bankruptcy.[41] However, the expansion in network capacity led to a significant fall in broadband prices and made possible the subsequent rapid growth in internet traffic, which spurred the growth of online TV services such as Netflix. A great number of other transformative technologies, including railways, bicycles and automobiles, owe their development to financial bubbles. A third social benefit of bubbles is that they can encourage more people to become entrepreneurs, driving competition and innovation, which ultimately feeds into future economic growth.

Booms and busts are simply the extreme tops and bottoms of market cycles. Markets exist for virtually everything. The cycle in any particular market represents the fluctuations in price caused by the interaction between demand and supply over time.[42] The commodity cycle for oil provides a good illustration of this. The oil embargo and Middle East unrest in the 1970s led to a surge in the oil price. This stimulated investments in new oil discoveries and alternative energies, which contributed to the low oil prices of the 1980s. In the early 2000s, surging Chinese energy demand and a perception that the world was running out of oil caused its price to shoot up once again. However, high fuel costs encouraged people to drive less or to buy more fuel efficient cars. They also attracted substantial investment into developing shale oil extraction technologies and electric vehicles. By the early 2010s, oil prices had once again fallen back far from their peak.

Fluctuations in energy costs had knock-on effects on demand in other markets too, as price rises reduced the amount of money consumers had to spend on other goods and services, and *vice versa*.

Distilled to its essence, the economy is simply the aggregate of all the overlapping and interconnected markets within it. When booms and busts occur in any given market, therefore, they can have a significant impact on other markets and on the overall economy.

In their study of financial bubbles spanning some 400 years, the academics William Quinn and John Turner identify three components that are required to form financial bubbles: (i) marketability of the asset (or how easily it can be bought and sold); (ii) the availability of money and credit; and (iii) speculation (or the level of willingness to buy something on the expectation that its price will rise in the future). They also find that bubbles typically require a catalyst in the form of either technological innovation or government policy.[43] Recognising that bubbles occur within market cycles and that markets are interlinked leads to two further observations. First, the larger the bubble, the more spectacular the bust tends to be. Second, the greater the interlinkages between the bubble market and other markets, the greater the destructive force of the bubble's bursting.

This explains why the US mortgage bubble led to one of the biggest financial crises in history. Almost everybody needs a home. Mortgage securitisation had transformed homes, which are fairly illiquid, into highly marketable assets that could be widely distributed and traded. This brought in a flood of new investment, particularly from overseas, and there was a general belief that home prices would keep going up over time. The innovation of CDSs had further created the illusion that risk had virtually disappeared. All the while, incentives at every level had been underpinned by government policies to encourage home ownership. Crucially, the mortgage bubble was supercharged by credit, the availability of which affects price levels across *all* asset classes, as well as consumption and investment in the real economy. In retrospect, it should have been little surprise that, when home prices fell, it would lead to a cascade of losses across multiple markets, leaving in their wake a trail of massive economic destruction. But what explains the increasing *frequency* of financial crises?

★★★

The past 50 years have been a period of breakneck financial innovation. In aggregate, this has led to an increase in both the marketability of financial investments and the availability of credit. New financial instruments, such as ETFs, swaps and financial futures, have offered investors a much wider array of financial exposures. The establishment of ICSDs and the development of the repo market have massively increased the efficiency with which holders of financial securities can borrow against them. The sum effect of this has been an explosion in financial activity, reflected in a surge in market liquidity. In 1976, world stock market turnover as a percentage of market capitalisation was around 39 percent;[44] by 2020, this figure had risen to 169 percent.[45]

Liquidity is sometimes thought of as cash in the form of bank deposits. In financial markets, it is more accurate to think of liquidity in terms of the *sources of funds* available for use. These include secured and unsecured funding from domestic private sector institutions, such as banks, non-bank creditors (or 'shadow banks') and corporates; foreign investors and lenders; and, as we have seen more and more following the 2008 GFC, central banks. It is estimated that the pool of global liquidity available today totals around $130 trillion, a figure some two-thirds larger than world GDP. In effect, money itself can be seen as a commodity, whose price increases or decreases inversely with its availability.[46] More money being available means greater *market liquidity*.

'Market liquidity' refers to the ability to buy or sell a large quantity of something with minimal price impact. The growth in market liquidity since the 1970s has yielded many benefits. When there are more buyers and sellers, the spread between the bid (price offered for a security) and ask (price sellers are willing to sell at) tends to compress, reducing transaction costs for investors. Lower transaction costs tend to reduce the cost of capital for issuers needing to raise money. This should stimulate more economic activity. However, there are also adverse consequences associated with the rise in liquidity.

Increased leverage has made the financial system more fragile. Greater reliance on credit has exacerbated the procyclicality of market cycles. When the value of assets collateralising loans goes up, borrowers can increase their credit. The increased supply of money allows more projects to get financed and causes asset prices to rise. This is the upward part of the credit cycle. As the cycle ascends to its peak, more and more money begins to chase fewer and fewer sound investments, and lenders tend to take on more risk. Eventually, poor lending decisions lead to defaults, causing lenders to become more risk averse. When the credit cycle shifts into its downswing, it becomes more difficult to borrow, with lenders demanding higher interest rates and more collateral. Borrowers who are unable to refinance their loans are forced to sell assets, driving down prices. This contraction in credit (or 'deleveraging') can lead to a vicious circle, in which falls in asset prices lead to a further tightening of credit, and so on. The deleveraging phase of the credit cycle can have serious negative consequences for the real economy, including a spiral of falling consumption and employment.

The increasing complexity of financial markets has obscured the extent of increased leverage in the system. Derivatives allow speculators to take huge leveraged positions in markets without any explicit borrowing showing up in standard measures of financial debt in the economy, such as debt-to-GDP ratios. The shadow banking system, made up of non-bank creditors such as MMFs, is less transparent and less regulated than traditional bank lending in many markets. Further, cross-border lending by foreign financial institutions often falls outside national jurisdictions, making it harder to monitor and control.

Along with the increase in leverage in the financial system, there has also been a deterioration in the *quality* of liquidity. Liquidity quality is measured in two ways: the duration of credit backing an investment; and the riskiness of the underlying collateral. The rise of repos and other forms of short-term financing has led to a shortening of loan maturities, increasing refinancing risks. Meanwhile, we have also witnessed increasing volatility in the financial instruments used to collateralise this short-term lending, such as the March 2020 yield spike in US Treasuries.

Developments in financial markets have both reflected and driven shifts in the real economy. Globalisation of manufacturing has led to a lengthening of global supply chains, with producers becoming more dependent on short-term credit to finance their inventories.[47] This has made the real economy more vulnerable to shocks in the financial markets.

If financial innovations have elevated both marketability and credit within the financial system, then what of that third component required to inflate bubbles: *speculation*? Students of financial history will be sceptical of any claim that human nature has changed fundamentally since the days of the Dutch tulip mania (1636–1637) or the South Sea Bubble (1719–1720). Speculation is difficult to measure and it would be hard to assert that the nature of the greed that drove speculative excesses during the 1990s Dot-com era, the subprime bubble or the 2015 Chinese stock market boom was any different to that which propelled past boom-and-bust cycles. However, technology has made it easier to participate in financial speculation. Nowadays, all it takes is a few taps on a smartphone to execute a trade. In the UK, one in 10 investors today is a novice who opened an online brokerage account during the Covid-19 pandemic, spurred on by traders boasting of profits in social media chat rooms.[48]

Evidence of increasing speculative activity in financial markets is not just limited to retail investors opening online brokerage accounts though, and it is certainly not just a phenomenon related to the pandemic lockdowns. In recent years, high frequency traders (HFTs) have accounted for around 50–60 percent of all trading in the US stock market.[49] HFTs employ computer algorithms to execute large numbers of trades, profiting from very small price movements. They have been a major driver behind rising stock market turnover, and the additional liquidity they bring has helped reduce frictional trading costs. However, given their massive volumes and the speed and automated nature of their activities, they have also been accused of exacerbating market volatility. The 6 May 2010 'flash crash', when the Dow Jones Industrial Average dropped almost 10 percent in a matter of minutes, was closely associated with algorithmic trading strategies.[50] Perhaps more importantly though,

HFTs only trade in secondary markets and do not provide capital to the real economy, which is perhaps why the social value of their activities is often questioned.

There is nowhere easier to make (or lose) a fortune than in financial markets. In March 2021, Archegos, a fund that managed the personal wealth of a formerly little known trader called Bill Hwang, blew up, causing billions of dollars in losses for creditors, including Crédit Suisse and Nomura. A former *protégé* of legendary hedge fund investor Julian Robertson, Hwang had reportedly parlayed just over $200 million into a fortune that peaked at around $30 billion through highly leveraged stock market bets, before losing it all in just a matter of days.[51] Beyond the matter of market risks associated with certain types of financial activity, it is reasonable to ask whether or not the growth in secondary trading has come at the expense of investment in the real economy. If the structure and incentives of financial markets today are found to be diverting capital away from being used to drive improvements in economic productivity, then perhaps policies to curb financial speculation, such as financial transaction taxes, ought to be considered – although fiscal competition between financial centres has discouraged this in the past.

Rising marketability, credit and speculation have led to a substantial rise in global equity prices. In theory, share prices are supposed to track earnings. However, during the 20-year period of the 1980s and 1990s, the S&P Composite index rose by more than 13 times, compared with an increase in earnings of only three times. US equity exposure over the same period rose from around 14 percent to a staggering 42 percent of national financial wealth.[52] It is also notable that equity market performance has far more closely tracked the rise in global liquidity, rather than earnings,[53] corroborating what many experienced investors have believed for a long time: that fundamentals now play little role in financial markets.

Following the massive losses incurred in the 2008 GFC and the Covid-19 recession, it might have been expected that global markets would have to undergo a long period of deleveraging. Indeed, increased regulatory capital and liquidity requirements for banks have reduced their capacity to extend credit. However, after brief contractions, global liquidity has continued to grow. This has been driven significantly by central bank monetary policy actions.[54] There is no doubt that, under crisis circumstances, radical steps were required to maintain economic and social stability. *But has the path chosen stored up further problems for the future?*

Funny Money

In the deleveraging phase of a credit cycle, there are four ways to reduce the debt burden. In practice, all four tend to be employed. However, the degree to which each is pursued depends on government policy, which must take into account domestic politics and geopolitical factors. Each path towards deleveraging involves its own risks and challenges.

First, spending is cut. Overextended consumers, corporates and governments are forced to reduce their outlays in order to repay their debts. The problem with this is that, on a macroeconomic level, when overall consumption and investment fall, it leads to a reduction in incomes, dragging economic activity down further and making it even more difficult to service borrowings. Rising unemployment also leads to a reduction in income, while government expenditures on social welfare tend to rise.

Second, where debts are simply too large to be repaid, borrowers may default. In such an event, creditors may agree to renegotiate debt terms to reduce the interest rate, extend maturities or write down part of what is owed. This allows distressed borrowers to achieve a more sustainable level of debt servicing, and can help maintain spending and save jobs. However, this is offset by losses imposed on creditors, which negatively impact credit availability and economic activity. Borrowers' ability to renegotiate debt terms also depends on the prevailing policy framework and political environment. Up until 1869, borrowers who defaulted on their debts in Britain were thrown into debtors' prison, thereby making default a last resort option. Not only was this rather unpleasant for the unfortunate defaulters, it may not even have been in the best interests of creditors (since an incarcerated debtor was impeded from working to pay down *any* of the defaulted debt).[55]

Government defaults are more complex and have wider-ranging impacts. Where foreign creditors are involved, sovereign defaults can have severe diplomatic consequences. For much of history, it was not uncommon for creditors to employ military force to coerce defaulting nations to honour financial commitments. In the 19th and early 20th centuries, colonial powers used gunboat diplomacy to enforce debt repayment on numerous occasions.[56] Nowadays, it is more likely to be the risk of being locked out of international bond markets than outright foreign invasion that deters governments from defaulting on their debts. However, sovereign defaults can still spark serious international tensions.

Both spending cuts and defaults are inherently deflationary. The third means of reducing debt burdens is through wealth redistribution. Most commonly, this involves imposing higher taxes on those most able to pay, such as the rich. Raising taxes simply to pay down debt is certainly deflationary. However, taxation is not a zero-sum game. In an economic downturn, savings may be hoarded or capital might be put to unproductive uses. If governments put the increased tax revenues to more productive uses, then higher taxation on those with surplus wealth could stimulate economic growth.

This is particularly important when it comes to long-term investments whose economic benefits are less tangible in the short term, which are often among the first forms of spending to be cut when budgets are squeezed. In the 1980s, spending by a large number of US states on primary and secondary education collapsed in relative terms. By the mid-2010s, the chances of attending university was just 20 to 30 percent for children of the poorest parents, compared with 90 percent for the children of the richest parents.[57] As advances in technology have made economic productivity ever more dependent on the workforce's skills, rather than just its size, ensuring broad-based access to high quality education has become critical to economic competitiveness and long-term growth. It is likely that past cutbacks on US public spending on education have contributed to falling productivity growth in recent years. During a deleveraging, therefore, it is vital to ensure that fiscal policy takes into account not just short-term financial effects, but also longer-term social and economic factors.

The fourth way to reduce the debt burden is to expand the monetary base – in other words, to print more money in order to reduce the value of the debt in real terms. This is generally considered to be inflationary – and it is. However, if the expansion of the money supply simply offsets

the reduction in spending, it will not necessarily lead to a rise in inflation. This is a fine balance though and, in practice, central bankers are
not able to control the money supply with a high degree of precision.[58]
Since resorting to the printing presses is relatively easy compared with
other means of reducing the debt burden, it is also tempting to rely
excessively on this lever. This is what led to highly destabilising hyperin-
flation in Germany in the 1920s.

After Paul Volcker tamed inflation by hiking interest rates in the
early 1980s, the US came to rely more heavily on monetary policy to
control economic cycles. In response to the Black Monday stock market
crash of October 1987, Alan Greenspan aggressively bought US Treasuries to bring down the cost of borrowing from the Fed.[59] This quickly
reflated asset prices and prevented the crash from spilling over into the
real economy. It was a policy widely cheered on Wall Street. In what
became known as the 'Greenspan put', the US began to follow a highly
asymmetrical monetary policy, whereby the Fed eased monetary policy
in response to asset price falls, but eschewed intervention to prevent the
formation of price bubbles in the first place – even as the epic Dot-com
bubble formed during the 1990s.

In the wake of the GFC and in response to the Covid-19 pandemic,
the Federal Reserve and other major central banks have engaged even
more extensively in monetary expansion through quantitative easing.
In deciding to do so, policymakers drew heavily from the lessons of the
1930s, when the rigidities of the gold standard and central banks' failure
to sufficiently ease the money supply resulted in the Great Depression.
Ben Bernanke's quick and decisive actions in 2008 certainly avoided a
more calamitous financial collapse at the time. However, he and his successor Janet Yellen were both candid about the limitations of monetary
policy. Simply expanding the money supply does not guarantee that
money flows to where it is most needed or where it can be most productively utilised.

To avoid an unstable deleveraging process, monetary policy must be
balanced with spending cuts, reductions in credit, and adjustments to
fiscal policy. Bernanke and Yellen's warnings went largely unheeded. Rock
bottom interest rates and quantitative easing led to a surge in asset prices
that most benefited the wealthy, but few countries increased taxes. Not
only did political ideology impede necessary fiscal policy adjustments in

the US, but tax cuts for the wealthiest Americans in the form of Donald Trump's 2017 tax reforms threw additional fuel on the fire. Meanwhile, longstanding policies that encouraged share buybacks and the hoarding of cash offshore by US corporations further limited investment needed to drive long-term productivity growth. Perhaps rather than focusing so heavily on the mistakes that led to the Great Depression, policymakers should have considered the lessons of an earlier financial crisis.

★★★

The Spanish War of Succession (1701–1714) left France with an unprecedented level of public debt. In 1715, the French national debt stood at over two billion livres, somewhere between 83 and 167 percent of GDP. In the face of its acute debt problem, France imposed a write-down on creditors, devaluing some short-term debt by around two-thirds. Financiers were charged with profiteering and their assets confiscated. The currency was debased, with coins being stamped with lower gold and silver content at least four times between 1701 and 1718. However, even with a severe austerity programme, interest payments still exceeded the state's income by more than 40 million livres annually. Of course, another option would have been to raise taxation, but this would have forced those in political power to assume a greater share of the burden, so was avoided.[60] Instead, to solve the country's precarious finances, the Duc d'Orléans, Regent during the minority of Louis XV, turned to one of the more unlikely figures to grace the annals of financial history.

John Law, born in Edinburgh in 1671, was a convicted murderer and compulsive gambler. The heir to Lauriston Castle, at the age of 21 he moved to London, where he began to squander his inheritance on gambling and various business ventures. After being sentenced to death for killing his neighbour in a duel, he fled to Amsterdam where he became fascinated by the financial innovations taking place there at the time. Notwithstanding his admiration for the financial ingenuity he witnessed, he puzzled at what he saw as the excessive conservatism of the Dutch. Given the high demand for the Dutch East India Company's shares, *why restrict the supply of them?* The *Wisselbank*, a forerunner of modern central banks, had been formed in 1609 to facilitate payments between merchants in different currencies, but deposits were almost fully backed by reserves of coins and precious metals. Insightfully, Law saw the opportunity for credit creation on a substantial scale through more aggressive leveraging of the bank's reserves. The ambitious Scot therefore devised a system that combined the properties of a monopoly trading company and a public bank with note issuing powers.

Law tried unsuccessfully to sell his idea to the Italian city-states of Genoa and Turin, as well as to his native Scotland. Eventually, he arrived in Paris in 1715 and, by the following year, had successfully petitioned for the establishment of the *Banque Générale* under his direction. Although nominally a private company, Law knew that its success depended on the backing of the political authorities. For this reason, he ensured that influential members of the aristocracy were offered a large allocation of the shares. Political support was further guaranteed when the Regent became a large early depositor. Favourable legislation duly followed. In 1717, the government decreed that all taxes should be paid in notes issued by the Banque Générale, at a stroke creating a substantial source of demand for the bank's paper. The following year, the bank was nationalised, yielding its initial shareholders an impressive 35 percent annualised return.[61]

The attraction of Law's scheme to the French authorities was that the bank issued paper money, enabling it to expand credit to help revive France's economy. As money was invested in the bank, the government could also consolidate its huge debt. The fact that France was ruled by an absolute monarch, however, meant that there was no institutional constraint on how the bank's power to create credit might be abused.

Having gained credibility from the spectacular capital gains generated for the Banque Générale's shareholders, Law was ready to expand the scope of his ventures. He obtained a charter for the establishment of the *Compagnie d'Occident* ('Company of the West') in 1717. The initial remit of the company was to develop land near the Mississippi River. The company's capital was fixed at 100 million livres and shares were priced at 500 livres each. Investors were encouraged to purchase the shares by exchanging their holdings of French government bonds, which were to be retired and converted into perpetual bonds yielding four percent interest.[62] The essence of the scheme was to enable the government to reduce its debt, as the interest rate on the bonds exchanged by investors was higher than the interest on the perpetual bonds that the government paid to the company. Although this was a self-evidently bad deal for the company's shareholders, Law was able to induce them to invest by creating a perception that the company's shares would go up in price.

The Compagnie d'Occident spent its initial capital on acquiring the Senegal Company and a monopoly on tobacco production. Three additional share issues in 1719 raised close to 1.6 billion livres. These funds were used to purchase concessions that gave the company the rights to conduct almost all French overseas trade, mint coins, and collect taxes equivalent to around 85 percent of state revenues. Following its takeover of the East India and China companies, the Compagnie d'Occident was renamed the *Compagnie des Indes*, better known as the Mississippi Company.

Law's vision of marrying a monopoly trading company with a note issuing bank was fully realised when the Mississippi Company took over the Banque Générale in February 1720. If this wasn't already an invitation to set self-serving monetary policies, he was also appointed France's Minister of Finance at around the same time. Incredibly, this put the Scotsman simultaneously in charge of the country's monetary, trade and fiscal policy, while at the same time running a private commercial enterprise. Such concentrated power over the financial system in the hands of one man with such an obvious conflict of interest was bound to end in disaster.

The average yield on the French government bonds that the Mississippi Company had received from subscribers to its shares after the 1719 issues was 4.5 percent. Meanwhile, the interest rate on the total loans it had made to the government was just 3 percent, implying a negative spread of 1.5 percent for investors. Nevertheless, this mattered little when Law had all the financial levers of the state at his disposal to keep inflating the share price. He used the Banque Générale to expand the money supply, so that there were ample funds with which to purchase the stock. In the second half of 1719, total notes in circulation grew fivefold from 200 million livres to 1 billion livres. He also allowed shareholders to leverage their purchases of shares by demanding only an initial 10 percent down payment for them. He drummed up excitement through the government-controlled media and, when the shares flagged, created an informal futures market to prop up their price. Shareholders who had bought shares at 140 to 160 livres saw their price surge to more than 10,000 livres just a couple of years later.[63]

The laws of financial gravity could not remain in suspense forever, however. The company's shares soon began to fall. Meanwhile, the huge expansion in the money supply was causing rapid consumer price inflation. By September 1720, prices in Paris were around twice what they had been two years previously. Anticipating a devaluation of the paper currency, people started to revert to transacting in gold and silver. Law sought to stop this by banning the export of these precious metals and making it illegal for a private citizen to possess more than 500 livres in metal coins. In an attempt to make banknotes more attractive to the public than coins, he adjusted the official exchange rate to gold and silver no fewer than 35 times between September 1719 and December 1720. All this achieved was to further sap economic confidence. Having peaked at 10,100 livres on 8 January 1720, the Mississippi Company's share price slumped to 1,000 livres by the end of the year.[64]

The meltdown led to a violent public outcry, forcing John Law to flee France. The government attempted to rebuild the monetary and financial system, setting up an instrument called the *Visa*, to which all assets related to Law's scheme were submitted, along with a statement on how the assets were obtained. Those with smaller holdings were bailed out, leaving the state with annual interest obligations of 87 million livres after the Visa was wound up in 1724.[65] The result was to leave the French state financially crippled, and to turn the French off the stock market and paper money for generations. Fiscally constrained, the reigns of Louis XV and Louis XVI lurched from one abortive reform to another before the state's bankruptcy finally precipitated the French Revolution.[66]

The parallels between the Mississippi Bubble and America's policy direction following the GFC should perhaps give policymakers some pause. Obviously, no individual American financial official has held as much power as John Law did over the French financial system in 1720. Indeed, the Federal Reserve has a high degree of independence to set monetary policy. Nevertheless, as the US entered into the deleveraging phase of its long-term credit cycle, banks and investors were bailed out from their poor decisions, while the political environment precluded raising taxes on the rich. This left the system heavily reliant on quantitative easing and other forms of monetary tinkering by the Federal Reserve. Monetary expansion is a blunt tool, however.

The Fed's options are limited to buying up financial assets, which it has done on an unprecedented scale, but it cannot force private creditors to lend and it is not able to direct spending to where it is most needed. In fact, it has been suggested that extended low interest rates have actually had adverse economic effects. Low or negative interest rates reduce bank profitability, inhibiting their capacity to expand credit. Further, reduced inflationary expectations and interest income on deposits can force savers to increase their demand for 'safe' assets. Meanwhile, the rise in the value of risk assets is likely to have reduced the potential for future capital gains, leading to greater risk aversion.[67]

If monetary policy and the private sector are unable to drive consumption and investment to where they are most needed, then, as John Maynard Keynes argued, there is no option but for the government to step in and start spending. However, as the French found out in the wake of the Mississippi Bubble, a country in a financially precarious condition can easily undermine confidence in its currency.

***

Much like any commodity, when money is debased through dilution or adulteration, demand for it would be expected to fall. Falling demand leads to a fall in price. Most people think of the price of money in terms of the rate of interest charged or received on it, but the true price of money is actually its rate of exchange either into goods and services, or into other currencies. When the supply of a currency in international markets increases through persistent trade deficits or monetary expansion, its exchange rate versus other currencies should drop, and the same amount of money will be able to purchase fewer goods and services. This redistribution of relative purchasing power is an important rebalancing mechanism. While the impact of inflation can fall unevenly, a lower exchange rate makes financially weaker countries' goods and services cheaper (helping to stimulate economic growth through higher exports) and allows countries with stronger economies to consume more. In the case of the dollar, however, this mechanism has been turned on its head.

Demand for the dollar as a utility in global trade and finance has blunted the US currency's ability to properly adjust to new economic realities. As the Federal Reserve massively expanded the US monetary base following the GFC, the dollar's exchange rate versus other major currencies actually *rose* and, by and large, it has continued to hold up, notwithstanding growing questions over America's national finances.

While this anomaly could persist for a long time yet, we could find that we are actually now living in a financial bubble of spectacular proportions. If it bursts, the pop is likely to echo thunderously around the world.

Two starkly differing responses to this dollar phenomenon have emerged. On the one hand, some have been enthusiastically embracing potential alternative currencies. On the other, some believe that the dollar has entered a new paradigm that US policymakers should embrace.

The most novel challengers to the dollar have been cryptocurrencies. Among these, the most prominent is Bitcoin. Invented as the GFC was roiling markets in 2008 by a so-far-unidentified individual or group of people using the name Satoshi Nakamoto, Bitcoin began use in 2009.

Bitcoin operates as a decentralised digital currency on a peer-to-peer network, with no single administrator or central bank. Transactions are verified cryptographically through 'nodes' on the network and recorded on a public distributed ledger called a 'blockchain'. The anonymised nature of Bitcoin transactions and the inability of any individual or group to cancel or amend a transaction that has taken place renders it difficult – if not impossible – for any government to control or manipulate the currency.[68] Further, the total number of Bitcoins that can be issued is capped at 21 million, ensuring their value cannot be diluted by expanding their supply beyond that cap.

Hidden in the jumble of code of the first 50 Bitcoins, known as the 'genesis block', was the text: 'The Times 03/Jan/2009 Chancellor on the brink of second bailout for banks'. This referred to an article in *The Times* of London about the breakdown of the banking system amidst the GFC[69] and has been interpreted as a 'battle cry' against the fiat money system.[70] Astonishingly, this movement caught on and spawned a market that has since topped $2 trillion in size.[71] The first known commercial transaction took place in 2010, when 10,000 Bitcoins were used to purchase two Papa John's pizzas. Since then, the value of the cryptocurrency (as expressed by its conversion rate into US dollars) has seen a meteoric rise to surpass $60,000 per Bitcoin in March 2021.

Bitcoin's surge has spawned the creation of a raft of other cryptocurrencies. As of April 2021, there were roughly 4,200 cryptocurrencies in existence,[72] and a large number of cryptocurrency exchanges have been launched to facilitate trading in them. In December 2017, both the Chicago Board Options Exchange (CBOE) and the CME launched trading in Bitcoin futures, further endorsing Bitcoin's status as part of the mainstream financial system. When the cryptocurrency exchange Coinbase listed on Nasdaq in April 2021, its market value briefly topped $100 billion, making it the largest exchange in the world by market capitalisation.[73] In June 2021, El Salvador even passed legislation to make Bitcoin legal tender.[74]

The rapid growth of cryptocurrencies has stirred debate about the very nature of currencies, including whether they actually require state control and support. After all, private currencies issued by commercial banks, railroad companies and religious institutions had been widespread in the US until the National Bank Acts of the 1860s established government supervision over the banking sector and helped establish a national currency. As the historian Niall Ferguson succinctly put it, at its core, money is simply 'trust inscribed'.[75] Anything can serve as a currency – from cowrie shells or lumps of metal to bits of data on computer servers – so long as people *believe* in it. Where faith in a state-issued currency is undermined, the private sector will inevitably innovate to create substitutes.

Nevertheless, Bitcoin is beset by challenges that make it unlikely that it will pose any serious challenge to the dollar. First, the lengthy processing time required to complete a Bitcoin transaction renders it impractical as a currency for everyday payments. The Bitcoin network has a capacity of just 7 transactions per second (TPS). By comparison, Visa's network handles around 1,700 TPS and the payments company claims to be able to handle up to 24,000 TPS.[76] Second, its high level of price volatility makes Bitcoin an unreliable store of value. From a high of over $60,000 in April 2021, its price had roughly halved just two months later.[77] Third, a large amount of electricity is required to create (or 'mine') new Bitcoins, making it both costly and environmentally unfriendly. The Bitcoin network's annualised electricity consumption of

130 TWh exceeds that of even some advanced countries, including the Netherlands and Norway.[78] Fourth, its role in facilitating illicit transactions undermines state authorities and, for this reason, governments are likely to intervene to limit Bitcoin's use. During 2021, China intensified a crackdown on the trading and mining of the cryptocurrency,[79] and ultimately outlawed it altogether. However, it is one of Bitcoin's greatest attractions that is likely to prove its fatal flaw in achieving universal adoption. The absolute limit on supply to 21 million Bitcoins makes it even less flexible than the gold standard. When economic conditions require expansion in the money supply, Bitcoin's very design makes this impossible.

Bitcoin's shortcomings do not necessarily rule out other cryptocurrencies from posing a serious challenge to the dollar though. This is a relatively nascent technology and there will likely be further innovations and design improvements over time. Notably, Ethereum, the second most popular cryptocurrency by market value, already features significant modifications compared with Bitcoin to improve its attractiveness as a currency. By employing a different cryptographic protocol,[80] Ethereum is far more energy efficient than Bitcoin. Through a technology called 'sharding', whereby the blockchain is split up into multiple parts to process transactions, and 'Layer Two' solutions that work via 'side chains' off the main Ethereum blockchain, Ethereum's transaction capacity could be increased to around 100,000 TPS.[81] Crucially, Ethereum is also designed to allow it to be inflationary. In time, other more credible challengers are likely to emerge. This has started to make governments and central banks nervous.

In June 2019, a Facebook-led consortium, including some of the biggest names in payments technologies, announced plans to launch a new digital currency called Libra. Libra was designed as a 'stablecoin' – meaning that it was to be fully asset-backed, rather than fiat-based as Bitcoin and Ethereum are. The assets backing Libra were to be a basket of national currencies. Given Facebook's billions of users, Libra had the potential to achieve widespread international uptake and, therefore, posed a considerable threat to national currencies and governments' monetary sovereignty. After both US and European regulators expressed serious concerns,[82] a number of the consortium members, including both MasterCard and Visa, backed out. Eventually, Facebook announced significantly scaled-back digital currency plans in late 2020 under the brand 'Diem'.[83]

Facebook's Libra proposal catalysed central banks around the world to begin taking digital currencies far more seriously, and to launch a series of efforts of their own. By January 2021, 86 percent of central banks were actively investigating the possibility of launching central bank digital currencies (CBDCs), 60 percent were already conducting experiments or proofs-of-concept on them, and 14 percent had moved onto development and pilot arrangements.[84]

National currencies have significant advantages over private ones. Not only do they enjoy the backing of accountable public institutions but, as seen with John Law's Banque Générale, the state's power to require payment of taxes in the national currency creates substantial natural demand that private currencies cannot easily replicate. The advent of CBDCs could bring about a wide range of public benefits, including lowering the cost of payments across the economy; improved ability to monitor inflation and transmit monetary policy; and greater ability to combat tax evasion, money laundering and other financial crime.[85] Nevertheless, there are also significant challenges associated with them. In its 2021 Annual Report, the BIS noted in relation to CBDCs:

> *Technological development in money and payments could bring about wide benefits, but the ultimate consequences for the well-being of individuals in society depend on the market structure and governance arrangements that underpin it. The same technology could encourage either a virtuous circle of equal access, greater competition and innovation, or it could foment a vicious circle of entrenched market power and data concentration. The outcome will depend on the rules governing the payment system and whether these will result in open payment platforms and a competitive level playing field.[86]*

The key risks associated with CBDCs are: (i) they could give governments unprecedented levels of insight into individual citizens' private transactions, which gives rise to civil liberty concerns; (ii) they could disintermediate commercial banks, undermining the market's ability to price and create credit; and (iii) the use of CBDCs across borders could exacerbate the risk of national currencies being displaced.

The renminbi has long been viewed as an emerging rival to the dollar due to the scale and rapid growth of China's economy and international trade. China is also among the front runners in the development of CBDCs. In a step towards promoting greater international adoption of the renminbi, in 2019 the PBOC launched the digital renminbi (e-CNY,数字人民币), the first digital currency to be issued by a major economy. Use of e-CNY to invoice and settle payments in Chinese international trade could substantially reduce transaction costs by disintermediating banks and other financial intermediaries, thereby encouraging adoption. This could reduce the dollar's role in international trade settlement. However, a more profound impact of the transition to digital currencies could be a shift in the balance of power in the global financial system.

The new technology could well challenge the incumbency of key pillars of the plumbing of international finance. For example, digital currencies might operate on new messaging protocols, and messaging and settlement could be carried out as a single process. This could displace the SWIFT messaging network, undermining America's ability to impose financial sanctions. Further, new international financial infrastructures that emerge around digital currencies could transfer significant influence over the financial system to the parties that control them. These are the issues underlying American concerns over China's digital currency initiative,[87] and could incentivise the US to make further moves to constrain China's technological and financial development.

Yet, the greater challenge for the renminbi as a contender to the dollar's leading role continues to come from China itself. To foster international adoption of the renminbi, the Chinese government would need to allow an international system of renminbi-based credit to build up. This would require both much freer outbound capital flows by Chinese investors and the development of renminbi-based derivatives for financial hedging and speculation. Technology could help facilitate such steps by giving the Chinese authorities greater transparency and control over the use of the currency offshore, but gaining trust for the renminbi will likely require additional measures to enhance confidence in the Chinese legal system, which would mean putting certain constraints on the government's power.

New technologies have the potential to radically transform the global monetary system, and pose the greatest threat to the dollar's global dominance in at least a generation. Nevertheless, it is still possible that the dollar is usurped not because of the strength of the alternatives, but due to America's pursuit of self-destructive policies that undermine its own currency. In this regard, a theory being promoted by certain US academics and policymakers could well lead to the dollar's undoing if adopted as policy.

Modern Monetary Theory (MMT) asserts that rising fiscal deficits don't matter to governments that issue their own fiat currencies, since they can always print more money to finance them. MMT's proponents argue that government deficits should not be capped by any arbitrary public debt-to-GDP ratio, but rather can be allowed to rise to the level at which they do not generate excessive inflation. Drawing in certain respects on Keynesian theory, they assert that suppressing public spending below this level unnecessarily exacerbates involuntary unemployment. In other words, so long as inflation doesn't go up too much, the US government should just keep printing money and spending until unemployment goes away.[88] MMT can be thought of as the monetary equivalent to a no-limit credit card whose bill never has to be settled.

What sounds too good to be true usually is though. MMT overlooks the fact that fiat currencies rely on confidence, which is a fragile commodity. The precise tipping point at which an expansion in money supply unconnected to underlying economic productivity growth will precipitate a collapse in confidence is unknown. However, there *is* a tipping point. Perhaps more importantly, MMT's proponents appear to have forgotten the fundamental social purpose for which money was invented in the first place. Money is a tool that allows markets to organise and harness society's resources. History has shown clearly that an absence of budgetary or fiscal constraints inevitably leads to significant resource misallocation, resulting in economic and social decay.

For more than seven decades, the global monetary system has been underpinned by the US dollar. However, the structure of the dollar-based system depended on the US being able to continuously match or exceed economic productivity growth in other major economies. That assumption was always flawed. In addition, excessive faith in markets' ability to self-correct, coupled with flawed incentive structures, has led to severe global imbalances that are both leading to more financial shocks and exacerbating their impact. The result has been rising inequality that has driven escalating tensions, both at the national and international levels. While it is easy to cast blame though, these are collective problems that require collective solutions.

We're All in the Same Boat

Towards the end of the Cold War, Ronald Reagan put a question to Mikhail Gorbachev during a private walk, with only their translators present: If planet Earth were invaded by hostile Martians, how would the USSR and the US respond? At first, the Russian translator misunderstood the question and his translation raised eyebrows: *was President Reagan informing the Soviet leader that Martians had just invaded Earth?*

After the confusion was cleared up, however, Gorbachev got the point.[89] Reagan's simple point is as true today as it was back then. China and the US co-exist on the same planet and share many fundamental common interests. The challenges of the Covid-19 pandemic and global climate change have highlighted clearly the importance of global cooperation.

Financial markets, like the natural world around us, are made up of complex ecosystems. They thrive on equilibrium and are strengthened through competition. When functioning properly, markets are a powerful organising tool for society, providing a mechanism for surplus capital to be allocated to its most productive uses and for risks to be shared. In so doing, they support innovation and enable mankind to undertake giant ventures.

However, financial ecosystems, like ecosystems in nature, are cyclical and have intricate interdependencies. They are highly sensitive to the environment around them, relying on and responding to incentives created by the institutional frameworks within which they operate. When distortions occur in one market, they can lead to severe imbalances throughout the economy.

As international trade and financial investment have grown in recent decades, so have the dependencies between the participants in the global financial system. As the two largest economies in the world, America and China sit at the apex of this system and share a common interest in keeping the system in equilibrium. Notwithstanding the challenges and frictions in the Sino-US relationship, both countries' interests clearly lie in each other's social and economic wellbeing, and in avoiding any further escalation in tensions. Let us therefore turn to how the two countries might work together to address the imbalances in the global financial system.

Chapter 8

Avoiding the Thucydides Trap

I think a resumption of the Cold War would be a historic tragedy. If a conflict is avoidable, on a basis reflecting morality and security, one should try to avoid it.

– Henry A. Kissinger

For the vast majority of the world's population, the structure of the global financial system seems pretty abstract from their daily lives, and the policies, regulations and infrastructures that determine how international financial markets operate are seldom considered. This book has attempted to show what a profound influence financial markets have both on individual livelihoods and on society as a whole, and to explain how the global financial system as we know it today has come about. Given the extent to which we have come to depend on it, everyone has an interest in ensuring that this system operates properly to serve the common good.

Notwithstanding the passage of more than three-quarters of a century since the Bretton Woods Agreement and Richard Nixon's formal abandonment of it in 1973, the dollar-centric international financial system it created remains with us today. If anything, given accelerated globalisation and the massive expansion of financial markets in the intervening decades, the world is even more dependent on the US dollar today than it was back then. While the dollar's global utility status has provided many benefits to participants in international trade and investment and has been a considerable source of power for the US, it has also been a key source of international financial imbalances. It is the first major argument of this book that the costs of a dollar-based global monetary system now outweigh its benefits to the world and even to the US itself.

China's phenomenal economic rise over the past four decades has exacerbated the imbalances inherent in the dollar-based monetary system. The path of development China pursued reflected the enormous challenges and internal conflicts the country had to confront as it emerged from the chaos of the Cultural Revolution, as well as its unique national history and experience. In particular, the government's instinct to place stability above all else has meant that the state has kept tight control over the domestic financial system, inhibiting the development of China's financial markets. While this approach has seen China achieve a long period of rapid economic growth, it has also contributed to deep structural imbalances in its economy. The second major argument of this book is that, given the rising risk of resource misallocation and significant demographic challenges, China's development model is reaching its limits and further structural reforms are required.

The third major argument of this book is that policies that China and America have each pursued have led to rising inequality in both countries. These have included fiscal, industrial and monetary policies that have favoured large corporations and the wealthy. This has driven an increase in social tensions, which are contributing to escalating Sino-US conflicts. The proximate causes of growing inequality differ in each country, but common root causes lie in government policies that have entrenched incumbent elites and suppressed social mobility. History has shown that, over time, elite capture of the economy and political system has stifled competition and innovation, leading to a reduction in opportunity and prosperity for society as a whole.

It is unlikely that these financial imbalances will lead *directly* to war between China and the US. Both sides are acutely aware of the potentially catastrophic consequences of military conflict. However, there are numerous other points of tension in the Sino-US relationship where even a small incident could spark a conflict that ignites into a major conflagration. These range from disputes in the South China Sea, to the question over the future status of Taiwan, to the unresolved conflict on the Korean Peninsula, or even the management of new cyber capabilities.[1] As the Opium War highlighted, the persistence of financial imbalances can only add to the risk that an accident or miscalculation might spiral out of control into a full-blown war.

The continuing ratcheting-up of geo-economic measures against each other has added to the tensions.[2] This is ironic, since mutual economic dependencies mean that both countries have a strong interest in each other's social and economic wellbeing. This is the fourth major argument of this book. Geo-economic warfare imposes a high cost on *both* countries. American tariffs on Chinese goods raises costs for US consumers and adds to inflationary pressures. Equally, although in theory China could put pressure on the US government by dumping its sizeable US Treasury holdings, the ensuing market chaos would cause significant harm to China's own economy.[3]

War between China and the US is not only *avoidable*, it is manifestly in both countries' interests *to avoid it*. This chapter focuses on how to de-escalate the financial sources of Sino-US conflict.

Admitting the Problems

In his book *Destined for War*, which highlighted the risk of the Thucydides Trap between China and America, Graham Allison wrote:

> *Honest observers in both societies are increasingly recognising that neither 'decadent' democracy nor 'responsive' authoritarianism is fit for meeting the twenty-first century's severest tests.*[4]

Since the first step in resolving any problem is admitting that there is one, for China and the US to avoid the Thucydides Trap, it is critical for each of them to recognise and reflect on their own shortcomings. This is needed for them to be open to the inevitable accommodations that are required to solve common problems.

Despite their belief in their own respective exceptionalism, neither the Chinese nor the US system of governance is perfect. Indeed, both systems' failure to check growing inequality has been a major underlying contributor to the rising tensions between them. Addressing wealth and income inequality would be a major step towards de-escalating conflicts that have arisen.

In America, dogmatic adherence to free market ideology has, in fact, undermined the proper functioning of markets to serve their fundamental social purposes. Corporate consolidation and the 'winner-takes-all' dynamics of certain new technology sectors have significantly eroded competition. In some instances, larger scale has led to lowered consumer prices in the short term, but over time it has also stifled innovation, reduced investment and compressed wages. A return to more rigorous antitrust enforcement is long overdue. Incumbents will inevitably denounce moves to rein in or break up industry leaders, and argue that this will inhibit their ability to compete in the global marketplace. Similar arguments were made in the face of rising competition from Japanese conglomerates in the 1970s.[5] However, as the break-up of AT&T demonstrated, break-ups of monopoly players to enhance competition can actually strengthen US industries' global competitiveness and spawn entirely new areas of growth.[6]

More directly contributing to rising inequality in the US has been the turn since the 1980s towards increasingly regressive tax policies, which have unfairly favoured corporate and wealthy interests. Sharply more progressive levels of taxation are needed not only to address inequality, but also to tackle America's unsustainable rising public debt. The highest levels of taxation should not be set at punitive levels that discourage enterprise, as they were in the 1970s. Nor should 'fairness' in the tax system be taken to mean absolute equality of outcomes. Differences in ability, aptitude, industry and luck are a part of life and will inevitably play a big role in individuals' lifetime earnings and wealth accumulation. However, those who are most able should bear the largest burden, and the fiscal system should be calibrated to avoid the entrenchment of class divides through the passing down of very large inheritances.

Further, while enterprise should be rewarded, it is hard to justify on the basis of equity substantially lower rates of taxation on capital income versus labour income. In practice, the main justification for taxing capital income at much lower rates is the risk of capital flowing elsewhere due to fiscal competition from other jurisdictions. Combatting the race to the bottom in international tax rates will inevitably require cooperation and coordination with other countries. While much still rests on the details and ultimate implementation, the G-7 global tax reforms initiated by the Biden Administration and announced in June 2021 appear to be a step in the right direction.

Closely tied to the question of fiscal revenues is the allocation of government spending. Markets tend to have a short-term outlook and the capitalist system is designed to allocate resources based on the ability to pay, rather than pure merit. The government is a steward of the nation not only for the present generation, but also for generations to come. In recent decades, America has wasted resources on costly wars of choice and neglected investment in education and public infrastructure at home. This has not only sapped national resources and undermined the social fabric, but it has also diminished future prosperity.

It is unavoidable that the children of middle class and wealthy parents will have substantial advantages over the children of poorer families; however, education is a major leveller that can help drive fairer outcomes for talented and industrious young people who start with fewer advantages in life. Moreover, as advances in technology have increased the value of intellectual capital versus manual labour, future growth and prosperity will depend to an ever greater degree on a well-educated population and on investments in further technological progress.

Similarly, to help drive long-term productivity improvements, America desperately needs public investment to enhance its crumbling domestic infrastructure and to fund long-term research. The nature of the private sector means that businesses tend only to invest once the commercial opportunity is clear. Governments, in contrast, have unmatched resources to take a longer-term view. In the words of the economist Mariana Mazzucato, 'there is a role for the public sector to make [innovation] happen, rather than sitting back and hoping'.[7]

In China, rapid economic growth and improvements in living standards in recent decades have meant that the issue of wealth inequality is, as yet, less acute than in the US. Restrictions on media freedoms have also limited public discourse on the matter. Nonetheless, as demographic pressures drag on future growth, social tensions are likely to increase. Like that in America, the Chinese tax system is structured to favour the wealthy and will require reforms to prevent further exacerbating already high levels of inequality. Vast changes in the country's social architecture since the 1980s, including urbanisation and the loosening of traditional family structures, will also necessitate further enhancements in social welfare provision. However, addressing inequality in China is not just a matter of fiscal policy.

The country's accelerated development has only been possible through the suppression of consumption to drive investment. This was a highly successful strategy for a long time but, given the stage of development that China has now reached, a continued top-down investment-driven approach is likely to lead to growing resource misallocations. This is evidenced in China's drive in recent years to export its surplus capacity through initiatives such as the BRI. In many cases, this initiative has backfired and given rise to international conflicts.

Policies that have helped keep wages low have directly profited exporters at the expense of Chinese workers. Tight controls over the banking system, financial markets and the currency have further denied Chinese savers access to higher returns on their savings. This has allowed the government to channel cheap capital to favoured sectors, but has limited the spending power of ordinary citizens, stifled competition and increased the scope for official corruption. It has also contributed to the build-up of substantial trade and financial imbalances that have been a major driver of Sino-US tensions.

President Xi's dual circulation strategy, announced in 2020, is a recognition that more emphasis needs to be placed on developing China's domestic consumer economy. As the manuscript for this book was being finalised, Xi had just further called for the country to pursue 'common prosperity' (共同富裕) and signalled a shift towards more explicit measures of wealth and income redistribution. It remains to be seen what the details of these policies are, how effective they will be, and what second and third order effects they may have. However, it is commendable that China appears to be taking proactive steps towards addressing its domestic inequality.

As the US and China begin to pursue policies to improve wealth and income distribution at home, care must be taken to ensure that their respective policies do not collide with each other to create unintended consequences. This will require coordination between the two of them, as well as with other countries. Importantly, it must be recognised that domestic policy adjustments to reduce inequality are only a first step.

At the core of global financial imbalances today is the role played by the US dollar. At the end of WW2, the US accounted for around half of the world's economic output. The relative size of its economy and its financial markets made it possible for the US to step into the role of the world's consumer of last resort, and for it to absorb large capital flows from other countries. Today, the US accounts for less than a quarter of global output and it is clear that it is unsustainable for America to continue to borrow and consume as it has done in the past.

Many commentators have blamed the mercantilist policies of countries with export surpluses for America's deficits.[8] This is unfair: it has been a choice that America has taken. That choice allowed US policymakers to defer difficult budgetary decisions and it has hugely enriched the US financial services industry, while manufacturers and exporters have paid the price. Nevertheless, if America had not been willing to run large deficits, global economic growth would have been much lower not only due to reduced US consumption, but also because of the dollar liquidity shortage this would have caused in the international financial system.

All else being equal, if America were to address its wealth inequality problem, this would most likely lead to higher disposable incomes for lower-wage earners. This would result in an increase in US consumption that would only further exacerbate its deficits. Corresponding policies to raise consumption in China would help to balance the equation, but that is hardly a comprehensive solution. Although the US and China are the two largest economies in the world, together they only account for just over 40 percent of world GDP. Even if trade between the two of them were balanced, disequilibrium in the rest of the world could still lead to significant global financial imbalances. Moreover, given that cross-border capital flows now vastly outstrip the flow of trade in goods and services, a comprehensive rebalancing must involve reforms to the global monetary system.

A New Bretton Woods?

The predicament in which America finds itself today has many parallels with that of the UK at the end of WW2. Overextended due to the costs of the war and with its industrial base badly frayed, it was clear that Britain was no longer able to absorb a large portion of the world's balance of payments disequilibria. However, in 1947 sterling still made up 87 percent of global foreign exchange reserves. Even excluding the balances held by the colonies, sterling accounted for roughly four times the value of official US dollar reserves at that time.[9] And the 35 countries and colonies that made up the sterling area continued to account for around half of global trade during the 1950s. Sterling's international role was a source of considerable influence and national pride but, when it ultimately came down to it, British governments were unwilling to support the international role of sterling at the expense of domestic interests.

Unilateral imposition of foreign exchange controls by the British government discouraged the use of sterling in international trade. Nevertheless, it was difficult to shake off the shackles of sterling's status as a global reserve currency. It took a decade (and a 30 percent devaluation of the pound) before the dollar's share of global reserves exceeded that of sterling and, even by 1970, sterling still accounted for around 7 percent of global reserves,[10] compared with 4.7 percent at the end of 2020.[11] The reasons it took so long for sterling's role as a reserve currency to be wound down were varied.

First, the role of inertia should not be underestimated. Sterling's role as a reserve currency was embedded into established customs and reinforced by institutional arrangements, which created numerous network externalities that reinforced its use.

Second, Britain's borrowing during WW2 had left a huge amount of sterling-denominated debt outstanding internationally.[12] Many countries had also pegged their currencies to the pound. This gave other countries a significant interest in upholding the value of sterling, and slowed the process of converting their reserve balances into other currencies.

Third, much of this British government debt was owed to British colonies and Commonwealth countries (including some £1.3 billion in outstanding balances held by India), which gave Britain some moral obligation to avoid default. More practically though, British prosperity was still highly dependent on trade with these countries and a sudden default or devaluation would have led to a harmful rupture in trade flows.

The retreat of sterling as a global reserve currency was therefore not the ignominious decline that it is often portrayed as, but rather a calculated strategy in the face of changed realities, the execution of which was managed with the support of other major countries.

Of course, not all parts of the British establishment were supportive of the withdrawal of sterling from its international role. The Bank of England, keen to protect the interests of the City of London, vigorously resisted exchange controls that restricted the international commercial use of sterling. However, the emergence of the Eurodollar market and London's capture of it gradually reduced the importance of sterling to Britain's financial services sector. And following Britain's accession to the EEC, rising trade with Europe reduced Britain's dependence on the former sterling area.[13]

Like Britain at the end of WW2, America is severely overextended and faces a quagmire that is compounded by the dollar's global role. A first hurdle is a choice that must be made between the 'impossible trinity' of: (i) control over the exchange rate; (ii) free capital flows; and (iii) monetary independence. Governments can choose to maintain two of the three, but must sacrifice the third. Today, America enjoys free capital flows and monetary independence, but the cost of this is that the dollar's exchange rate fluctuates independently. In contrast, Mainland China has chosen to retain a high degree of control over the renminbi's exchange rate and monetary independence, but has had to maintain controls over flows of capital in and out of the country. A third option is the one chosen by Hong Kong (and many emerging markets): pegging the currency to a major currency, maintaining free capital flows, but effectively importing another country's monetary policy. Each of these options has a cost. The price that America has paid has been currency volatility and a structurally overvalued dollar. Mainland Chinese businesses and individuals are saddled with cumbersome capital controls when conducting international transactions. Hong Kong, with its US dollar peg, has faced frequent booms and busts in asset prices due to periodic misalignments between monetary policy and real economic conditions. The peg has required the territory to track extraordinarily low US interest rates since the GFC, notwithstanding buoyant local economic conditions driven by China's strong growth, thereby worsening Hong Kong's severe problem of unaffordable housing.

Britain's path to freeing itself from sterling's reserve currency status involved several devaluations over three decades and was aided by the high inflation environment of the 1970s. Throughout that period, the UK imposed capital controls and was dependent on funding assistance from the IMF and other countries. Surplus countries also had the alternative of the dollar (and later the Deutschmark) into which they were able to diversify newly accumulated reserves. If the US were to contemplate a similar reduction in the dollar's global role, it would face a far more complex journey.

Enormous growth in global trade and financial markets in recent decades means that the dollar is even more embedded into the structure of the global economy than sterling was at the end of WW2. Further, the scale of Britain's budget and current account deficits was nowhere near as large as America's has been in recent years. During the 1950s, the UK's current account balance saw an average *surplus* of 0.8 percent of GDP. The largest UK current account deficit during that period (in 1951, during the Korean War) was 2.1 percent of GDP.[14] From 2002 to 2008, the US current account deficit never fell below 4 percent, peaking at 5.9 percent in 2006. While this receded following the GFC, in 2019, before the Covid-19 pandemic struck, America's current account deficit of 2.2 percent of GDP was still comparatively high.[15] Any move to rapidly devalue the dollar would lead to a sudden withdrawal of US consumption, posing severe risks to the global economy.

Employing the framework of the impossible trinity, if the US were to try unilaterally to engineer a sustained devaluation of the dollar today, there is no obvious anchor for the dollar to be pegged to, so the alternative would be to impose capital controls. However, capital controls on the dollar would bring global trade and investment to a virtual standstill, plunging the world economy into a tailspin that would be immensely destructive to the US itself.

An alternative to devaluation would be for the US to pursue higher inflation in order to erode the real value of its public debt, or even a default. It is likely that US policymakers will use inflation as one means of reducing the debt burden, but they can only do so up to a point. While foreigners hold a huge amount of US Treasuries, almost three-quarters of the US federal debt is held domestically.[16] Among the largest domestic holders are social security trust funds, private pension funds and US households. Any attempt to inflate away or write down the public debt would upend the savings and retirement plans of millions of Americans, rendering it politically unacceptable.

What about imposing a write-down just on foreign holders of US Treasuries? A selective default targeted just at foreign holders is practically infeasible, as the structure of the Treasury market makes it difficult to discern between foreign holders and US holders holding securities via overseas funds or accounts.[17] Besides, any default in the Treasuries market would trigger global economic turmoil that could well worsen America's problems.

While a selective default on foreign holdings of US Treasuries would certainly lead to a sharp devaluation of the dollar, it would also make it difficult for the US to raise debt in international markets going forward. A devaluation would make US exports more competitive, but adjustments in international trade flows would take time and there would likely be a considerable lag before this was reflected in the US government budget position. This means that the US government would face substantial funding risks in the interim. It is also highly likely that a selective US default would be met with economic retaliation by other countries, so there is no guarantee that this option would lead to a sustainable improvement in the US balance of payments.

It is clear, therefore, that there is no realistic unilateral path towards meaningfully devaluing the dollar and that, given global dependence on the US currency and the scale of imbalances, it is ultimately in the interests of other countries to cooperate in seeking a gradual path towards resolution. But how could a 21st century version of the Bretton Woods 'grand bargain' on a new international monetary system be structured?

***

The principal American preoccupation will be to address the structural overvaluation of the dollar in order help restore the competitiveness of US industry. In addition, the US government's huge anticipated refinancing requirements mean that continued access to international bond markets will be of at least equal concern. Other countries, including Eurozone nations and China (on whose support any agreement on reforms hinges), will be most concerned with maintaining currency stability, given the potential impact on trade and the value of their US dollar assets. To a greater or lesser degree, they will also wish to prevent any one country from gaining hegemony over the international financial system. Any proposal for reforms must take all of these concerns into account.

For the purposes of providing a framework for consideration, three broad paths of reform are reviewed here. It is not the intention of this volume to advocate for any particular one, but rather to explore how each structure might work and the associated challenges, in the hope of driving forward the public debate. It is also important to emphasise two points up front. First, there is no silver bullet. The history of financial markets examined in this book shows that international trade and capital flows are continually evolving. Key challenges for policymakers are to keep abreast of and to understand changes in order make timely adjustments where appropriate. Second, a rebalancing of the global monetary system must take place at a very measured pace (if dangerous instability is to be avoided). Britain took more than three decades to dismantle sterling's global role. Given the far greater scale of imbalances today, the restructuring of the dollar-based system could take even longer.

The first potential path of reform harks back to John Maynard Keynes' Bancor proposal, replacing the US dollar and other national currencies with a new reserve currency issued by a multinational institution. As advocated by the PBOC, this could be done by expanding the role and usage of the IMF's SDRs – though there would be some substantial hurdles to overcome.

As the problems of using a national currency as a reserve asset encapsulated in the Triffin Dilemma became apparent in the early 1960s, confronting the world with a liquidity shortage, governments began multilateral discussions through the G-10 and the IMF on reforms to the international monetary system. However, those discussions were confounded by a lack of consensus on the nature of the problem and consequent ambiguity of purpose.

Bretton Woods had established a system that pegged all currencies to the US dollar, which in turn was pegged to gold. To keep the world supplied with sufficient liquidity, the US had to keep increasing the supply of dollars. While, on the one hand, America was caught in a bind by the gold supply's inability to keep pace with the growth in global liquidity needs, on the other, reserve holders were becoming increasingly anxious about the rising amount of dollars relative to US gold reserves. From the American perspective, the question came down to how to provide that liquidity without requiring the US to continually increase its indebtedness. From the perspective of the EEC – and the French in particular – the main problem was how to restrict the expansion of US dollar liquidity to prevent the value of their reserve holdings from being eroded. This key difference drove a rather tortuous and inconclusive debate over whether this new reserve asset should be considered 'money' (effectively 'paper gold') or 'credit' (which would need to be repaid). Failure to fully resolve this issue was what led to the somewhat anodyne and ambiguous name of the new reserve asset created: 'Special Drawing Rights'.[18]

When they were finally created and allocated among IMF members in proportion to their quotas, SDRs were a compromise that failed to resolve the fundamental problem of expanding dollar reserves backed by a shrinking ratio of gold. Neither did they replace national currencies as reserves or redistribute the burden of adjustment between countries with balance of payments of surpluses and those with deficits. Three allocations totalling 9.3 billion SDRs were made between 1970 and 1972, bringing their share of the world's non-gold reserves to 9.5 percent.[19] By the time of the third allocation, however, President Nixon had suspended the Bretton Woods system and floated the dollar, and a substantial expansion in the US money supply had resulted in a surge in international liquidity. This removed the main impetus behind further development of SDRs and they fell away from prominence until the GFC, when an additional 182.6 billion were allocated to bolster liquidity in the global financial system.[20]

Today, the value of SDRs is based on a narrow basket of five currencies, including the US dollar, the euro, the renminbi, the Japanese yen and the British pound. Their weightings within the basket are reviewed by the IMF every five years.[21] Since they cannot be held by private parties, SDRs primarily serve as a unit of account for the IMF, rather than as a payments currency. Countries wishing to utilise their SDR holdings must first convert them into the currency they need, and the lack of a private secondary market makes them relatively illiquid.

Although there have been repeated proposals to substitute existing reserve currency holdings for SDRs, these have always gone nowhere due to a lack of commitment from the US. Were existing reserve currencies exchanged for SDRs, large debtor countries would need to pay interest based on prevailing SDR interest rates and face exchange rate risks. Understandably, the US has been unwilling to give up the advantages of issuing debt in dollars and of seigniorage without a firm assurance that countries with persistent balance of payments surpluses would have to revalue their currencies upward or take other adjustment measures.[22]

There is also an important question of governance, which affects the elasticity of reserve supply. Under the dollar-based system, the supply of dollars depends on the US balance of payments position and can therefore expand in response to an increase in demand or other exogenous factors affecting the US deficit. In contrast, the supply of SDRs depends on administrative decisions made by the IMF.[23] At issue is the power to determine whether the global monetary environment should be inflationary or deflationary. As seen during the euro crisis, however, international disagreements can paralyse decision making at multilateral institutions, causing delays that can have severe economic consequences.

Finally, tied up in the governance question is the issue of what is the most appropriate method for allocating SDRs. At present, SDRs continue to be allocated based on IMF quotas that also determine each member country's voting rights. Quota sizes were historically determined and do not necessarily reflect each country's share of global GDP, trade or other more relevant measures. Any changes in quotas must be approved by an 85 percent majority of the total voting power. Since the US has 16.5 percent of the voting rights,[24] it has the power to block any adjustments.

None of these hurdles are insuperable, however, and the Covid-19 pandemic may have served as a major catalyst for expanding the role of SDRs. As markets went into a tailspin in March 2020, liquidity in emerging markets rapidly dried up, shutting some of the world's poorest countries out of the capital markets at precisely the time when their governments desperately needed funds to help combat the impact of the global pandemic. While the Fed provided support to numerous rich country central banks, no such facility was available for less advanced nations. As a result, the IMF found itself inundated with requests for support from more than 80 countries.[25] At the time, a bold proposal was put forward calling for at least $500 billion worth of new SDRs to be issued to bolster the reserves of cash-strapped countries.[26]

While this idea was welcomed by emerging markets, support was not universal. Opponents to the proposal pointed out that, given the small share of IMF quotas held by emerging markets, the bulk of any such issue would end up going to wealthy nations. It was also argued that SDRs would do little to help indebted poor countries if they were just used to pay down existing debt. It was therefore argued that countries in need should seek to make use of IMF lending facilities instead.[27] An underlying concern was also that a major expansion in SDR issuance would dilute the influence America enjoys through the Fed's power to grant US dollar swap lines.[28] Nevertheless, given the scale of the pandemic's hit to the global economy and to emerging markets in particular, the IMF's Board took a major step forward in expanding the global pool of SDRs by approving in July 2021 the issuance of $650 billion worth of new SDRs (in the form of new money, rather than credit requiring repayment).[29]

Expanding the amount of SDRs in issue is just one hurdle though, and further steps would be required to enable them to take over the baton from the dollar in the global monetary hierarchy. These steps would include making SDRs more representative of the global economy and international trade flows. This would involve widening the basket of currencies against which SDRs are referenced. Over time, SDRs would also need to become the key reference unit for other currencies' exchange rates, requiring far more frequent adjustments in the unit's reference exchange rates and interest rates.

A key decision would be on the role to be played by the enhanced SDRs: *should they remain a reserve asset just for transactions between the IMF and central banks, or should private parties be allowed to transact in SDRs?* Keynes' proposal envisaged that Bancor would serve as a unit of settlement between central banks to manage balance of payments surpluses and deficits. He proposed that the ICB would pool excess reserves, which could be lent to deficit countries in the form of 'unsecured overdrafts', and that beyond certain quota limits surplus countries would be subject to mandatory exchange rate appreciation, while deficit countries would be forced to depreciate.[30] Although this proposal had the advantage of automatically stimulating a rebalancing of trade, it failed to fully address the credit risks arising from chronic deficit countries or instances where borrowers were unwilling to repay. Keynes' plan also assumed that capital controls would be 'a permanent feature of the postwar system'[31] – something which seems unpalatable for businesses and individuals used to relatively free capital flows nowadays.

These issues might be addressed by opening up SDRs to private sector use, which would encourage market pricing of credit and exchange rates. Private sector use of SDRs would need to be developed along two lines: (i) pricing, accounting and payments; and (ii) as a store of value. These two lines are very much interconnected, since a currency's usage in trade depends on the recipient's ability to purchase other goods and assets with the currency. Sovereign states and international institutions would have to play a role in generating these assets by issuing bonds and other instruments denominated in SDRs. This may, in fact, be an attractive option for countries that find it difficult to issue debt in their own currencies, since SDRs' basket composition provides a better hedge against foreign exchange volatility than debt issued in a single currency, such as US dollars.[32] Nevertheless, although long-term public sector holders such as central banks and SWFs are likely to be attracted to the market, they tend to be 'buy and hold' investors. Marketing of these securities to fund managers and retail investors will be critical to building market liquidity, which is needed to drive down transaction costs. The development of hedging tools and a repo market would also need to be encouraged to support trading liquidity.

Countries that are able to invoice and settle in their home currencies will continue to have incentives to do so, but there are ways to accelerate adoption of SDRs in global trade. For example, international accounting rules for multinational companies could be amended to require reporting in SDRs. Countries that currently peg their currencies to the US dollar might also find the SDR to be preferable if it better reflects the composition of their balance of payment flows.[33]

Ultimately, however, whether or not SDRs can replace existing reserve currencies will depend on achieving international agreement on their governance. This will require striking an appropriate balance of fairness to different stakeholders; establishing a robust system of exchange rate adjustments that discourages countries from undervaluing their currencies to gain trade advantages; minimising political interference in monetary policy; and supporting the US in gradually winding down the dollar's global role. This can all be done, but it will require resolute political determination.

The second broad path of reform would involve rebalancing the mix of reserve holdings to reduce the role of the dollar. This is, in effect, the path followed by sterling in the decades after WW2 and could come about naturally as China continues to expand its international trade and to develop its financial markets. Nevertheless, this path would still require active coordination between the major economies, and a willingness on the part of individual countries to make significant policy adjustments.

Since it is practically infeasible for the US to follow Britain's strategy of imposing capital controls, it would be reliant to a great degree on voluntary policy reforms by large surplus countries, such as China and Germany, to increase consumption. Although the falling marginal benefits (and rising collateral costs) of its investment-led economic model would suggest that encouraging domestic consumption is in China's own interests, it is not clear that such reforms would go as far or as fast as may be needed to effect the level of rebalancing required. Further, demographic decline will create a headwind limiting the absolute growth in Chinese consumption for the foreseeable future.

For a rebalancing to take place, the rate of growth in US Treasury issuance would need to be below that of alternative reserve assets. Slowing (or reversing) the growth of dollar reserves would likely require the US to undergo a period of fiscal austerity. The impact of this could be managed through tax reforms to increase the tax burden on the wealthy, while limiting the impact on lower-wage earners. Nevertheless, political resistance is likely to be considerable.

The biggest challenge to this approach, however, is likely to come from the markets. In financial markets, there are significant benefits in terms of cost and efficiency from concentrating liquidity around the leading benchmark. This has helped entrench the dollar's pre-eminent role. If the renminbi and the euro were to take on a greater role at the dollar's expense, liquidity in dollar-based financial instruments such as interest rate and currency swaps would be split, reducing overall market efficiency. For this reason, market forces may resist efforts to move to a more balanced mix in the international use of the major currencies.

Further, while it has been argued that there is space for more than one international currency in the global financial system,[34] the experience of the transition from sterling to the dollar as the leading international currency suggests that the market will ultimately congregate around one dominant currency. As discussed in Chapter 5, increasing the international use of the renminbi is likely to require the Chinese government to pursue a number of reforms, including further relaxations of capital controls and improvements in property protections. Anticipated growth in future government borrowing needs provides a significant incentive for China to pursue these reforms. Nevertheless, Chinese policymakers' have historically had three key reservations about free-floating currencies and open capital flows. First are the social risks potentially posed by sudden large speculative flows. Second, any move in this direction for China would involve ceding significant control over the domestic financial system. Third, US control over the arteries of global capital flows means that this would expose China to much greater risk of US financial sanctions. On this third point, US fears of China exploiting a more global renminbi to target America with sanctions could incentivise US policymakers to try to thwart the rise of the renminbi.

Setting aside individual Chinese and US policies, however, it is questionable whether a system that relies on voluntary policy adjustments can avoid countries seeking trade advantages by taking measures to undervalue their currencies. Further, this option relies on several large countries to bear a disproportionate burden of supplying global liquidity, with no in-built mechanism for adjusting for possible changes in countries' relative economic and financial conditions that might occur in the future – for example, through the further growth and development of large countries such as India.

The third potential option is to leave the current international monetary framework broadly intact, keeping the US dollar as the primary global reserve currency. This would require the same voluntary steps on the part of surplus countries to increase consumption, and on the part of the US to contain its fiscal deficits. However, it would also involve an explicit acknowledgement of the role that the US plays in supplying global liquidity through some form of compensation arrangement.

This approach would avoid the challenge of establishing a new global reserve asset, and minimises the upheaval to existing networks supporting the international monetary system. If, following voluntary steps to effect a rebalancing, the US continues to suffer substantial deficits due to its role in supplying the world with dollar liquidity, countries with excess reserves over a certain level (or which run persistent current account surpluses) could be required to provide rebates to the US. If this is not sufficient incentive for them to balance their trade flows, then at least the rebates might serve to compensate the US for supplying a global utility and help reduce its national debt.

Of course, the idea of *paying* another country for running budget deficits would be politically difficult to justify, particularly if the quantum of rebates were to be large enough to make any material difference to America's sizeable national debt. Further, it does not directly redress the burden borne by US manufacturers due to the structural overvaluation of the dollar. From the Chinese perspective, this option also fails to address US dominance over the international financial system and China's consequent geo-economic vulnerability, thereby disincentivising more substantial steps to relax its capital controls.

Looking back, the geopolitical context that brought about the 1944 Bretton Woods Agreement was, of course, unique. Further, Bretton Woods' architects were perhaps excessively focused on the problems of the 1920s and 1930s, without sufficiently taking into account how the world was poised to change, and were certainly overly optimistic about the sustainability of the system that the agreement created. Notwithstanding the global common interest in effecting a smooth rebalancing of the international financial system today, achieving consensus will be a major challenge. Nevertheless, unless the system that we have inherited is reformed, the continued build-up of imbalances may well lead to a sudden and violent rupture in the future. None of the options reviewed here is perfect, but each of them could serve as a basis for discussions that could lead to a solution. In the present geopolitical environment, however, a lack of trust is the principal barrier to progress. Perhaps, therefore, we must first find a way to address the trust deficit.

MAD for Markets

Throughout the history of international commerce, various *entrepôts* have emerged to bridge linguistic, cultural and ideological divides, and support the smooth flow of trade. From Medieval Venice, which facilitated trade between the Byzantine Empire and Europe; to London, which has hosted the transatlantic trade in Eurodollars; to Hong Kong, which has bridged trade and investment between the East and the West since the 1840s, these *entrepôts* have shared certain important commonalities.

First, they have been situated in fortuitous geographic locations. Second, they were open to immigration and hosted diverse populations. Third, they permitted relatively high levels of intellectual freedom. Fourth – and most importantly – they featured robust legal systems, which provided strong property protections. These features created 'neutral ground' on which trust could be built, which in turn facilitated the flow of commerce and investment.

However, trust is a fragile commodity that can quickly dissipate. After elite capture in the late 13th and early 14th centuries undermined Venice's pluralistic institutions, trust rapidly evaporated and the city fell into a long decline. Over the long run, the evolving nature of human societies means that political institutions will continually be challenged and tested. From time to time, some changes will undermine trust.

Certain aspects of our modern world can also make trust harder to establish and maintain. Advances in communications and transport have vastly extended our horizons, but have contributed to an erosion in the bonds of traditional communities. The winner-takes-all dynamics of a number of new technologies have, in many instances, opened the door to abuses. These developments have also affected the financial world. Before the explosive growth of the Eurodollar market, the City of London operated as a sort of club, where regulators could rely on personal relationships to instil standards of behaviour. With the arrival of many more international banks from the 1960s onwards, traditional values gave way to greater reliance on codified rules and regulations. In the financial markets infrastructures that have been established to support greater globalisation of capital flows, substantial benefits are derived from scale. However, this also puts enormous power in the hands of the party controlling that infrastructure.

In response to the threat of America exploiting the dollar's global role to exert geo-economic pressure on it, China has sought to insulate itself by developing its own international market infrastructures (such as CIPS as an alternative to the SWIFT network). While there are benefits that can arise from greater competition in the global financial system, this has also given rise to four problems. First, splitting the infrastructure supporting international financial flows into two (or more) parallel operating systems raises costs and reduces efficiency for users. Second, if the world becomes divided into two separate international financial networks, it could lead to a reduction in overall global trade and investment, negatively impacting the world economy. Third, separate networks for financial flows do not provide perfect protection to either set of users where the two systems need to interact. Fourth, China's attempts to create a competing international financial system are perceived as a strategic threat by the US, elevating Sino-US tensions.

To reduce the risk of conflict, neutral ground should be cherished and protected. Specifically, in capital markets, Hong Kong's role as an international financial centre has been of great value to both China and the US. Both countries have an interest in the territory continuing to serve as a bridge between their two distinct financial systems. Following local unrest in 2019 and the passage of the NSL, the situation in Hong Kong at the time of writing remains sensitive. An extremely judicious approach towards the application of the NSL would help set international investors' minds at ease. Equally, it would be in the interests of the West not to undermine Hong Kong's judicial system. Since the return of sovereignty to China in 1997, foreign judges from other common law jurisdictions have served on Hong Kong's CFA, which has reinforced the independence of the territory's judicial system. Given the substantial volume of international investment passing through Hong Kong, this arrangement would appear to be helpful in upholding common interests. Therefore, comments by the British Foreign Secretary in November 2020 questioning 'whether it continues to be appropriate' for British judges to serve in Hong Kong[35] seemed counter to the West's *own* interests. Ideally, both sides should work to restore trust as quickly as possible.

However, if neither side is ready to fully trust each other yet, then perhaps there is another way of bridging the trust deficit.

Taking a leaf out of the nuclear deterrent strategy that was developed during the Cold War, rather than engaging in a geo-economic 'arms race', a financial version of the MAD doctrine could be pursued. This would involve deepening financial interdependencies in a way that would make it unthinkable for either the US or China to wield their financial arsenals against each other in capital markets, thereby enhancing safety for both on the international capital highways.

To give a specific example of how this might work, key financial structures under Western and Chinese jurisdiction with complementary roles could be linked. Since the launch of the Stock Connect and Bond Connect programmes, Hong Kong's securities depositories have become the world's largest offshore custodians of international investors' holdings of Mainland Chinese securities.[36] These holdings represent a huge potential collateral pool. However, there are, as yet, limited options for international investors to borrow against their Mainland Chinese securities holdings to raise liquidity in offshore markets. This is a key inhibitor to further increasing foreign investor demand for Chinese sovereign bonds at a time when China's government borrowing requirements to meet rising social welfare needs are expected to increase sharply. LCH, operating and regulated in London, is the dominant clearer in the global swaps markets and could significantly stimulate demand for Chinese government debt were it to begin accepting CGBs held in Hong Kong's bond depository to meet its margin requirements. By linking London's clearing infrastructure with Hong Kong's depository in this manner, a mutually beneficial co-dependency would be created, whereby the international investor community would be dependent on Hong Kong for the safekeeping of their Chinese securities holdings, while the Chinese government would be dependent on London for supporting international demand for its sovereign debt.[37] Under this arrangement, any action by either China or the US to attack each other's financial infrastructure or to limit the other's use of their own, would be self-defeating, since it would be met by equally damaging retaliation from the other party.

Taking this concept a step further, there could be other benefits to this arrangement. International investors choose to invest in Mainland

Chinese capital markets via Hong Kong to avail themselves of the protections of Hong Kong's legal and regulatory system. Further development of Hong Kong as a depository centre for Chinese investors' holdings of international securities would address Chinese concerns about transparency and vulnerability to foreign sanctions. This could encourage Chinese policymakers to open their market to greater outward portfolio investment, enabling Chinese investors to access a greater diversity of investments to support their retirement saving needs. For the West, this would provide an opportunity to access investment from China's giant $33 trillion pool of bank deposits. It would also reduce security concerns related to Chinese investment in foreign markets, since the purchase of a few shares each by many individual Chinese investors for their retirement accounts would not raise the concerns about government control or technology transfer associated with FDI by Chinese corporates.[38]

A rebalancing and deepening of the Sino-US financial relationship would help reduce tensions and bring substantial benefits to both countries. Given the lack of trust that currently exists, there should be no illusion that this will be easy. Much will depend on leaders on both sides having the vision and willingness to take the first step.

It All Starts with Leadership

Leaders' ability to shape the course of events is always circumscribed by the historical context within which they must operate. Drawing on the experience of his long and distinguished career as a diplomat and statesman, Henry Kissinger observed that:

> [*Political leaders*] *may deviate from the previous trajectory only within a finite margin. The great statesmen act at the outer limit of that margin.*[39]

There is no doubt that pushing the edge of the boundaries requires both skill and courage. Amidst the international outcry following the Tiananmen incident, it was at considerable political risk to himself that President George H.W. Bush extended an olive branch to Deng Xiaoping, kept open diplomatic channels of communication, and restrained other world leaders in the sanctions that were ultimately imposed on China. Likewise, when it looked like a conservative backlash in the early

1990s might derail China's economic reforms, Deng Xiaoping demonstrated political dexterity and bravery in challenging the next generation of CCP leaders through his Southern Tour. We must hope that Chinese and American leaders today will have the same courage and determination to restore harmony to relations between the two countries.

Sometimes courageous leadership is not demonstrated by sticking to established convictions, but by admitting errors and being willing to change course, notwithstanding the personal political risks that might entail for individual leaders. In the Sino-US relationship, there are three course corrections that great statesmen might now pursue.

First: *stop threatening each other.* The war of words has only undermined security and increased animosity, forcing both sides into an escalating conflict. Reining in the rhetoric on both sides would go a long way towards improving relations. Disagreements will inevitably occur, but leaders should take care to be respectful in their public comments and to avoid using threatening language.

Beyond rhetoric, disputes in the South China Sea run a particularly high risk of miscalculations or accidents that could spiral out of control. The constant US presence in waters near China's coastline and regular intelligence flights are unwelcome legacies of a past era.[40] In the late 19th century, America was unwilling to tolerate a substantial British naval presence in the Western Hemisphere and began ratcheting up the cost to Britain of maintaining it. War was avoided by Britain's willingness to make a graceful exit.[41] America might now consider following that example in the South China Sea. However, the Chinese leadership should also recognise that America's presence is welcomed by other countries in the region because China's neighbours see China as a threat. Seeking peaceful resolution to Chinese territorial claims through compromise would go a long way towards removing any continuing need or excuse for a sizeable US naval presence in these waters.

Second: *abide by international rules.* Both the US and China have shown a propensity to ride roughshod over established international rules and act unilaterally outside multinational organisations. The problem is that, each time one of them does so, it encourages others to do the same, undermining the rules-based international order. Without limits, there is no order. It is in America's and China's mutual interests for them both to limit themselves, and to operate within the framework of multinational bodies and international laws.

Of course, to have legitimacy, multinational bodies must also be seen to be fair and broadly representative. Institutions that were established in the post-WW2 era do not adequately reflect the new global environment. IMF quotas today clearly are not reflective of the contributions of China and emerging markets to the world economy. As a venue for arbitrating trade disputes, the WTO has been discredited by perceptions of systematic bias in favour of rich countries; manipulation of the organisation's rules; and the Trump Administration's wilful undermining of the body.[42] Where these organisations need reforms and improvements, the US and China should engage to pursue these.

Third: *invest in leadership*. If we are to transmit our world greater, better and more beautiful onto future generations, then we must invest in future generations of leaders. The Covid-19 pandemic has demonstrated clearly the importance of good government, and the need for transparency and competence in our leadership.

Cultivating good leaders begins with education, not just in vocational subjects, but also in morals and civic responsibilities. Given the greater risks of one-sided echo chambers posed by the rise of social media, it is vital that our future leaders be trained to see issues from multiple perspectives, and that they develop empathy. The state must invest to ensure that a top quality education is available not only to the sons and daughters of the wealthy, but to all young people. Well-educated populations not only provide a larger pool of leadership talent, but they also demand higher standards of their leaders.

Both the US and China would further benefit from following Singapore's example in remunerating their public servants well. Given the importance of government, it is in our interests to ensure that the public sector is able to compete with the private sector for the best talent. Better pay would reduce the incentives for corruption. At the same time, greater restrictions should be placed on moves from the public into the private sector to remove improper incentives inherent in the revolving door.

For the system to survive and thrive over the long term, leaders must be held to account. Their respective national histories have bequeathed China and the US with vastly different systems of political governance, each with its own merits and disadvantages. In the interests of stability, it is preferable for change to be evolutionary. Nevertheless, both systems must guard against elite capture of the state. In America, campaign finance reforms to reduce the influence of wealthy interests appear to be long overdue. Meanwhile, greater press freedoms in China would help increase political accountability.

Our current generation of leaders has inherited many challenges, both domestic and global. History has taught us that, in our highly interconnected world, no country can be immune from events that occur elsewhere and that we must all face these challenges together. Imbalances in the global financial system have contributed significantly to tensions between China and the US. The problems are large and complex but, with courage, Chinese and American leaders can find a way to work together to resolve them.

Afterword

I began writing this book in 2020, as the Covid-19 pandemic forced people around the world to confine themselves to their homes. However, the ideas that drove me to write it began to form many years earlier.

When my wife and I moved back to Hong Kong in 2008 after years of living and working overseas, I found it had changed from the place I had known in my youth. Some of these changes were for the better. The city was richer and more vibrant, with a far greater range of entertainment and cuisines. Long gone were the days when local Chinese were discriminated against based on race. Further, China's rapid growth was creating greater opportunity for many businesses and, in particular, those in the financial services industry. Nevertheless, what struck me more was an increased sense of social polarisation and a loss of the territory's famed 'Lion Rock Spirit' (獅子山精神) – the 'get-up-and-go' and perseverance that had driven huge socioeconomic mobility in the decades post-WW2 (so-named after the popular 1973 television series *Under the Lion Rock* (獅子山下)).

Hong Kong has always featured a large divide between the 'haves' and 'have-nots'. However, previously, there had been a strong belief that, with hard work and determination, those in the lower socioeconomic strata stood a good chance of bettering their lot and even rising to the top. By 2008, that sense of hope that had powered the territory's rapid growth in prosperity in earlier decades had faded and had been replaced by a growing sense of cynicism and resentment towards those at the top of the economic pile.

This was something that I had witnessed before, when working as an investment banker in London in the early 2000s. Ordinary Londoners, feeling the squeeze of the rising cost of living as global capital flowed into the city, were not shy about expressing their resentment about a system they felt was rigged in favour of overpaid investment bankers and hedge fund managers. But my years away from Hong Kong had accentuated my sense of the shift in attitudes here and made it seem far starker. And perhaps it was. After all, Hong Kong was well on its way to becoming one of the most unequal developed economies on Earth.

In Hong Kong, *nouveaux riches* Mainlanders and their conspicuous consumption became a particular focus of resentment among those struggling to get by. This almost certainly contributed to growing calls for universal suffrage as a means of selecting the territory's leader and sowed the seeds of rising antipathy towards Mainland China among those who had not benefited from the country's growth.

Certainly, Hong Kong's post-1997 political structure was one factor underlying the growing wealth and income disparities. Adhering to the principle of One Country Two Systems, the Chinese government had relied on Hong Kong people to govern their own affairs, but the electoral system heavily concentrated power in the hands of local tycoons and business interests. Thus, the Hong Kong government continued to follow the *laissez faire* approach laid down by John Cowperthwaite in the 1960s, notwithstanding vast changes in the territory's internal and external environments. Hong Kong was also buffeted by numerous exogenous factors outside the government's control, not least the Asian Financial Crisis, the SARS epidemic, and the 2008 GFC. As a small, open economy, the territory has long been vulnerable to shocks in international financial markets. As its economy came to depend more and more on financial services, any form of fiscal redistribution through tax increases was precluded, since that would risk driving business to other centres, such as Singapore. Echoing the experience of Medieval Venice, the capture of Hong Kong's government by vested interests diverted it from addressing core social problems, such as the city's low housing affordability and highly unequal educational access.

As asset price inflation driven by extraordinary monetary policies in the wake of the GFC pushed Hong Kong's housing prices to ever more unaffordable levels, popular frustrations began to boil over, fanning political unrest. Some calling for democratic reforms waved Hong Kong's colonial flag in protest at the lack of progress. This was highly ironic, since not a single one of Hong Kong's colonial era governors had been democratically elected. What was really at stake were livelihood issues and the deeply inequitable distribution of opportunity and of the fruits of economic growth. Moreover, as the turbulence of the GFC ignited waves of popular dissatisfaction around the world, it did not appear that democratic countries were faring much better.

The impact of financial phenomena, in terms of prices, consumption and employment, and their knock-on effects on social stability seemed obvious. The better off would ignore this at their own peril. From my work and travel, it was also clear that Hong Kong was not unique in facing these pressures, but rather was at the forefront of a wider global trend of rising social tensions brought on by widening inequality, which were gradually spilling over into international conflicts.

★★★

In 2015, we were blessed with the birth of our two sons. Fatherhood has provided me with new perspectives and focused my mind of how recent developments will affect our boys' futures. There is profound wisdom in that oft-cited African proverb, 'It takes a village to raise a child.' Beyond the simple truth it encapsulates, it reminds us of the common endeavour in which we as human beings are all engaged, of our shared aspirations, and of the duties we each owe to society and to future generations. The research for this book has further led me to three key observations:

1. For each of us and our loved ones to enjoy security, we must have care for the security of others.
2. Social stability and progress rest on fair access to opportunity, an appropriate balance of incentives and community support, and the ability to pursue diverse forms of fulfilment, which provide for a level of human dignity.
3. Markets are a valuable tool, but governments play a critical role in regulating the allocation of society's resources in a way that balances the interests of different groups within it and of current and future generations.

Although substantial inequality has persisted for long periods over the course of history, highly inegalitarian regimes have tended to be maintained through high levels of violence. This almost always ends badly. It is estimated that governments killed as many as 625 million people before the 20th century. Meanwhile, between the years 600 and 1800, one in eight European monarchs was murdered in office.[1] Even in modern times, countries with high wealth and income disparities have been associated with high levels of kidnappings and other crimes.[2] The costs to our security of sustaining high levels of wealth disparity are therefore steep, even for those at the top of the wealth pyramid.

Significant social changes accompanying industrialisation, such as urbanisation and higher education levels, and more recently through massive advances in communications, have made severe inequality harder to justify. Although the residents of developed countries today on average enjoy far higher absolute living standards and life expectancies than the even the wealthiest of earlier periods, *relative* equality and the *perception* of fairness are far more important to the maintenance of social stability than *absolute* levels of income or wealth. The trajectory is also critically important. Student debts and sharp rises in housing costs have left a large proportion of young people in the West today poorer than their parents at the same stage in life.[3] This has put the family life to which many aspire out of reach, stoking widespread dissatisfaction.

Of course, not all quality-of-life factors that contribute to societal harmony can be measured in economic terms. Beyond a certain basic level of subsistence, human beings also have a need for other forms of fulfilment. What makes life worth living encompasses social, intellectual, spiritual, environmental and many other aspects of our existence. For many, fulfilment is derived from having purposeful work. As the forces of technology march on, the coming years are likely to see a wave of automation across the professional services sectors, which had previously been largely untouched in earlier periods of industrial sector automation. This will bring about considerable benefits in terms of increased efficiency and reduced costs. However, it will also displace millions of service sector workers.

In response, there have been calls for a 'universal basic income' to guarantee that each citizen's minimum needs are met. The idea that redistribution of the rewards of technological automation could free people to pursue a range of interests outside of work is alluring and warrants exploration. In fact, financial relief dispensed during the Covid-19 pandemic provided the largest ever real-world experiment on the effects of universal basic income, which should better inform future policymaking in this area.[4] However, one earlier study found that the largest increase in time usage among non-working prime-age men was in 'screen time' in front of the television or internet, creating greater risks of social disaffection.[5] If universal basic income were to remove incentives to work, it could also hold back further social and economic advancement, which would likely render it unsustainable in the long run.

Order within states ultimately rests on the social contract between governments and their citizens. In earlier times, governments' role was limited to providing citizens with minimum protections, such as a military force to ward off invasion and courts of law to adjudicate disputes. During the 19th and 20th centuries, states began to develop more elaborate public infrastructure and social welfare systems to meet the needs of the modern world. The demands on government finances rose commensurately. There are three basic means for governments to fund their spending: (i) taxation; (ii) sale of the state's natural resources; and/ or (iii) borrowing. Each involves decisions on how the community's resources should be allocated between different stakeholders and has wider social ramifications.

Beyond simply funding the functions of government, taxation plays a critical role in the modern social contract in other ways. First, it binds the political elite to the broader citizenry through financial dependency. It has been argued that rentier states that can rely largely on natural resource endowments for their funding are less responsive to society.[6] Second, it is a key mechanism for income and wealth redistribution, which helps avoid the entrenchment of class hierarchies. Third, fiscal policy is an important driver of incentives, which play a critical role in supporting wider social objectives, innovation, and overall economic vibrancy.

Natural resource endowments can be a blessing but, for states that become over-reliant on this form of income, the risks of resource misallocation, corruption, waste, and inefficiency are well documented.[7] Many such endowments, such as oil reserves, are also finite, risk being rendered obsolete by technological advancements, and expose the state to substantial fluctuations in global supply and demand.

The evolution of financial markets has given modern states unprecedented ability to raise debt. Where borrowing is used to fund sound investments, this has helped to accelerate development, substantially raising living standards and improving future prosperity. However, where it is squandered on current consumption or where investment is misallocated, it can create a burden on later generations that imperils future prosperity or even social stability. It is alarming, therefore, that both China and America have heavily mortgaged their younger generations' futures and misallocated capital on a substantial scale – America on unnecessary wars, and China on continuing to build more industrial capacity in the face of its steep demographic cliff.

Further, it is not only in monetary terms that we have borrowed from future generations. Since the world began to industrialise, enhancements in our lifestyles and consumption have come at an enormous environmental cost. It is critical to mankind's long-term survival that governments serve as stewards of our planet and its resources not only for the current generation, but also for future generations. This naturally raises the question of the optimal political model to allow governments to achieve this.

★★★

Throughout this book, I have emphasised the importance of the rule of law as a check and balance on the power of government. However, I have not expressed a view as to whether America's liberal democratic model or China's responsive one-party model is superior – a key *ideological* difference between the two countries.

Winston Churchill famously advocated for democracy not based on its strengths, but on the weakness of the alternatives, stating that it is the 'worst form of Government except for all those other forms that have been tried from time to time. . .' The UK has not experienced violent regime change since the English Civil War (1642–1651).[8] Over the same period, the incumbent Chinese government has been violently overturned on four occasions,[9] not to mention many more uprisings and rebellions that were quashed. Democracy's greatest weakness is that the selection of leaders by popular vote doesn't necessarily guarantee the best leadership. In fact, it specifically incentivises political leaders to focus on short-term and populist policies, driven by the exigencies of election cycles.

China's governance model allows for longer-term policy setting, without the need to pander to electoral agendas. Nevertheless, this does not mean that the Chinese government has been able to avoid short-term or ill-considered policies on many occasions. China has found it just as difficult as Western democracies to raise the pension age and reform entitlements, and Chinese government officials also often pursue short-term measures to advance their careers.

The portrayal of Sino-US relations as a clash of cultures, or an inevitable clash of ideas, is far from helpful. Rather than focusing on whether one system is inherently superior or inferior to the other, we should acknowledge that each has its merits and that both have been susceptible to corruption. Warren Buffett tries to invest in businesses 'that are so wonderful that an idiot can run them. Because sooner or later, one will.' Perhaps it is possible to find companies with such strong business models that that the quality of management doesn't matter. Unfortunately, no equivalent political model has yet been devised. Leadership is therefore critical. Governments must from time to time take unpopular decisions, particularly if they are to balance the interests of present and future generations. This places an emphasis on developing political leaders who are not only skilful, but who also have the strength of character to communicate clearly and honestly with their people about the issues they must confront.

Recent events offer a glimpse of the scale of the financial challenges Chinese and American leaders face as the world emerges from a state of suspended animation induced by Covid-19.

On 24 July 2021, China's State Council announced a ban on for-profit tuition centres engaged in the teaching of the school curriculum. These centres had proliferated amidst China's highly competitive examination system for university entrance, spawning a multi-billion dollar industry. Coming on the heels of sweeping measures to rein in the monopoly power and activities of some of the country's largest tech giants, the move spooked markets. The first trading day following the State Council's announcement saw $16 billion wiped off the market value of the top three listed Chinese education companies and Hong Kong's leading index of Chinese enterprises fell by 4.9 percent.[10]

Some in the Western media have interpreted this as the Chinese government turning away from capitalism and the legendary former hedge fund manager George Soros wrote an article in the *Wall Street Journal* criticising leading US fund managers for continuing to allocate capital to China.[11] The scale of the market reaction seemed to take Chinese policymakers by surprise and the CSRC was reported to have convened foreign financial firms in a bid to restore calm.[12] In many ways, Chinese policymakers' moves were commendable. The rising power of large technology platforms has been a challenge for governments globally, given the scope for abuse of their monopoly positions. Set against the backdrop of China's demographic challenges, the rise of for-profit tuition centres not only increased the risk of compounding wealth and income inequality, but created greater financial pressures for parents, thereby contributing to lower birth rates. It would be mistaken to see these steps as a signal that China is turning away from markets. Chinese policymakers have stressed that President Xi's common prosperity initiative does not mean absolute equality of outcomes or an elimination of markets' role in resource allocation, nor is it a repudiation of private enterprise.[13]

Nevertheless, Chinese leaders should pay close attention to the market reaction and to the views of Western commentators. The country's rapidly aging demographic profile will inevitably place considerable pressures on its national finances, and China will need access to international financial markets. While investors' views on the attractions of China's markets in light of more redistributive policies will vary, it is the lack of transparency and due process in the government's pursuit of such policies that poses the greatest risk to the country being able to attract international capital. Inadequate public debate on new policy initiatives also raises the risk of unintended consequences. In light of China's fiercely competitive university entrance system, it is likely that parents will continue to seek ways of giving their children the best advantages. Shutting off for-profit tuition centres may simply lead the wealthiest parents to turn to private home tuition, thereby compounding the advantages their children already enjoy.

On 20 September, Hong Kong's Hang Seng Index plunged again by as much as 4.2 percent on growing fears of a debt default by the Evergrande Group (恒大集团).[14] China's second largest property developer by sales, Evergrande had racked up debts exceeding $300 billion, and its financial troubles had been the subject of speculation for many months. Some in the financial media rushed to declare this was China's 'Lehman moment'.[15] The company's debts equal around two percent of Chinese GDP, and it owes money to 128 banks and over 121 non-banking institutions.[16] It also has some $37 billion in bills and trade payables due to contractors and suppliers in the next 12 months,[17] and around 1.6 million customers who have made down payments for apartments yet to be completed.[18] In addition, the company employs some 200,000 people directly and another 3.8 million contracted workers on its construction projects.[19] The risk of economic contagion from Evergrande's failure is therefore real. However, for this precise reason, it is highly unlikely that the government will allow a disorderly collapse. Indeed, following the stock market plunge, the PBOC injected $18.6 billion in liquidity into the banking system in a bid to alleviate fears that Evergrande's problems might further roil financial markets.[20]

Ultimately, the Chinese government has sufficient capacity to contain the fallout in this situation, and Evergrande will likely fade into the annals of financial history. However, Evergrande's travails are a further symptom that China's top-down investment-led economic growth model has reached its limits.

In recent years, China's property sector has been fuelled by credit and a belief that prices will go on rising. Around 78 percent of Chinese household wealth is invested in real estate compared with just 35 percent in the US. With property prices in Beijing, Shanghai and Shenzhen running at over 40 times median household disposable incomes compared with 22 times in London and 12 times in New York, top Chinese cities are arguably facing a severe property price bubble.[21] A major precipitator of the Evergrande's liquidity crunch was a 2020 PBOC mandate to the banking sector to cut back on their mortgage lending to tame property prices. This resulted in a $60 billion reduction in the amount of new mortgage lending during 2021.[22] With China's real estate and construction sectors accounting for an eye-popping 29 percent of

2016 GDP and around one-fifth of urban non-private employment though, it is hard to see that this bubble can be deflated without incurring severe economic pain. In the face of China's demographic decline, it is easy to draw comparisons with the Japanese property bubble of the 1980s, when the market value of Japan's real estate soared to twice that of the US compared with just one-third of the value today.[23]

The challenges facing US policymakers are no less daunting. Post-GFC monetary policies had already fuelled rising inequality, feeding rising social tensions. Persisting with Fed policies implemented during the Covid-19 pandemic poses even greater risks.

Unlike the GFC, which hit consumption *demand*, the Covid-19 pandemic has largely impacted the *supply* of goods and services. Stimulating demand through loose monetary policy at a time when global supply chains have been disrupted is likely simply to fuel price inflation, as more money chases a restricted supply of goods. As John Maynard Keynes noted, inflation is not just simply a rise in prices, but a form of wealth transfer between different segments of society. Runaway inflation would hurt millions of middle class savers and could further undermine social stability. Nevertheless, political gridlock continues to impede the search for a solution.

Withdrawing monetary stimulus and raising interest rates would inevitably hit asset prices, which would have knock-on macroeconomic consequences. In order for monetary rebalancing to be effected without causing widespread hardship, the government will have to engage fiscal levers to support employment and investment. The Biden Administration has put forward such a proposal in the form of the Build Back Better Act, a 10-year $3.5 trillion dollar programme to modernise America's infrastructure, provide for a transition to cleaner energy, increase investment in education, and provide greater support to working families. It is proposed that this would be funded by raising the corporate tax rate from 21 percent to 26 percent, increasing the top income tax rate for Americans earning over $400,000 per year from 37 percent to 39.6 percent, and upping the top capital gains tax rate from 20 percent to 25 percent. The effectiveness of Biden's proposal will hinge on the details of implementation. The tax increases, expected to yield an additional $2 trillion in government revenues over 10 years, may be insufficient. At the time of writing, not only does passage of the Act remain stalled, but Congress is mired in another self-defeating fight over extending the US debt ceiling.

Set against their respective domestic challenges, President Biden and President Xi held their first phone call in seven months on 9 September in a bid to 'ensure competition does not veer into conflict.'[24] Since that call, the US has dropped its case against the Huawei executive Meng Wanzhou, allowing her to return to China. In turn, China has released the two Canadians it had detained following her arrest. Offsetting this apparent progress, on 15 September, the US entered into the AUKUS security pact with the UK and Australia, under which the US and the UK will help Australia acquire nuclear submarines to counter Chinese influence in the Indo-Pacific region. Meanwhile, the PLA has pursued further moves to test Taiwan's air defences.[25]

Two decades after 9/11, the US finally withdrew from Afghanistan in August 2021. The 20-year occupation of the country not only sad-dled the US with enormous debts, but it also failed to make the world feel more secure, and the Taliban's rapid return to power has dealt the greatest blow to American prestige since its defeat in the Vietnam War. This should prompt serious reflection by both US and Chinese leaders on the slippery slope of military engagement in the name of 'just causes'.

Both China and America have serious challenges to address, neces-sitating deep reforms. However, it would be a grave mistake for their leaders to cast each other as strategic enemies in order to generate the momentum for those reforms. We must hope that they will pay heed to the lessons of history and avoid the catastrophic mistakes made by earlier generations. In meeting their own respective and common challenges, both countries have far more to gain from cooperation than through confrontation.

– James A. Fok
Hong Kong
4 October 2021

Cast of Characters

ADAMS, John Quincy (1767–1848). American statesman. Secretary of State, 1817–1825. President, 1825–1829.

ADVANI, Alokik (1978–). Banker and investor. Made the initial approach to HKEX on behalf of Tradeweb to partner on what became the Bond Connect programme.

AISIN GIORO Hongli (爱新觉罗 弘历) (Emperor Qianlong, 乾隆) (1711–1799). Fifth Qing emperor of China, 1735–1796. One of the longest-reigning monarchs in history. Expanded the empire significantly in Central Asia, but the latter years of his rule were marked by increasing corruption.

AISIN GIORO Mianning (爱新觉罗 绵宁) (Emperor Daoguang, 道光) (1782–1850). Seventh Qing emperor of China, 1820–1850. His Reign was confronted with China's growing opium problem.

AISIN GIORO Puyi (爱新觉罗 溥仪) (Emperor Xuantong, 宣统) (1906–1967). Last emperor of the Qing Dynasty, 1908–1912. Ascended to the throne aged two and forced to abdicate in 1912.

AISIN GIORO Yinzhen (爱新觉罗 胤禛) (Emperor Yongzheng, 雍正) (1678–1735). Fourth Qing emperor of China, 1722–1735. Father of Emperor Qianlong.

AISIN GIORO Yiwei (爱新觉罗 奕纬) (1808-31). Emperor Daoguang's eldest son and presumed heir. Believed to have been an opium addict.

AISIN GIORO Yixin (爱新觉罗 奕䜣, 'Prince Gong') (1833–1898). Manchu statesman and moderniser. Brother of Emperor Xianfeng. Regent to the Emperor Tongzhi, 1861–1865.

AISIN GIORO Yizhu (爱新觉罗 奕詝) (Emperor Xianfeng, 咸丰) (1831–1861). Seventh Qing emperor of China. His reign saw several domestic rebellions, including the Taiping Rebellion, as well as the Arrow War.

AISIN GIORO Yongyan (爱新觉罗 颙琰) (Emperor Jiaqing, 嘉庆) (1678–1735). Sixth Qing emperor of China, 1796–1820. Son of Emperor Qianlong.

AISIN GIORO Zaichun (爱新觉罗 载淳) (Emperor Tongzhi, 同治) (1856–1875). Eighth Qing emperor of China, 1861–1875. Overshadowed by his mother, Empress Dowager Cixi, he had little influence over state affairs.

AISIN GIORO Zaitian (爱新觉罗 载湉) (Emperor Guangxu, 光绪) (1871–1908). Ninth Qing emperor of China, 1875–1908. Initiated the Hundred Days' Reform but was foiled by a coup by Empress Dowager Cixi in 1898 and spent the rest of his reign under house arrest.

AL SAUD, Abdulaziz bin Abdul Rahman ('Ibn Saud') (1875–1953). Arab tribal leader who founded Saudi Arabia and ruled as its king until his death.

AL SAUD, Faisal bin Abdulaziz ('King Faisal') (1906–1975). King of Saudi Arabia, 1964–1975. Withdrew Saudi oil from world markets in protest at Western support for Israel during the 1973 Arab-Israeli War, sparking a sharp increase in oil prices. Later agreed to channel oil export surpluses into US Treasury bonds.

ALDER Ashley I. (1959–). English lawyer and regulator. CEO of Hong Kong's SFC since 2011. Chairman of the International Organisation of Securities Commissions since 2016.

ALEXANDER, Henry C. (1902–1969). American banker. Chairman of Morgan Guaranty, 1959–1967. Predicted that President Kennedy's IET would lead to a large-scale migration of dollar bond issuance to London.

AMHERST, Lord (William Pitt) (1773–1857). British diplomat and colonial administrator. Governor-general of India, 1823–1828. Appointed Ambassador Extraordinary to China in 1816 but failed to receive an audience due to disagreements over diplomatic protocol.

ANGELL, R. Norman (1872–1968). British author and Labour politician. Winner of the Nobel Peace Prize in 1933. Wrongly predicted before WW1 that tight economic integration meant that war between European nations would not occur.

BALDWIN, Stanley (1867–1947). British politician. Leader of the Conservative Party, 1923–1937. Prime Minister on three occasions: 1923–1924; 1924–1929; and 1935–1937.

BATTUTA, Ibn (1304–c.1369). Muslim Moroccan explorer. Visited most of southern Eurasia, leaving an account titled *A Gift to Those Who Contemplate the Wonders of Cities and the Marvels of Travelling*.

BAYH, Birch Evans ('Evan') (1955–). American politician. Democratic Senator for Indiana, 1999–2011. Governor of Indiana, 1989–1997. Criticised the dysfunctional state of US politics when he resigned from the Senate.

BERNANKE, Ben S. (1953–). American economist. Chairman of the Federal Reserve, 2006–2014. Pioneered extraordinary monetary measures to rescue the US economy in the wake of the 2008 Global Financial Crisis.

BERNARD, Andrew T.C. (1962–). English financial executive. Head of Tradeweb Asia, 2014–2017. Steered Tradeweb to work with HKEX to create the Bond Connect programme.

BIDEN Jr., Joseph R. ('Joe') (1942–). American politician. Democratic Senator for Delaware, 1973–2009. Vice President, 2009–2017. President since 2021.

BIN LADEN, Osama (1957–2011). Radical Islamic terrorist. Born into a wealthy Saudi Arabian family, founded Al Qaeda, which launched the 11 September 2001 attacks on the US.

BLAIR, Anthony C.L. ('Tony') (1953–). British Prime Minister, 1997–2007. Under his leadership, the Labour Party moved away from hard-left socialism to a more centrist political agenda.

BOTERO, Giovanni (c.1544–1617). Italian priest, philosopher, and diplomat. His thinking on the political economy set out clear circumstances in which the state should be involved in commercial enterprise.

BUFFETT, Warren E. (1930–). American businessman. Chairman of Berkshire Hathaway and widely considered to be one of the most successful investors in the world.

BURNS, Arthur F. (1904–1987). American economist. Chairman of the Federal Reserve, 1970–1978. Had a reputation for being overly influenced by political pressure in his monetary policy decisions.

BUSH, George H.W. (1924–2018). US President, 1989–1993. Steered the US diplomatic response following the 1989 Tiananmen Square incident. Assembled the international coalition that repelled Iraqi forces from Kuwait in the 1991 Gulf War.

BUSH, George W. (1946–). US President, 2001–2009. Son of President George H.W. Bush. Launched America's War on Terror in the aftermath of the 9/11 terrorist attacks.

BÜNDCHEN, Gisele C. (1980–). Brazilian model. Famously requested for her fees to be paid in euros instead of dollars in 2007.

CAMDESSUS, Michel (1933–). French economist. Governor of the Banque de France, 1984–1987. Managing Director of the IMF, 1987–2000. Oversaw the controversial IMF response to the 1997 Asian Financial Crisis.

CARTER Jr., James E. ('Jimmy') (1924–). US President, 1977–1981. His presidency was marred by a host of foreign policy and domestic challenges. In response to Soviet aggression in Afghanistan, he articulated clearly that the US would use military force to defend its interests in the Persian Gulf.

CARVILLE Jr., (Chester) James (1944–). American political consultant. Lead strategist behind Bill Clinton's successful 1992 presidential campaign.

CHA, Laura M. (史美伦) (1949–). Hong Kong regulator and politician. Deputy Chairman of the SFC, 1998–2001. Vice Chairman of the CSRC, 2001–2004. Member of the Executive Council of the Hong Kong Special Administrative Region since 2004. Chairman of HKEX since 2018.

CHEN Yun (陈云) (1905–1995). Chinese Communist revolutionary and political leader. Second most powerful person in the CCP after Deng Xiaoping in the 1980s and 1990s. Regarded as conservative, he often tempered the pace of economic and political reforms.

CHENEY, Richard B. ('Dick') (1941). American politician and businessman. White House Chief of Staff, 1975–1977. Secretary of Defence, 1989–1993. Chairman and CEO of oil services company Halliburton, 1995–2000. Vice President, 2001–2109. Key decision maker behind US decision to invade Iraq in 2003.

CHENG Ho-ming (郑可明) (c.1943–). Hong Kong businessman. Chairman of East Asia Holdings Limited. One of the early Hong Kong entrepreneurs to set up manufacturing operations in Shenzhen.

CHIANG Ching-kuo (蒋经国) (1910–1988). Taiwanese politician. The only biological son of Chiang Kai-shek. President of the Republic of China, 1978–1988. Under his tenure, Taiwan began to pursue gradual political liberalisation.

CHIANG Kai-shek (蒋介石) (1887–1975). Chinese Nationalist politician and military leader. Leader of the Republic of China, 1928–1975. Defeated by the Communists in the civil war, his government retreated to Taiwan in 1949.

CHURCHILL, Winston (1874–1965). British statesman. Chancellor of the Exchequer, 1924–1929; Prime Minister, 1940–1945 and 1951–1955. Returned sterling to the gold standard in 1925.

CI'AN (慈安, Empress Dowager) (1837–1881). Shared power as Regent during the reign of Emperor Tongzhi and Emperor Guangxu but focused on family affairs and seldom intervened in politics.

CIXI (慈禧, Empress Dowager) (1835–1908). Mother of Emperor Tongzhi. Effectively controlled the Qing government from 1861 until her death.

CLÉMENCEAU, Georges (1841–1929). French statesman. Prime Minister, 1906–1909 and 1917–1920. One of the key figures at the Paris Peace Conference in 1919, where the terms ending WW1 were negotiated.

CLINTON, Hillary D.R. (1947–). American politician and diplomat. Secretary of State, 2009–2013. Senator for New York, 2001–2009. Democratic presidential candidate who ran against Donald Trump in 2016. Wife of Bill Clinton.

CLINTON, William J. ('Bill') (1946–). US President, 1993–2001. His administration led the negotiations that brought China into the WTO.

CLIVE, Robert (1725–1774). First British Governor of Bengal. Credited for laying the foundations of the British Empire in India.

COLUMBUS, Christopher (1451–1506). Italian explorer and navigator. His voyage in 1492 to seek a westward sea passage to the East Indies led to the European discovery of the Americas.

CONFUCIUS (孔子) (551–479 BC). Chinese philosopher of the Spring and Autumn period. His teachings, which emphasised social morality and filial piety, underpin Chinese traditional beliefs and remain highly influential across East Asia today.

CONNALLY Jr., John B. (1917–1993). American statesman Secretary of the Navy, 1961. Governor of Texas, 1963-69. Secretary of the Treasury, 1971–1972. Presided over the suspension of the US dollar's convertibility to gold in 1971.

COOK, Robert F. ('Robin') (1946–2005). British Labour Party politician. Secretary of State, 1997-2001). Leader of the House of Commons, 2001–2003. Resigned from the Cabinet in protest at the government's decision to commit troops to the US-led invasion of Iraq in 2003.

COWPERTHWAITE, John J. (1915–2006). British civil servant. Financial Secretary of Hong Kong, 1961–1971. Strongly advocated free market economic policies in Hong Kong.

CRABBE, George (1754–1832). English poet, surgeon, and clergyman. First prescribed opium in 1790 to relieve pain, he continued to use it for the rest of his life.

CUOMO, Andrew M. (1957–). American politician. Governor of New York, 2011–2021. Received national attention for his handling of the Covid-19 pandemic in New York.

DE GAULLE, Charles (1890–1970). French military officer and statesman. Prime Minister, 1958–1959. President, 1959–1969. Led the Free French forces during WW2 and founded the French Fifth Republic. He was a fierce critic of the dollar's central position in the world economy.

DE QUINCEY, Thomas (1785–1859). British writer and romantic poet. Best known for his work *Confessions of an English Opium-Eater.*

DENG Pufang (邓朴方) (1944–). Deng Xiaoping's eldest son. He was left a paraplegic after being injured by Red Guards during the Cultural Revolution.

DENG Xiaoping (邓小平) (1904–1997). Chinese revolutionary and statesman. As paramount leader from 1978 until 1989, steered the PRC on a path of economic modernisation.

DENG Zhifang (邓质方) (1951–). Chinese businessman. Deng Xiaoping's youngest son. Studied in the US in the 1980s, obtaining a doctorate degree in quantum physics.

DIAS, Bartolomeu (c.1450–1500). Portuguese mariner and explorer. First European navigator to round the southern tip of Africa, establishing the sea route between Europe and Asia.

DICAPRIO, Leonardo W. (1974–). American actor. Among many memorable roles, played Frank Abagnale in Steven Spielberg's biographical crime drama *Catch Me If You Can.*

DRAGHI, Mario (1947–). Italian economist, central banker and politician. Governor of the Bank of Italy, 2006–2011. President of the European Central Bank, 2011–2019. Italian Prime Minister since 2021. Credited with steering Europe out of the euro crisis in 2012.

DU PLESSIS, Armand Jean (Cardinal de Richelieu) (1585–1642). French clergyman and statesman. First Minister of State, 1624–1642. An astute practitioner of power politics in foreign policy.

EDWARD I (King of England) (1239–1307). Reigned from 1272 until 1307. Best known for colonising Wales and his conflict with the Scots. Met with Rabban Sawma in 1288.

EISENHOWER, Dwight D. (1890–1969). American military officer and politician. US President, 1953–1961. Presciently warned Americans against the risk of the country's growing military-industrial complex.

ELGIN, Lord (James Bruce) (1811–1863). British colonial administrator and diplomat. As High Commissioner and Plenipotentiary in China between 1857 and 1861, it was he who ordered the sacking of the Summer Palace in Beijing in 1860.

ELLIOT, Charles (1801–1875). British naval officer and colonial administrator. Chief Superintendent of British Trade in China, 1836–1841. Most senior British official in China at the outbreak of the Opium War.

ENGELS, Friedrich (1820–1895). German political theorist and revolutionary socialist. Co-authored *The Communist Manifesto* with Karl Marx, which whom he developed what is now known as Marxism.

FAMA, Eugene F. (1939–). American economist and Nobel laureate. Professor of Finance at the University of Chicago, best known for his work on portfolio theory, asset pricing and the efficient-market hypothesis.

FERDINAND II of Aragon (1452–1516). Together with his wife, Isabella I of Castile, ruled over a dynastically unified Spain. Financed Christopher Columbus' 1492 voyage that discovered the Americas.

FISCHER, Robert J. ('Bobby') (1943–2008). American chess grandmaster. Became the 11th World Chess Champion in 1972 after beating Boris Spassky of the USSR.

FORRESTAL, James V. (1892–1949). American financier and politician. Under Secretary of the Navy, 1940–1944. Secretary of the Navy, 1944–1947. Secretary of Defence, 1947–1949.

FRANZ FERDINAND, Archduke of Austria (1863–1914). His assassination in Sarajevo sparked the chain of events that led to WW1.

FRASER, Ian (1923–2003). British merchant banker. One of the small group of bankers at S.G. Warburg who completed the first ever Eurobond issue in 1963.

FRIEDMAN, Milton (1912–2006). American economist. Renowned for his monetary economic theories, he was a vocal supporter of floating exchange rates and an influential force behind America's turn towards monetarist policies in the late 1970s.

FU Hao (傅浩, 'Harry') (1971–). Chinese financial executive. Head of the Global Business Development Department of the SSE. A key architect of the Shanghai-Hong Kong Stock Connect programme.

GALBRAITH, John Kenneth (1908–2006). Canadian-American economist, diplomat and public official. Active in Democratic Party politics. US Ambassador to India, 1961–1963.

GAO Jian (高坚) (1949–). Chinese financial official. Introduced the Dutch auction mechanism in Chinese government bond syndications.

GEITHNER, Timothy F. ('Tim'). American financial official. President of Federal Reserve Bank of New York 2003–2009. Secretary of the Treasury 2009–2013. A key figure in formulating the US policy response to the 2008 GFC.

GISCARD D'ESTAING, Valéry (1924–2020). French politician. Minister of Economy and Finance, 1962–1966 and 1969–1974. President, 1974–1981. Famously coined the term 'exorbitant privilege' to characterise US dollar hegemony under the Bretton Woods system.

GORBACHEV, Mikhail (1931–). Soviet Communist Party leader and statesman. General Secretary of the Communist Party, 1985–1991. Last president of the USSR, 1990–1991. Pursued political liberalisation and economic modernisation in the Soviet Union.

GRANT, Duncan (1885–1978). British painter and designer. Member of the Bloomsbury Set of writers and artists, and a one-time lover of John Maynard Keynes.

GRASSLEY, Charles E. (1939–). American politician. Republican Senator for Iowa since 1981. Chair of the Senate Finance Committee, 2001; 2003–2007; and 2019–2021.

GREENSPAN, Alan (1926–). American economist. Chairman of the Federal Reserve, 1987–2006. Some consider that the 'easy-money' policies pursued by the Fed under him contributed to both the late 1990s Dot-com bubble and the 2008 subprime mortgage bubble.

GUI Minjie (桂敏杰) (1953–). Chinese financial official. Chairman of the SSE, 2012–2016. Made the initial approach to HKEX to set up Shanghai-Hong Kong Stock Connect.

GUO Guangchang (郭广昌) (1967–). Chinese businessman. Chairman and co-founder of Fosun International Limited.

GUO Shuqing (郭树清) (1956–). Chinese banker, financial regulator, and politician. Chairman of the CSRC, 2011–2013. Governor of Shandong, 2013–2017. Chairman of the China Banking Regulatory Commission, 2017–2018. Chairman of the China Banking and Insurance Regulatory Commission since 2018.

GYATSO, Tenzin (14th Dalai Lama) (1935–). Spiritual leader of Tibet. Established the Tibetan government in exile in India after fleeing Chinese-controlled Tibet in 1959.

HAMILTON, Alexander (1755–1804). American revolutionary and statesman. First Secretary of the Treasury, 1789–1795.

HAMMURABI (c.1810–1750 BC). Sixth king of the First Babylonian Dynasty, reigning from 1792 until 1750 BC. Best known for having issued the Code of Hammurabi, an influential early code of laws.

HANKS, Thomas J. ('Tom') (1956–). American actor and two-time Academy Award winner. Played Agent Hanratty in Steven Spielberg's *Catch Me If You Can*.

HART, Robert (1835–1911). British diplomat and official in the Qing government. Inspector-General of China's Imperial Maritime Customs Service, 1863–1911.

HOBBES, Thomas (1588–1679). English philosopher. Best known for his 1651 book *Leviathan*, which expounds on the theory of the social contract between the state and its citizens.

HOBSBAWM, Eric J.E. (1917–2012). British Marxist historian. Served as President of Birkbeck College of the University of London from 2002 until his death.

HONG, Xiuquan (洪秀全) (1814–1864). Chinese revolutionary. Led the Taiping Rebellion, a Christian-inspired movement, which occupied significant parts of southern China in the mid-1800s, establishing an alternative capital in Nanjing.

HU Jintao (胡锦涛) (1942–). Chinese politician. General Secretary of the CCP, 2002–2012. President, 2003–2013.

HU Yaobang (胡耀邦) (1915–1989). Chinese politician and reformer. Chairman / General Secretary of the CCP, 1981–1987. His death sparked the 1989 student movement.

HUA Guofeng (华国锋) (1921–2008). Chinese politician. Premier, 1976–1980. Chairman of the CCP, 1976–1981. Chairman Mao's chosen successor. Took the first step on China's path to reform when he arrested and prosecuted the Gang of Four.

HUANG Ju (黄菊) (1938–2007). Chinese politician. First Vice Premier, 2003–2007. A *protégé* of Jiang Zemin who held responsibility for the financial sector. When he was forced to step aside in 2005 due to ill health, the PBOC lost a key supporter for further banking reforms.

HUANG Yongsheng (黄永胜) (1910–1983). Chinese military officer. PLA General, 1955–1971. Served as Chief of Staff to Defence Minister Lin Biao during the Cultural Revolution. Proposed invading Hong Kong during the 1967 pro-Communist riots.

HUSSEIN, Saddam (1937–2006). Iraqi dictator. President, 1979–2003. Ordered the invasion of Kuwait in 1990, sparking the Gulf War. Toppled by the US invasion of Iraq in 2003.

HWANG, Sung Kook ('Bill') (1964–). Korean-born New York-based investor. Came to public prominence when his family office, Archegos Capital Management, reportedly lost $20 billion over 10 days in March 2021.

ISABELLA I of Castile (1451–1504). Together with her husband, Ferdinand II of Aragon, ruled over a dynastically unified Spain. Financed Christopher Columbus' 1492 voyage that discovered the Americas.

JARDINE, William (1784–1843). Scottish physician and merchant. Co-founded the trading conglomerate Jardine Matheson, which played a leading role in the opium trade in China.

JIANG Qing (江青) (1914–1991). Chairman Mao's third wife. Major political figure during the Cultural Revolution and a member of the radical group known as the 'Gang of Four'.

JIANG Zemin (江泽民) (1926–). Chinese politician. General Secretary of the CCP, 1989–2002. President, 1993–2003. Emerged as the compromise candidate to lead the country after the Tiananmen incident. Continuing market reforms under him saw China achieve rapid economic growth.

JOHNSON, Lyndon B. (1908–1973). US President, 1963–1969. Expanded American social welfare provision under his Great Society programme. Also responsible for the escalation of US involvement in the Vietnam conflict in the 1960s.

JUNCKER, Jean-Claude (1954–). Luxembourgish politician. Minister for Finance, 1989–2009. Prime Minister, 1995–2013. President of the European Commission, 2014–2019.

KENNAN, George F. (1904–2005). American diplomat. Key architect of America's Cold War containment strategy towards the USSR.

KENNEDY, Edward M. ('Ted') (1932–2009). American politician. Younger brother of President John F. Kennedy. Served as a Democratic Senator for Massachusetts for 47 years. His death in 2009 deprived the Obama Administration of a Democratic majority in Congress.

KENNEDY, John F. (1917–1963). US President, 1961–1963. His administration faced the challenges of heightened Cold War tensions and rising capital outflows. Launched the Apollo space programme and the IET.

KEYNES, John Maynard (1883–1946). British economist. Advocated greater government intervention in the economy. Led the British delegation at Bretton Woods and originally opposed putting the dollar at the centre of the global monetary system.

KHOMEINI, Sayyid Ruhollah Musavi (Khomeini Ayatollah) (1900–1989). Iranian political and religious leader. Founded the Islamic Republic of Iran after overthrowing the Shah in 1979.

KHRUSHCHEV, Nikita S. (1894–1971). Soviet politician. First Secretary of the Soviet Communist Party, 1953–1964. His denouncement of policies Stalin's policies after his death contributed to the souring of Sino-Soviet relations.

KISSINGER, Henry A. (1923–). American statesman. National Security Advisor, 1969–1975. Secretary of State, 1973–1977. His 1971 secret visit to China to meet with Zhou Enlai kicked off the process of Sino-US rapprochement.

KRAUTHAMMER, Charles (1950–2018). American political columnist. His essay 'The Unipolar Moment', published shortly after the fall of the Berlin Wall, defined the US role as the sole superpower after the USSR's collapse.

KRUGMAN, Paul (1953–). American economist. Awarded a Nobel Prize in 2008 for his contributions to New Trade Theory, Neo-inflationism and New Economic Geography.

KUNG Hsiang-hsi (孔祥熙, 'H.H.') (1881–1967). Chinese banker and Nationalist politician. Premier of the Republic of China, 1938–1939. Vice Premier of the Republic of China, 1939–1945. China's representative at Bretton Woods. Brother-in-law of Chiang Kai-shek.

LAI Chee-Ying (黎智英, 'Jimmy') (1947–). Hong Kong media tycoon and political activist. Founder of Next Digital and the popular newspaper *Apple Daily*.

LAM, Carrie (林郑月娥) (1957–). Hong Kong public servant and politician. Secretary for Development, 2007–2012. Chief Secretary for Administration, 2012–2017. Chief Executive of Hong Kong since 2017.

LAW, John (1671–1729). Scottish financier. Minister of Finance for France, 1720. His financial dealings inflated the Mississippi Bubble and ultimately led to the financial crippling of the French state.

LE CARRÉ, John (David John Moore Cornwell) (1931–2020). British author best known for his Cold War era espionage novels.

LEE Kuan Yew (李光耀) (1923–2015). Singaporean statesman, recognised as the nation's founding father. Prime Minister, 1959–1990.

LEE Teng-hui (李登辉) (1923–2020). First democratically elected leader of the Republic of China (Taiwan). President, 1988–2000.

LEE, Charles Y.K. (李业广) (1936–). Hong Kong lawyer and politician. SEHK Chairman, 1999–2006.

LEUNG, Francis (梁伯韬) (1955–). Hong Kong investment banker. Credited as the father of red chip shares.

LI Guixian (李贵鲜) (1937–). Chinese politician and central banker. Governor of the PBOC, 1988–93.

LI Hongzhang (李鸿章) (1823–1901). Chinese military officer and statesman. Played important roles in supressing the Taiping Rebellion and in the Self-strengthening Movement. A controversial figure due to his role in negotiating China's unequal treaties.

LI Keqiang (李克强) (1955–). Chinese politician. Rose through the ranks via the Communist Youth League. Premier of China since 2013.

LI Peng (李鹏) (1928–2019). Chinese politician. Premier, 1988–1998. Closely associated with the Chinese government's handling of the 1989 Tiananmen Square incident.

LI, Shimin (李世民) (Emperor Taizong, 太宗) (598–649). Reigned as the second Tang Dynasty emperor from 626 until 649. Religiously open, he allowed the establishment of a Christian church in his capital.

LINCOLN, Abraham (1809–1865). American President, 1861–1865. Led the nation through the American Civil War, preserving the Union and abolishing slavery.

LIN, Zexu (林则徐) (1785–1850). Chinese scholar-official. Appointed Special Commissioner to Canton in 1839 to suppress the opium trade. Exiled in the wake of the Opium War.

LIU Hongru (刘鸿儒) (1930–). Chinese financial official. First Chairman of the CSRC, 1992-95.

LIU Shaoqi (刘少奇) (1898–1969). Chinese Communist revolutionary and politician. Chairman of the PRC, 1959–1968. Denounced and tortured to death during the Cultural Revolution.

LIU Xiaobo (刘晓波) (1955–2017). Chinese writer, human rights activist, and political dissident. Imprisoned for 'inciting subversion of state power' in 2009. Awarded the Nobel Peace Prize in 2010.

LLOYD GEORGE, David (1863–1945). British Liberal politician. Prime Minister, 1916–1922. As Chancellor of the Exchequer, introduced the redistributive 'People's Budget' in 1909 to fund new social welfare programmes. A leading figure of the 1919 Paris Peace Conference.

LOEVINGER, Lee (1913–2004). American jurist and public official. Attorney General of the Department of Justice Antitrust Division, 1961–1963. Commissioner of the FCC, 1963–1968.

LOUIS XV, King of France (1710–1774). His reign, from 1715 until 1774, is generally criticised by historians for corruption and financial mismanagement.

LOUIS XVI, King of France (1754–1793). Reigned from 1774 until 1792. Executed by guillotine following the French Revolution.

MA, Jack (马云) (1964–). Chinese business magnate. Co-founder of internet giant Alibaba Group.

MACARTNEY, Lord (George) (1737–1806). British statesman and diplomat. Led the first British diplomatic mission to be received by the Qing court in 1793.

MACHIAVELLI, Niccolò (1469–1527). Italian diplomat and philosopher. Best known for his political treatise *The Prince*.

MACMILLAN, Harold (1894–1986). British Conservative politician. Prime Minister, 1957–1963.

MAO Zedong (毛泽东) (1893–1976). Communist revolutionary and a founder of the PRC. Ruled China as Chairman of the CCP from 1949 until his death.

MARX, Karl H. (1818–1883). German political theorist and socialist revolutionary. Working with Friedrich Engels, he developed the political theory now known as Marxism.

MASTERS, Blythe (1969). British financial executive. At 28, became the youngest female Managing Director in JPMorgan's history. Credited with the creation of CDSs.

MATHESON, James N.S. (1796–1878). Scottish merchant. Co-founded the trading conglomerate Jardine Matheson, which played a leading role in the opium trade in China.

MCGOVERN, George S. (1922–2012). American politician. Democratic Senator for South Dakota, 1963–1981. He was the Democratic nominee for President in 1972, but lost to Richard Nixon.

MELAMED, Leo (1932–). American financial executive. Chairman of the CME since 1969. Drove CME's entry into the financial futures business in the 1970s.

MENCIUS (孟子) (c.371–289 BC). Chinese philosopher of the Warring States period. Further developed Confucian ideology. Teachings included the obligations of rulers to the masses.

MENG Wanzhou (孟晚舟) (1972–). Chinese businesswoman. Chief Financial Officer of telecoms giant Huawei. Arrested in Canada in 2018 at the request of US authorities and subjected to lengthy extradition proceedings.

MERTON, Robert C. (1944–). American economist and Nobel laureate. One of the creators of the Black-Scholes option pricing model, and a partner in the failed hedge fund LTCM.

MEYER Jr., John M. (1907–1996). American banker. Chairman of Morgan Guaranty, 1969-71. Negotiated the establishment of Euroclear and subsequently co-founded DTCC.

MILL, John Stuart (1806–1873). British philosopher, political economist and public servant. His views were highly influential on classic liberal thinking.

MILLER, G. William (1925–2006). American economist and central banker. Chairman of the Federal Reserve, 1978–1979. Secretary of the Treasury, 1979–1981.

MIZUTA Mikio (1905–1976). Japanese educator and politician. Founded Josai University in 1965. Served as Finance Minister at the time Richard Nixon suspended the dollar's fix to gold.

MOHAMAD, Mahathir (1925–). Malaysian statesman. Prime Minister, 1981–2003 and 2018–2020. Has, at various times, been critical of both US and Chinese policies in Southeast Asia.

MORGENTHAU Jr., Henry (1891–1967). Secretary of the Treasury, 1934–1945. Untrained in economics, he depended greatly on and became a powerful patron for Harry White.

NAKAMOTO, Satoshi (age unknown). Presumed pseudonym of the creator(s) of Bitcoin.

NASSER, Gamal Abdel (1918–1970). Egyptian revolutionary and moderniser. President, 1956-70. Anti-imperialist who supported decolonisation and pan-Arabism. His nationalisation of the Suez Canal in 1956 sparked the Suez Crisis.

NIXON, Richard M. (1913–1994). US President, 1969–1974. His presidency was marred by the Watergate scandal, but he left significant legacies in a number of areas. Notably, these included the abandonment of the dollar's fix to gold and US rapprochement with China.

NORMAN, Montagu C. (1871–1950). British banker. Governor of the Bank of England, 1920–1944. Strong advocate for returning sterling to the gold standard in the 1920s.

OBAMA, Barack H. (1961–). US President, 2009–2017. First African American elected to the White House. His time in office was heavily occupied with dealing with the aftermath of the 2008 GFC.

PALMERSTON, Lord (Henry John Temple) (1784–1865). British statesman. Secretary of State for Foreign Affairs, 1830–1834; 1835–1841; and 1846–1851. Prime Minister, 1855–1858 and 1859–1865. Dominant figure in British foreign policy from 1830 until 1865.

PAN Gongsheng (潘功胜) (1963–). Chinese financial official and reformer. Deputy Governor of the PBOC since 2012. A key figure behind the launch of the Bond Connect programme.

PARSONS, Maurice H. (1910–1978). British banker. Deputy Governor of the Bank of England, 1966–1970. Opposed restricting British banks from building up US dollar deposits in the 1950s.

PAULSON Jr., Henry M. ('Hank') (1946–). American banker and statesman. Chairman and CEO of Goldman Sachs, 1998–2006. Secretary of the Treasury, 2006–2009. A key figure in formulating the US policy response to the 2008 GFC.

PENG Dehuai (彭德怀) (1898–1974). Chinese Communist revolutionary and military commander. Minister of Defence, 1954–1959. Purged after criticising Chairman Mao's policies during the Great Leap Forward.

PEREIRA, Thomas (1645–1708). Portuguese Jesuit scientist who served at the Qing court. Acted as an interpreter during negotiations between the Qing Empire and Russia over the Treaty of Nerchinsk.

PERRY, Matthew C. (1794–1858). Commodore of the US Navy. Played a leading role in Japan's opening to the West.

PETROV, Stanislav (1939–2017). Soviet military officer. In charge of the Serpukhov-15 bunker during the 1983 nuclear false alarm incident, his cool head averted a US-Soviet nuclear war.

PHILIPPE II, Duc d'Orléans (1674–1723). French statesman. Regent during the minority of Louis XV. Countenanced the financial dealings of John Law, which led to the Mississippi Bubble.

PHILIPPE IV, King of France (1268–1314). Reigned 1285–1314. Received the first diplomatic mission from China to France.

PHILLIPS, A. William H. ('Bill') (1914–1975). New Zealand economist. Best known for the Phillips curve, which hypothesised an inverse relationship between the rates of wage increases and unemployment.

POLO, Marco (1254–1324). Venetian merchant and explorer. Best known for his account of Yuan Dynasty China.

POTTINGER, Henry (1789–1856). British military officer and colonial administrator. First colonial Governor of Hong Kong, 1843–1844.

PRELLER, Ludwig (1897–1974). German Social Democrat politician. Member of the Bundestag, 1951–1953.

PRINCIP, Gavrilo (1894–1918). Bosnian Serb nationalist. His assassination of Archduke Franz Ferdinand sparked the chain of events that led to WW1.

PUTIN, Vladimir V. (1952–). Russian politician. Prime Minister, 2008–2012. President, 1999–2008 and since 2012.

QIN Shi Huang (秦始皇) (259–210 BC). First emperor of the Qin Dynasty, who conquered all other Warring States to unify China.

QISHAN (琦善) (1786–1854). Mongolian nobleman and official of the Qing Dynasty. As governor-general of Zhili province, he was tasked with diplomatic negotiations with the British during the Opium War.

RANIERI, Lewis S. (1947–). Bond trader. Widely credited for having created the MBS market while at Salomon Brothers in the 1970s and 1980s.

RAZAK, Najib (1953–). Malaysian politician. Prime Minister, 2009–2018. Arrested in 2018 on suspicion of corruption in relation to the Malaysian public investment company 1MDB.

REAGAN, Ronald W. (1911–2004). American actor-turned-politician. US President, 1981–1989. Pursued low-tax and deregulatory policies to spur economic growth.

REN Zhengfei (任正非) (1944–). Chinese entrepreneur. Founder and CEO of the telecoms company Huawei.

RENÉ, Duc d'Anjou (1409–1480). Great grandson of Jean II of France. Reigned as King of Naples, 1435-42. Christopher Columbus served him during his attempt to conquer Naples.

RICCI, Matteo (1552–1610). Italian Jesuit priest. One of the first Europeans to be admitted to the Ming imperial court.

ROBERTSON Jr., Julian H. (1932–). American hedge fund manager. Founded Tiger Management, an early hedge fund, and invested in a number of funds run by former employees, known as the 'Tiger cubs'.

ROCKEFELLER, David (1915–2017). American banker. A grandson of John D. Rockefeller, he served as Chairman and CEO of the Chase Manhattan Corporation from 1969 until 1981.

ROCKEFELLER, John D. (1839–1937). American business magnate. Founder of the Standard Oil Company and widely considered to be the wealthiest Americans of all time.

ROOSEVELT Jr., Theodore ('Teddy') (1858–1919). US President, 1901–1909. Pursued an assertive agenda both internationally and domestically. Noted for his antitrust crackdown on US monopolies.

ROOSEVELT, Franklin D. (1882–1945). US President, 1933-45. Coming to power amidst the Great Depression, he implemented the New Deal programme of reforms and economic stimulus.

ROSS, Stanley D.L. (1930–2014). British bond trader. One of the pioneers of the Eurobond market.

RUBIN, Robert E. (1938–). American investment banker and government official. Chairman of Goldman Sachs, 1990–1993. Secretary of the Treasury, 1995–1999.

RUMSFELD, Donald H. (1932–2021). American government official. Ambassador to NATO, 1973–1974. White House Chief of Staff, 1974–1975. Secretary of Defence, 1975–1977 and 2001–2006.

SAMUELSON, Paul A. (1915–2009). American economist and Nobel laureate. A founder of neo-Keynesian economics and a major contributor to the development of neoclassical economics.

SANTELLI, Rick J. (1956–). American financial reporter. His broadcast from the CME on 19 February 2009 is widely considered to have been a catalyst for the Tea Party movement.

SATŌ Eisaku (1901–1975). Japanese politician. Prime Minister, 1964–1972. Presided over a period of rapid Japanese economic growth. His government was shaken by Nixon's suspension of the dollar's fix to gold and by Kissinger's secret visit to China.

SAWMA, Rabban (c.1220–1294). Diplomat of the Nestorian Church of East in China. Led the first diplomatic mission from China to Europe in 1287.

SCHOLES, Myron S. (1941–). Canadian American economist and Nobel laureate. One of the creators of the Black-Scholes option pricing model, and a co-founder of the failed hedge fund LTCM.

SCHUMPETER, Joseph A. (1883–1950). Austrian political economist. Popularised the term 'creative destruction'.

SCHWAB, Klaus M. (1938–). German engineer and economist. Founder and executive chairman of the World Economic Forum.

SCHWARTZ, Anna (1915–2012). American economist. Co-author (with Milton Friedman) of *A Monetary History of the United States, 1867–1960*.

SEIDMAN, L. William ('Bill') (1921–2009). American economist and public official. Advisor to three presidential administrations. Chair of the FDIC, 1985–1991.

SIMON, William E. (1927–2000). American investment banker and public official. Director of the Federal Energy Office, 1973–1974. Secretary of the Treasury, 1974–1977. Brokered the deal for Saudi Arabia to purchase US Treasuries with its oil surpluses.

SONG Jian (宋健) (1931–). Chinese scientist and politician. Director of the State Science and Technology Commission, 1985–1898. State Councillor, 1986–1998. His demographic projections in the 1970s led to China's one child policy.

SOONG Ching-ling (宋庆龄) (1893–1981). Chinese political figure. Sun Yat-sen's American-educated wife, she was also sister-in-law to Chiang Kai-shek. Became a strong supporter of the CCP.

SOONG May-ling (宋美龄) (1898–2003). Chinese political figure. Wife of Chiang Kai-shek, she played a prominent role in the politics of the Republic of China.

SOONG Tse-vung (宋子文, 'T.V.') (1894–1971). Chinese businessman and Nationalist politician. Brother-in-law to Sun Yat-sen and Chiang Kai-shek, he served in a succession of high offices in Chiang's government.

SOROS, George (1930–). Hungarian-born American billionaire investor and philanthropist. Founder of Soros Fund Management, most famous for 'breaking the Bank of England' when he made over $1 billion in profits during the 1992 sterling crisis that led to the UK's withdrawal from the European Exchange Rate Mechanism.

SŌSUKE Uno (1922–1998). Japanese politician. Minister of International Trade and Industry, 1983. Minister for Foreign Affairs, 1987–1989. Prime Minister, 1989. Along with President George H.W. Bush, urged moderation in international sanctions on China after the Tiananmen incident.

SPASSKY, Boris V. (1937–). Russian chess player. World Chess Champion, 1969–1972. Lost the title to Bobby Fischer in 1972.

SPIELBERG, Steven A. (1946–). American movie director, producer, and screenwriter. Holds two Academy Awards for Best Director.

STALIN, Joseph V. (1878–1953). Soviet revolutionary and political leader. Governed the USSR from 1924 until 1953. Supported the CCP into power but pursued a realist approach towards relations with China.

SUGIHARA Chiune (1900–1986). Japanese diplomat. Stationed as vice-consul in Lithuania during WW2, he risked his career to help thousands of Jews flee Europe by issuing them with Japanese transit visas.

SUHARTO (1921–2008). Indonesian military officer and politician. President, 1967–1998. His government was toppled by social unrest sparked by the Asian Financial Crisis.

SUN Yat-sen (孙中山) (1866–1925). Chinese revolutionary and statesman. First provisional president of the Republic of China and founder of the Nationalist Party.

TAYLOR COLERIDGE, Samuel (1772–1834). English poet, literary critic, philosopher, and theologian. One of the founders of the Romantic Movement in England, he had lifelong addiction to opium.

THATCHER, Margaret H. (1925–2013). British politician. Prime Minister, 1979–1990. Her government emphasised deregulation and low taxes and pursued a wide-ranging privatisation programme.

THORP, Edward O. (1932–). American mathematics professor and hedge fund manager. His book *Beat the Dealer* used probability theory to show how blackjack players could beat the house. He later turned his skills to the fund management industry.

TRENCH, David C.C. (1915–1988). British military officer and colonial official. Governor of Hong Kong 1964–1971. Introduced social reforms after the 1967 pro-Communist riots.

TRIFFIN, B. Robert (1911–1993). Belgian American economist. Best known for his critique of the Bretton Woods system, known as the Triffin Dilemma.

TUNG Chee-hwa (董建华) (1937–). Hong Kong businessman and politician. First post-colonial Chief Executive of Hong Kong. His administration was confronted with the Asian Financial Crisis and the SARS epidemic.

VINER, Jacob (1892–1970). Canadian economist and a leading figure of the Chicago school. It was he who first invited Harry White to Washington DC. He later presciently foresaw the problems of the dollar-centric Bretton Woods system.

VOLCKER Jr., Paul A. (1927–2019). American economist and public servant. Chairman of the Federal Reserve, 1979–1987. His tight monetary policies tamed US inflation, but contributed to the LDC crisis.

VON BISMARCK, Otto (1815–1898). German statesman. Chancellor, 1871–1890. A shrewd diplomat, he cooperated with Wilhelm I of Prussia to unify the various German states.

WANG Qishan (王岐山) (1948–). Chinese politician. A seasoned veteran of China's financial and economic reforms, he served as Secretary of the Central Commission for Discipline Inspection, 2012–2017. Vice President since 2018.

WARBURG, Felix M. (1871–1937). German-born American banker. A member of the Warburg banking dynasty, he worked as a partner at the Wall Street firm Kuhn, Loeb & Co.

WARBURG, Paul M. (1868–1932). German-born American banker. A partner of the Wall Street firm Kuhn, Loeb & Co., he was influential behind the establishment of the Federal Reserve and served on the Fed's Board of Governors from 1914 to 1918.

WARBURG, Siegmund G. (1902–1982). German-born British banker. A member of the Warburg banking dynasty, his firm pioneered the issuance of Eurobonds in London.

WHITE, Harry D. (1892–1948). US Treasury department official. He was the key architect behind the Bretton Woods system.

WILSON, T. Woodrow (1856–1924). US President, 1913–1921. A progressive on matters of foreign policy, he was the leading architect of the League of Nations.

WOOLF, Leonard S. (1880–1969). British intellectual and civil servant. Husband of Virginia Woolf, he was a member of the Bloomsbury Set to which Maynard Keynes belonged.

WOOLF, Virginia (1882–1941). British author. Member of the Bloomsbury Set to which Maynard Keynes belonged.

WRISTON, Walter B. (1919–2005). American banker. Chairman and CEO of Citibank / Citicorp, 1967–1984.

XI Jinping (习近平) (1953–). President of the PRC since 2013. Has led a more assertive foreign policy and cracked down on domestic corruption.

XI Zhongxun (习仲勋) (1913–2002). Chinese Communist revolutionary and politician. Vice Chairman of the Standing Committee of the NPC, 1980–1983. Secretary General of the State Council, 1954–1965. Father of President Xi Jinping. Advocated decentralisation of economic decision making in Guangdong in 1979.

XIAO Gang (肖钢) (1958–). Chinese financial official. CSRC Chairman, 2013–2016. Stepped down from the CSRC following the 2015 Chinese stock market crash.

XIAO Jianhua (肖建华) (c.1972–). Chinese Canadian businessman. Reported to have been abducted by Mainland Chinese agents from Hong Kong's Four Seasons Hotel in 2017.

XU Caihou (徐才厚) (1943–2015). Chinese military officer. Vice Chairman of the Central Military Commission, 2005–2013. One of the highest profile PLA officers to be prosecuted for corruption under President Xi Jinping.

XU Jiatun (许家屯) (1916–2016). Chinese politician. Director of the *Xinhua* News Agency in Hong Kong, China's *de facto* representative office in the territory before 1997. Lived in exile in the US after sympathising with student protesters in 1989.

XUANZANG (玄奘) (602–664). Chinese Buddhist monk and traveller. Undertook a 17-year overland journey to India and translated key Buddhist texts from Sanskrit to Chinese.

YASSUKOVITCH, Stanislas M. (1935–). Paris-born American banker. Partner of White, Weld & Co., 1969–1973. Chief Executive of the European Banking

Group, 1983–1985. Chairman of Merrill Lynch Europe, 1985–1989. A key pioneer of the Eurobond market.

YELLEN, Janet L. (1946–). American economist and public servant. Chair of the Federal Reserve, 2014–2018. Secretary of the Treasury since 2021.

YELTSIN, Boris N. (1931–2007). First post-Soviet president of Russia, in office from 1991 until 1999.

YI Gang (易纲) (1958–). Chinese financial official. Deputy Governor of the PBOC, 2007–2018. Governor of the PBOC since 2018. Echoed his predecessor in calling for an expanded role for the IMF'S SDRs in 2020.

YUAN Shikai (袁世凯) (1859–1916). Chinese military and government official. Negotiated the abdication of Emperor Xuantong. President of the Republic of China, 1912–2015. Precipitated the splitting of the country when he declared himself emperor in 1915.

ZHAO Ziyang (赵紫阳) (1919–2005). Chinese politician and reformer. Premier, 1980–1987; General Secretary of the CCP, 1987–1989.

ZHENG He (郑和) (1371–1435). Chinese mariner and court eunuch. Commanded the Ming Dynasty treasure fleet, which visited as far as East Africa and the Gulf of Hormuz in the early 1400s.

ZHOU Enlai (周恩来) (1898–1976). Chinese Communist revolutionary and politician. Premier, 1949–1976. One of few top officials not to have been purged during the Cultural Revolution, his secret meeting with Henry Kissinger in 1971 kick-started Sino-US rapprochement.

ZHOU Xiaochuan (周小川) (1948–). Chinese financial official and reformer. CSRC Chairman, 2000–2002. Governor of the PBOC, 2002–2018. One of the major figures behind China's banking and financial market reforms.

ZHOU Yongkang (周永康) (1942–). Chinese politician. Minister of Land and Resources, 1998–2099. Party Secretary of Sichuan Province, 2000–2002. Minister of Public Security, 2002–2007. Secretary of the Central Political and Legal Affairs Commission, 2007–2012. The most senior Chinese official to have been convicted in President Xi's anti-corruption campaign.

ZHU Di (朱棣) (Emperor Yongle, 永乐) (1360–1424). Third emperor of the Ming Dynasty, 1402–1424. He ordered the construction of the Forbidden City and China's treasure fleet.

ZHU Rongji (朱镕基) (1928–). Chinese politician and reformer. Vice Premier, 1993–1998. Premier, 1998–2003. A key figure behind China's economic reforms in the 1990s and entry into the WTO in 2001.

ZHU Yijun (朱翊钧) (Emperor Wanli, 万历) (1563–1620). Reigned as 14th emperor of the Ming Dynasty, 1572–1620. Welcomed the Jesuit missionary Matteo Ricci into his court.

ZHU Yuanzhang (朱元璋) (Emperor Hongwu, 洪武) (1328–1398). Founder of the Ming Dynasty, who reigned from 1368 to 1398.

ZHU Yunwen (朱允文) (Emperor Jianwen, 建文) (1377–1402). Second emperor of the Ming Dynasty, 1398–1402. He was overthrown in a coup by his uncle, who became Emperor Yongle.

Bibliography

Abrams, M. H. (1971). The Milk of Paradise: The Effect of Opium Visions on the Words of DeQuincey, Crabbe, Francis Thompson and Coleridge. New York: Octagon Books.

Acemoglu, D., & Robinson, J. A. (2012). Why Nations Fail: The Origins of Power, Prosperity and Poverty. New York: Crown Business.

Adler, D., & Arauz, A. (2020, 23 March). It's Time to End the Fed's 'Monetary Triage'. Retrieved July 2021, from The Nation: https://www.thenation.com/article/economy/economy-fed-imf/

Ahamed, L. (2009). Lords of Finance: The Bankers Who Broke the World. New York: Penguin.

Allison, G. (2017). Destined For War: Can America and China Escape Thucydides's Trap? New York: Houghton Mifflin Harcourt.

Allison, G., & Blackwill, R. D. (2013). Lee Kuan Yew: The Grand Master's Insights on China, the United States and the World. Cambridge, MA: MIT Press.

Appelbaum, B. (2019). The Economists' Hour: How the False Prophets of Free Markets Fractured Our Society. London: Picador.

Appelbaum, B., & Hershey Jr., R. D. (2019, 10 December). Paul A. Volcker, a Stolid Crusader Against Inflation, Is Dead at 92. New York Times, p. 28.

Apple Daily. (2020, 8 November). Wang Qishan's speech at the Bund Summit 2020 in Shanghai. Retrieved January 2021, from Apple Daily: https://hk.appledaily.com/opinion/20201108/YHH7LSBH35AQFHCXBNBQ4KPNUY/

Areddy, J. T. (2021, 5 April). China Creates Its Own Digital Currency, a First for Major Economy. Retrieved May 2021, from Wall Street Journal: https://www.wsj.com/articles/china-creates-its-own-digital-currency-a-first-for-major-economy-11617634118

Arnold, C. (2020, July 10). Pandemic speeds largest test yet of universal basic income. Retrieved September 2021, from Nature: https://www.nature.com/articles/d41586-020-01993-3

Asia Asset Management. (2015, 17 November). CSRC vice chairman detained under suspicion of corruption. Retrieved December 2020, from Asia Asset Management: https://www.asiaasset.com/post/5789-csrcvc-ch1611

Ax, J., Viswanatha, A., & Nikolaeva, M. (2014, 1 July). U.S. imposes record fine on BNP in sanctions warning to banks. Retrieved May 2021, from Reuters: https://www.reuters.com/article/us-bnp-paribas-settlement-idUSKBN0F52HA20140701

BBC. (2020, 1 May). Coronavirus: Trump stands by China lab origin theory for virus. Retrieved August 2020, from BBC News: https://www.bbc.com/news/world-us-canada-52496098

BIS. (2021). CBDCs: an opportunity for the monetary system. BIS Annual Economic Report, 65-95.

Backhouse, E., & Bland, J. O. (1914). Annals and Memoirs of the Court of Peking. Boston, MA: Houghton Mifflin.

Baccardax, M. (2021, September 20). China Faces 'Lehman Moment' With Evergrande Collapse, So What Are The Risks? Retrieved October 2021, from The Street: https://www.thestreet.com/markets/china-faces-lehman-moment-in-evergrande-bust-what-are-the-risks

Baker, L. B., Toonkel, J., & Seetharaman, D. (2014, 19 September). Alibaba IPO prices at top of range, raising $21.8 billion. Retrieved January 2021, from Reuters: https://www.reuters.com/article/us-alibaba-ipo/alibaba-ipo-prices-at-top-of-range-raising-21-8-billion-idUSKBN0HD2CO20140918

Barrett, C. (2021, 12 March). Is day trading ever a winning investment strategy? Retrieved May 2021, from Financial Times: https://www.ft.com/content/3df7bdb0-2c87-478f-bc3c-636a73a73712

Barton, S. (2021, 18 February). Yuan's Popularity for Global Payments Hits Five-Year High. Retrieved March 2021, from Bloomberg: https://www.bloombergquint.com/onweb/yuan-s-popularity-for-cross-border-payments-hits-five-year-high

Berger, M. (2021, 16 April). What are economic sanctions, and how did they become Washington's foreign policy tool of choice? Retrieved June 2021, from Washington Post: https://www.washingtonpost.com/world/2021/04/15/faq-united-states-economic-sanctions/

Bernanke, B. S. (2015). The Courage to Act: A Memoir of a Crisis and Its Aftermath. New York: W. W. Norton.

Binder, A. J. (2014, September/October). Why Are Harvard Grads Still Flocking to Wall Street? Retrieved April 2021, from Washington Monthly: https://washingtonmonthly.com/magazine/septoct-2014/why-are-harvard-grads-still-flocking-to-wall-street/

Blackwill, R. D., & Harris, J. M. (2016). War by Other Means: Geoeconomics and Statecraft. Cambridge, MA: Belknap Press.

Bloomberg News. (2021, July 28). China Convenes Banks in Bid to Restore Calm After Stock Rout. Retrieved October 2021, from Bloomberg: https://www.bloomberg.com/news/articles/2021-07-28/china-convenes-banks-in-bid-to-restore-market-calm-after-rout?sref=u5WI0AVD

Brands, H. (2020, 7 July). The Upside of a New Cold War With China. Retrieved August 2020, from Bloomberg: https://www.bloomberg.com/view/articles/2020-07-07/new-cold-war-with-china-can-make-u-s-democracy-stronger

Breckenfelder, J. (2019). Competition among high-frequency traders, and market quality. Frankfurt: European Central Bank.

Brooke, J. (1995, 7 April). Kidnappings Soar in Latin America, Threatening Region's Stability. Retrieved September 2021, from New York Times: https://www.nytimes.com/1995/04/07/world/kidnappings-soar-in-latin-america-threatening-region-s-stability.html

Brown, P., & Horowitz, J. (2018, 15 June). CNN. Retrieved February 2021, from Trump announces tariffs on $50 billion worth of Chinese goods: https://money.cnn.com/2018/06/14/news/economy/trump-china-tariffs/index.html?adkey=bn

CFTC & SEC. (2010). Findings Regarding the Market Events of May 6, 2010: Report of the Staffs of the CFTC and SEC to the Joint Advisory Committee on Emerging Regulatory Issues. Washington DC: CFTC & SEC.

Capo McCormick, L., & Kruger, D. (2009, 29 May). Bond Vigilantes Confront Obama as Housing Falters. Retrieved August 2020, from Bloomberg: https://web.archive.org/web/20110805042208/http://www.bloomberg.com/apps/news?pid=newsarchive&sid=a6eMpGVUDeeE&refer=home

Carney, M. (2019, 23 August). The Growing Challenges for Monetary Policy in the current International Monetary and Financial System. Retrieved July 2021, from BIS: https://www.bis.org/review/r190827b.pdf

Carter, Z. D. (2020). The Price of Peace: Money, Democracy, and the Life of John Maynard Keynes. New York: Random House.

Chan, H. (2021, 12 August). Hong Kong experiences 'alarming' population drop, but government says not all 90,000 leaving city because of national security law. Retrieved September 2021, from South China Morning Post: https://www.scmp.com/news/hong-kong/society/article/3144845/hong-kongs-experiences-alarming-population-drop-government

Chang, J. (2019). Big Sister, Little Sister, Red Sister: Three Women at the Heart of Twentieth-Century China. London: Penguin.

Chang, J. (2013). Empress Dowager Cixi: The Concubine Who Launched Modern China. New York: Alfred A. Knopf.

Chang, J., & Halliday, J. (2006). Mao: The Unknown Story. New York: Anchor Books.

Chau, C. (2020, 24 November). Foreign minister says UK is considering whether to withdraw British judges from Hong Kong's top court. Retrieved June 2021, from Hong Kong Free Press: https://hongkongfp.com/2020/11/24/

foreign-minister-says-uk-is-considering-banning-british-judges-from-sitting-on-hong-kongs-top-court/

Cheah, C., & Fok, J. A. (2020). The renminbi and China's capital markets: The geopolitical realities. China Asset Management at an Inflection Point, pp. 11–12.

Chen, B. X. (2021, 20 March). There Is No Rung on the Ladder That Protects You From Hate. Retrieved March 2021, from New York Times: https://www.nytimes.com/2021/03/20/technology/personaltech/asian-american-wealth-gap.html?referringSource=articleShare

Chen, T., & Chen, T. (2021, September 22). China Injects $18.6 Billion Into Banking System During Evergrande Crisis. Retrieved October 2021, from Bloomberg: https://www.bloomberg.com/news/articles/2021-09-22/china-maintains-liquidity-support-amid-evergrande-s-debt-crisis?sref=u5WI0AVD

Chen, Y., & Lawder, D. (2018, 18 September). China says Trump forces its hand, will retaliate against new U.S. tariffs. Retrieved February 2021, from Reuters https://www.reuters.com/article/us-usa-trade-china-tariffs/trump-slaps-tariffs-on-200-billion-in-chinese-goods-threatens-267-billion-more-idUSKCN1LX2M3

Cheng, J., Wessel, D., & Younger, J. (2020, 1 May). How did COVID-19 disrupt the market for U.S. Treasury debt? Retrieved March 2021, from Brookings Institution: https://www.brookings.edu/blog/up-front/2020/05/01/how-did-covid-19-disrupt-the-market-for-u-s-treasury-debt/

Cheung, G. (2020, 23 June). National security law: chief executive picking judges to hear cases undermines judiciary, warns former Hong Kong chief justice. Retrieved July 2021, from South China Morning Post: https://www.scmp.com/news/hong-kong/politics/article/3090156/national-security-law-chief-executive-picking-judges-hear

Cheung, G. (2020, 3 September). Remembering Hong Kong's unsung role in Shenzhen's glory – 40 years on, have fortunes reversed? Retrieved November 2020, from South China Morning Post: https://www.scmp.com/news/hong-kong/politics/article/3099919/remembering-hong-kongs-unsung-role-shenzhens-glory-40-years

Cheung, G., & Cheung, J. (2006, 27 September). Keep the laissez-faire policy, economist Friedman urges. Retrieved January 2021, from South China Morning Post: https://www.scmp.com/article/565533/keep-laissez-faire-policy-economist-friedman-urges

Chiu, J. (2019, 16 May). Former JPMorgan Banker Charged With Bribery in 'Sons and Daughters' Program. Retrieved January 2021, from Wall Street Journal: https://www.wsj.com/articles/former-jpmorgan-banker-charged-with-bribing-client-11558000123

Ciampaglia, G. L., & Menczer, F. (2018, 21 June). Biases Make People Vulnerable to Misinformation Spread by Social Media. Retrieved March 2021, from Scientific

American: https://www.scientificamerican.com/article/biases-make-people-vulnerable-to-misinformation-spread-by-social-media/

Clark, D. (2016). Alibaba: The House That Jack Ma Built. New York: Harper Collins.

Clark, M. (2021, 23 June). What we know about China's cryptocurrency crackdown. Retrieved July 2021, from The Verge: https://www.theverge.com/2021/6/23/22544367/china-crypto-crackdown-bitcoin-mining-sichuan-ban-hydro-cryptocurrency-trading

Cole, R. J. (1989, 31 October). Japanese Buy New York Cachet With Deal for Rockefeller Center. Retrieved December 2020, from New York Times: https://www.nytimes.com/1989/10/31/business/japanese-buy-new-york-cachet-with-deal-for-rockefeller-center.html

Congressional Budget Office. (2010, 5 August). Historical Data on Federal Debt Held by the Public. Retrieved December 2020, from Congressional Budget Office: https://www.cbo.gov/publication/21728

Congressional Research Service. (2019, 30 August). The International Monetary Fund. Retrieved August 2020, from Congressional Research Service: https://crsreports.congress.gov/product/pdf/IF/IF10676/6

Connolly, K. (2010, 16 September). What exactly is the Tea Party? Retrieved September 2020, from BBC News: https://www.bbc.com/news/world-us-canada-11317202

Cox, M., & Kennedy-Pipe, C. (2015). The tragedy of American diplomacy? Rethinking the Marshall Plan. Journal of Cold War Studies, 7(1), 97–134.

Crawford, N. C. (2019, 13 November). United States Budgetary Costs and Obligations of Post-9/11 Wars through FY2020: $6.4 Trillion. Retrieved August 2020, from Costs of War Research Series: https://watson.brown.edu/costsofwar/files/cow/imce/papers/2019/US%20Budgetary%20Costs%20of%20Wars%20November%202019.pdf

Creery, J. (2019, 25 June). Exclusive: Pro-Beijing lawmaker Regina Ip on Hong Kong's extradition row and history repeating itself. Retrieved February 2021, from Hong Kong Free Press: https://hongkongfp.com/2019/06/25/exclusive-pro-beijing-lawmaker-regina-ip-hong-kongs-extradition-row-history-repeating/

Davidson, H. (2021, 6 January). Dozens of Hong Kong pro-democracy figures arrested in sweeping crackdown. Retrieved February 2021, from The Guardian: https://www.theguardian.com/world/2021/jan/06/dozens-of-hong-kong-pro-democracy-figures-arrested-in-sweeping-crackdown

Davidson, P. (2010). Making dollars and sense of the U.S. government debt. Journal of Post Keynesian Economics, 32(4), 661–666.

Davis, J. (2011, 3 October 3). The Crypto-Currency. Retrieved May 2021, from New Yorker: https://www.newyorker.com/magazine/2011/10/10/the-crypto-currency

Davison, L., & Versprille, A. (2021, 8 January). Carried Interest Tax Break Restricted in New IRS Regulations. Retrieved March 2021, from Bloomberg: https://www.bloomberg.com/news/articles/2021-01-07/carried-interest-tax-break-restricted-in-new-irs-regulations-kjniat0e?sref=u5WI0AVD

DeLong, J. B. (2007). Right from the Start? What Milton Friedman Can Teach Progressives. Democracy: A Journal of Ideas, 4(Spring), 108–115.

Diamond, J. (2005). Guns, Germs, and Steel: The Fates of Human Societies. New York: W. W. Norton.

Dudziak, M. L. (2000). Cold War Civil Rights: Race and the Image of American Democracy. Princeton, NJ: Princeton University Press.

Eberstadt, N., & Abramsky, E. (2021, February 8). What Do Prime-Age 'NILF' Men Do All Day? A Cautionary on Universal Basic Income. Retrieved September 2021, from Institute for Family Studies: https://ifstudies.org/blog/what-do-prime-age-nilf-men-do-all-day-a-cautionary-on-universal-basic-income

Ebrahimy, E., Igan, D., & Martinez Peria, S. (2020). The Impact of COVID-19 on Inflation: Potential Drivers and Dynamics. Washington DC: IMF.

Economist. (2010, 9 December). Keqiang ker-ching. Retrieved October 2020, from The Economist: https://www.economist.com/asia/2010/12/09/keqiang-ker-ching

Economist. (2017, 16 November). What annual reports say, or do not, about competition. Retrieved August 2020, from The Economist: https://www.economist.com/finance-and-economics/2017/11/16/what-annual-reports-say-or-do-not-about-competition

Egan, M. (2021, September 16). China faces a potential Lehman moment. Wall Street is unfazed. Retrieved October 2021, from CNN Business: https://edition.cnn.com/2021/09/16/business/wall-street-evergrande-china/index.html

Eisenman, J., & Heginbotham, E. (2020). China's Relations with Africa, Latin America, and the Middle East. In D. Shambaugh, China & the World (pp. 291–312). New York: Oxford University Press.

Elliott, F. (2009, 3 January). Chancellor Alistair Darling on brink of second bailout for banks. Retrieved May 2021, from The Times: https://www.thetimes.co.uk/article/chancellor-alistair-darling-on-brink-of-second-bailout-for-banks-n9l382mn62h

European Commission. (2016, 30 August). State aid: Ireland gave illegal tax benefits to Apple worth up to €13 billion. Retrieved March 2021, from European Commission: https://ec.europa.eu/commission/presscorner/detail/en/IP_16_2923

European Commission. (2020, 25 September). Statement by Executive Vice-President Margrethe Vestager on the Commission's decision to appeal the General Court's judgment on the Apple tax State aid case in Ireland. Retrieved March 2021, from European Commission: https://ec.europa.eu/commission/presscorner/detail/en/STATEMENT_20_1746

Fallows, J. (1989, April). Japan: Let Them Defend Themselves. The Atlantic, 264(4), 34–38.

Federal Trade Commission. (2020, 9 December). FTC Sues Facebook for Illegal Monopolization. Retrieved April 2021, from Federal Trade Commission: https://www.ftc.gov/news-events/press-releases/2020/12/ftc-sues-facebook-illegal-monopolization

Feng, C., & Pan, C. (2021, 13 April). US-China tech war: supercomputer sanctions on China begin to bite as Taiwan's TSMC said to suspend chip orders. Retrieved July 2021, from South China Morning Post: https://www.scmp.com/tech/tech-war/article/3129362/us-china-tech-war-supercomputer-sanctions-china-begin-bite-taiwans

Ferguson, N. (2020, 5 July). America and China Are Entering the Dark Forest. Retrieved August 2020, from Bloomberg: https://www.bloomberg.com/opinion/articles/2020-07-05/is-the-u-s-in-a-new-cold-war-china-has-already-declared-it

Ferguson, N. (2008). The Ascent of Money: A Financial History of the World. New York: Penguin.

Fioretti, J., Hu, B., & Hunter, G. S. (2020, 2 November). Ant Group Trades at 50% Premium in Hong Kong Gray Market. Retrieved January 2021, from Bloomberg: https://www.bloomberg.com/news/articles/2020-11-02/ant-group-said-to-trade-at-50-premium-in-hong-kong-gray-market?sref=u5WI0AVD

Fok, J. A. (2019, May). Connecting China, Connecting the World. ISSA Newsletter, pp. 3–5.

Foy, H. (2018, 3 October). Can Russia stop using the US dollar? Retrieved September 2020, from Financial Times: https://www.ft.com/content/a5187880-c553-11e8-8670-c5353379f7c2

France 24. (2015, 8 July). Almost half of China's firms halt trading as market dives. Retrieved January 2021, from France 24: https://www.france24.com/en/20150708-almost-half-chinese-firms-suspend-trading-market-dives

Frankopan, P. (2015). The Silk Roads: A New History of the World. New York: Alfred A. Knopf.

Frederickson, H. G. (2010). Social Equity and Public Administration: Origins, Developments and Applications. Armonk: M. E. Sharpe.

Friedman, M. (1970, 13 September). A Friedman doctrine: The Social Responsibility of Business Is to Increase Its Profits. New York Times, p. 17.

Friedman, M. (1997, 31 December). The Real Lesson of Hong Kong. (National Review) Retrieved January 2021, from Hoover Institution: https://www.hoover.org/research/hong-kong-experiment

Fukuyama, F. (1992). The End of History and the Last Man. New York: The Free Press.

Gaddis, J. L. (2005). The Cold War: A New History. New York: Penguin.

Gallagher, K. P., Ocampo, J. A., & Volz, U. (2020, 26 March). IMF Special Drawing Rights: A key tool for attacking a COVID-19 financial fallout in developing countries. Retrieved July 2021, from Brookings Institution: https://www.brookings.edu/blog/future-development/2020/03/26/imf-special-drawing-rights-a-key-tool-for-attacking-a-covid-19-financial-fallout-in-developing-countries/

Gallagher, K. P., Ocampo, J. A., & Volz, U. (2020, 20 March). It's time for a major issuance of the IMF's Special Drawing Rights. Retrieved July 2021, from Financial Times: https://www.ft.com/content/43a67e06-bbeb-4bea-8939-bc29ca785b0e

Gao, J. (2007). Debt Capital Markets in China. Hoboken, NJ: John Wiley & Sons.

Garbade, K. D. (2012). Birth of a Market: The U.S. Treasury Securities Market from the Great War to the Great Depression. Cambridge, MA: The MIT Press.

Gates, B. (2021). How to Avoid a Climate Disaster: The Solutions We Have and the Breakthroughs We Need. New York: Alfred A. Knopf.

Ghose, R., Zhang, J., Tian, Y., Master, K., & Shah, R. S. (2021). Future of Money: Crypto, CBDCs and 21st Century Cash. New York: Citigroup.

Gilmour, R. S., & Jensen, L. S. (1998, May–June). Reinventing Government Accountability: Public Functions, Privatization and the Meaning of 'State Action'. Public Administration Review, 58(3), 247–258.

Global Times. (2019, 29 July 29). Traitors seek to separate Hong Kong and fuel street violence. Retrieved February 2021, from Global Times: https://www.globaltimes.cn/content/1159595.shtml

Godfrey, M. (2012, 28 May). Norwegian salmon exporters feel China's wrath. Retrieved February 2021, from SeafoodSource: https://www.seafoodsource.com/news/supply-trade/norwegian-salmon-exporters-feel-china-s-wrath

Goodkind, D. (2018). If Science Had Come First: A Billion Person Fable for the Ages (A Reply to Comments). Demography, 55, 743–768.

Goodstadt, L. F. (2018). A City Mismanaged: Hong Kong's Struggle for Survival. Hong Kong: Hong Kong University Press.

Goodstadt, L. F. (1972). Mao Tse-tung: The Search for Plenty. Hong Kong: Longman.

Gray, M. (2011). A Theory of 'Late Rentierism' in the Arab States of the Gulf. Qatar: Center for International and Regional Studies Georgetown University School of Foreign Service in Qatar.

Green, J. (2019, 8 July). Inventions we use every day that were actually created for space exploration. Retrieved April 2020, from USA Today: https://www.usatoday.com/story/money/2019/07/08/space-race-inventions-we-use-every-day-were-created-for-space-exploration/39580591/

Green, M. J. (2017). By More Than Providence: Grand Strategy and American Power in the Asia Pacific Since 1783. New York: Columbia University Press.

Greenhalgh, S. (2003, June). Science, Modernity, and the Making of China's One-Child Policy. Population and Development Review, 29(2), 163–196.

Harari, Y. N. (2015). Sapiens: A Brief History of Mankind. New York: HarperCollins.

Hargreaves, D. (2019). Are Chief Executives Overpaid? Cambridge: Polity Press.

Hawkins, J. (2021, 14 June). Can Bitcoin become a real currency? Here's what's wrong with El Salvador's crypto plan. Retrieved July 2021, from The Conversation: https://theconversation.com/can-bitcoin-become-a-real-currency-heres-whats-wrong-with-el-salvadors-crypto-plan-162348

Hayton, B. (2020). The Invention of China. New Haven, CT: Yale University Press.

Heng, C., & Bray, C. (2021, 7 January). How Donald Trump has targeted Chinese companies with executive orders, sanctions. Retrieved March 2021, from South China Morning Post: https://www.scmp.com/business/companies/article/3116682/how-donald-trump-has-targeted-chinese-companies-executive-orders

Heng, C. (2021, September 20). Hong Kong stocks sink on tech, developers fallout while Evergrande roils market as mainland funds take a breather. Retrieved October 2021, from South China Morning Post: https://www.scmp.com/business/companies/article/3149371/hong-kong-stocks-sink-tech-china-evergrande-fallout-without

Hille, K. (2021, October 3). China sends record number of warplanes towards Taiwan. Retrieved October 2021, from Financial Times: https://www.ft.com/content/f83e7f68-12d2-438d-a0cd-64c586995166

Hobsbawm, E. (1990, October). Goodbye to All That. Marxism Today, 18–23.

Hoffman, D. (1999, 10 February). 'I Had A Funny Feeling in My Gut'. Retrieved February 2021, from Washington Post: https://www.washingtonpost.com/wp-srv/inatl/longterm/coldwar/soviet10.htm

Howell, M. J. (2020). Capital Wars: The Rise of Global Liquidity. Cham: Palgrave Macmillan.

Hsü, I. C. (2000). The Rise of Modern China. New York: Oxford University Press.

IMF. (2011). Enhancing International Monetary Stability – A Role for the SDR? Strategy, Policy, and Review Department. Washington DC: IMF.

IMF. (2014). Global Financial Stability Report: Risk Taking, Liquidity, and Shadow Banking. Washington DC: IMF.

Inglis, B. (1976). The Opium War. London: Hodder & Stoughton.

Irwin, D. A. (2013, January). The Nixon shock after forty years: the import surcharge revisited. World Trade Review, 12(1), 29–56.

Jacobs, J. (2021, 4 June). Biden Blocks 59 Chinese Companies in Amended Trump Order. Retrieved June 2021, from Bloomberg: https://www.bloomberg.com/news/articles/2021-06-03/biden-to-blacklist-59-chinese-companies-in-amended-trump-order?sref=u5WI0AVD

Javers, E. (2011, 16 March). Citigroup Tops List of Banks Who Received Federal Aid. Retrieved August 2020, from CNBC: https://www.cnbc.com/2011/03/16/citigroup-tops-list-of-banks-who-received-federal-aid.html

Jay, S., Batruch, A., Jetten, J., McGarty, C., & Muldoon, O. T. (2019, September/October). Economic inequality and the rise of far-right populism: A social psychological analysis. Journal of Community & Applied Social Psychology, 29(5), 418–428.

Jenson, J. (2008). Government Spending on Health Care Benefits and Programs: A Data Brief. Domestic Social Policy Division. Washington DC: Congressional Research Service.

Jim, C. (2021, September 14). Explainer: How China Evergrande's debt troubles pose a systemic risk. Retrieved October 2021, from Reuters: https://www.reuters.com/business/how-china-evergrandes-debt-troubles-pose-systemic-risk-2021-09-14/

Jones, L. (2020, 24 August). The myth of China's 'debt-trap diplomacy'. Retrieved February 2021, from Spectator: https://www.spectator.co.uk/article/the-myth-of-china-s-debt-trap-diplomacy-

Jung, J., & Shiller, R. J. (2005, April). Samuelson's Dictum and the Stock Market. Economic Inquiry, 43(2), 221–228.

Kahneman, D. (2011). Thinking, Fast and Slow. New York: Farrar, Straus and Giroux.

Kaplan, E., & Rodrik, D. (2001, 26 February). Did the Malaysian Capital Controls Work? National Bureau of Economic Research Working Paper, w8142, 393–440.

Kelton, S. (2020). The Deficit Myth: Modern Monetary Theory and the Birth of the People's Economy. New York: PublicAffairs.

Kennan, G. F. (1946, 22 February). The Charge in the Soviet Union (Kennan) to the Secretary of State. Retrieved February 2021, from George Washington University: https://nsarchive2.gwu.edu/coldwar/documents/episode-1/kennan.htm

Kennan, G. F. (1947, July). The Sources of Soviet Conduct. Retrieved February 2021, from Foreign Affairs: https://www.foreignaffairs.com/articles/russian-federation/1947-07-01/sources-soviet-conduct

Kennedy, P. (1981). The Realities Behind Diplomacy: Background Influences on British External Policy 1865–1980. Glasgow: William Collins Sons.

Kennedy, P. (1987). The Rise and Fall of the Great Powers: Economic Change and Military Conflict from 1500 to 2000. New York: Random House.

Kessler, G. (2019, 17 October). Are jobs lost due to 'bad trade policy' or automation? Retrieved March 2021, from Washington Post: https://www.washingtonpost.com/politics/2019/10/17/are-jobs-lost-due-bad-trade-policy-or-automation/

Kharpal, A. (2021, 6 April). Cryptocurrency market value tops $2 trillion for the first time as ethereum hits record high. Retrieved May 2021, from CNBC: https://www.cnbc.com/2021/04/06/cryptocurrency-market-cap-tops-2-trillion-for-the-first-time.html

Killian, S. (2006). Where's the harm in tax competition? Lessons from US multinationals in Ireland. Critical Perspectives on Accounting, 17, 1067–1087.

Kissinger, H. A. (2012). On China. New York: Penguin.

Kissinger, H. A. (2014). World Order. New York: Penguin.

Klein, M. C., & Pettis, M. (2020). Trade Wars Are Class Wars: How Rising Inequality Distorts the Global Economy and Threatens International Peace. New Haven, CT: Yale University Press.

Knapp, A. (2019, 20 July). Apollo 11's 50th Anniversary: The Facts And Figures Behind The $152 Billion Moon Landing. Retrieved April 2020, from Forbes: https://www.forbes.com/sites/alexknapp/2019/07/20/apollo-11-facts-figures-business/

Kolchin, K. (2020). SIFMA Insights: COVID-19 Related Market Turmoil Recap: Part II. New York: SIFMA.

Kolodko, G. W. (2020). China and the Future of Globalization: The Political Economy of China's Rise. New York: I. B. Tauris.

Korhonen, I. (2019, December). Economic Sanctions on Russia and Their Effects. CESifo Forum, 20(4), 19–22.

Koty, A. C. (2021, May 12). What's Next for Australian Wine in China? Retrieved June 2021, from China Briefing: https://www.china-briefing.com/news/whats-next-for-australian-wine-in-china/

Krauthammer, C. (1990). The Unipolar Moment. Foreign Affairs, 70(1), 23–33.

Kristof, N. D. (1989, 16 April). Hu Yaobang, Ex-Party Chief in China, Dies at 73. Retrieved 2020 November, from New York Times: https://www.nytimes.com/1989/04/16/obituaries/hu-yaobang-ex-party-chief-in-china-dies-at-73.html

Ku, D., & Shen, S. (2010, 2 November). CCB to raise $9.2 billion through rights issue. Retrieved January 2021, from Reuters: https://www.reuters.com/article/us-ccb-idUSTRE6A10EF20101102

Kurlantzick, J. (2020, 30 January). Vietnam, Under Increasing Pressure From China, Mulls a Shift Into America's Orbit. Retrieved February 2021, from World Politics Review: https://www.worldpoliticsreview.com/insights/28502/as-china-vietnam-relations-deteriorate-hanoi-mulls-closer-ties-with-the-u-s

Kynge, J., & Wheatley, J. (2020, 12 December). China pulls back from the world: rethinking Xi's 'project of the century'. Retrieved February 2021, from Financial Times: https://www.ft.com/content/d9bd8059-d05c-4e6f-968b-1672241ec1f6

Köppel, J. (2011). The SWIFT Affair: Swiss Banking Secrecy and the Fight against Terrorist Financing. Retrieved July 2020, from http://books.openedition.org/iheid/225

Lam, W. W.-L. (2020). The Fight for China's Future: Civil Society vs. the Chinese Communist Party. Abingdon: Routledge.

Lee, A. (2020, 15 December). China debt: how big is it and who owns it? Retrieved January 2021, from South China Morning Post: https://www.scmp.com/economy/china-economy/article/3084979/china-debt-how-big-it-who-owns-it-and-what-next

Lee, D., & Cheng, L. (2021, 30 January). Hong Kong BN(O): Britain stands firm on visa offer after Beijing declares the passports will no longer be recognised for travel, identification. Retrieved February 2021, from South China Morning Post: https://www.scmp.com/news/hong-kong/politics/article/3119885/hong-kong-bno-britain-stands-firm-visa-offer-after-beijing

Lee, G. (2018a, 2 June). China's moves to cap first-day IPO gains prove to be a winning ticket for issuers and investors. Retrieved January 2021, from South China Morning Post: https://www.scmp.com/business/markets/article/2148899/chinas-moves-cap-first-day-ipo-gains-prove-be-winning-ticket

Lee, K.-F. (2018). AI Superpowers: China, Silicon Valley, and the New World Order. New York: Houghton Mifflin Harcourt.

Lee, Y., Lague, D., & Blanchard, B. (2020, 10 December). Special Report-China launches 'gray-zone' warfare to subdue Taiwan. Retrieved February 2021, from Reuters: https://www.reuters.com/article/hongkong-taiwan-military-idUSKBN28K1GS

Leigh, L., & Podpiera, R. (2006). The Rise of Foreign Investment in China's Banks – Taking Stock. IMF, Asia and Pacific Department. IMF.

Leng, S. (2020, 30 August). China censors Thomas Piketty's book that touches on nation's growing inequality. Retrieved January 2021, from South China Morning Post: https://www.scmp.com/economy/china-economy/article/3099460/china-censors-thomas-pikettys-book-touches-nations-growing

Levathes, L. E. (1994). When China Ruled the Seas: The Treasure Fleet of the Dragon Throne, 1405–1433. New York: Open Road Distribution.

Levy, A. (2021, 14 April). Coinbase closes at $328.28 per share in Nasdaq debut, valuing crypto exchange at $85.8 billion. Retrieved July 2021, from CNBC: https://www.cnbc.com/2021/04/14/coinbase-to-debut-on-nasdaq-in-direct-listing.html

Lewis, L. (2021, 31 January). Companies consider writing Hong Kong out of legal contracts. Retrieved February 2021, from Financial Times: https://www.ft.com/content/1070440a-0993-4c19-9797-2c0e781fd7db

Lewis, M. (2010). Liar's Poker: Rising Through the Wreckage on Wall Street. New York: W. W. Norton.

Litan, R. E. (2002, 1 December). The Telecommunications Crash: What To Do Now? Retrieved April 2021, from Brookings: https://www.brookings.edu/research/the-telecommunications-crash-what-to-do-now/

Liu, C. (2020, 28 December). Alibaba Probe Stirs Worry About What's Next for Chinese Tech. Retrieved January 2021, from Bloomberg: https://www.bloomberg.com/news/articles/2020-12-28/alibaba-hikes-share-buyback-plan-to-10-billion-from-6-billion?sref=u5WI0AVD

Liu, J. (2017, 13 February). 30 million Chinese men to be wifeless over the next 30 years. Retrieved January 2021, from China Daily: https://www.chinadaily.com.cn/china/2017-02/13/content_28183839.htm

Locke, R. (2006). Japan, Refutation of Neoliberalism. In E. Fullbrook, Real World Economics: A Post-Autistic Economics Reader (pp. 237–258). New York: Anthem Press.

Lockett, H. (2021, 26 July). Crackdown on education companies sparks sharp sell-off for Chinese stocks. Retrieved September 2021, from Financial Times: https://www.ft.com/content/d6d2f31e-72dd-4d22-aa2a-907990d43e97

Lovell, J. (2019). Maoism: A Global History. London: Penguin.

Lowenstein, R. (2011). When Genius Failed: The Rise and Fall of Long-Term Capital Management. New York: Random House.

Luhby, T. (2020, January 11). Many millennials are worse off than their parents -- a first in American history. Retrieved October 2021, from CNN: https://edition.cnn.com/2020/01/11/politics/millennials-income-stalled-upward-mobility-us/index.html

Lung, N. (2021, 4 March). Hong Kong Dumped From Economic Freedom List It Had Dominated. Retrieved March 2021, from Bloomberg: https://www.bloomberg.com/news/articles/2021-03-04/hong-kong-dumped-from-economic-freedom-index-it-used-to-dominate?sref=u5WI0AVD

MSCI. (2017, 10 November). Assets in Global Equity ETFs linked to MSCI Indexes Reach All-Time High of $707 Billion. Retrieved February 2021, from MSCI: https://www.msci.com/documents/10199/6de39767-c42a-47ba-ab8c-11a6205e397c

Macartney, J. (2008, 9 August). Olympics: the power and the glory China leaves world awestruck. Retrieved December 2020, from The Times: https://www.thetimes.co.uk/article/olympics-the-power-and-the-glory-china-leaves-world-awestruck-253m0gmwtpp

Magnus, G. (2018). Red Flags: Why Xi's China Is In Jeopardy. New Haven, CT: Yale University Press.

Mahbubani, K. (2020). Has China Won? The Chinese Challenge to American Primacy. New York: PublicAffairs.

Makepeace, M. (2020). FTSE: The inside story of the deals, dramas and politics and that revolutionized financial markets. Boston, MA: Nicholas Brealey.

Mandeng, O. J. (2020, 20 March). IMF SDR allocation: Interesting in theory. Retrieved July 2021, from Economics Advisory: https://www.economicsadvisory.com/comments/20-03-20-SDR-allocation.html

Mann, J. (1989, 25 June). Turmoil In China: Crackdown on Dissent: Picture of Jiang Emerges From Interview After 1986 Unrest: New Party Chief at Home With Lincoln, Marx. Retrieved November 2020, from Los Angeles Times: https://www.latimes.com/archives/la-xpm-1989-06-25-mn-6439-story.html

Marks, H. (2018). Mastering the Market Cycle: Getting the Odds On Your Side. New York: Houghton Mifflin Harcourt.

McSheaffrey, P., Robson, B., & Huang, A. (2019). The rise of the tech giants. Hong Kong: KPMG.

Melamed, L. (1988, Fall). Evolution of the International Monetary Market. Cato Journal, 8(2), 393–404.

Melamed, L. (2013). The Birth of FX Futures. Retrieved August 2020, from CME Group: https://www.cmegroup.com/content/dam/cmegroup/education/interactive/fxproductguide/birthoffutures.pdf

Micklethwait, J., & Wooldridge, A. (2020). The Wake-Up Call: Why the Pandemic Has Exposed the Weakness of the West, and How to Fix It. New York: HarperVia.

Milanovic, B. (2019). Capitalism, Alone: The Future of the System that Rules the World. Cambridge, MA: Belknap.

Milesi-Ferretti, G. M. (2021, 14 April). The US is increasingly a net debtor nation. Should we worry? Retrieved July 2021, from Brookings Institution: https://www.brookings.edu/blog/up-front/2021/04/14/the-us-is-increasingly-a-net-debtor-nation-should-we-worry/

Mitter, R., & Johnson, E. (2021, May–June). What the West Gets Wrong About China. Harvard Business Review, 42–48.

Mo, Y. (1999). A review of recent banking reforms in China. In BIS, Strengthening the Banking System in China: Issues and Experience (pp. 90–109). Basel: BIS.

Morton, K. (2020). China's Global Governance Interactions. In D. Shambaugh, China & the World (pp. 156–180). New York: Oxford University Press.

Mouawad, J. (2008, 3 March). Oil Prices Pass Record Set in '80s, but Then Recede. Retrieved December 2020, from New York Times: https://www.nytimes.com/2008/03/03/business/worldbusiness/03cnd-oil.html

Naughton, B. (2019). China's Domestic Economy. In J. deLisle, & A. Goldstein, To Get Rich Is Glorious: Challenges Facing China's Economic Reform and Opening at Forty (pp. 29–52). Washington DC: Brookings Institution.

Naughton, B. (2020). China's Global Economic Interactions. In D. Shambaugh, China & the World (pp. 113–136). New York: Oxford University Press.

Nikkei Asian Review. (2019, 8 October). US sanctions 8 China tech companies over role in Xinjiang abuses. Retrieved September 2020, from Nikkei Asian Review: https://asia.nikkei.com/Economy/Trade-war/US-sanctions-8-China-tech-companies-over-role-in-Xinjiang-abuses

Norman, P. (2007). Plumbers and Visionaries: Securities Settlement and Europe's Financial Market. Chichester: John Wiley & Sons.

O'Clery, C. (2011). Moscow, December 25, 1991: The Last Day of the Soviet Union. New York: PublicAffairs.

O'Connor, N. (2017). Three Connections between Rising Economic Inequality and the Rise of Populism. Irish Studies in International Affairs, 28, 29–43.

O'Connor, S. (2018, February 23). Millennials poorer than previous generations, data show. Retrieved October 2021, from Financial Times: https://www.ft.com/content/81343d9e-187b-11e8-9e9c-25c814761640

O'Mahony, P. (2019, 1 October). Do stock buybacks constitute a 'licence to loot'? Retrieved April 2021, from Irish Times: https://www.irishtimes.com/business/personal-finance/do-stock-buybacks-constitute-a-licence-to-loot-1.4031567

O'Malley, C. (2015). Bonds Without Borders: A History of the Eurobond Market. Chichester: John Wiley & Sons.

OXFAM Hong Kong. (2018). Hong Kong Inequality Report. Hong Kong: OXFAM Hong Kong.

Obinger, H., & Schmitt, C. (2011, April). GUNS AND BUTTER? Regime Competition and the Welfare State during the Cold War. World Politics, 63(2), 246–270.

Oi, J. C. (2019). Reflections on Forty Years of Rural Reform. In J. deLisle, & A. Goldstein, To Get Rich Is Glorious: Challenges Facing China's Economic Reform and Opening at Forty (pp. 55–86). Washington DC: Brookings Institution.

Olson, E. S. (2011). Zero-Sum Game: The Rise of the World's Largest Derivatives Exchange. Hoboken, NJ: John Wiley & Sons.

Outram, Q. (2001). The Socio-Economic Relations to Warfare and the Military Mortality Crises of the Thirty Years' War. Medical History, 45(2), 151–184.

Parsons, K. (2018, 29 August). Paleo diet gains populatory. Retrieved April 2021, from Orlando Sentinel: https://www.orlandosentinel.com/health/get-healthy-orlando/os-paleo-diet-benefits-20180822-story.html

Paulson Jr., H. M. (2015). Dealing With China: An Insider Unmarks the New Economic Superpower. New York: Hachette.

Paulson Jr., H. M. (2020, 19 May 19). The Future of the Dollar: U.S. Financial Power Depends on Washington, Not Beijing. Retrieved May 2020, from Foreign Affairs: https://www.foreignaffairs.com/articles/2020-05-19/future-dollar

Peltier, H. (2020, January). The Cost of Debt-financed War: Public Debt and Rising Interest for Post-9/11 War Spending. Retrieved August 2020, from Costs of War Research Series: https://watson.brown.edu/costsofwar/files/cow/imce/papers/2020/Peltier%202020%20-%20The%20Cost%20of%20Debt-financed%20War.pdf

Phillips, M. (2019, 18 September). Wall Street Is Buzzing About Repo Rates. Here's Why. New York Times.

Picchi, A. (2018, November 20). Millennials are much poorer than their parents. Retrieved October 2021, from CBS News: https://www.cbsnews.com/news/millennials-are-much-poorer-than-their-parents-data-show/

Piketty, T. (2020). Capital and Ideology. Cambridge, MA: Harvard University Press.

Pillsbury, M. (2015). The Hundred-Year Marathon: China's Secret Strategy to Replace America as the Global Superpower. New York: Henry Holt & Company.

Pinker, S. (2011). The Better Angels of Our Nature: Why Violence Has Declined. New York: Viking Penguin.

Platt, S. R. (2018). Imperial Twilight: The Opium War and the End of China's Last Golden Age. New York: Alfred A. Knopf.

Prasad, E. S. (2017). Gaining Currency: The Rise of the Renminbi. New York: Oxford University Press.

Prasad, E. S. (2019, September). Has the dollar lost ground as the dominant international currency? Retrieved June 2020, from Global Economy and Development at Brookings: https://www.brookings.edu/wp-content/uploads/2019/09/DollarInGlobalFinance.final_.9.20.pdf

Prasad, E. S. (2014). The Dollar Trap: How the U.S. Dollar Tightened its Grip on Global Finance. Princeton, NJ: Princeton University Press.

Quinn, W., & Turner, J. D. (2020). Boom and Bust: A Global History of Financial Bubbles. Cambridge: Cambridge University Press.

Rajan, A. (2007, 6 November). New low for the dollar as top-paid model demands her fees in euros. Retrieved September 2020, from The Independent: https://www.independent.co.uk/news/world/americas/new-low-for-the-dollar-as-top-paid-model-demands-her-fees-in-euros-399173.html

Rajan, R. (2019). The Third Pillar: How Markets and the State Leave Community Behind. New York: Penguin.

Rappeport, A. (2021, 9 July). I.M.F. Board Backs $650 Billion Aid Plan to Help Poor Countries. Retrieved July 2021, from New York Times: https://www.nytimes.com/2021/07/09/us/politics/g20-imf-vaccines.html?referringSource=articleShare

Reid-Henry, S. (2019). Empire of Democracy: The Remaking of the West Since the Cold War, 1971–2017. New York: Simon & Schuster.

Reuters. (2010, 2 July). Bank of China plans rights issue for $8.8 billion. Retrieved January 2021, from Reuters: https://www.reuters.com/article/us-boc-idUSTRE66128020100702

Richter, P. (1989, 27 September). Sony to Buy Columbia, Says Americans Will Run Studio: 1st Sale of Film Maker to Japanese. Retrieved December 2020, from Los Angeles Times: https://www.latimes.com/archives/la-xpm-1989-09-27-mn-335-story.html

Rogoff, K. S., & Yang, Y. (2020). Peak China Housing. Cambridge, MA: National Bureau of Economic Research.

SAFE. (2021, 13 January). Qualified Domestic Institutional Investors (QDIIs) with Investment Quotas Granted by the SAFE. Retrieved January 2021, from SAFE: https://www.safe.gov.cn/en/file/file/20210113/d99ad2a5cd4c-4f06a9567a795f0f6d74.pdf?n=QDIIs(January13%2C2021)

Sargent, G. (2011, 30 September). 'There's been class warfare for the last 20 years, and my class has won'. Retrieved September 2020, from Washington Post: https://www.washingtonpost.com/blogs/plum-line/post/theres-been-class-warfare-for-the-last-20-years-and-my-class-has-won/2011/03/03/gIQApaF-bAL_blog.html

Saunders, P. C. (2020). China's Global Military-Security Interactions. In D. Shambaugh, China & the World (pp. 181–207). New York: Oxford University Press.

Schatzker, E., Natarajan, S., & Burton, K. (2021, 1 May). Before he lost US$20 billion, Bill Hwang was the greatest trader you had never heard of. Retrieved May 2021, from South China Morning Post: https://www.scmp.com/magazines/post-magazine/long-reads/article/3131610/he-lost-us20-billion-bill-hwang-was-greatest

Schenk, C. R. (2010). The Decline of Sterling: Managing the Retreat of an International Currency, 1945–1992. Cambridge: Cambridge University Press.

Schenk, C. R. (1998, April). The Origins of the Eurodollar Market in London: 1955–1963. Explorations in Economic History, 35(2), 221–238.

Schwab, K. (2019, 2 December). What Kind of Capitalism Do We Want? Retrieved August 2020, from TIME: https://time.com/5742066/klaus-schwab-stakeholder-capitalism-davos/

Schwartz, S. (2020, 15 April). Japan's Coronavirus Response Increases Public Debt Challenge. Retrieved February 2021, from Fitch Ratings: https://www.fitch-ratings.com/research/sovereigns/japan-coronavirus-response-increases-public-debt-challenge-15-04-2020#:~:text=Japan's%20gross%20government%20debt%20ratio,GDP%20and%20interest%20rate%20assumptions

Scott, S.V., & Zachariadis, M. (2012). Origins and Development of SWIFT, 1973–2009. Business History, 54(3), 462–482.

Sen, C. (2021, 25 February). Fixing the Supply Chain Will Help Beat Inflation. Retrieved March 2021, from Bloomberg: https://www.bloomberg.com/opinion/articles/2021-02-25/inflation-is-more-about-supply-chain-shortages-than-price-hikes?sref=u5WI0AVD

Shamapant, N. (2021, 26 April). Etherium, The Triple Halving. Retrieved September 2021, from Squish Chaos: https://squish.substack.com/p/ethereum-the-triple-halving

Shambaugh, D. (2020). China and the World: Future Challenges. In D. Shambaugh, China & the World (pp. 343–367). New York: Oxford University Press.

Shan, W. (2019). Out of the Gobi: My Story of China and America. Hoboken, NJ: John Wiley & Sons.

Sharma, R. (2019, 24 June). Elizabeth Warren and Donald Trump Are Wrong About the Same Thing. Retrieved May 2020, from New York Times: https://www.nytimes.com/2019/06/24/opinion/elizabeth-warren-donald-trump-dollar-devalue.html

Shen, S. (2016, 6 February). How China's 'Belt and Road' Compares to the Marshall Plan. Retrieved February 2021, from The Diplomat: https://thediplomat.com/2016/02/how-chinas-belt-and-road-compares-to-the-marshall-plan/

Shen, S., Stanway, D., Jim, C., Westbrook, T., Cushing, C., & Holmes, S. (2021, August 25). Evergrande supplier threatens lawsuit over late payment. Retrieved October 2021, from Reuters: https://www.reuters.com/world/china/pipe-producer-yonggao-says-may-take-action-against-china-evergrande-over-unpaid-2021-08-25/

Sheng, A., & Ng, C. (2016). Shadow Banking in China: An Opportunity for Financial Reform. Hoboken, NJ: Wiley.

Sheridan, M. (2007, 24 June). Revealed: the Hong Kong invasion plan. Retrieved February 2021, from The Sunday Times: https://www.thetimes.co.uk/article/revealed-the-hong-kong-invasion-plan-b0xpm60xd2h

Shih, V. C. (2007). Factions and Finance in China: Elite Conflict and Inflation. Cambridge: Cambridge University Press.

Sin, N. (2019, 5 September). Explainer: How important is Hong Kong to the rest of China? Retrieved February 2021, from Reuters: https://www.reuters.com/article/us-hongkong-protests-markets-explainer-idUSKCN1VP35H

Smialek, J. (2021, 16 March). The Financial Crisis the World Forgot. Retrieved March 2021, from New York Times: https://www.nytimes.com/2021/03/16/business/economy/fed-2020-financial-crisis-covid.html

Smith, C., & Wigglesworth, R. (2020, 29 July). US Treasuries: the lessons from March's market meltdown. Retrieved March 2021, from Financial Times: https://www.ft.com/content/ea6f3104-eeec-466a-a082-76ae78d430fd

So, A. Y. (2019). The Rise of Authoritarianism in China in the Early 21st Century. International Review of Modern Sociology, 45(1), 49–70.

Sobel, M. (2020, 24 March). Coronavirus SDR allocation not the answer. Retrieved July 2021, from OMFIF: https://www.omfif.org/2020/03/coronavirus-sdr-allocation-not-the-answer/

Song, H. (2021, September 22). China's Property Sector Will Muddle Through Rest of Year. Retrieved October 2021, from MacroPolo: https://macropolo.org/china-property-sector-evergrande/?rp=m

Soros, G. (2021, 6 September). BlackRock's China Blunder. Retrieved September 2021, from Wall Street Journal: https://www.wsj.com/articles/blackrock-larry-fink-china-hkex-sse-authoritarianism-xi-jinping-term-limits-human-rights-ant-didi-global-national-security-11630938728

Stacey, K., Greeley, B., & Murphy, H. (2019, 17 October). Federal Reserve sets out regulatory challenges facing Facebook's Libra. Retrieved July 2021, from Financial Times: https://www.ft.com/content/ef650f9a-f052-11e9-ad1e-4367d8281195

Stearns, J. (2018, 18 November). EU Set to Tighten Rules on Foreign Investment to Fend Off China. Retrieved February 2021, from Bloomberg: https://www.bloomberg.com/news/articles/2018-11-18/eu-set-to-tighten-rules-on-foreign-investment-to-fend-off-china?sref=u5WI0AVD

Steil, B. (2013). The Battle of Bretton Woods: John Maynard Keynes, Harry Dexter White, and the Making of a New World Order. Princeton, NJ: Princeton University Press.

Steil, B. (2018). The Marshall Plan: Dawn of the Cold War. New York: Simon & Schuster.

Steil, B., & Litan, R. E. (2006). Financial Statecraft: The Role of Financial Markets in American Foreign Policy. New Haven: Yale University Press.

Stevenson, A., & Li, C. (2021, September 19). Evergrande Gave Workers a Choice: Lend Us Cash or Lose Your Bonus. Retrieved October 2021, from New York Times: https://www.nytimes.com/2021/09/19/business/china-evergrande-debt-protests.html

Stewart, P. M. (2019, 25 March). Trump's Search for Absolute Sovereignty Could Destroy the WTO. Retrieved June 2021, from World Politics Review: https://www.worldpoliticsreview.com/insights/27692/wto-reforms-are-needed-but-trump-s-demands-could-destroy-the-organization

Stine, D. D. (2009). The Manhattan Project, the Apollo Program, and Federal Energy Technology R&D Programs: A Comparative Analysis. Washington DC: Congressional Research Service.

Sutter, R. (2020). China's Relations with the United States. In D. Shambaugh, China & the World (pp. 211–232). New York: Oxford University Press.

Sweeney, P. (2021, 26 July). Chinese communists are souring on capitalism. Retrieved September 2021, from Reuters: https://www.reuters.com/break-ingviews/chinese-communists-are-souring-capitalism-2021-07-26/

Tang, F. (2020, 7 December). China estimates shadow banking worth US$12.9 trillion as it moves to clean up high-risk sector. Retrieved January 2021, from South China Morning Post: https://www.scmp.com/economy/china-economy/article/3112892/china-estimates-shadow-banking-worth-us129-trillion-it-moves

Tanjangco, B., Cao, Y., Nadin, R., Borodyna, O., Calabrese, L., & Chen, Y. (2021). Pulse 2: China navigates its Covid-19 recovery – outward investment appetite and implications for developing countries. London: Overseas Development Insitute.

Tartar, A. (2019, 12 June). China Sets the Pace in Race to Build the Factory of the Future. Retrieved January 2021, from Bloomberg: https://www.bloomberg.com/graphics/2019-china-factory-future-automation/?sref=u5WI0AVD

Tepper, J., & Hearn, D. (2019). The Myth of Capitalism: Monopolies and the Death of Competition. Hoboken, NJ: John Wiley & Sons.

Thayer, F. C. (1996, April). Balanced Budgets and Depressions. American Journal of Economics and Sociology, 55(2), 211–212.

The White House. (2021, September 9). Readout of President Joseph R. Biden Jr. Call with President Xi Jinping of the People's Republic of China. Retrieved October 2021, from The White House: https://www.whitehouse.gov/briefing-room/statements-releases/2021/09/09/readout-of-president-joseph-r-biden-jr-call-with-president-xi-jinping-of-the-peoples-republic-of-china/

Theriault, S. (2014, 10 January). Polarization we can live with. Partisan warfare is the problem. Retrieved September 2020, from Washington Post: https://www.washingtonpost.com/news/monkey-cage/wp/2014/01/10/polarization-we-can-live-with-partisan-warfare-is-the-problem/

Thorp, E. O. (2017). A Man for All Markets: From Las Vegas to Wall Street, How I Beat the Dealer and the Market. New York: Random House.

Tiezzi, S. (2020, 20 August). US Becomes Latest Country to Suspend Extradition Treaty With Hong Kong. Retrieved February 2021, from The Diplomat: https://thediplomat.com/2020/08/us-becomes-latest-country-to-suspend-extradition-treaty-with-hong-kong/

Tooze, A. (2018). Crashed: How a Decade of Financial Crises Changed the World. New York: Viking.

Tooze, A. (2014). The Deluge: The Great War and the Remaking of the Global Order. New York: Penguin.

Tooze, A. (2020, 30 July). Whose century? Retrieved March 2021, from London Review of Books: https://lrb.co.uk/the-paper/v42/n15/adam-tooze/whose-century

Turbiville, G. H. (1996). Weapons proliferation and organized crime: The Russian military and security force dimension. Colorado Springs: Air Force Academy, Institute for National Security Studies.

Union of Concerned Scientists. (2015). Close Calls with Nuclear Weapons. Cambridge, MA: Union of Concerned Scientists.

United States Department of Defence. (2020). Military and Security Developments Involving the People's Republic of China 2020. Washington DC: US Department of Defence.

Vinograd, C., & Jaffe, A. (2016, 2 May). Donald Trump in Indiana Says China Is 'Raping' America. Retrieved June 2021, from CNBC: https://www.cnbc.com/2016/05/02/donald-trump-in-indiana-says-china-is-raping-america.html

Vogel, E. F. (2011). Deng Xiaoping and the Transformation of China. Cambridge, MA: Belknap Press.

WTO. (2019). World Trade Statistical Review. Geneva: WTO.

Waley, A. (1958). The Opium War Through Chinese Eyes. London: George Allen & Unwin.

Walter, C. E., & Howie, F. J. (2006). Privatizing China: Inside China's Stock Markets (2nd Edition). Singapore: John Wiley & Sons.

Walter, C. E., & Howie, F. J. (2012). Red Capitalism: The Fragile Financial Foundation of China's Extraordinary Rise. Singapore: John Wiley & Sons.

Wang, G. (2019). China Reconnects: Joining a Deep-rooted Past to a New World Order. Singapore: World Scientific.

Wang, X. (2020, 6 March). Why it's time for China to cut its 45 per cent income tax rate. Retrieved March 2021, from South China Morning Post: https://www.scmp.com/week-asia/opinion/article/3124143/why-its-time-china-cut-its-45-cent-income-tax-rate

Westad, O. A. (2017). The Cold War: A World History. New York: Hachette.

Westcott, B. (2019, 1 August). China is blaming the US for the Hong Kong protests. Can that really be true? Retrieved August 2020, from CNN: https://www.cnn.com/2019/07/31/asia/us-china-hong-kong-interference-intl-hnk/index.html

Wheelock, D. C. (1995, March/April). Regulation, Market Structure, and the Bank Failures of the Great Depression. Federal Reserve Bank of St. Louis Review, 77(2), 27. Retrieved June 2020, from Federal Reserve Bank of St. Louis: https://files.stlouisfed.org/files/htdocs/publications/review/95/03/Regulation_Mar_Apr1995.pdf

Wigglesworth, R., & Janiaud, A. (2020, 8 January). Index funds break through $10tn-in-assets mark amid active exodus. Retrieved February 2021, from Financial Times: https://www.ft.com/content/a7e20d96-318c-11ea-9703-eea0cae3f0de

Wildau, G. (2015, 26 November). China's 'national team' owns 6% of stock market. Retrieved January 2021, from Financial Times: https://www.ft.com/content/7515f06c-939d-11e5-9e3e-eb48769cecab

Williamson, J. (2009). Understanding Special Drawing Rights (SDRs). Washington DC: Peterson Institute for International Economics.

Winn, P. (2016, 27 September). Trump says US jobs get 'stolen' by China. Well, here are the countries 'stealing' Chinese jobs. Retrieved March 2021, from The World: https://www.pri.org/stories/2016-09-27/trump-says-us-jobs-get-stolen-china-well-here-are-countries-stealing-chinese-jobs

Wise, P. (2020, 29 January). Portugal set to curb tax breaks for wealthy foreigners. Retrieved March 2021, from Financial Times: https://www.ft.com/content/88f3b958-41ee-11ea-a047-eae9bd51ceba

Wolkonowski, J. (2018, January). NATO defense expenditures in 1949-2017. SHS Web of Conferences. 57, pp. 1–13. Les Ulis: EDP Sciences.

Wong, A. (2016, 31 May). The Untold Story Behind Saudi Arabia's 41-Year U.S. Debt Secret. Retrieved June 2020, from Bloomberg: https://www.bloomberg.com/news/features/2016-05-30/the-untold-story-behind-saudi-arabia-s-41-year-u-s-debt-secret

Wong, B. (2020, 26 May). How Chinese Nationalism Is Changing. Retrieved February 2021, from The Diplomat: https://thediplomat.com/2020/05/how-chinese-nationalism-is-changing/

Wong, F., & Shen, S. (2010, 11 November). ICBC to raise $6.8 bln in HK, Shanghai rights issue. Retrieved January 2021, from Reuters: https://www.reuters.com/article/icbc-idUSTOE6A90AY20101111

Wong, J. (2015). Zhu Rongji and China's Economic Take-off. Hackensack, NJ: Imperial College Press.

Wood, M. (2020). The Story of China: A Portrait of a Civilisation and its People. London: Simon & Schuster.

Wordie, J. (2012, 24 June). Writers blocked. Retrieved January 2021, from South China Morning Post: https://www.scmp.com/article/1004758/writers-blocked

Wu, T. (2018). The Curse of Bigness: Antitrust in the New Gilded Age. New York: Columbia Global Reports.

Wudunn, S. (1995, 11 April). Chen Yun, a Chinese Communist Patriarch Who Helped Slow Reforms, Is Dead at 89. Retrieved November 2020, from New York Times: https://www.nytimes.com/1995/04/11/obituaries/chen-yun-a-chinese-communist-patriarch-who-helped-slow-reforms-is-dead-at-89.html

Xie, S.Y., & Yang, J. (2020, 25 August). Inside Ant Group's Giant Valuation: One Billion Alipay Users and Big Profit Margins. Retrieved June 2021, from Wall Street Journal: https://www.wsj.com/articles/jack-mas-ant-group-files-ipo-listing-documents-11598349802

Xie, Y. (2020, 24 September). Wall Street Journal. Retrieved February 2021, from China's Bonds Win Third Key Index Inclusion: https://www.wsj.com/articles/chinas-bonds-win-third-key-index-inclusion-11600994714?st=sgpp655sospibn8&reflink=article_email_share

Xie, Y., & Zheng, W. (2019, 20 May). China's former securities regulator Liu Shiyu is probed over family members' alleged insider trading and favouring hometown IPOs, sources say. Retrieved December 2020, from South China Morning Post: https://www.scmp.com/business/banking-finance/article/3010965/chinas-former-securities-regulator-liu-shiyu-probed-over

Yahuda, M. (2020). China's Relations with Asia. In D. Shambaugh, China & the World (pp. 270–290). New York: Oxford University Press.

Yan, X., & Huang, J. (2017). Navigating Unknown Waters: The Chinese Communist Party's New Presence in the Private Sector. The China Review, 17(2), 37–63.

Yang, J., & Ng, S. (2020, 3 November). Ant's Record IPO Suspended in Shanghai and Hong Kong Stock Exchanges. Retrieved January 2021, from Wall Street Journal: https://www.wsj.com/articles/ant-group-ipo-postponed-by-shanghai-stock-exchange-11604409597

Yergin, D. (2020). The New Map: Energy, Climate, and the Clash of Nations. London: Allen Lane.

Yergin, D. (1991). The Prize: The Epic Quest for Oil, Money, and Power. New York: Free Press.

Yergin, D. (2011). The Quest: Energy, Security, and the Remaking of the Modern World. New York: Penguin.

Yergin, D. (2020, 15 December). The World's Most Important Body of Water. Retrieved February 2021, from The Atlantic: https://amp-theatlantic-com.cdn.ampproject.org/c/s/amp.theatlantic.com/amp/article/617380/

Yi, G. (2020, 16 July). The IMF should turn to special drawing rights in its Covid-19 response. Retrieved March 2021, from Financial Times: https://www.ft.com/content/e7efef20-3960-46e7-922b-112dba8f2def

Yoshii, M. (2008). The Creation of the 'Shock Myth': Japan's Reactions to American Rapprochement with China, 1971–1972. The Journal of American-East Asian Relations, 15, 131–146.

Young, P. L. (2019). Victory or Death? Blockchain, Cryptocurrency & the Fintech World. Valletta: DV Books.

Yu, H., Cheng, S., & Zhang, T. (2021, September 11). In depth: What's standing in way of China's 'common prosperity'? Retrieved October 2021, from Nikkei Asia: https://asia.nikkei.com/Spotlight/Caixin/In-depth-What-s-standing-in-way-of-China-s-common-prosperity

Zhang, L. (2002). The Tiananmen Papers: The Chinese Leadership's Decision to Use Force Against Their Own People – In Their Own Words. (A. J. Nathan, & P. Link, Eds) New York: PublicAffairs.

Zhang, S. (2020, February 19). China's stock accounts top 160 million, equal to world's ninth-largest population, outpacing Communist Party's membership.

Retrieved January 2021, from SCMP: https://www.scmp.com/business/china-business/article/3051412/chinas-stock-accounts-top-160-million-equal-worlds-ninth

Zhao, Y. (2020, 22 January). China's Two-Child Policy. Retrieved January 2021, from Bloomberg: https://www.bloomberg.com/quicktake/china-s-two-child-policy?sref=u5WI0AVD

Zhao, Z. (2009). Prisoner of the State: The Secret Journal of Zhao Ziyang. New York: Simon & Schuster.

Zheng, S., & Mai, J. (2019, 2 August). US President Donald Trump calls protests 'riots' and an issue between Hong Kong and Beijing. Retrieved February 2021, from South China Morning Post: https://www.scmp.com/news/hong-kong/politics/article/3021067/chinas-top-diplomat-yang-jiechi-accuses-us-fanning-fires

Zhou, C. (2021, 14 March). China's plan to raise retirement age will be gradual process, government researcher insists. Retrieved March 2021, from South China Morning Post: https://www.scmp.com/economy/china-economy/article/3125403/chinas-plan-raise-retirement-age-will-be-gradual-process

Zhou, X. (2009, 23 March). Reform the international monetary system. Retrieved August 2020, from BIS: https://www.bis.org/review/r090402c.pdf

Zhu, R. (2015). Zhu Rongji on the Record: The Road to Reform 1998-2003. Washington DC: Brookings Institution Press.

Zhu, R. (2013). Zhu Rongji on the Record: The Road to Reform, 1991-1997. Washington DC: Brookings Institution Press.

Zhu, R. (2018). Zhu Rongji on the Record: The Shanghai Years, 1987-1991. Washington DC: Brookings Institution Press.

Zhu, R. (2011). Zhu Rongji meets the press. Hong Kong: Oxford University Press.

中国人口网. (2010, 20 August). Total population, CBR, CDR, NIR and TFR of China (1949–2000). Retrieved January 2021, from China Daily: http://www.chinadaily.com.cn/china/2010census/2010-08/20/content_11182379.htm

周, 鹏. (2009, 21 January). 国债市场仍存行政隐痛. Retrieved January 2021, from Sina 新闻中心: http://news.sina.com.cn/c/2009-01-21/092617088899.shtml

Notes

Preface

1. See (Allison, 2017).

Chapter 1: Introduction

1. (Fukuyama, 1992).
2. *IMF* data, which can be accessed at: https://data.imf.org. Figure given is for 31 December 2020.
3. A 'Gilt' is the common term used for a British government bond.
4. (Rajan, 2019, p. 248).
5. See, for example, (Klein & Pettis, 2020) and (Magnus, 2018).
6. See (Kolodko, 2020).
7. (Saunders, 2020).
8. China conducted a series of live-fire exercises in the Taiwan Strait in the run-up to Taiwan's presidential election on 23 March 1996 to express displeasure at the apparent independence leanings of Taiwanese President Lee Teng-hui (李登辉).
9. (Yergin, The New Map: Energy, Climate, and the Clash of Nations, 2020, p. 138).
10. (Wong, 2015, p. 14).
11. (Naughton, 2020, p. 129).
12. (Wong, 2015, p. 14).
13. In 2018, before worsening Sino-US relations and the 737 Max recall affected its sales, China accounted for 13.6 percent of Boeing's worldwide revenues. Notwithstanding ongoing trade tensions, China contributed 18.8 percent, 11.0

percent and 9.3 percent, respectively, of the worldwide sales of Nike, Starbucks and Disney in 2020.

14. See (Magnus, 2018) and (Mahbubani, 2020).

15. *HKEX* and *Dealogic* data for the 10 years up to 31 December 2020.

16. For the 10 years ending 31 December 2020, Mainland China-listed A-shares traded at an average premium of 18.2 percent versus their Hong Kong-listed H-share counterparts.

17. (Mahbubani, 2020, pp. 33–37).

18. For example, President Trump suggested publicly that the Covid-19 virus originated in a Chinese laboratory. See (BBC, 2020). Meanwhile, the Chinese Foreign Ministry accused the US of inciting anti-government protests in Hong Kong in 2019. See (Westcott, 2019).

19. (Ferguson, 2020).

20. (Brands, 2020).

21. (Klein & Pettis, 2020, p. 96).

22. (Sargent, 2011).

23. (Blackwill & Harris, 2016, p. 49).

24. See (Steil, 2013) and (Klein & Pettis, 2020, pp. 19–23).

25. (Steil & Litan, 2006, pp. 2–3).

Chapter 2: How the US Dollar Took Over the World

1. (Barton, 2021) and *IMF* data, which can be accessed at: https://data.imf.org.

2. (WTO, 2019).

3. *World Bank* data. Figure is for 2019 and can be accessed at: https://data.worldbank.org.

4. (Paulson Jr., 2020).

5. (Sharma, 2019). Emphasis added.

6. (Tooze, 2014, p. 33).

7. (Ahamed, 2009, p. 135).

8. (Steil, 2013, p. 34).

9. (Steil, 2013, p. 55).

10. (Steil, 2013, p. 28).

11. (Steil, 2013, pp. 55–56). Quote attributed to Henry Morgenthau III.

12. (Steil, 2018, p. 89).

13. (Steil, 2013, p. 72).

14. (Ahamed, 2009, p. 131).

15. In 1933, Cornell professor of farm management George Warren, along with two colleagues, published a title *Wholesale Prices for 213 Years: 1720–1923*, in which they documented a strong correlation between trends in commodity prices and the global supply and demand for gold. One of their conclusions was that, if commodity prices fell because of a gold shortage, raising the price of gold (in other words, devaluing the currency against gold) would be a means of reversing falling prices. This argument was to become influential on

the Roosevelt Administration as it battled deflation brought on by the Great Depression in the 1930s.

16. (Ahamed, 2009, pp. 159–161).
17. (Ahamed, 2009, p. 100).
18. (Ahamed, 2009, pp. 218–219).
19. (Steil, 2013, p. 74).
20. (Ahamed, 2009, pp. 241–268).
21. (Carter, 2020, p. 130)
22. Fractional reserve banking is a system in which only a fraction of bank deposits is backed by actual cash on hand and available for withdrawal. This system frees up more capital for lending, allowing the economy to expand more quickly.
23. (Wheelock, 1995).
24. (Steil, 2013, p. 157).
25. (Ahamed, 2009, p. 491).
26. (Steil, 2013, p. 207).
27. Under both the Atlantic Charter and Article VII of Lend-Lease, the US had sought to put an end to Britain's Imperial Preference system that provided preferential trade terms within the British Commonwealth.
28. (Steil, 2013, p. 129).
29. (Steil, 2013, p. 219).
30. (Steil, 2013, pp. 472–487).
31. Notwithstanding the prefix 'Euro-', the term 'Eurodollar' refers to all US dollar deposits held at banks outside the US and are therefore not under the jurisdiction of the Federal Reserve. Thus, a US dollar-denominated deposit at a bank in Hong Kong or Tokyo would be likewise deemed a Eurodollar deposit.
32. (O'Malley, 2015, p. 13).
33. (O'Malley, 2015, p. 13).
34. (Schenk, 1998, p. 222).
35. The spot market is where financial instruments are traded for immediate delivery.
36. Threadneedle Street in the City of London is the location of the Bank of England and is commonly used to refer to the UK's central bank.
37. (Schenk, 1998, pp. 224-227).
38. (O'Malley, 2015, p. 13).
39. (O'Malley, 2015, p. 14).
40. (O'Malley, 2015, p. 17).
41. (O'Malley, 2015, p. 17). Quote attributed to John Craven.
42. (O'Malley, 2015, p. 18). Quote from a speech by Lord Cromer, Governor of the Bank of England, at the Lord Mayor's Banquet in October 1962.
43. (O'Malley, 2015, p. 18).
44. Although there are claims that other issuers may have gone before Autostrade, as the first publicly issued Eurocurrency offering with an active secondary market, Autostrade is generally recognised as the first Eurobond issue.
45. (O'Malley, 2015, p. 23).

46. 'Coupon clipping' refers back to a time when bonds came printed with coupons on them. To receive the interest payments, the bondholder would clip off each coupon as its payment came due and redeem it for cash.
47. (O'Malley, 2015, p. 23–24). 'Throgmorton Street' refers to the London Stock Exchange, which was located there from 1972 until 2004.
48. (O'Malley, 2015, p. 25).
49. (Norman, 2007, p. 18).
50. (O'Malley, 2015, p. 25).
51. (O'Malley, 2015, p. 27–30).
52. (O'Malley, 2015, p. 35–36).
53. (O'Malley, 2015, p. 36).
54. (Norman, 2007, p. 22).
55. A 'repo' is a repurchase agreement. This is a form of short-term collateralised borrowing. The borrower sells securities (usually government or other highly rated bonds) to the lender in return for short-term funds and, by agreement between the two parties, buys them back at a future date, usually at a higher price to reflect interest costs.
56. (Phillips, 2019).
57. *SWIFT* data, which can be accessed at: https://www.swift.com/swift-resource/249851/download.
58. Based on *BIS* and *SIFMA* figures, which can respectively be accessed at: https://stats.bis.org/statx/toc/SEC.html and https://www.sifma.org/wp-content/uploads/2020/09/US-Fact-Book-2020-SIFMA.pdf.
59. The Guam Doctrine is also known as the Nixon Doctrine. By the time that Nixon came to office in 1969, the US was financially and militarily overstretched by the Cold War and the Vietnam War. Recognising that the US was realistically unable to maintain all the commitments it had previously made, President Nixon first articulated a retrenchment in US foreign commitments at a press conference in Guam on 25 July 1969, whereby he stated that henceforth the US 'would assist in the defence and developments of allies and friends' but would not 'undertake all the defence of the free nations of the world'. Implicitly, this was an abandonment of the Southeast Asian Treaty Organisation (SEATO).
60. (Klein & Pettis, 2020, pp. 192–193).
61. These were known as 'Roosa bonds', named after Treasury official Robert Roosa.
62. (Steil, 2013, p. 495).
63. (Reid-Henry, 2019, p. 58).
64. Emphasis added.
65. (Thorp, 2017, p. 202).
66. For the story of the rise and fall of LTCM, see (Lowenstein, 2011).
67. These currencies were: British pounds, Canadian dollars, Deutschmarks, Japanese yen, Mexican pesos and Swiss francs.

68. (Yergin, 1991, pp. 597–607).
69. (Mouawad, 2008).
70. *BIS* data as of 31 December 2020, which can be accessed at: https://stats.bis.org.
71. *World Federation of Exchanges* data as of 31 December 2020, which can be accessed at: https://statistics.world-exchanges.org.
72. *BIS* data as of 31 December 2020, which can be accessed at: https://stats.bis.org.
73. This is the risk of default by the opposite party to a trade. Clearing houses act as a central counterparty to all traders within a market and collect margin funds from all participants in order to insure against the default of any one party to a trade.
74. *US Treasury Department* data, which can be accessed at: www.publicdebt.treas.gov.
75. Based on *US Treasury Department* data for Treasury securities held by the public, which can be accessed at: https://ticdata.treasury.gov/Publish/mfh.txt. This figure may misstate the true proportion of US Treasury securities held by foreigners, since US securities held in overseas custody accounts may not be attributed to the actual owners.
76. (Garbade, 2012, p. 1).
77. (Garbade, 2012, p. 44).
78. (Davidson, 2010, p. 664).
79. *US Treasury Department* data, which can be accessed at: https://fiscaldata.treasury.gov/datasets/.
80. (Congressional Budget Office, 2010).
81. (Yergin, 1991, p. 616).
82. (Yergin, 1991, p. 409).
83. Based on *US Treasury Department* data, which can be accessed at: https://ticdata.treasury.gov/Publish/mfhhis01.txt and https://fiscaldata.treasury.gov/datasets/historical-debt-outstanding/historical-debt-outstanding.
84. Pursuant to the Dodd-Frank Wall Street Reform and Consumer Protection Act (Pub.L. 111-203), effective since 21 July 2010.
85. *Bloomberg* data.
86. (Richter, 1989).
87. (Cole, 1989).

Chapter 3: Whose Problem?

1. (Irwin, 2013, p. 33).
2. (Irwin, 2013, pp. 33–34).
3. (Irwin, 2013, p. 38).
4. (Irwin, 2013, pp. 39–40).
5. (Irwin, 2013, p. 42).
6. (Wolkonowski, 2018). Even adjusting for the decline in its expenditure on the Vietnam War, America's share of total NATO expenditure fell from around 70 percent in 1970 to 60 percent in 1975.

7. (Fallows, 1989).
8. (Yergin, 1991, p. 753).
9. (Yergin, 1991, p. 755).
10. (Reid-Henry, 2019, p. 285).
11. (Yergin, 1991, p. 758).
12. On 12 September 2001, Australian Prime Minister John Howard invoked the Australia, New Zealand, United States Security Treaty (ANZUS), declaring: 'Australia will provide all support that might be requested of us by the United States in any action that might be taken'. German Chancellor Gerhard Schröder showed similar support, stating that the attacks were 'a declaration of war against the civilised world'. British Prime Minister Tony Blair despatched his top intelligence personnel to Washington DC in the wake of the attacks, while NATO also placed itself at the disposal of the US. See (Reid-Henry, 2019, p. 504).
13. (Yergin, 2011, p. 145).
14. (Reid-Henry, 2019, p. 521).
15. (Reid-Henry, 2019, p. 521). Cook was referring to the extremely narrow victory that George W. Bush had scored over the Democratic contender, Vice President Al Gore, in the 2000 presidential election, in which there had been a hand recount of votes cast in four counties in Florida.
16. (Reid-Henry, 2019, p. 521).
17. (Yergin, 2011, p. 523).
18. (Reid-Henry, 2019, p. 522).
19. (Crawford, 2019).
20. (Peltier, 2020).
21. (Steil, 2013, p. 372).
22. (Tooze, 2018, p. 372). This would appear to be proof that some people *really do* read *Playboy* for the articles!
23. (Reid-Henry, 2019, pp. 70–71).
24. (Reid-Henry, 2019, p. 90).
25. (Carter, 2020, p. 468).
26. (DeLong, 2007, p. 110).
27. (Carter, 2020, p. 495).
28. (Reid-Henry, 2019, p. 32).
29. Data on federal income tax rates is sourced from the *Tax Foundation* and can be accessed at: https://files.taxfoundation.org/legacy/docs/fed_individual_rate_history_nominal.pdf.
30. (Carter, 2020, p. 463).
31. (Friedman, 1970).
32. (Schwab, 2019).
33. Enron Corporation was a Texas-based company that operated in energy and commodity markets. It went bankrupt in 2001 after it was discovered that its senior management had used accounting loopholes to hide billions of dollars

of debt from failed deals and projects. Several senior executives were jailed in connection with the scandal, which also led to the collapse of Arthur Anderson, one of the five largest global accountancy firms at the time. Following the scandal, the US introduced major new regulations and legislation to improve the accuracy of public companies' financial disclosures.

34. (Tepper & Hearn, 2019). Quote attributed to Edward Queen, Director of Ethics and Servant Leadership at the Emory Centre for Ethics.
35. Emphasis added.
36. (Tepper & Hearn, 2019, p. 119).
37. (Tepper & Hearn, 2019, p. 198).
38. (Tepper & Hearn, 2019, p. 8).
39. (Economist, 2017).
40. (Tepper & Hearn, 2019, pp. 35–62).
41. (Tepper & Hearn, 2019, p. 154).
42. (Milanovic, 2019, p. 57).
43. (Reid-Henry, 2019, p. 151).
44. (Milanovic, 2019, pp. 56–57).
45. (Mahbubani, 2020, pp. 112–114).
46. (Westad, 2017, p. 287). Quote from Eisenhower's televised address, 17 January 1961.
47. (Mahbubani, 2020, p. 107).
48. The chairman of the Defence Board in question was Richard Perle.
49. (Reid-Henry, 2019, p. 566).
50. (Carter, 2020, p. 485).
51. (Carter, 2020, p. 487).
52. (Carter, 2020, p. 492).
53. (Reid-Henry, 2019, pp. 557–558).
54. (Capo McCormick & Kruger, 2009).
55. (Steil & Litan, 2006, p. 11).
56. (Steil & Litan, 2006, p. 13).
57. (Steil & Litan, 2006, p. 13).
58. (Steil & Litan, 2006, p. 13).
59. (Steil & Litan, 2006, p. 14).
60. (Steil & Litan, 2006, p. 14).
61. Paul Volcker's former boss at the New York Fed was Robert Roosa.
62. (Appelbaum & Hershey Jr., 2019).
63. (Appelbaum & Hershey Jr., 2019).
64. (Appelbaum & Hershey Jr., 2019).
65. *Federal Reserve Bank of St. Louis* data, which can be accessed at: https://fred.stlouisfed.org.
66. (Schwartz, 2020).
67. (Tooze, 2018, p. 32).
68. (Prasad, 2014, p. 60).

69. (Prasad, 2014, p. 53).
70. (Steil & Litan, 2006, p. 83).
71. While the US held only 16.5 percent of the voting power on the IMF as of 17 July 2021, it has a unique veto power over major policy decisions. For details, see (Congressional Research Service, 2019) and the *IMF* website: https://www.imf.org/external/np/sec/memdir/members.aspx#U.
72. (Steil & Litan, 2006, pp. 93–94).
73. (Steil & Litan, 2006, p. 84).
74. (Prasad, 2014, pp. 66–67).
75. (Steil & Litan, 2006, p. 85).
76. (Kaplan & Rodrik, 2001, p. 393).
77. (Steil & Litan, 2006, pp. 91–92).
78. (Steil & Litan, 2006, p. 17).
79. (Steil & Litan, 2006, p. 20).
80. (Steil & Litan, 2006, p. 23).
81. This included the 1989 Financial Institutions Reform, Recovery and Enforcement Act, requiring thrift institutions to maintain minimum capital ratios of at least three percent, and the Federal Deposit Insurance Corporation Improvement Act of 1991, which allowed regulators to seize and close down a bank if its capital ratio fell below two percent.
82. *IMF* data, which can be accessed at: https://data.imf.org.
83. Based on *PBOC* data as of 28 February 2021, China's foreign exchange reserves stood at $3.3 trillion. This data can be accessed at: http://www.pbc.gov.cn/eportal/.
84. *Bloomberg* data.
85. (Appelbaum & Hershey Jr., 2019).
86. For an excellent account of the history of the development of the mortgage-backed securitisation business, see (Lewis, 2010).
87. (Tooze, 2018, p. 50).
88. (Tooze, 2018, p. 47).
89. (Tooze, 2018, p. 62).
90. (Tooze, 2018, pp. 62–63).
91. (Reid-Henry, 2019, p. 605).
92. (Tooze, 2018, p. 64).
93. (Reid-Henry, 2019, p. 605).
94. (Bernanke, 2015, p. 47).
95. (Bernanke, 2015, p. 21)
96. For a more detailed account of regulatory and policy actions during the GFC, see (Bernanke, 2015) and (Tooze, 2018).
97. (Bernanke, 2015, pp. 427–428).
98. (Javers, 2011).
99. (Tooze, 2018, pp. 109–110).

100. (Tooze, 2018, p. 207).
101. (Tooze, 2018, p. 89).
102. These included the Banco Central do Brasil, Banco de México, Bank of Japan, Bank of Canada, Bank of England, Bank of Korea, Danmarks Nationalbank, the ECB, the Monetary Authority of Singapore, Norges Bank, the Reserve Bank of Australia, Reserve Bank of New Zealand, Sveriges Riksbank, and the SNB.
103. (Tooze, 2018, pp. 213–214).
104. (Rajan, 2007).
105. (Zhou, 2009).
106. (Tooze, 2018, pp. 241–242).
107. (Bernanke, 2015, p. 505).
108. (Bernanke, 2015, p. 348).
109. (Bernanke, 2015, pp. 469–470).
110. (Theriault, 2014).
111. (Bernanke, 2015, pp. 623–624).
112. (Bernanke, 2015, p. 518).
113. (Reid-Henry, 2019, p. 658).
114. (Prasad, 2014, p. 6).
115. (Prasad, 2014, pp. 6–7).
116. (Tooze, 2018, p. 564).
117. (Winn, 2016).
118. At the end of 2020, Japan held $1.25 trillion in US Treasury securities. *US Treasury Department* data, which can be accessed at: https://ticdata.treasury.gov/Publish/mfh.txt.
119. Based on *PBOC* data as of 31 December 2020, China's foreign exchange reserves stood at $3.2 trillion. This data can be accessed at: http://www.pbc.gov.cn/eportal/.
120. (Howell, 2020, p. 143).
121. *World Bank* data. Figure is for 2019 and can be accessed at: https://data.worldbank.org.
122. (Klein & Pettis, 2020). Based on *BIS* data for 2017.
123. (Kelton, 2020, p. 61). Refers to the Tax Cuts and Jobs Act of 2017.
124. (Brown & Horowitz, 2018).
125. (Chen & Lawder, 2018).
126. For the case that reserve currency issuers do need to run deficits, see (Thayer, 1996) and (Kelton, 2020). For the case against, see (Prasad, 2017, pp. 125–127).
127. *IMF* data as of 30 September 2020, which can be accessed at: https://data.imf.org.
128. (Barton, 2021).
129. For further details on the Federal Reserve programmes announced between March and June 2020, see (Kolchin, 2020, pp. 8–10).

130. *Federal Reserve Bank of St. Louis* data, which can be accessed at: https://fred. stlouisfed.org/series/WALCL.
131. (Howell, 2020, pp. 141–176).
132. (Tooze, 2018, pp. 471–483).
133. *US Treasury Department* and *Federal Reserve Bank of St. Louis* data, which can respectively be accessed at: www.publicdebt.treas.gov. and https://fred. stlouisfed.org.
134. *US Treasury Department* data, which can be accessed at: https://ticdata.treasury. gov/Publish/mfhhis01.txt.
135. *Federal Reserve Bank of St. Louis* data, which can be accessed at: https://fred. stlouisfed.org.
136. *Bloomberg* data.
137. See (Sen, 2021) and (Ebrahimy, Igan, & Martinez Peria, 2020).
138. On 5 June 2021, G-7 finance ministers agreed to tax reforms comprising two key pillars: the first will enable countries to tax big companies based on the revenue they generate in that country, rather than where the company is located for tax purposes; and the second sets a minimum global corporate tax rate of 15 percent.

Chapter 4: From First World to Third and Back Again

1. (Levathes, 1994, pp. 144–145).
2. (Diamond, 2005, p. 364).
3. (Diamond, 2005, p. 279).
4. (Wang, 2019, pp. 103–108).
5. For an account of the nation building efforts of Chinese revolutionaries and the legacies they have left, see (Hayton, 2020).
6. (Hayton, 2020, p. 160).
7. (Wood, 2020, p. 144).
8. (Levathes, 1994, pp. 107–122).
9. Thomas Pereira and fellow Jesuit Jean-François Gerbillon served as translators between the Manchus and the Russians during negotiations of the 1689 Treaty of Nerchinsk, which defined the border between the Manchu and Russian empires. More than serving as just linguistic translators, the Jesuits played a crucial role in translating the concept of the nation state, established by the Westphalian treaties in 1648, to the Manchus. See (Hayton, 2020, pp. 17–23).
10. (Diamond, 2005, p. 485).
11. (Kennedy, 1987, pp. 4–8).
12. (Hsü, 2000, p. 124). Quote attributed to Hsiao Kung-ch'üan.
13. See (Abrams, 1971).
14. (Hsü, 2000, p. 149).
15. (Hsü, 2000, p. 168).

16. (Hsü, 2000, p. 149).
17. (Inglis, 1976, p. 38).
18. (Hsü, 2000, pp. 147–148).
19. (Inglis, 1976, p. 53).
20. (Backhouse & Bland, 1914, pp. 322–331).
21. A tael is equivalent to one and a third ounces.
22. (Chang, 2013, pp. 20-21).
23. (Hsü, 2000, p. 162).
24. See (Hsü, 2000, pp. 168–172) and (Platt, 2018, pp. 287–291).
25. (Platt, 2018, p. 289).
26. (Waley, 1958, pp. 11–157).
27. (Inglis, 1976, p. 149).
28. (Inglis, 1976, p. 152).
29. (Inglis, 1976, p. 193).
30. Also known as the 'Bogue' or the 'Humen Strait' (虎门), this is a narrow stretch of the Pearl River Delta separating the Shizi Channel (狮子洋) in the north and the Lingding Channel (伶仃洋) in the south.
31. Also referred to as the Convention of Chuenpi (穿鼻草约).
32. (Hsü, 2000, p. 187).
33. Also referred to as the Treaty of Nanking (南京条约).
34. (Inglis, 1976, p. 228).
35. (Economist, 2010).
36. (Hsü, 2000, pp. 221–223).
37. (Kissinger, 2012, p. 65).
38. Also referred to as the Second Opium War.
39. Also referred to as the Treaty of Tientsin (天津条约), signed in June 1858.
40. Dengzhou (now known as Penglai, 蓬莱); Hankou (汉口); Jiujiang (九江); Nanjing; Newchwang (now known as Yingkou, 营口); Qiongzhou (now part of Qiongshan, 琼山); Shantou (汕头); Taiwanfu (台湾府); Tamsui (*Danshui*, 淡水); and Zhenjiang (镇江).
41. (Hsü, 2000, pp. 398–404).
42. (Chang, 2013, p. 298).
43. (Chang, 2019, p. xv).
44. (Wood, 2020, pp. 457–458). Quote from the diary of Liu Dapeng.
45. (Wang, 2019, p. 43).
46. (Hsü, 2000, p. 572).
47. (Chang, 2019, p. 231).
48. (Hsü, 2000, p. 652).
49. (Wong, 2015, p. 41).
50. (Goodstadt, 1972, p. 10).
51. (Westad, 2017, p. 236).
52. (Hsü, 2000, p. 675).
53. (Hsü, 2000, p. 652).

54. (Hsü, 2000, p. 654).

55. (Chang & Halliday, 2006, p. 511).

56. (Hsü, 2000, pp. 655–658).

57. (Chang & Halliday, 2006, p. 575).

58. (Westad, 2017, p. 234).

59. (Chang & Halliday, 2006, p. 587).

60. (Westad, 2017, p. 242).

61. (Goodstadt, 1972, p. 33).

62. The 'Long March' (长征) was a military retreat by the CCP's Red Army in 1934 and 1935 against a campaign of extermination by Nationalist forces. Over harsh conditions and with the Nationalist army trying to encircle them, the CCP forces retreated from Jiangxi to Yan'an (延安) in Shaanxi (陕西) province. The Long March later acquired an almost mythical status in Chinese Communist history.

63. (Lovell, 2019, p. 134).

64. For a highly readable first-hand account of one youth who was sent down to the countryside during the Cultural Revolution, see (Shan, 2019).

65. See, for example, (Chang & Halliday, 2006).

66. (Kissinger, 2012, pp. 101–103).

67. In addition to Jiang Qing, the Gang of Four included Zhang Chunqiao (张春桥), Yao Wenyuan (姚文元) and Wang Hongwen (王洪文). This group both exerted a heavy influence on Chairman Mao during the Cultural Revolution and were used by him to orchestrate many of the political campaigns and purges of the era.

68. (Harari, 2015, pp. 227–232).

69. (Vogel, 2011, p. 279).

70. (Vogel, 2011, p. 390).

71. (Zhao, 2009, p. 134).

72. (Vogel, 2011, p. 443).

73. (Vogel, 2011, p. 309).

74. (Vogel, 2011, p. 531).

75. (Vogel, 2011, p. 533).

76. (Vogel, 2011, p. 541).

77. (Cheung, 2020. Remembering Hong Kong's unsung role in Shenzhen's glory – 40 years on, have fortunes reversed?).

78. (Vogel, 2011, p. 394).

79. (Vogel, 2011, p. 398).

80. (Vogel, 2011, p. 402).

81. (Vogel, 2011, p. 427).

82. (Vogel, 2011, p. 403).

83. (Vogel, 2011, p. 407).

84. (Vogel, 2011, p. 406).

85. (Vogel, 2011, p. 401).

86. (Vogel, 2011, p. 450).
87. (Vogel, 2011, p. 450).
88. (Vogel, 2011, p. 470).
89. (Zhao, 2009, pp. 219–221).
90. (Kristof, 1989).
91. (Zhao, 2009, pp. 156–157).
92. (Zhao, 2009, p. 157).
93. (Zhao, 2009, pp. 249–252).
94. (Kissinger, 2012, p. 416).
95. *World Bank* data, which can be accessed at: https://data.worldbank.org.
96. (Shih, 2007, pp. 142–143).
97. (Vogel, 2011, p. 670).
98. (Zhao, 2009, pp. 111–113).
99. (Wong, 2015, p. 56).
100. (Wong, 2015, p. 53).
101. (Shih, 2007, p. 145).
102. (Shih, 2007, p. 146).
103. (Shih, 2007, p. 146).
104. The Sixteen Measures were: (1) controlling money supply; (2) prohibiting raising capital illegally; (3) actively leveraging interest rates; (4) prohibiting 'chaotic' fund raising; (5) controlling lending; (6) paying back depositors; (7) strengthening financial reforms; (8) reforming investment and financing structures; (9) national debt issues; (10) refine the management of issuing and trading shares; (11) restructuring the foreign exchange market; (12) strengthening control over the real estate market; (13) tightening tax loopholes; (14) stopping construction projects; (15) price controls; and (16) controlling purchasing power.
105. (Magnus, 2018, p. 46).
106. (Wong, 2015, pp. 52–54).
107. (Green, 2017, p. 426).
108. (Wong, 2015, p. 57).
109. (Green, 2017, pp. 471–472).
110. (Wong, 2015, p. 95).
111. (Magnus, 2018, p. 54).
112. See (Wong, 2015, p. 170) and *State Council* news release, which can be accessed at: http://www.gov.cn/shuju/2021-02/09/content_5586245.htm.
113. (Shih, 2007, p. 193).
114. (Wong, 2015, p. 59).
115. (Macartney, 2008).
116. *World Bank* data. Figure is for 1997–2007 and can be accessed at: https://data.worldbank.org.
117. (Paulson Jr., 2015, p. 214).
118. (Vogel, 2011, p. 423).

119. (Wang, 2019, p. 101).
120. (Mitter & Johnson, 2021).
121. (Vogel, 2011, p. 714).

Chapter 5: Two Steps Forward, One Step Back

1. (Naughton, 2019).
2. (Klein & Pettis, 2020, p. 105).
3. (Naughton, 2019, pp. 30–31).
4. (Klein & Pettis, 2020, p. 113).
5. (Klein & Pettis, 2020, p. 113).
6. See (Howell, 2020, pp. 63–69). Over the period 1981–2019, China enjoyed 7.3 percent annualised growth in real productivity versus 1.5 percent for the US.
7. (Klein & Pettis, 2020, p. 110).
8. (Klein & Pettis, 2020, p. 111).
9. (Naughton, 2019, pp. 39–40).
10. Since renamed China Mobile (中国移动).
11. (Paulson Jr., 2015, pp. 49–50).
12. (Paulson Jr., 2015, p. 54).
13. (Paulson Jr., 2015, pp. 62-63).
14. (Wong, 2015, pp. 56, 95).
15. For a detailed and excellent account of the development of China's various securities markets, see (Walter & Howie, 2006).
16. Not to be confused with Charles Li Xiaojia (李小加), who served as CEO of HKEX from 2010 to 2020.
17. (Walter & Howie, 2006, p. 55).
18. Although government bond futures were relaunched on the China Financial Futures Exchange (CFFEX, 中国金融期货交易所) in 2013, it was not until February 2020 that it was announced that banks – which generally have the greatest need to hedge interest rates through bond futures – would be allowed to participate in the market again.
19. Laura Cha was appointed Chairman of HKEX in 2018.
20. (Walter & Howie, 2007, pp. 61–65).
21. See (Walter & Howie, 2007, pp. 60–61), (Xie & Zheng, 2019) and (Asia Asset Management, 2015).
22. (Zhang, 2020).
23. (Walter & Howie, 2007, pp. 131–164).
24. (Walter & Howie, 2007, pp. 149–151).
25. (Wildau, 2015).
26. For the ten years ending 31 December 2020, Mainland China-listed A-shares traded at an average premium of 18.2 percent versus their Hong Kong-listed H-share counterparts.
27. (Lee, 2018).

28. The SSE's Science and Technology Innovation Board, known as 'STAR', was established in July 2019 to attract new technology companies that found the rules governing the SSE's Main Board unattractive. Specifically, the STAR Market has lower financial hurdles for issuers, does not have valuation caps, allows for non-standard voting structures, and features a shortened approvals process. The SZSE also launched a tech-focused board with lower listing hurdles called ChiNext (创业板) in October 2009.
29. The remark was made during a private conversation in the author's presence in 2013.
30. (Wong, 2015, p. 56).
31. (Mo, 1999, p. 91).
32. Data sourced from: (中国金融年鉴) 1998-2000 整理计算.
33. (Walter & Howie, 2012, p. 57).
34. (Mo, 1999, pp. 93-94).
35. See the discussion on the GFC and the euro crisis in Chapter 3. For further reading, see (Ahamed, 2009) and (Tooze, 2018).
36. Dubbed the 'S&L Crisis', this involved the bankruptcy of 1,043 out of 3,234 savings and loan associations in the US between 1986 and 1995.
37. The four AMCs were: China Great Wall Asset Management (中国长城资产管理) – ABC; China Orient Asset Management (中国东方资产管理) – BOC; China Cinda Asset Management (中国信达资产管理) – CCB; and China Huarong Asset Management (中国华融资产管理) – ICBC.
38. (Walter & Howie, 2012, p. 44).
39. (Walter & Howie, 2012, pp. 60-61).
40. (Walter & Howie, 2012, p. 44).
41. (Leigh & Podpiera, 2006, p. 12).
42. (Tooze, 2018, pp. 239-251).
43. (Gao, 2007, pp. 106-107).
44. (Walter & Howie, 2012, p. 100).
45. This is an auction method whereby the price is reduced until all securities on offer are sold.
46. (周, 2009).
47. (Walter & Howie, 2012, p. 118).
48. (Walter & Howie, 2012, pp. 131-141).
49. (Walter & Howie, 2012, p. 116).
50. See (Prasad, 2017, pp. 204-207) and (Magnus, 2018, pp. 5-10).
51. (Magnus, 2018, p. 57).
52. (Magnus, 2018, p. 42).
53. *Fitch* and *CEIC* data, which can respectively be accessed at: https://www.fitchratings.com/research/sovereigns/what-investors-want-to-know-china-household-debt-15-04-2021#:~:text=China's%20household%20debt%20continued%20to,9pp%20from%20end%2D2018%20levels and https://www.ceicdata.com/en/indicator/china/household-debt--of-nominal-gdp.

54. Definitions of shadow banking vary, but it can include: (i) 'entrusted loans', which involve non-financial corporations as borrowers and lenders (sometimes with banks acting as intermediaries); (ii) 'trust loans', which are financial transactions undertaken by trust companies, which are regulated separately from banks; (iii) 'bank acceptances', which are instruments issued by banks that pay a fixed amount over a fixed period and are backed by deposits of the ultimate borrower; and (iv) other credit instruments, such as peer-to-peer lending, financial leasing and credit provided by pawnshops.

55. (Tang, 2020).

56. (IMF, 2014).

57. For further reading on shadow banking in China, see (Sheng & Ng, 2016).

58. (Lee, 2020).

59. (Paulson Jr., 2015, p. 179). References remarks by President Xi Jinping.

60. (Prasad, 2017, p. 287).

61. Based on disclosures by China Central Depository and Clearing (中央国债登记结算) and Shanghai Clearing House (上海清算所) as of 31 December 2020, which can be accessed at: https://www.chinabond.com.cn/Channel/19012917# and https://www.shclearing.com/sjtj/tjyb/.

62. *SAFE* data as of 30 September 2020, which can be accessed at: https://www.safe.gov.cn/en/2018/0928/1459.html.

63. (SAFE, 2021).

64. The six cities included were: Chongqing (重庆), Shanghai, Shenzhen, Tianjin, Wenzhou (温州) and Wuhan.

65. (Prasad, 2017, p. 182).

66. (Prasad, 2017, pp. 28-29).

67. (Prasad, 2017, pp. 82-87).

68. (Prasad, 2017, p. 200).

69. At the time, the PBOC was applying for the renminbi to be included in the basket of currencies underlying the IMF's SDRs. A more market-driven exchange rate was also a condition required to achieve this inclusion.

70. (Prasad, 2017, p. 92).

71. (Prasad, 2017, p. 73).

72. (Paulson Jr., 2015, p. 337).

73. (Clark, 2016, p. 24).

74. (Clark, 2016, p. 94).

75. (Xie & Yang, 2020).

76. (Baker, Toonkel, & Seetharaman, 2014).

77. (Milanovic, 2019, p. 88).

78. (Prasad, 2017, p. 42).

79. For an engaging account of the emergence of China's technology sector, see (Lee K.-F. , 2018).

80. (Milanovic, 2019, pp. 91-96).

81. (Milanovic, 2019, pp. 103-106).

82. (Wong, 2015, p. 316).
83. (Lam, 2020, p. 73). References Wu Jinglian (吴敬琏), an economist at the Development Research Centre of the State Council.
84. (Chiu, 2019).
85. Defined as the sum of investment income, rental income and other property income.
86. Notably, President Xi Jinping heaped praise on French academic Thomas Piketty's 2013 book *Capital in the 21st Century*, which chronicled rising wealth inequality in the US and Europe. However, after Piketty refused to acquiesce to the censorship of data on rising wealth inequality in China in his 2019 book *Capital and Ideology*, publication of it in China was banned. See (Leng, 2020).
87. (Milanovic, 2019, pp. 97-106).
88. (Milanovic, 2019, pp. 107-109).
89. (Paulson Jr., 2015, pp. 357-363).
90. For a detailed account of the Xi Administration's curtailment of Chinese civil liberties, see (Lam, 2020).
91. (Yan & Huang, 2017).
92. (Lam, 2020, p. 204).
93. (Yang & Ng, 2020).
94. (Apple Daily, 2020).
95. (Fioretti, Hu, & Hunter, 2020).
96. It is stressed that the author has no inside knowledge of Chinese regulators' decision-making process specifically relating to the suspension of Ant Group's IPO in November 2020 and these observations are simply an interpretation based on publicly available information.
97. (中国人口网, 2010).
98. (Greenhalgh, 2003, p. 181).
99. (Magnus, 2018, pp. 113-119).
100. (Goodkind, 2018).
101. (Magnus, 2018, p. 112).
102. (Magnus, 2018, p. 119). These figures do not take into account the effects of the Covid-19 pandemic, which are as yet unclear.
103. (Magnus, 2018, pp. 119-128).
104. (Tartar, 2019).
105. (Liu, 2017).
106. (Pinker, 2011, pp. 104-106).
107. (Zhou, 2021).
108. (Zhao, 2020).
109. *PBOC* data as of December 2020. Includes corporate demand deposits, corporate time deposits and personal deposits: http://www.pbc.gov.cn/diaochatongjisi/116219/116319/3959050/3959052/index.html.
110. Based on the market capitalisation of Chinese equity markets and Chinese domestic bonds outstanding as of September 2020, less foreign holdings as

disclosed by the *PBOC*: http://www.pbc.gov.cn/diaochatongjisi/resource/cms/2020/11/2020110417475871026.pdf.

111. *Federal Reserve* data as of September 2020, which can be accessed at: https://www.federalreserve.gov/releases/z1/default.htm.

112. For Northbound investors, eligible stocks were those included in the SSE 180 and SSE 380 indices. For Southbound investors, eligible stocks were the constituents of the Hang Seng Composite LargeCap Index and the Hang Seng Composite MidCap Index. In addition, all stocks dual-listed in both markets were eligible.

113. The Sino-British Joint Declaration was the agreement signed on 19 December 1984 between China and the UK on the future governance of Hong Kong under Chinese sovereignty after 1 July 1997, when a 99-year lease over Hong Kong's New Territories was set to expire.

114. Hong Kong Basic Law, Chapter IV: Political Structure.

115. 全国人民代表大会常务委员会关于香港特别行政区2012年行政长官和立法会产生办法及有关普选问题的决定 (2007年12月29日第十届全国人民代表大会常务委员会第三十一次会议通过).

116. Under electoral reforms enacted in March 2021, the number of seats on Legco will be increased to 90, of which 20 will be directly elected geographic constituencies, 30 will be be indirectly elected trade-based functional constituencies, and 40 will be elected by a newly created 'Election Committee'.

117. (Lung, 2021). Hong Kong's crown was lost in 2020 to Singapore, which topped the Heritage Foundations' ranking that year, with Hong Kong coming in second place. In 2021, the Heritage Foundation announced that it would no longer distinguish Hong Kong from Mainland China in its rankings.

118. (Cheung & Cheung, 2006).

119. (Friedman, 1997).

120. (OXFAM Hong Kong, 2018, p. 11).

121. (Goodstadt, 2018, pp. 90-91).

122. (Wordie, 2012).

123. (Goodstadt, 2018, p. 69).

124. For a more in-depth discussion of the policy failures of successive Hong Kong administrations, see (Goodstadt, 2018).

125. Following a scandal involving melamine-tainted baby formula milk in Mainland China in 2008, there was a surge in Mainland demand for foreign formula milk sold in Hong Kong. The impact of this demand on local supply was so strong that the Hong Kong Government had to impose a two-can restriction on the export of formula milk.

126. There were a number of significant implementation errors in the Shanghai-Hong Kong Stock Connect scheme. One of the most notable was the requirement for Northbound investors to transfer shares from their custodian to the execution broker one day before selling the shares. This was not only operationally cumbersome, but it also created a risk that their trading intentions would be leaked, impacting the price of the shares ahead of the time of

trading. This arose out of HKEX's insufficient understanding of the needs of its end customers. This and other errors have been subsequently rectified.

127. A joint notice by the MOF, SAT and CSRC on 14 November 2014 clarified that Northbound investors would be exempted from capital gains tax and would be subject to a 10 percent withholding tax on dividends.

128. Two of the most important regulators whose approval was required were the Central Bank of Ireland and Luxembourg's Commission de Surveillance du Secteur Financier, which regulated the largest number of funds subject to the European Undertakings for Collective Investment in Transferable Securities (UCITS) Directive.

129. (Prasad, 2017, p. 200).

130. (France 24, 2015).

131. Based on a conversation between the author and a senior representative of the SWF in 2018.

132. At inception, Bond Connect only allowed Northbound investment by international investors into China. Southbound Bond Connect, which allowed Mainland Chinese investors to invest in bonds traded overseas was launched on 24 September 2021.

133. As things turned out, Bloomberg had vastly underestimated the intricacies of implementing a major cross-border market access programme in China. The *Bloomberg News* website had been blocked in China since in 2012 after it published an article detailing the wealth accumulated by family members of China's leadership, and Bloomberg's negotiations with CFETS ultimately stalled.

134. For an interesting insider's account of the growth of the indexing business, see (Makepeace, 2020).

135. (Makepeace, 2020, p. 7).

136. (Wigglesworth & Janiaud, 2020).

137. (MSCI, 2017).

138. (Xie, 2020, Wall Street Journal).

139. For further reading on the renminbi's internationalisation, see (Prasad, 2017).

140. *PBOC* data. Most recent figure is as of 31 March 2021. Data can be accessed at: http://www.pbc.gov.cn/diaochatongjisi/resource/cms/2021/04/2021043016025378006.htm.

141. *HKEX* data.

142. *PBOC* data. Data can be accessed at: http://www.pbc.gov.cn/diaochatongjisi/resource/cms/2021/04/2021043016025378006.htm.

143. (Sheridan, 2007).

144. (Sin, 2019).

145. (Vogel, 2011, pp. 490–491).

146. Such accusations were not entirely without foundation, given Tung's infamous grant of the highly profitable Cyberport property development project to Richard Li (李泽楷), the second son of fellow Hong Kong tycoon Li Ka-shing (李嘉诚), without any competitive tender process.

147. In the US, the 1947 National Security Act imposes penalties for treason and subversion; the Patriot Act enacted in the wake of the 11 September 2011 terrorist attacks provides for monitoring of citizens' information and the detention of non-US persons on security grounds; and the 1938 Foreign Agents Registration Act and 1982 Foreign Missions Act provide for certain controls over the actions of foreign individuals and institutions in the US. Changes to Spain's national security legislation were also seen as an attempt to curtail the activities of separatist movements.
148. See (Zheng & Mai, 2019) and (Creery, 2019).
149. (Global Times, 2019).
150. Notably, a bipartisan US Congressional commission received testimony from Hong Kong pro-democracy activist Joshua Wong in September 2019.
151. (Davidson, 2021).
152. Countries that have suspended extradition arrangements with Hong Kong include Australia, Canada, France, New Zealand, the UK and the US. See (Tiezzi, 2020).
153. On 17 June 2021, Hong Kong authorities froze the assets of Next Digital, Apple Daily's parent company. Unable to pay its wage and utility bills, Apple Daily was forced to cease operations.
154. The full CFA decision on the matter of Jimmy Lai's bail application can be found at: https://www.hklii.hk/eng/hk/cases/hkcfa/2021/3.html.
155. (Cheung, National security law: chief executive picking judges to hear cases undermines judiciary, warns former Hong Kong chief justice, 2020).
156. (Lewis, 2021).
157. (Lee & Cheng, 2021).
158. (Chan, 2021).
159. (Shen, 2016).
160. (Shambaugh, 2020, pp. 358-360).
161. (Sutter, 2020).
162. (Yahuda, 2020, pp. 275-277).
163. *SAFE* data, which can be accessed at: https://www.safe.gov.cn/en/DataandStatistics/index.html.
164. *Japan Ministry of Finance* data, which can be accessed at: https://www.mof.go.jp/english/policy/international_policy/reference/index.html.
165. *Bureau of Economic Analysis* data, which can be accessed at: https://www.bea.gov.
166. *Bureau of Economic Analysis* data. Figures shown are as of 31 December 2019 and can be accessed at: https://www.bea.gov. See also (Milesi-Ferretti, 2021).
167. (Prasad, 2017, pp. 213-244).
168. (Morton, 2020).
169. See (Magnus, 2018, pp. 167-168) and (Stearns, 2018).
170. 1Malaysia Development Berhad, better known as 1MDB, was established in 2008 by the Malaysian government as a strategic development company. In

2015, the company was placed under investigation for money laundering, fraud and theft, with billions of dollars alleged to have been improperly expropriated.

171. (Yahuda, 2020, p. 276).
172. (Eisenman & Heginbotham, 2020, p. 301).
173. (Shambaugh, 2020, p. 359).
174. (Jones, 2020).
175. China Development Bank (国家发展银行) and the Export-Import Bank of China (中国进出口银行).
176. (Eisenman & Heginbotham, 2020, pp. 298-299).
177. (Kynge & Wheatley, 2020).
178. (Tanjangco, et al., 2021, p. 24).

Chapter 6: A New Cold War?

1. (Outram, 2001).
2. (Kennan, 1946).
3. (Ahamed, 2009, pp. 19-21).
4. (Yergin, The World's Most Important Body of Water, 2020).
5. (Tooze, 2020).
6. (Gaddis, 2005, pp. 73-76).
7. The Congressman killed on board Korea Air Lines Flight 007 was Larry McDonald, a Democratic member of the House of Representatives from Georgia.
8. (Hoffman, 1999).
9. (Union of Concerned Scientists, 2015).
10. (Pillsbury, 2015, pp. 72-79).
11. (Frankopan, 2015, pp. 458-463).
12. (Gaddis, 2005, p. 272).
13. Data sourced from Our World in Data and can be accessed at: https://ourworldindata.org/grapher/us-education-expenditure-as-share-of-gdp-public-and-private-institutions.
14. (Jenson, 2008).
15. (Turbiville, 1996).
16. (Knapp, 2019).
17. (Stine, 2009).
18. McCarthyism refers to the heightened political repression and persecution of left-wing individuals in the US during the 1940s and 1950s, when Senator Joseph McCarthy led a campaign spreading fear of communist and socialist influences in the US. This resulted in numerous false accusations of subversion and treason.
19. (Steil, 2018, pp. 341-342).
20. (Gaddis, 2005, p. 130).
21. (Green, 2019).

22. (Reid-Henry, 2019, p. 72).
23. (Hobsbawm, 1990).
24. (Obinger & Schmitt, 2011, p. 252).
25. (Reid-Henry, 2019, p. 32).
26. (Obinger & Schmitt, 2011, p. 248).
27. (Dudziak, 2000, pp. 220-231).
28. (Obinger & Schmitt, 2011, pp. 253-254).
29. (Piketty, 2020, pp. 420-424).
30. (Piketty, 2020, pp. 445-451).
31. (Piketty, 2020, pp. 420-424).
32. (Piketty, 2020, pp. 362-371).
33. The principle of free capital movement was later incorporated into the 1992 Maastricht Treaty.
34. Treasury Decision 8697.
35. (Klein & Pettis, 2020, pp. 30-34).
36. (Piketty, 2020, pp. 679-683).
37. (Killian, 2006, p. 1076).
38. (European Commission, 2016).
39. (European Commission, 2020).
40. (Killian, 2006, pp. 1073-1074).
41. For example, Sweden, which is viewed as a highly egalitarian society, moved away from progressive taxation on capital income to a flat tax of 30 percent on interest and dividends in the early 1990s. In the mid-2000s, it abolished progressive inheritance and wealth taxes. See (Piketty, 2020, pp. 923-926). After the GFC roiled its economy, Portugal rolled out a low-tax offer to so-called 'non-habitual residents' in order to attract wealthy foreigners to relocate and invest there. See (Wise, 2020).
42. (Davison & Versprille, 2021).
43. (Wang, 2020).
44. See (Jay, Batruch, Jetten, McGarty, & Muldoon, 2019), (O'Connor, 2017) and (Piketty, 2020, pp. 862-965).
45. (Vinograd & Jaffe, 2016).
46. (Kessler, 2019).
47. (Mahbubani, 2020, pp. 25-47).
48. (Piketty, 2020, pp. 693-696).
49. (So, 2019).
50. The term 'wolf warrior diplomacy' was coined after the Chinese patriotic action movie Wolf Warrior 2 (战狼2).
51. Examples of this can been seen in US support for General Augusto Pinochet's anti-leftist military junta in Chile from 1973 until 1990, as well as continuing close ties with Saudi Arabia, which has been branded an authoritarian regime.
52. (Chen, 2021).

53. (Ciampaglia & Menczer, 2018).
54. (Blackwill & Harris, 2016, pp. 87-91).
55. (Blackwill & Harris, 2016, p. 155).
56. (Steil & Litan, 2006, pp. 40-42).
57. (Godfrey, 2012).
58. (Allison & Blackwill, 2013, pp. 4-6).
59. (Yergin, The New Map: Energy, Climate, and the Clash of Nations, 2020, pp. 142-146).
60. (Yergin, The New Map: Energy, Climate, and the Clash of Nations, 2020, p. 138).
61. (Blackwill & Harris, 2016, pp. 112-114).
62. (Koty, 2021).
63. (Blackwill & Harris, 2016, p. 93).
64. (United States Department of Defence, 2020).
65. (Lee, Lague, & Blanchard, 2020).
66. (Wong, 2020).
67. (Kurlantzick, 2020).
68. (Köppel, 2011).
69. In fact, the Committee on Foreign Investment in the United States (CFIUS) demonstrated this precisely when in 2019 it forced Beijing Kunlun Tech, a Chinese company, to dispose of Grindr, a gay dating app that was deemed to give rise to the risk of giving Chinese intelligence to potentially sensitive information on US persons.
70. (Korhonen, 2019).
71. (Berger, 2021).
72. For further reading, see (Steil & Litan, 2006).
73. These included HikVision (海康威视); iFLYTEK (科大讯飞); Megvii (旷视), SenseTime (商汤科技); Xiamen Meiya Pico Information (厦门美亚柏科信息); Yitu Technologies (依图科技); Yixin Science and Technology (颐信科技); and Zhejiang Dahua (浙江大华技术).
74. (Heng & Bray, 2021).
75. (Jacobs, 2021).
76. (Mahbubani, 2020, p. 59).
77. (Ax, Viswanatha, & Nikolaeva, 2014).
78. (Foy, 2018).
79. *World Bank* data, which can be accessed at: https://data.worldbank.org.
80. (Prasad, 2017, pp. 28-29).
81. (Howell, 2020, p. 234).
82. (Cheah & Fok, 2020).
83. (Yi, 2020).
84. For example, the US Foreign Account Tax Compliance Act (FATCA) of 2010 requires all financial institutions to disclose financial information they hold on US persons to the US authorities. Non-US financial institutions that

fail to comply may be denied access to US financial markets and the dollar payments system.
85. (Fok, 2019).
86. For example, SWIFT.
87. For example, Clearstream, DTCC and Euroclear.
88. For example, in 2018, Euroclear and Clearstream were forced to suspend settlement of securities transactions involving US-sanctioned Russian companies and individuals.
89. (Prasad, 2017, pp. 114-118). CIPS was established as a Chinese alternative to the SWIFT payment network.
90. *LCH* data as of 1 June 2021.

Chapter 7: The Role of Markets in the 21ˢᵗ Century

1. See, for example, (Harari, 2015).
2. A diet based on food types presumed to have been eaten by early humans, consisting primarily of meat, fish, vegetables and fruit, and excluding dairy or cereal products and processed foods. In 2013, 'paleo' was the most Googled diet term.
3. (Pinker, 2011, pp. 31-42, 284-288).
4. See (Diamond, 2005), (Acemoglu & Robinson, 2012) and (Frankopan, 2015).
5. This was illustrated by Adam Smith in *An Inquiry into the Nature and Causes of the Wealth of Nations* (1776) through his example of a pin maker that substantially raised its output by dividing its manufacturing process into 18 distinct operations, with each handled by a specialist.
6. (Klein & Pettis, 2020, p. 67).
7. See (Ferguson, 2008, pp. 27-31) and (Harari, 2015, pp. 173-187).
8. (Prasad, 2017, p. 1).
9. (Harari, 2015, p. 184).
10. See (Ferguson, 2008, pp. 27-52) and (Young, 2019, pp. 63-83).
11. (Ferguson, 2008, pp. 69-76).
12. The prize was shared with Lars Peter Hansen and Robert J. Shiller.
13. For further reading on human irrationality in financial decision making, see (Kahneman, 2011).
14. (Jung & Shiller, 2005).
15. (Gates, 2021, p. 29).
16. (Yergin, The New Map: Energy, Climate, and the Clash of Nations, 2020, p. xix).
17. See (Gilmour & Jensen, 1998) and (Frederickson, 2010).
18. (Micklethwait & Wooldridge, 2020).
19. (Frederickson, 2010, p. 86).
20. (Gates, 2021, p. 29).
21. (Frankopan, 2015, pp. 132-153).
22. (Acemoglu & Robinson, 2012, pp. 152-156).

23. See (Acemoglu & Robinson, 2012) and (Rajan, 2019).
24. See (Wu, 2018) and (Tepper & Hearn, 2019).
25. (Wu, 2018, p. 78).
26. (Wu, 2018, pp. 93-98).
27. (Wu, 2018, pp. 108-109).
28. *Wikipedia* data.
29. See (Federal Trade Commission, 2020). In June 2021, Facebook won a court ruling dismissing two antitrust suits brought by the Federal Trade Commission.
30. *S&P Dow Jones* data for the years 2009–2020.
31. (Tepper & Hearn, 2019, p. 205).
32. (O'Mahony, 2019).
33. (Tepper & Hearn, 2019, pp. 205-206).
34. (Hargreaves, 2019).
35. (Binder, 2014).
36. (Ferguson, 2008, p. 5).
37. *Federal Reserve Bank of St. Louis* data, which can be accessed at: https://fred.stlouisfed.org.
38. See (Quinn & Turner, 2020, pp. 214-215) and (Howell, 2020, pp. 6-7).
39. (Quinn & Turner, 2020, pp. 16-37).
40. See (Ahamed, 2009).
41. (Litan, 2002).
42. For a useful practitioner's perspective on market cycles, see (Marks, 2018).
43. (Quinn & Turner, 2020, pp. 4-11).
44. *World Bank* data, which can be accessed at: https://data.worldbank.org.
45. *World Federation of Exchanges* data.
46. (Howell, 2020, pp. 17-28).
47. (Howell, 2020, pp. 146-148).
48. (Barrett, 2021).
49. (Breckenfelder, 2019).
50. (CFTC & SEC, 2010).
51. (Schatzker, Natarajan, & Burton, 2021).
52. (Howell, 2020, p. 228).
53. (Howell, 2020, p. 17).
54. (Howell, 2020, pp. 1-8).
55. The incarceration of debtors in default in Great Britain was ended with the Debtors Act 1869.
56. (Piketty, 2020, pp. 283-287).
57. (Piketty, 2020, pp. 534-538).
58. (Howell, 2020, pp. 119-129).
59. Greenspan's actions to increase the money supply in 1987 brought down the cost of borrowing from the Fed by almost two percent in just 16 days.
60. (Quinn & Turner, 2020, pp. 16-17).
61. (Quinn & Turner, 2020, p. 18).

62. (Ferguson, 2008, pp. 140-141).
63. (Quinn & Turner, 2020, pp. 18-20).
64. (Ferguson, 2008, pp. 149-152).
65. (Quinn & Turner, 2020, p. 22).
66. (Ferguson, 2008, p. 154).
67. (Howell, 2020, p. 102).
68. In theory, a government could shut down access to Bitcoin by shutting down the internet within its national borders. However, modern societies have become so dependent on the internet that a complete shutdown of the network would likely be unfeasible in practice.
69. (Elliott, 2009).
70. (Davis, 2011).
71. (Kharpal, 2021).
72. (Ghose, Zhang, Tian, Master, & Shah, 2021, p. 10).
73. (Levy, 2021).
74. Admittedly, El Salvador making Bitcoin legal tender is perhaps less significant than if other countries were to do so, since the Central American nation had already abandoned its own currency, the colón, in favour of the US dollar in 2001. See (Hawkins, 2021).
75. (Ferguson, 2008, p. 30).
76. (Ghose, Zhang, Tian, Master, & Shah, 2021, p. 56).
77. *CoinDesk* data.
78. (Ghose, Zhang, Tian, Master, & Shah, 2021, p. 73).
79. (Clark, 2021).
80. Ethereum has adopted a 'proof-of-stake' algorithm instead of Bitcoin's 'proof-of-work' methodology. Under this system, instead of all nodes on the network being incentivised to devote maximum computing power to solve each cryptographic puzzle (as under the proof-of-work system), a proof-of-stake miner is limited to mining a percentage of transactions reflective of its ownership stake. For further details, see (Ghose, Zhang, Tian, Master, & Shah, 2021).
81. (Shamapant, 2021).
82. Concerns publicly expressed by regulators and policymakers tended to focus on consumer protection, data privacy and anti-money laundering, rather than the specific threat that Libra potentially posed to national monetary sovereignty. In light of Facebook's alleged role in election interference, data privacy concerns were certainly genuine. However, it is fair to say that the challenge that Libra might have posed to national currencies was a major factor underlying the authorities' reaction.
83. Among the key changes in the design features of Diem versus Libra are a series of single currency stablecoins, which complement existing fiat currencies.
84. (Ghose, Zhang, Tian, Master, & Shah, 2021, p. 22).
85. For further reading about the benefits of CBDCs, see (BIS, 2021).
86. (BIS, 2021, p. 66).

87. (Areddy, 2021).
88. For further reading on MMT, see (Kelton, 2020).
89. (Allison, 2017, p. 227).

Chapter 8: Avoiding the Thucydides Trap

1. For a more detailed description of potential Sino-US military flashpoints, see (Allison, 2017, pp. 154-184).
2. (Feng & Pan, 2021).
3. In fact, as the GFC was unfolding in 2008, Russian officials made a top-level approach to China with a suggestion that they conduct a coordinated sale of American securities to place pressure on the US government. It was unclear how serious the Russian proposal was, but the Chinese did not pursue this – most likely because they were well aware that this would be harmful to China's own economy. See (Paulson Jr., 2015, p. 249).
4. (Allison, 2017, p. 238).
5. (Appelbaum, 2019, pp. 146-151).
6. This was also true in the case of the break-up of Standard Oil in 1911. Competition between the former Standard Oil entities spurred innovation in the US oil industry, which continues to play a leading role in the global oil market. See (Yergin, 1991).
7. (Appelbaum, 2019, p. 284).
8. For a well-argued recent piece of scholarship taking this position, see (Klein & Pettis, 2020).
9. (Schenk, 2010, p. 30). It should be noted that gold still predominated at that time and foreign exchange made up only around 30 percent of global reserves. However, gold holdings were highly concentrated in the US. Excluding the US, foreign exchange constituted around half of global reserves.
10. (Schenk, 2010, pp. 30, 117).
11. *IMF* data, which can be accessed at: https://data.imf.org.
12. Gross sterling liabilities to overseas lenders in December 1945 stood at over £3.5 billion. See (Schenk, 2010, p. 39).
13. For an authoritative account of the decline of sterling as a global reserve currency, see (Schenk, 2010).
14. (Schenk, 2010, p. 13).
15. *World Bank* data, which can be accessed at: https://data.worldbank.org.
16. Based on data from the *Federal Reserve Bank of St. Louis*, which can be accessed at: https://fred.stlouisfed.org.
17. (Prasad, 2014, pp. 89-122).
18. (Williamson, 2009, pp. 1-2).
19. (Williamson, 2009, p. 2).
20. *IMF* data, which can be accessed at: https://www.imf.org/en/About/Factsheets/Sheets/2016/08/01/14/51/Special-Drawing-Right-SDR.

21. As of 15 March 2021, the currency weightings within the SDR basket were: US dollar (41.73 percent); euro (30.93 percent); renminbi (10.92 percent); Japanese yen (8.33 percent); and pound sterling (8.09 percent).

22. (Williamson, 2009, p. 2).

23. (Williamson, 2009, p. 4).

24. *IMF* data as of 17 July 2021. America's voting rights are below its share of IMF quotas, which stand at 17.43 percent. Details can be accessed at: https://www.imf.org/external/np/sec/memdir/members.aspx#1.

25. (Gallagher, Ocampo, & Volz, IMF Special Drawing Rights: A key tool for attacking a COVID-19 financial fallout in developing countries, 2020).

26. (Gallagher, Ocampo, & Volz, It's time for a major issuance of the IMF's Special Drawing Rights, 2020).

27. See (Sobel, 2020) and (Mandeng, 2020).

28. (Adler & Arauz, 2020).

29. (Rappeport, 2021).

30. (Steil, 2013, pp. 182-223).

31. (Steil, 2013, p. 211).

32. (IMF, 2011, pp. 14-15).

33. (IMF, 2011, pp. 13-14).

34. (Schenk, 2010, p. 426).

35. (Chau, 2020).

36. Based on *HKEX* data, 70 percent of all international investors' holdings of Mainland Chinese domestic equities are held via Stock Connect. Based on *CCDC* and *PBOC* data, 22.6 percent of international investors' holdings of Mainland Chinese domestic bonds were held via Bond Connect as of March 2021. See https://www.chinabond.com.cn/cb/cn/yjfx/zzfx/yb/20210407/156852275.shtml and http://www.pbc.gov.cn/diaochatongjisi/resource/cms/2021/04/2021043016025378006.htm.

37. As the dominant centre for dollar and euro swaps clearing, LCH already plays a vital role in the market for US Treasuries and European government bonds. Since the UK voted to leave the EU in 2016, there have been calls by European policymakers to repatriate the clearing of euro contracts to the Eurozone. If this does eventuate, however, it would significantly increase costs for market participants by eliminating netting efficiencies derived from pooling euro and US dollar clearing in a single clearing house.

38. (Cheah & Fok, 2020).

39. (Kissinger, 2014, p. 255).

40. (Allison, 2017, pp. 159-160).

41. See (Allison, 2017, pp. 89-94).

42. (Stewart, 2019).

Afterword

1. (Pinker, 2011, p. 159).
2. (Brooke, 1995).
3. See (Luhby, 2020), (Picchi, 2018) and (O'Connor, 2018).
4. (Arnold, 2020).
5. (Eberstadt & Abramsky, 2021).
6. For further reading, see (Gray, 2011).
7. See (Gray, 2011).
8. It should be noted that James II of England and VII of Scotland was deposed in the Glorious Revolution of 1688 after he suspended the English and Scottish parliaments to rule by decree; however, that revolution was bloodless.
9. The four violent changes in China's regime were: the transition from the Ming to the Qing Dynasty (1644); the republican revolution (1911); Chiang Kai-shek's seizure of power (1928); and the Communist defeat of the Nationalists (1949).
10. (Lockett, 2021).
11. See (Sweeney, 2021) and (Soros, 2021).
12. (Bloomberg News, 2021).
13. (Yu, Cheng, & Zhang, 2021).
14. (Heng, 2021)
15. See, for example, (Baccardax, 2021) and (Egan, 2021).
16. (Jim, 2021).
17. (Shen, et al., 2021).
18. (Stevenson & Li, 2021).
19. (Jim, 2021).
20. (Chen & Chen, 2021).
21. (Rogoff & Yang, 2020).
22. (Song, 2021).
23. (Rogoff & Yang, 2020).
24. (The White House, 2021).
25. (Hille, 2021).

Index